WITHDRAWN

Violence at Work

What Everyone Should Know

*Nothing can guarantee that an employee will not become a victim of
workplace violence. There are steps, however, that can help reduce the odds.*

— OSHA, U.S. Department of Labor

In Memory of Our Daughter,
Marijke Joi (Van Fleet) Silvent
4/01/1973–2/19/2014

The unexpected work experiences she encountered in
her short lifeinspired us to write this book.

Violence at Work

What Everyone Should Know

by

Ella W. Van Fleet
Professional Business Associates

David D. Van Fleet
Arizona State University

INFORMATION AGE PUBLISHING, INC.
Charlotte, NC • www.infoagepub.com

Library of Congress Cataloging-in-Publication Data

A CIP record for this book is available from the Library of Congress
http://www.loc.gov

ISBN: 978-1-62396-685-0 (Paperback)
978-1-62396-686-7 (Hardcover)
978-1-62396-687-4 (ebook)

Some material in this book is from Van Fleet, E. W. & Van Fleet, D. D. 2007. Work-place Survival: Dealing with Bad Bosses, Bad Workers, Bad Jobs. Frederick, MD: PublishAmerica. Copyright the authors and used with permission of the authors.

Printed in the United States of America

CONTENTS

PREFACE

Every day we wake up, send our children to school, go to work, attend sports or other entertainment events, and so on. Then suddenly the unexpected happens. This day will not end like yesterday and a thousand other days. Our lives are changed forever. Suddenly we realize how precious and fragile life is, and we question whether we could have done something to prevent this emergency event.

We have become accustomed to violence, but we do not need to accept it. Our study of workplace violence, terrorism, and other forms of dysfunctional behavior associated with work suggests that both managers and nonmanagers would like to reduce the risks associated with violence at the workplace. The book is designed to help do just that.

No job is completely safe, of course; there are a lot of ways to get hurt at work. You can cut yourself with a letter opener, accidentally staple your finger, smash the wrong nail with a hammer, or experience an accident while driving a company car. You can slip, trip, stumble, and fall. You can take an aching back home with you after slumping in front of an improperly adjusted computer monitor, sitting in an ergonomically poor chair, or standing too long on an uncushioned surface. But the larger problems that we want to cover include physical or emotional hurt that result from the behaviors of others.

You can be underpaid, overworked, or get fired even though you are performing well. You can be a victim of sabotage or harassment even though—or sometimes because!—you are doing an outstanding job. You can be a victim on company premises of an angry, psychologically impaired, or chemically dependent manager, nonmanager, former coworker, spouse, or even a stranger. The violent act you face may have stemmed from coworker interaction, worker-boss relations, a sick corporate environment, or even family problems.

Top executives and other managerial and nonmanagerial personnel clearly need to take steps toward reducing the threat of workplace violence. Numerous studies have been done regarding workplace problems, resulting in numerous books and professional journal articles. Some books, articles, workshops, seminars, and the like proffer general advice to managers. However, virtually all of that advice has come from psychologists, physicians, and lawyers. And very little counsel is provided to nonmanager employees on dealing with problems that involve coworkers or managers. What has been lacking is advice that would reduce the threat of workplace violence and therefore (a) reduce stress, (b) enable organizations to develop potential competitive advantages in terms of their personnel and productivity, and (c) guide organizational personnel in their efforts to solve problems before they culminate in violent actions.

This book fills that need. We believe it is the first to offer both general and specific information and advice from a managerial point of view. The authors have spent their careers intimately involved with the practice, teaching, and research on management and organizations.

STANDARDS

This book follows five standards: readable, interesting, up-to-date, accurate, and unique. The first two assure that the book is readily understandable by a diverse audience while the latter two assure that it is of high quality.

Readable

To ensure readability, *Violence at Work* avoids unnecessary jargon and detailed summaries of research findings. As authors, our job is to read and interpret research, then write so that the material flows smoothly and logically from one point to another throughout the book. The use of straightforward language that involves the reader, a logical sequencing of material, and the use of numerous examples all contribute to making the material clear and understandable to the reader.

Interesting

Violence at Work tries to make the learning job easier and more enjoyable by making the material realistic and therefore more interesting. Three Appendages provide real-world examples from individuals and organizations from all sectors and walks of life. Everything is done to make applications of the material relevant and understandable to readers.

Up-to-Date

To be on the cutting edge means to have the most up-to-date material. *Violence at Work* is current and timely in its content.

Accurate

Violence at Work is firmly grounded in research but not burdened with references. Careful use of current research assures that the material is correct, while the use of relevant practical examples assures that it is believable.

Unique

Violence at Work is different from others that deal with workplace violence. Most others focus on one type of problem (e.g., bullying) or one type of organization (e.g., public schools). Ours provides advice that covers a broad field of either proscribed criminal acts or coercive behavior that occur in the course of performing any work-related duty. Some books provide coverage only of psychological problems that lead to violent acts. Others attempt to serve as self-help counseling material by creating artificial stereotypes fitted with clever little labels rather than letting the "real world of work" speak for itself in all of its complexity. Thus, while some of these may be interesting to read, they tend not to be very satisfactory in terms of providing useful information to real-world members of organizations. Nor do they provide any theoretical basis for dealing with the issue of workplace violence. Our book recognizes that problems can result from actions or inactions of managers, coworkers, or the organization itself. For that reason, our readers are asked to look inside themselves rather than risk facing the same relationship problems in a new department or job. And our book emphasizes the importance of knowing your four options when facing workplace problems.

AUDIENCE

Violence at Work was written primarily for managers and workers in all types of business and government organizations, including law enforcement. The book should also be especially useful for those teaching or doing research about workplace violence in business schools, criminal justice programs, law enforcement programs, and schools of education or other academic or trade programs.

It is written at a level that is appropriate for individuals in either self-study, training, or classroom settings. It could also be used as a supplement in business, education, criminal justice, or law enforcement classes. Top-level executives, who are generally somewhat removed from the types of behaviors described here, should also find the material useful in improving their organizations.

The reader needs no business, organizational, or technical background to understand this book. The more experience in organizations that the reader has, the more the reader will recognize the value of the material; but the less experience that the reader has, the more he or she probably needs the information presented in the book.

This book could be used as a text or supplement for both graduate and undergraduate courses as well as by organizations (private/public, profit/nonprofit) in training programs. The subject matter and writing style are geared to a general audience, but especially practicing managers, others in organizations, and those in the criminal justice and law enforcement fields.

This book would be a natural companion volume to the authors' earlier book, *The Violence Volcano: Reducing the Threat of Workplace Violence* (2010, Charlotte, NC: Information Age Publishing).

CHAPTER 1

INTRODUCTION

Violence is the last refuge of the incompetent.
—Isaac Asimov, *Foundation*

In Oakland, California, the four police officers killed at a routine traffic stop came to work that day knowing that their lives were always in danger. On the other hand, do you suppose in another city the plant supervisor who insisted that his young employee wear safety glasses ever thought that this managerial act would cost him his life? Not likely. In the 1970s, most postal workers felt safe going to work in their mailrooms. Not anymore — not after the '80s and '90s, the era of "going postal".

The nurses at Mercy hospital, especially in the emergency room, were always on guard against unstable or agitated patients, but the pharmacist at the local drugstore was not expecting to be shot in the face when he told the robber that he could not unlock the safe where the drugs were kept. Did the parents in Littleton, Colorado, and Newtown, Connecticut, think that their children might not return from school that day? Of course not— schools are safe. The five Wendy's employees in New York City must have been caught totally by surprise when a former employee vented his anger on them. But 2,000 miles away, the 38-year-old father of three children, angry because his request for a schedule change was denied, probably knew that he would return the next day and shoot his boss and three coworkers.

Violence at Work: What Everyone Should Know, pp. 1–14
Copyright © 2014 by Information Age Publishing
All rights of reproduction in any form reserved.

Is it safe for anyone in any company to go to work after a coworker has been terminated? Not anymore.

Violence in society is as old as time itself.[1] It is documented in Biblical writings and other tales of religion-based wars, ancient hieroglyphics and literature, and stories of the Mafia, street gangs, organized crime, and "the Mob." However, such acts were considered as "criminal acts" that involved various elements of society; and even if they happened to have occurred in the workplace, they were not seen as having anything in particular to do with the workplace or the organization. They did not have a direct impact on most citizens and didn't change conditions at work. Violence in the workplace, even though it was not new, was thought to be relatively uncommon. Not anymore.

The pertinent question, then, is whether an organization has a propensity for violence. More specifically, what about *your* organization? Have there been instances of bullying or harassment? Are employees nervous about coming to work? Are they tense around managers or some workers? Do they feel that the organization doesn't really care about its people, caring instead only about the "bottom line"? Are you aware of instances of anonymous e-mails damaging someone's reputation? Do people tend to grumble, complain, and criticize one another? Has an employee erupted in uncontrollable temper outbursts? Are these becoming increasingly apparent? Are any of these evident in your organization? Hopefully not. But if you answered yes to one or more of these questions, you just might be dealing with an organization that has a high propensity for violence. If so, what can you do about it? This book is intended to help you answer that question.

DEFINITION

There is no single, accepted definition of what constitutes workplace violence. Ontario's Health and Safety act focuses on physical aspects of violence[2] and the International Labor Organization differentiates internal (between members of an organization) and external (between members of an organization and those outside of the organization).[3] The U.S. Occupational Safety and Health Administration has published at least two definitions both of which include threats, verbal abuse, physical assaults, and homicide.[4] ASIS International (formerly the American Society for Industrial Security) and SHRM (the Society for Human Resource Management) jointly developed a preparedness document with a more inclusive definition dealing with a "spectrum of behaviors."[5] For our purposes in this book, we will use one that we developed earlier:

Workplace Violence refers to willful or negligent acts, including either proscribed criminal acts or coercive behavior, that occur in the course of performing any work-related duty and that lead to significant negative results, such as physical or emotional injury, diminished productivity, and/or property damage.[6]

With that definition in mind, then, let's examine in a bit more detail the background of workplace violence.

ORIGINS[7]

Workplace violence, like other forms of violence, has always been around in some form or another, but only in the past quarter century has it received substantial attention. Increasingly, individuals have become less reluctant to talk about and report it. Scholars, government agencies, and professional organizations have developed better definitions and reporting processes. And the media are more likely to report it and even to sensationalize it. So while it may appear to be increasing, it may simply be that counting it and reporting it are better and more likely. While high-profile, tragic incidents grab the attention of the media and the public, more frequent but less tragic incidents garner little attention.[8] Although a 2012 survey found that over a third (36%) of organizations reported incidents of workplace violence, and some (40%) indicated that the frequency of incidents had decreased over the past 2 years, others (15%) reported an increase.[9] And workplace violence affects all demographic classifications. From 2005 to 2009, Hispanics had the lowest rate of nonfatal workplace violence (3 of every 1,000), and American Indians had the highest (13 per 1,000); the rate for males was 5.9 and for females it was 4.1.[10]

Workplace violence affecting businesses in the United States more or less started abroad, when in the 1970s American businessmen were kidnapped in South American countries and held for ransom. In the early 1980s, some American businessmen in the Middle East (Lebanon) were kidnapped and tortured for political purposes. Then in the 1980s, ordinary workers from little towns to big cities began to see and hear about lethal weapons used against employers and coworkers. At least twice in 1983 and twice in 1985, postal employees opened fire on supervisors and/or fellow employees. On August 19, 1986, Patrick Henry Sherrill shot 17 coworkers and himself at the U.S. Post Office in Edmond, Oklahoma. These incidents led to the coining of the term "going postal." At that point, violence in the workplace began to take on a different character; it was no longer an aberration. Suddenly workplace violence became a problem that could occur anywhere and anytime.

Two years later, a Merrill Lynch employee in Boston killed the supervisor who had fired him, and 250 passengers on Pan Am flight 103 were blown to pieces over Lockerbie, Scotland, by terrorists whose complaints and motives were unknown to the victims. The pace accelerated in 1991 when George Hennard executed 22 people in a Luby's cafeteria in Killeen, Texas, because he had lost his job as a merchant seaman two years previously and half a continent away; and Tom McIlvane shot 3 supervisors, himself, and 14 others after being dismissed as a mail carrier in Royal Oak, Michigan. Similar isolated incidents continued to make front-page news until February 16, 1993, when the bombing of the World Trade Center in New York City confirmed our worst fears that someday terrorists would find their way into our cosmopolitan centers. Then at 9:02 A.M. on Wednesday, April 19, 1995, an explosion outside the Federal Building in Oklahoma City really directed our attention to the vulnerability of innocent people at work or at play, everywhere, even in the nation's noncosmopolitan heartland—and at the hands of our own people.

In 2011, an employee of Lehigh Southwest Cement Permanente Plant in Cupertino, California, killed three workers.[11] In 2012, just outside the Empire State Building in New York, a man shot and killed another man who worked for the first man's former employer. The resulting confrontation with police led to nine other people being injured. That same year, an Apple Valley Farms employee shot two coworkers, and in an unrelated incident, a worker at ConAgra Foods in Indianapolis killed a coworker.[12]

Also in 2012, Minneapolis, Minnesota, incurred the deadliest incident of workplace violence since the state began tracking incidents when five people were killed and the gunman committed suicide at a signage firm.[13] And in the Washington, DC, area a sanitation work was fatally shot and another wounded at a garbage collection facility; an employee of a commercial cleaning company was killed by a former employee who thought his wife was having an affair with the first man; and an engineer at a hospital stabbed his supervisor to death as a result of receiving a poor performance evaluation.[14] But these are only a few of the many violent occurrences.

Soon other types of workplaces were experiencing attacks, expanding the list of violent incidents in the workplace. Healthcare, convenience stores, and fast-food restaurants became targets due to their handling medications or cash. Such violence resulted not only from workplace relationships but also from family and other off-site problems that led the culprit into the workplace to settle a perceived grievance. In less than 10 years (around 1990), the violence had spread to a different type of workplace—schools—and involved both personnel and students, both during the school day and after hours at school-related events. From 1999 to 2009, almost 300 school-related deaths were recorded, with students as young as 6 years of age shooting classmates and teachers (Trump, 2009). Then fellow students began "killing sprees" that took the lives of multiple students (e.g., Columbine High School, Northern Illinois University, Virginia Tech).

In 2012, a 20-year-old male made his way into Sandy Hook Elementary School in Newtown, Connecticut, and killed 26 children and adults after first killing his mother at home in her bed. In 2013, the shooting of teachers by 12- and 14-year-old students continued to cause alarm. We could no longer feel safe at work, not even in a child's schoolroom. And not just schools, but all forms of government have been impacted. Between 2002 and 2011, while serious violent crime was greater for the private sector, the rate of simple assault against government employees was more than three times that of private sector employees.[15] During that time period, virtually all (96%) workplace violence against government employees involved local, county, or state workers rather than those in the federal service.[16]

Even when the workplace involves sporting events, violence can occur.[17] While that violence may occur among players, it increasingly involves spectators.[18] But violence at sporting events may be more a form of terrorism than workplace violence. In 2013, for example, during the Boston Marathon, two pressure cooker bombs exploded, killing 3 people and injuring nearly 300.[19]

TARGETS OF VIOLENCE

In a relatively few years, then, workplace violence has become a serious problem potentially faced by employees at all levels.[20] Even though there is only a low probability that you or your company will be a target, you know it does happen in other places and could happen to you. The fear as much as the violence itself translates into uncertainty and anxiety that creates additional stress in the workplace, the costs of which are ultimately borne by all of society, not just managers and employees. The possibility of a violent event at work adds to the stress experienced on the job. "Not only must people perform well in a highly competitive, shrinking job market in a complex society functioning in a global economy, but now they must fear death or injury on their jobs unrelated to the nature of their work."[21] And while the focus is generally on deadly incidents, the nondeadly ones are also costly to both individuals and organizations.

Many of us generally seem to feel that prudent practices by most organizations and the presence of governmental regulation make our own workplaces safe. We tend to associate violence with hazardous occupations (e.g., fishing, logging, construction, transportation, material moving, mining) or vulnerable jobs (e.g., handling cash, working late at night, taxi drivers, food-service workers, convenience stores, gasoline stations). That is partially correct. But between 2005 and 2009, 28% of workplace homicides were in sales and related occupations, and another 17% were in protective service occupations.[22] And even though the vast majority of workplace homicides are committed by organizational outsiders (robbers and other assailants), 21% are committed by work associates.[23] Half of all firms with 1,000 or more employees reported experiencing a workplace violence incident in 2005.[24] Thus, the rising incidents of workplace violence—including negligence, sexual harassment, stalking, bullying, bad management, and even terrorism—are convincing everyone that all organizations are vulnerable to workplace violence, and something must be done. When *you* are the victim of violence, the odds do not offer a great deal of consolation.

Obviously, workplace violence occurs not only in big cities, big companies, or postal facilities but also in small towns, small businesses, public schools and universities, hospitals, eating establishments, beauty salons, bowling alleys, and everywhere. It is not only ubiquitous; it is costly and long-lasting—in terms of tardiness and absenteeism, lost productivity, turnover, stress, and damage.[25] Women in particular suffer increased tardiness and absenteeism after violent incidents.[26] And of course workplace violence can result in death.[27] Indeed, in 2011, nearly 17% of all fatal U.S. work injuries were the result of workplace violence.[28] Violent incidents can be particularly dangerous when individuals are taken captive.[29] Thus, members of all organizations clearly need to know how to reduce threats of violence and how to respond if they occur. Knowledge and awareness are the first steps to reduce the propensity for violence, and prevention is always preferable to reaction.[30]

CONTRIBUTORS TO VIOLENCE

Large or small, public or private, profit or nonprofit, all organizations are vulnerable; no organization is immune to violence. We now recognize that there are conditions and events—especially when cumulative—that can push a person toward violence. To defuse that tendency or cut short that potential, both managers and employees need to be able to recognize when an individual is moving toward explosive behavior as well as when and how to intervene.[31] As indicated in Figure 1.1, these influences include (a) the environment—economic, social, and political forces outside the organization; (b) the organization itself—its culture, managers, values, and mores; and (c) individuals—factors related to the members of organizations, inherent characteristics of those individuals and their reactions to situations both inside the workplace and those carried over from their life outside the workplace, and customers/clients of the organization.

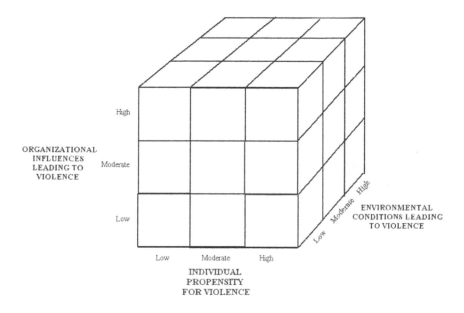

Source: Van Fleet, D. D., & Van Fleet, E. W. (2010). *The violence volcano: Reducing the threat of workplace violence.* Charlotte, NC: Information Age. Used with permission.

Figure 1.1. Environmental, individual, and organizational influences on work-place violence.

Environmental Influences

Environmental conditions can increase or decrease the potential for violence. While scholars have proffered different theories about workplace violence,[32] the socioeconomic environment is clearly at least a partial cause. In the troubling period of growing workplace violence that we mentioned earlier, many changes were facing individuals as well as the society at-large and the political and economic environment. A shrinking job market in an increasingly complex society and a global economy characterized by intense competition put additional stress on workers to perform at a higher level. Employees were laid off, especially as jobs were shipped overseas, usually resulting in the remaining managers and workers being expected to perform both their work and the duties of the laid-off workers as well. At the same time the aging population was subsisting on their dwindling fixed incomes, young families needing the income of two wage earners often found themselves with only one or none, and young educated adults were working for minimum wage, if at all.

Sociocultural forces may lead to feelings of social disenfranchisement and alienation in a complex and seemingly uncaring world; and those factors, in turn, may lead to an increase in the potential for violence. In like manner, various stressors play a role. Consider the many conditions in the environment that can cause stress. Economic conditions such as high unemployment, the movement of jobs to other areas including to other countries, shrinking and changing job markets, increased competition (particularly global competition), skyrocketing costs of health care, and the like all lead to increased stress on individuals. The nature of the workplace has changed, jobs have changed, technology changed, and the psychological contract that formerly assured continued employment for loyal, hard-working employees has changed in many organizations. All of these increase stress.

The sociocultural environment is changing with increased diversity, open acknowledgement of varying sexual preferences, the seeming increase in the types and usage of drugs, the presence of gangs, the incidence of terrorism, and a seeming high tolerance for violence in society as indicated by movies and video games. All contribute to increased stress than can push individuals toward violent responses. Dress and behavioral norms both on and off the job have changed and no doubt will continue to do so. Families and churches don't provide the levels of support that they did in the past.

Individual Factors

The potential for violence cannot be attributed solely to one's environment or workplace. This is true even for the U.S. Postal System, where so much violence occurred. Everyone comes into an organization with some potential tendency already to exhibit dysfunctional behavior.[33] Nevertheless, rarely does that result in a physical assault of one person by another. Most "bad" behavior involves low-level violent behavior such as shouting, spreading rumors, malicious gossip, or rudeness.[34] However, these can and sometimes do escalate to higher levels of violence.[35] The greater the individual's violence potential, the more likely the individual will actually "erupt," becoming dangerously violent, under some set of circumstances.[36]

Contrary to what you often hear, individuals don't just snap. Violence is a process. Frustrations and stresses build up over time, much like a volcano.[37] We have seen several examples of this in school shootings, where the aggressor appears to be finally reacting after months, if not years, of coping with bullying or other forms of insult. Another example is postal workers; they had been building grudges over many years, some toward bosses in their local post office, some toward bullying coworkers, and others resulting from negative feeling and hate that came from experiences that they probably didn't even remember at the time they "went postal." No doubt many of their criticisms were true and should have been dealt with by upper management; but the postal worker saw no hope in any change occurring and decided to take care of his own problem.

The backgrounds and personalities of individuals with a high propensity for violence have been the subject of research in an effort to identify them so as to prevent or minimize violence.[38] Other individual factors (e.g., drugs; alcohol; hostile attributional bias; and hatred based on race, religion, gender, sexual orientation, or other personal characteristics) have also been used to identify individuals likely to engage in aggression.[39]

But the best predictor of future behavior, including violence, is behavior. So most profiles of violence-prone individuals include those with a history of destructive, aggressive, and bullying behavior. They tend to be loners who have little support from family or friends. They have a difficult time with criticism and don't tolerate frustration. They complain and file grievances and become even more frustrated when nothing seems to happen. Eventually, they "take charge" and handle the problem themselves in the form of a violent act. On the other hand, we know there are individuals who do not fit that profile at all. They are quiet, passive noncomplainers who instead allow their frustrations and stress to build, invisible to most other persons, until they can no longer suffer in silence. They do not just "snap"—they successfully cope until "the cup runneth over" and they can cope no more. They, too, decide that "it's time to take charge" and remove their problem.

Like environmental forces, the backgrounds and personalities of individuals are only a partial explanation of the causes of workplace violence. People with a preoccupation with guns are sometimes mentioned as potentially violent workers. Other potential causes have been suggested, including overly stressful events such as a job termination, bankruptcy, divorce, or personal disputes. Yet no conclusive, indisputable explanations have been identified for predicting the potentially violent actor. True, the greater the individual's violence potential, the more likely the individual will actually "erupt"—become dangerously violent—under some set of circumstances,[40] but the organization itself can increase the likelihood of that occurring. Let's look at that next.

Organizational Factors

Job termination might not result in a person's becoming violent if it is handled properly by management, but it can serve (and has in many cases) as the final stimulus for a worker's retaliation against coworkers, managers, or the organization. The organization can be as incompetent as its terminated workers and as sick as any gun-toting individual. A member of an organization already stressed in his or her personal life—feeling a lack of resources for dealing with that stress—and also in a sick or stress-producing organizational environment is more likely to respond with violence. However, place that same individual in a supportive work environment and the propensity for violence is reduced substantially.[41] In other words, organizational factors (e.g., the workplace itself, overcontrolling supervision, perceived injustice, abusive coworkers, unsafe jobs) can increase or decrease the potential for violence.

Organizational cultures, including jobs and relationships, are changing. The demographics of those working in organizations are changing and becoming more diverse. Reengineering, reorganization, downsizing, global competition, and increased regulation all contribute to more stress on the job. No organization is safe anymore. Just as it is for individuals, organizations with histories of numerous grievances, disability claims, aggression among individuals, or other indications of a propensity for violence are more likely to experience violence. Organizations with a disregard for safety and security, those that haven't developed a workplace harassment and violence policy, those that do not provide assistance to employees in need, those that seem to care little about their members, and those that don't train managers and workers about the signs of violence building—all have increased propensities for violent eruptions.

Some of the signs of organizations (or parts of organizations) that may be increasing their potential for eliciting violent behavior include unusually high rates of turnover and absenteeism, lots of grievances, slowing productivity and growth, increasing costs per employee, increasing sizes of central staffs, and poor morale. Projects that seem to possess a lot of potential end up slowly grinding to a halt or failing altogether. And personality clashes become more common and pronounced. These organizations include managers who are defensive, responding to suggestions or criticisms with statements like, "You need to understand the situation" or "You don't see the big picture." Rather than analyze and try to understand, they justify their action or inaction, make excuses, or simply blame others or external forces. Those managers regard workers as adversaries rather than team members. They distrust and threaten workers. They may inadvertently encourage deviant behavior.[42] And, of course, abusive managers clearly increase the propensity for violence in their organizations.[43]

WHAT CAN BE DONE?

While the propensity for workplace violence is impacted by individual factors, environment conditions, and organizational influences, organizations and their members can nevertheless do a great deal to decrease the likelihood of violence.

True, they can't do much about the environment, as they cannot control the economic and other environmental forces in our society. Likewise, they cannot have a lot of influence on improving the nature of individuals as they cannot control the personal characteristics and previous experiences of individuals. But they can do something to effect changes within their own organizations. They are or should be able to make modifications that will reduce the propensity for violence in their organizations. Identifying those factors that increase the propensity for workplace violence and then either reducing or eliminating them would be a major contribution. Many organizations, through their managers and nonmanagers alike, are recognizing the pervasiveness and the costs of workplace violence and have initiated such actions already. They work to develop work environments and organizational cultures where people feel secure divulging concerns, and managers perform due diligence to investigate signs of problems.

In this book, therefore, we address the problems that stem from organizational factors, including the workplace itself, and also the personalities and behaviors of its managers and nonmanager employees. The things over which organizations and/or their members have considerable control—the things that they can do something about. That is what this book is all about. Toward that end, we include specific illustrations of real-world characteristics of violence-prone organizations and what to do about them. The more closely employers look at the workplace violence problem, the more they come to realize that there are steps that they can take to either eliminate or significantly reduce the risk of a workplace violence incident on their premises.

NOTES

1. Drake, H. A. (Ed.). (2006). Violence in late antiquity: Perceptions and practices. Burlington, VT: Ashgate.
2. Ontario, Canada. (2011). *Ontario's Health & Safety Act*. Retrieved from www.e-laws.gov.on.ca/html/statutes/english/elaws_statutes_90o01_e.htm
3. United Nations. International Labour Organization (ILO). (2003). Retrieved from www.ilo.org/wcmsp5/groups/public/@ed_protect/@protrav/@safework/documents/normativeinstrument/wcms_107705.pdf
4. U. S. Department of Labor. Occupational Safety and Health Administration. (2013). www.osha.gov/SLTC/workplaceviolence/; *OSHA Fact Sheet 2002*. www.osha.gov/OshDoc/data_General_Facts/factsheet-workplace-violence.pdf
5. ASIS International. (2011). *Workplace violence prevention and intervention* (ASSIS/SHRM WPVI.1-2011). Alexandria, VA: ASIS International, p. 3.
6. Van Fleet, D. D., & Van Fleet, E. W. (2010). *The violence volcano: Reducing the threat of workplace violence*. Charlotte, NC: Information Age Publishing.

7. This section is based primarily on *Ibid.*

8. Romano, S. J., & Rugala, E. A. (2008). *Workplace violence: Mind-set of awareness*, Spokane, WA: Center for Personal Protection and Safety; Rugala, E. A. & Fitzgerald, J. R. (2003). Workplace violence: from threat to intervention. *Clinics in Occupational and Environmental Medicine, 3*, 775–789.

9. Society for Human Resource Management. (2012). *Workplace violence.* Retrieved from http://www.shrm.org/Research/SurveyFindings/Articles/Pages/WorkplaceViolence.aspx

10. Morgan, L. A. (2013). *Workplace violence statistics & information.* Retrieved from work.chron.com/workplace-violence-statistics-information-13144.html

11. Walter, L. (2011). Workplace violence claims the lives of two workers every day. *EHS Today.* Retrieved from http://ehstoday.com/safety/news/workplace-violence-two-death-daily-1007

12. Segarra, M. (2012). Stopping workplace violence. *CFO.* Retrieved from www3.cfo.com/article/2012/12/workplace-issues_workplace-violence-workplace-fatalities-bureau-of-labor-statistics

13. Magan, C. (2012). Minneapolis workplace shooting the deadliest of its kind in Minnesota. *Pioneer Press.* Retrieved from www.twincities.com/localnews/ci_21655126/minneapolis-shooting-is-deadliest-incident-workplace-violence-minnesotas

14. Babay, E. (2012). Local workplace violence cases. *The Examiner.* Retrieved from http://washingtonexaminer.com/local-workplace-violence-cases/article/112964

15. Harrell, E. (2012). *Workplace violence against government employees, 1994–2011.* Washington, DC: U.S. Bureau of Justice Statistics. Retrieved from http://www.bjs.gov/index.cfm?ty=pbdetail&iid=4615

16. *Ibid.*

17. Wann, D. L., Melnick, M. J., Russell, G. W., & Pease D. G. (2001). *Sport fans: The psychology and social impact of spectators.* New York, NY: Routledge; Smith, M. D. (1988). *Violence and sport.* Toronto: Canadian Scholars' Press.

18. Aguirre, B. E. (2008). Sports Fan Violence in North America. *Contemporary Sociology: A Journal of Reviews, 37*(2), 157–158.

19. Levs, J., & Plott, M. (2013). *Boy, 8, one of 3 killed in bombings at Boston Marathon; scores wounded.* Retrieved from http://www.cnn.com/2013/04/15/us/boston-marathon-explosions

20. Neuman, J., & Baron, R. (1998). Workplace violence and workplace aggression: Evidence concerning specific forms, potential causes, and preferred targets. *Journal of Management, 24*(3), 391–419; Baron, R. A., & Neuman, J. H. (1996). Workplace violence and workplace aggression: Evidence on their relative frequency and potential causes. *Aggressive Behavior, 22*, 161–173.

21. Van Fleet & Van Fleet, *op. cit.*

22. Harrell, E. (2011). *Workplace violence, 1993–2009.* Washington, DC: Bureau of Justice Statistics. Retrieved from http://www.bjs.gov/content/pub/pdf/wv09.pdf

23. *Ibid.*

24. U.S. Department of Labor, Bureau of Labor Statistics. (2006). *The survey of workplace violence prevention, 2005*. Retrieved from Washington, DC. http://www.bls.gov/iif/oshwc/osnr0026.pdf

25. U.S. Department of Labor, Bureau of Labor Statistics. (2006). *Crime & victims statistics*. Wash Statistics; Nixon, W. B. (2009). *Workplace violence prevention: Assessing the risk to your business*. Retrieved from http://www.collegerecruiter.com/blog/2011/01/27/assessing-the-risk-of-workplace-violence-to-your-business/

26. O'Leary Kelly, A., & Reeves, C. (2007). The effects and costs of intimate partner violence for work organizations. *Journal of Interpersonal Violence, 22*(3), 327–344.

27. National Research Council and Institute of Medicine. (2003). In M. H. Moore, C. V. Petrie, A. A. Braga, & B. L. McLaughlin (Eds.), Case studies of school violence committee. *Deadly Lessons: Understanding lethal school violence*. Washington, DC: National Academies Press.

28. SIW Editorial Staff. (2012). *Feds: Workplace violence caused nearly 17 percent of all fatal U.S. work injuries in 2011*. Retrieved from http://www.securityinfowatch.com/news/10834285/feds-workplace-violence-caused-nearly-17-percent-of-all-fatal-us-work-injuries-in-2011

29. Booth, B., Vecchi, G., Finney, E., Van Hasselt, V., & Romano, S. (2009). Captive-taking incidents in the context of workplace violence: Descriptive analysis and case examples. *Victims and Offenders, 4*, 76–92.

30. Nixon, W. B. (2013). Prevention Outweighs Reaction. *The Workplace Violence Fact Sheet*. Lake Forest, CA: The National Institute for the Prevention of Workplace Violence.

31. Van Fleet, D. D., & Van Fleet, E. W. (2007). Preventing workplace violence: The violence volcano metaphor. *Journal of Applied Management and Entrepreneurship, 12*(2), 17–36; Van Fleet & Van Fleet (2010). *op. cit.*

32. Paetzold, R. L., O'Leary-Kelly, A., & Griffin, R. W. (2007). Workplace violence, employer liability, and implications for organizational research. *Journal of Management Inquiry, 16*, 362–370; Martinko, M. J., & Zellars, K. L. (1998). Toward a theory of workplace violence: A cognitive appraisal perspective. In R. W. Griffin, A. O'Leary-Kelly, & J. M. Collins (Eds.), *Dysfunctional behavior in organizations: Violent and deviant behavior* (pp. 1–42). Stamford, CT: JAI; O'Leary-Kelly, A. M., Griffin, R. W., & Glew. D. J. (1996). Organization-motivated aggression: A research framework. *Academy of Management Review, 21*, 225–253.

33. Van Fleet & Van Fleet (2010). *op. cit.*; Van Fleet, D. D., & Griffin, R. W. (2006). Dysfunctional organization culture: The role of leadership in motivating dysfunctional work behaviors. *Journal of Managerial Psychology, 21*(8), 698–708; Griffin, R. W., & Lopez, Y. P. (2004). Toward a model of the person-situation determinants of deviant behavior in organizations. Paper presented at the 64th Annual Meeting of the Academy of Management; Griffin, R. W., & Lopez, Y. P. (2005). "Bad behavior" in organizations: A review and typology for future research. *Journal of Management, 31*, 988–1005; Deneberg, R. & Braverman, M. (2001). *The violence-prone workplace: A new approach to dealing with hostile, threatening, and uncivil behavior*. Ithaca, NY: Cornell University Press.

34. Porath, C. L., & Erez, A. (2007). Does rudeness matter? The effects of rude behavior on task performance and helpfulness. *Academy of Management Journal, 50,* 1181–1197; Porath, C. L., & Erez, A. (2009). Overlooked but not untouched: How incivility reduces onlookers' performance on routine and creative tasks. *Organizational Behavior and Human Decision Processes, 109,* 29–44.
35. Elias, S. M. (2013). *Deviant and criminal behavior in the workplace.* New York: New York University Press; Coleman, L. (2004). The frequency and cost of corporate crises. *Journal of Contingencies and Crisis Management, 12*(1), 2–13.
36. Inness, M., Barling, J., & Turner, N. (2005). Understanding supervisor-targeted aggression: A within-person, between-jobs design. *Journal of Applied Psychology, 90*(4), 731–739.
37. Van Fleet & Van Fleet (2010). *op. cit.*; Bryngelson, J. (2000). *CARE (courtesy and respect empower).* Billings, MT: J Bryngelson; McMillan, R. (1999). The path of dialogue: Why smart people do dumb things and how they can stop. A presentation at the Executive Forum's *Management Forum Series, March 24, 1999.* Lake Oswego, OR: Executive Forum.
38. Kelloway, E. K., Barling, J., & Hurrell, J. J., Jr. (2006). *Handbook of workplace violence.* Thousand Oaks, CA: Sage; Griffin, R. W., & O'Leary-Kelly A. M. (Eds. 2004. *The dark side of organizational behavior.* San Francisco: Jossey-Bass; Sommers, J. A., Schell, T. L., & Vodanovich, S. J. (2002). Developing a Measure of individual differences in organizational revenge. *Journal of Business and Psychology, 17*(2), 207–222; Neuman & Baron (1998). *op. cit.*
39. Jacobs, J. L., & Scott, C. L. (2011). Hate crimes as one aspect of workplace violence: Recommendations for HRD. *Advances in Developing Human Resources, 13*(1), 85–98; LeBlanc, M. M., & Barling J. (2004). Workplace aggression. *Current Directions in Psychological Science, 13*(1), 9–12.
40. Inness, Barling, & Turner, *op. cit.*
41. Geddes D., & Stickney, L. T. (2011). The trouble with Sanctions: Organizational responses to deviant anger displays at work. *Human Relations, 64*(2), 201–230.
42. Neider, L. L., & Schriesheim, C. A. (2010). *The "dark" side of management.* Charlotte, NC: Information Age; Litzky, B. E., Eddleston, K. A., & Kidder, D. L.. (2006). The good, the bad, and the misguided: How managers inadvertently encourage deviant behaviors. *Academy of Management Perspectives, 20,* 91–103.
43. Liu, D., Liao, H., &. Loi, R. (2012). The dark side of leadership: A three-level investigation of the cascading effect of abusive supervision on employee creativity. *Academy of Management Journal, 55,* 1187–1212; Reio, T. G., Jr. (2011). Supervisor and coworker incivility: Testing the work frustration-aggression model. *Advances in Developing Human Resources, 13*(1) 54–68; Tepper, B. J., Moss, S. E., & Duffy, M. K. (2011). Predictors of abusive supervision: Supervisor perceptions of deep-level dissimilarity, relationship conflict, and subordinate performance. *Academy of Management Journal, 54,* 279–294.

SECTION I

MANAGER BEHAVIOR AND VIOLENCE

CHAPTER 2

MANAGER BEHAVIOR

How It Can Contribute to Violence

What we think depends upon what we perceive.
What we perceive determines what we believe.
What we believe determines what we take to be true.
What we take to be true is our reality.

——Gary Zukav

Frequently, people complain about their "job" when, in fact, their problem is not really the job. As indicated in the opening chapter, managers themselves can be a primary contributing factor to job dissatisfaction, even leading to workplace violence.[1] It is important to understand that the effectiveness of managers depends not only on their ability and personality but also on how others perceive their ability and personality. People do not react to reality; they react to their perception of it. Their perception is their reality.

The extent of the concern about bad managers is illustrated by the fact that Working America, a community affiliate of the AFL-CIO, sponsored a "My Bad Boss Contest"[2] in 2006 to give workers an opportunity to speak out about the difficulties they face every day on the job. Books, articles, workshops, and seminars proffer advice on how to be a "good" manager and how employees might cope with a "bad" manager.[3] Everyone needs to

---

Violence at Work: What Everyone Should Know, pp. 17–40
Copyright © 2014 by Information Age Publishing
All rights of reproduction in any form reserved.

17

be able to recognize a bad manager[4]—executives, so they can either alter the behavior of the bad managers or get rid of them before they do irreparable damage to the organization; the bad managers themselves, so they can change their behavior; and employees, so they can gather evidence for a grievance, change their behavior, or move to another job. In this chapter we will look at some of the problems caused by bad managers, and in the next two chapters we will focus on what managers and nonmanagers may be able to do about it.

The quality of supervision has long been known to be a powerful force influencing the attitudes and behavior of jobholders. Good managers can help obtain good performance. Poor managers, on the other hand, help to bring about inferior performance when, for example, they are overly controlling, abusive, or so insecure that they fail to perform their supervisory role properly. Furthermore, the way managers treat nonmanagers and handle complaints about bad coworkers affects workers' attitudes toward their coworkers as well as toward the job itself.

Bad managers have been cited as the primary reason why some employees commit workplace violence or become internal organizational terrorists[5] (members of an organization who create fear among others in the organization to achieve their own personal goals). Tired of perceived injustice, they decide to retaliate against their manager or against the organization. Depending on the type of workplace, there are many ways to "get back" if an employee decides to do that. They may slow down the work to prevent their manager from meeting his own deadlines or give him headaches by sabotaging his computer. Minor acts of retaliation can also escalate to full-blown acts of terrorism or to workplace violence aimed at the manager.

Even though the examples shown in Figure 2.1 and discussed below do not capture all the characteristics or behaviors associated with bad managers, elimination or reduction of these behaviors alone could improve overall performance markedly and decrease the fear and tension that can lead to violent behavior in the workplace.

ABUSE THEIR POWER

Abusive supervisors or managers are always high on the list of things that make a job seem bad. Most people who hold jobs expect to be treated in fair and professional ways. Being treated as adults is important to all workers of any age, and from the lowest status jobs to the highest trained and highest paid professionals. They do not expect to be yelled at, called unflattering names, cursed, threatened, bullied, or harassed. They expect to have mature and reasonable interactions with supervisors and coworkers and to be judged and rewarded fairly. They expect their managers to allow

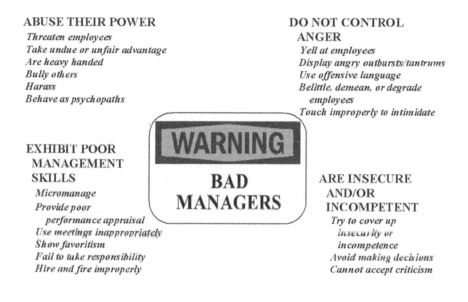

ABUSE THEIR POWER
Threaten employees
Take undue or unfair advantage
Are heavy handed
Bully others
Harass
Behave as psychopaths

DO NOT CONTROL
ANGER
Yell at employees
Display angry outbursts/tantrums
Use offensive language
Belittle, demean, or degrade
employees
Touch improperly to intimidate

EXHIBIT POOR
MANAGEMENT
SKILLS
Micromanage
Provide poor
performance appraisal
Use meetings inappropriately
Show favoritism
Fail to take responsibility
Hire and fire improperly

WARNING

BAD
MANAGERS

ARE INSECURE
AND/OR
INCOMPETENT
Try to cover up
insecurity or
incompetence
Avoid making decisions
Cannot accept criticism

Figure 2.1. Managers who contribute to increased propensity for workplace violence.

them to personalize their workspace to make it a more pleasant place, as they spend most of their waking hours inside that space. As experts in the jobs they perform day after day, they appreciate being asked for their input when impending decisions affect their jobs. When those conditions do not exist, jobholders have little incentive to perform at high levels or to keep their jobs.

It is important to note that the lowest performing employee is not necessarily the recipient of the manager's wrath. Not infrequently, the hardest worker or the most qualified one is subjected to the harshest criticism and treatment because the incompetent manager regards such individuals as a threat. That threat, though, is almost always in the mind of the beholder—the manager—and not the result of anything that the employee has done (except perform well!).

Managers who abuse their power are loathed by workers. Especially in a tight labor market when jobs are scarce, employees may feel that have little choice but to stay and subject themselves to the abuse. One might think then, that in a tight labor market when managers would be readily available for hire, top management would not hesitate to rid the organization of an abusive manager. However, that does not seem to be the case. Indeed, a tight labor market can have the opposite effect—nothing is done about the abusive manager because employees are not likely to complain or leave since there are no other jobs available. Just how abusive the manager becomes and how that behavior is brought to the attention of a manager's superiors will determine the organization's actions or lack thereof. When the manager's abusive behavior may subject the organization to legal action, upper management is more motivated to listen.

Managers need power, of course, in order to perform their functions within organizations. However, it is easy to abuse that power, especially when a manager feels either overly superior or inferior. For example, managers who feel they are truly the privileged elite at the workplace may abuse their power in an effort to remind themselves and the employees of their stature. On the other hand, managers who feel inferior may abuse their power because they fear losing control otherwise—or because that is the only way they can feel superior. We could include in this category those managers who use their power to gain sexual or other favors in the workplace.

Threaten Employees

Bad managers have many ways in which to abuse their power by threatening subordinates or making them feel threatened. They may threaten undesirable and perhaps embarrassing actions such as relocation, termination, changes in or additions to job duties and work assignments. They may threaten to give employees a difficult assignment that has a high probability of failure, an undesirable job assignment that the workers will not want, or menial tasks that assault their egos. Worse still, they may threaten to withhold pay increases or promotions unless employees follow their ethically questionable directions.

All of these are power plays that may be intended to show who is manager or perhaps to coax a worker to resign. Such threats are used sometimes as punishment for making a mistake, refusing questionable directions, failure to meet sales goals, expressing a difference in opinion, or even socializing with "higher-ups" or employees in a different department. Like horsemen who crack their whips, they hope that their scare tactics will elicit the desired behavior so that it will be unnecessary to do anything more. Other managers use threats to remind the employee that "I am the Boss—I have this power and am not afraid to use it." Some of these threatening managers may in fact carry through on their threats, but others are either bullies or shy and diffident managers who lack confidence in managing problems or people in a "healthy" way.

The threatened loss of a job has a deep psychological impact and is almost the worst kind of threat a worker can have outside of physical injury.

Various methods are used to deliver these threats. A worker may be told that he could lose his job if he stays home ill another day, or if he does not attend a conference at a time when he badly needs to finish a project or be available to a sick family member. A pregnant worker may be told that she will have to give up her job if she takes the full 6-week pregnancy leave. We are familiar with cases where an individual has been threatened with termination for interacting socially with individuals of higher rank in the organization. In one major international U.S company, employees were threatened with termination if they revealed their salaries to one another—or to their wives, who might share the information with another wife. Frequently, as sales people know, managers threaten termination if unrealistic sales goals are not met. Any one of these threats produces deep anxiety, affecting not only the worker's job performance but also his life outside the workplace. This is not to be confused with a manager's giving feedback or other forms of reminding or motivating employees to meet the organization's realistic productivity goals in order to stay employed at the company.

Take Undue or Unfair Advantage

By virtue of their power in their organizations, managers are in a position to take advantage of situations that should benefit their employees and their organizations. In the hands of bad managers, however, that power sometimes is used to gain undue or unfair advantage. Managers who have this motive are only one step away from managers who speak their threats, as discussed above. They, too, are generally despised by their workers. These managers will use their knowledge and connections to coerce employees to do as the manager wants, even though they are not technically threatening the worker. Nowhere is this more evident than in the manager's ability to determine what goes into the worker's personnel file, the size of salary increases, and whether the worker will be promoted. Unfortunately, some managers use their power to force an employee to do something unethical and/or illegal. Sexual harassment may also be included in this category. Another example you may be familiar with is a manager who pressures workers to contribute to a political candidate or cause, then reimburses them from company funds. Such illegal transactions may result from the pressure that the manager feels from his superiors, or it can result purely from greed—the manager expects to reap benefits from the person or organization that benefits from his employees' contributions.

Sometimes bad behavior results from managers' feeling that they are indeed superior to their workers and that they have a right to do whatever is needed to get the workers to produce. In some other cases, managers actually feel inferior in their jobs (or maybe in life also), and take unfair advantage or act heavy-handed as a way of convincing themselves and others that they are individuals with status or power. They defend their actions with "Because I Am The Boss." They function similar to threatening managers. Technically, though, these managers don't just threaten to, say, reassign workers to undesirable workstations, force workers to work overtime, relocate employees, reassign workers to undesirable workstations, or force unreasonable decisions (take promotion or get out). They just do it—usually without a word of explanation because they dislike something the person did or they just like to do it that way to remind all workers that they are the manager and they have power. On a more personal note, these power-wielding managers may take long lunch hours, come in late, or leave early. They may offer a worker a less-than-fair salary or a smaller salary increase because they know that the employee must "take it rather than leave it" since family responsibilities will not permit the worker to leave the area.

Heavy-Handed in Other Ways

Usually, abusive managers are only verbally abusive, but sometimes they may abuse their authority in other ways. For example, in what appears to be a vengeful or resentful decision, the manager may suspend employees or put them on administrative leave without thoroughly examining the facts. When an employee is unfairly singled out for harsher words or punishment than other employees receive, other workers are affected as well. They realize that managers who are unfair to one employee will likely mistreat another also. The stress is felt by most other employees because no one knows who will be next. Virtually all research and practical experience suggests that the use of coercive, punishing techniques is not good management. As the adage goes, "You can catch more flies with honey than with vinegar." This does not mean, of course, that managers should overlook poor performance; rather, it merely suggests that considerate and professional feedback to employees along with proper training and resources will yield better results than will abusive techniques.

Intentionally or unintentionally, managers can find many ways to be heavy-handed with the workers under their supervision. They can assign their own work (including personal work and errands) or an incompetent coworker's unfinished job to an efficient employee who they know will get the job done right and on time. They may change a worker's job duties without consulting the worker or HR. Other heavy-handed tactics include attempting to prohibit socializing, punishing a person in some way for seeking another job, and attempting to motivate workers by pitting them against each other. Employees are especially critical of managers who take a hard-line approach to granting them time off for important personal appointments during the workday.

The reasons for acting heavy-handed are as varied as the tactics—a desire to hold back a too-competent employee who may become a competitor for the manager, bad chemistry between the manager and employee, a psychological need for control, an attempt to pattern after a parent or former employer, an effort to persuade an employee to resign, and so on. No doubt the reasons are many. Consider these few examples: changing an employee's job requirements with no notice or appeal, demanding that the employee perform personal work for the manager on company time, or refusing to recommend a highly deserved promotion for any one of several personal reasons. Other heavy-handed ways include applying HR policies inappropriately, attempting to prohibit socializing, encouraging employees to "tattle" and exaggerate criticisms on one or more coworkers, misleading or overstating a problem to motivate, and even punishing an employee who is apparently looking for another job. There seems to be no limit to the number of ways that a person with some power can abuse an employee to persuade him or her to resign, including reassigning jobs or job duties that will result in unbearable stress and/or failure.

Bully Others[6]

Bullying is a form of workplace violence and should not be tolerated. Bullying by managers is a form of intra-office aggression that has negative effects on both productivity and morale. Furthermore, it can be emotionally, financially, and legally expensive to organizations. Frequently, since they have some amount of power as well as enforcement responsibility, managers become overly aggressive and, hence, develop into bullies—or become worse bullies. One recent survey found that negative managerial behavior that is directed at a particular employee especially in the presence of others is highly likely to be seen as bullying.[7] This suggests that one management adage possess a great deal of truth and can help to reduce the perception of bullying by managers: "Praise in public but criticize in private."

Experts and laymen have never established a firm agreement and definition as to what constitutes bullying versus what is aggressive behavior that may be acceptable or unacceptable.[8] This lack of a clear definition is especially important in the workplace, where individuals in supervisory roles are given some amount of power as well as enforcement responsibility. In the absence of precise definitions, office managers can at least learn from the efforts of scholars to understand these concepts.[9] It is also important to treat situations confidentially to protect the rights of all concerned.[10]

Harass Others

Bullying can take the form of harassment, but harassment is more. Generally speaking, harassment involves verbal or physical behavior based on legally protected characteristics (e.g., race, color, religion, sex, national origin, age [for those 40-years-old and over], disability, sexual orientation, or retaliation). Harassment may become a legal issue if the behavior creates a hostile work environment (an environment which interferes with work performance) or a change in an employee's employment status or benefits (demotion, transfer, or the like).

A few examples (but only a few) of behaviors that could constitute harassment include

- Using racially derogatory words.
- Negative or disparaging comments regarding an employee's gender or gender preference, race, religion or religious beliefs (or lack thereof), age (when referring to employees 40 and over), looks, clothing, body parts, mental or physical disabilities, or birthplace.
- Telling sexual jokes, hanging sexual calendars or posters, making sexual gestures, sending (or forwarding) sexually suggestive e-mails or images.
- Improper touching that makes someone uncomfortable.

Behaviors that aren't really serious are generally not regarded as harassment, especially if they are isolated incidents. Those would include offhand comments and teasing, again, so long as they are isolated and not serious. However, if someone complains about a behavior, don't simply "blow it off." Take the complaint seriously and correct the situation to assure that it isn't repeated.

Behave as Psychopaths

In many ways the worst type of manager and yet one of the hardest to readily identify is the psychopathic manager.[11] Psychopaths are charming but don't really have any feelings for others, so they lie and manipulate to achieve power over other people. They ruthlessly pursue their own selfish interests without regard for others (or the environment). Psychopathic managers tend to be overlooked so long as they are producing results—

profits, productivity, market share. But they may well be doing so in ways that are regarded as highly manipulative and deceitful. Chaotic situations, whether from the environment or from organizational change, are virtual breeding grounds for managerial psychopaths as they thrive on change and risk taking.

Psychopaths are generally likeable—until their "prey" find that they are just being used. Then the individuals feel betrayed and foolish. Psychopaths understand our emotions and can then manipulate them without feeling them in any way. People are simply tools or pawns to be used and sacrificed to accomplish the goals of the psychopath.

Psychologists H. M. Cleckley and R. D. Hare developed lists of characteristics of psychopaths (see Appendix: Psychopathy Indicators). Hare found that corporate psychopaths tend to score high on characteristics: Superficial Charm, Grandiose Self-Worth, Pathological Lying, Conning and Being Manipulative, Having a Lack of Remorse or Guilt, Having a Limited Range of Feeling (Shallow Affect); Callousness and Lack of Empathy; and a Failure to Accept Responsibility for One's Own Actions. Does this sound like your manager?

FAIL TO CONTROL THEIR ANGER

You don't need to be a psychiatrist to recognize managers who are ill-suited for managing employees because they either have not learned to manage their anger or have learned to express their anger inappropriately in a controlling, threatening way. In any setting and at any age, failure to control one's anger can create a myriad of problems. Nowhere is this truer perhaps than in the workplace where a manager yells at the workers or displays other angry outbursts and tantrums. Their anger creates a highly emotional state that results in a great many problems not only for them but also for those who interact with them. When managers do not control these feelings, they harm one or more persons and therefore the organization for which they work. Attempts to communicate while in a highly emotional state are likely to miss the mark.

Whether driven by power or because they are just plain malicious individuals, these bad managers may sometimes get good short-term results but eventually drive people off and generate lots of complaints or grievances. Long-term performance of their work groups is rarely more than just adequate.

Some of the tactics used most frequently by bad managers include yelling at employees, displaying angry outbursts or tantrums, using loud voices and negative body language, cursing or using offensive language, and other ways of demeaning or degrading employees.

Yell at Employees

Some managers yell or scream at others because they have become accustomed to using that technique to get their way—it's a habit. Perhaps they learned this behavior early in life from a parent, sibling, schoolmate, or teacher. They yelled and screamed until the adult or other child gave in to their demand, a behavior that is learned even before the age of 2 years. Others lack the confidence to obtain what they want by asking in a "normal," reasoning manner. Yelling is also a technique used by psychologically unstable individuals to embarrass or offend the ego of another person.

Many managers, like parents, tend to raise their voices unnecessarily and yell when they are overly stressed or when something meets their disapproval. Some do this because they believe that they must yell in order to prove their authority and elicit the behavior they want from the workers. They may yell and pound the table because that is how they think they should motivate the sales force. Or they yell, rant, and humiliate to hide insecurity; they aren't sure they can otherwise control workers. For similar reasons they may yell and belittle people who dare disagree with them; they cannot tolerate opinions that differ from theirs. Most of us have known a manager who yells at the top of his lungs to get his point across. After the explosion, fellow coworkers may cower and act as if they were walking on eggshells, not wanting to do anything to set him off. Some of our "interesting" managers yelled in an attempt to exert power and to intimidate people by inducing fear, especially when someone disagreed with their ideas or opinions. They could become very angry and aggressive, usually raising the voice (screaming mostly) and using curse words when expressing discontent that anyone dared disagree. And some managers would yell and mock a single individual whom they dislike just because they enjoy overpowering that person; they know he or she cannot retaliate or stand up for himself since the manager controls that person's job.

Managers don't necessarily confine their anger to their office staff; they can yell and berate outsiders such as suppliers, too. This is especially true in telephone interactions and electronic mail.

Display Angry Outbursts and Tantrums

Unfortunately, some managers go even further than yelling at their employees by displaying really angry outbursts or tantrums. Such behavior can genuinely frighten employees to the point where it not only interferes with their happiness and productivity at work but also carries over into their life after work, leading to unnecessary family stress as well. Many employees will not continue to work for a manager who resorts to such unnecessary tactics. Others may spend as much time thinking and talking about the incidents and dreading the next one as they do in carrying out the tasks for which they are paid.

Rather than conversing calmly, these managers use body language, tone of voice, hand gestures, and spoken words to instill fear—especially when employees are made to fear they will be fired. We found examples of managers "going ballistic," including punching and kicking walls and furniture while threatening to fire employees, and also throwing cake and drinks in the breakroom while demanding that everyone go back to work. Others throw tantrums or other objects to express disappointment over sales figures or anything else that may be happening in their life at that time. The result may be throwing papers on the floor, shouting, humiliating some individuals, and then storming out of the room—or, in the case of a dentist, throwing instruments at his assistant.

Nowadays, some managers have resorted to electronic mail as a means of displaying their anger. It apparently feels easier to express hostile feelings in the temporary anonymity that may be felt when the receiver is at a distance rather than face-to-face. Unfortunately for these managers, their outbursts and tantrums do not go away—they remain in the computer's memory forever and can easily come back to hit the writer in the face.

Use Offensive Language

Employees often criticize their managers for using offensive language when yelling, screaming, or otherwise attempting to communicate with employees. While in most companies the choice of bad words is considered unprofessional and unnecessary by virtually all employees, this habit is especially offensive and degrading to employees who are not accustomed to hearing foul language. The problem is that we do not all agree on what is socially acceptable and what is too offensive, but most would agree that habitually using foul language is not acceptable.

Some managers resort to using offensive language in reaction to the bearer of bad news. One CEO will rip the messenger to shreds, using comments such as "pull your head out of your *?*." The location of the foul-mouthed manager on a conference call, in a meeting, in his office, or in the hallway may intensify the impact and worsen the perception of other employees. A few managers will use foul language for the express purpose of coercing a person they would label a moralistic, narrow-minded person into resigning.

We should note that for some individuals foul or offensive language is simply their "vocabulary style." They do not mean to offend; they just cannot deviate from their established vocabulary, especially when deep in problem-solving thought and hence not thinking about what they are saying. We are not including them as bad managers. If they make it into a management position, they and upper management will usually warn potential employees and assign to him only workers who can overlook or tolerate the "colorful" language.

Belittle, Demean, or Degrade Employees

Yelling, having temper tantrums, and using foul language are generally viewed as demeaning or degrading; but some bad managers find even more ways, including illegal and/or unethical behavior, to accomplish the same improper mission. Examples of illegal or unethical behavior appear all too frequently on the pages of newspapers and business magazines. For the most part those are unusual and extreme incidents, but similar types of behavior on a smaller scale also occur more frequently than anyone would wish. Consider these additional examples of demeaning or degrading behavior.

Carrying over their childhood habits, some managers direct their anger toward a single individual by mocking, criticizing, or otherwise "putting down" an employee in the presence of his coworkers. This bully manager is likely to get his or her way by making the singled-out person feel low, "crawl into a shell," and therefore not participate in the discussions. Belittling or demeaning an individual worker in front of his peers or in emails is one method of assaulting another individual's ego. Employees may be treated like children, or like outcasts. They may be given "labels" that embarrass them or they may be bullied to instill fear. Depending on a worker's psychological makeup, a manager who belittles or demeans may seem even worse than one who yells or has tantrums.

One of the older managers we heard about uses emails the way some managers use their voices to put down employees. He uses words that are sarcastic or belittling, making employees feel that they have terrible skills and cannot communicate effectively. When some managers send what should be, at best, a private critical note to the worker, they also send CCs to others, further embarrassing the individual. Do they not have the nerve to say these things face-to-face but can write them to a person while not looking him in the eye? Has this type of communication always been their style, and they are not technically savvy enough to know that those same words in email messages today can be saved and used to build a case against them?

Young workers, in particular, encounter employers who treat them as if they were children. The manager insults them by talking down to them—

talking to them as if they were children and not adults at work. The tone of voice and body language can intensify the situation and create worse feelings. For example, in a meeting ostensibly to solve a problem, one manager forced each employee to indicate their participation in an incident, bringing to the open that this was really a problem with the rumor mill. But he intensified the situation and made it worse. He threatened all employees with "writing them up" if they were ever again caught "gossiping." He went as far as not allowing them to whisper in the office or to have private conversations unless it was done outside the office on their own time, which he could not control.

Belittling and demeaning behavior by the manager can lead to other employees joining in the teasing and hazing of the manager's "outcast" or using a "label" to embarrass an employee. One such case that we knew about involved targeting a 40-something female office worker with what they considered as "harmless behavior," such as moving things around on her desk while she was gone, and openly deriding her appearance and her age. It changed from "funny" to an expensive liability suit when someone pulled her chair out from under her as she was in the process of sitting down in a crowded meeting room, and she landed on her tailbone hard enough to knock the wind out of her and place her on bed rest for 3 days. Management, as well as everyone else, was aware of the teasing and the fact that it got out of hand. While it may be unbelievable to you that a manager would consciously or unconsciously reward the other employees for participating in such behavior, there definitely was no indication that management disapproved. Instead, there seemed to be a silent approval by management that "the weak" in this case would be driven off through the process of teasing and hazing.

Touch Improperly to Intimidate Person

Physical acts such as threatening posture, touching improperly, inappropriate physical contact, and other gestures and speech are sometimes used to intimidate others in the workplace. Such acts are prohibited, of course, but they happen nevertheless, especially involving minorities at the work site. We are perhaps most familiar with such behavior as it is directed toward women in a heavily male-oriented workplace. Sexual harassment has been a major problem to which many research studies, books, and articles have been devoted. Hopefully, current laws, training, and publicity are already helping to minimize the inappropriate touching of others to intimidate. Unfortunately, we may not yet have seen the peak of demeaning, degrading, or embarrassing individuals through emails or other forms of social media.

LACK MANAGEMENT SKILLS

When employees are asked to describe bad managers, they commonly cite examples of managers with poor management skills instead of or in addition to social or personal skills that we discussed above. These managers may (or may not) possess the right "personality" but lack the necessary managerial skills to make them successful or acceptable. For example, they may not have learned to trust anyone else to perform at the level they expect or to appraise employees objectively and provide proper feedback. Others may erroneously think that the best way to motivate a worker is to correct and humiliate him in the presence of his peers. They think they are "managing" when they harass employees, discriminate against those who don't fit the manager's concept of what a good employee should be, invade the privacy of employees, or even disregard the legal rights of employees. These are especially dangerous to organizations because not only do they jeopardize productivity but they also put their organizations at risk of potentially costly legal action as well as lowered morale and productivity

Many of the criticisms mentioned previously could also be tied to poor management skill, but here we address behaviors such as micromanaging, giving improper performance feedback, showing favoritism, and using meetings inappropriately.

Fail to Use Participative Management

As indicated in the introduction, a telling characteristic of many if not most bad managers is that they do not use participative management. Instead of involving their employees or even asking for their ideas or suggestions, they may wield their power like a club, put on a caring face for their employees while treating them poorly behind their backs, or justify their actions by the fact that they are the manager. They may be bullies, weak, incompetent, political, insecure, trying to perform beyond their level of competence, or some unfortunate combination of one or more of these.

Insecure, incompetent upper-level managers are usually opposed to asking those below them whether they have a solution to a problem or know how to do a job better or faster. The managers do not invite or accept input from those under their supervision. Yet these lower-level supervisors or their workers justifiably feel that they are more knowledgeable than are the upper-level managers about the job they are doing. Thus, they resent the fact that they are not asked or allowed to make suggestions for improving the job. Feeling that management is too incompetent, the individuals may ultimately come to resent the entire organization and to feel that their skills would be better used and rewarded elsewhere.

Micromanage

Managers who micromanage are also the curse of workers and supervisors, especially the more productive ones. Again, the manager, not the job, may be the culprit. Micromanagers are managers who cannot hand over a worker's job to the worker. They feel a need to tell the worker in minute detail how to perform a particular job, and then they still stay in control every step of the way. Overcontrolling or micromanaging has long been recognized as a sign of weak or poor management. Harry Chambers, an Atlanta-based workplace specialist, maintains that over 80% of all workers say they have been victimized by a micromanager.[12]

Micromanaging is more than merely bothersome to workers; it also lowers morale and performance on the job. Micromanaging means that the manager is paying extreme attention to small details—details that the worker should be taking care of while the manager is performing managerial work. Such meddling is not only counterproductive for the manager but also interferes with the worker's concentration and productivity. It sends the message that the manager thinks the worker does not know how to do his job. When a manager lacks faith in the worker, the worker either will lose faith in herself or will resent the manager's mistaken judgment and conclude that his or her skills would be better used elsewhere.

To micromanagers, it's more than just "getting there"—it's also about how the worker gets there. They must absolutely control every detail of how work gets done, and they demand constant activity. Individuals who shared their stories with us point out that micromanaging managers focus on activity instead of results and constantly check on employees. They tend to employ deadlines for everything, no matter how minor. Some even seem to believe that any sort of work break is unnecessary and bad—lunch, rest, bathroom, or whatever—things over which the micromanager has little or no control. In four words or less, they drive workers crazy. They command unjustifiable adherence to the manager's method, even to the point sometimes of dictating employee response to in-house surveys.

Some micromanagers behave as they do because they are insecure; they lack self-confidence. Or maybe they have too much self-confidence; no one can do the job as well as they can. Either way, they fear that subordinates might make mistakes that would reflect negatively on the manager. They are the only ones who can do the job right.

Perhaps micromanagers are insecure in their ability to lead. They fear "losing control" of people under their supervision or facing criticism for errors made by subordinates, so they require their personal approval before a subordinate can act. When promoted to the first managerial job, a manager may have begun by consciously or unconsciously demonstrating the new-manager syndrome. He may even have been encouraged by his managers to be vigilant and not let anything get "out of control"—micromanage to show power. But micromanaging then became his style. However, we also know that other micromanagers are motivated more by the love of the power, which they either have or want.

Even if a worker does not know how to do a job correctly, micromanaging is not the solution; it is not a substitute for training. Micromanaging is the method used by a manager who either doesn't trust the ability of his employees, believes that his way is the only way, believes that he or she is the only one who is capable of performing the job, doesn't want the employee to succeed without the manager's input—or perhaps all of the above. Whatever the cause, an overly controlling supervisor creates under-producing employees.

Micromanaging, for whatever the reason, is a manager's work style, not an indication of a worker's ability. It is a style that workers detest but that a manager is unlikely to change. It slows the productivity of competent workers and tells them that the manager does not trust their competency. If the organization hires competent workers, there is no need to have managers looking over the shoulders of their employees.

Provide Poor Performance Appraisal

Managers are responsible for providing feedback to each employee about how well he or she is performing the assigned tasks. Bad managers don't have a clue what their subordinates are doing or how well they are doing it. Or even if they do, these managers invariably are poor communicators and provide poor or no feedback about their subordinates' job performance. They are almost invisible in terms of helping subordinates or facilitating the work of the organization.

Workers need fair performance appraisals and timely feedback so that they know how well they are meeting the organization's expectations and where they may need to improve. Without that feedback, employees cannot know for sure how well they are perceived as performing their jobs. They probably won't improve in weak areas if they are not shown the areas that need improvement. They may not continue effective performance if it is not reinforced. Thus, managers who do not provide this appraisal and feedback are impeding the worker's growth and presumably his productivity.[13]

Despite the fact that there are numerous training programs, software packages, and even Internet sites to assist managers in conducting performance appraisals and feedback, some managers don't do it very well. Why? Perhaps the most innocent explanation is misplaced goal emphasis.

On the other hand, we have heard several examples of managers giving low evaluations with the intent to use those against the worker in the future—often to justify withholding raises or promotions, or even to fire the worker. Making false accusations and dishonest evaluations to support low performance ratings is among the more serious actions that a manager can take against his employee. The appraisal/feedback process is not working as intended when low performance ratings are assigned arbitrarily to the worker. When the feedback session is used to humiliate and instill fear in the worker, the manager is misusing the technique, thus highlighting his lack of management skills.

Use Meetings Inappropriately

A common complaint in most organizations is that there are too many meetings or that meetings are run poorly and are unnecessarily long. Meetings are meant to be a constructive means of giving information to, or getting information from, a group of individuals. As such, they serve as important functions within organizations. They provide a mechanism whereby information can be exchanged among several participants at the same time, thus enabling efficient communication within the organization. They are important to the efficient operation of organizations as they facilitate upward as well as downward and lateral communication.

However, meetings can be dysfunctional and unproductive if used inappropriately; that is, scheduled because someone thinks that everybody needs to get together, allowed to consume too much time, or are the manager's attempt to look engaged or to remind everyone "who's the boss." A few bad managers use meetings as dreadful "show and tell" sessions. Tension is great when group meetings are held to ridicule those who failed to meet goals, to intimidate by pointing out individuals' errors, or to humiliate individuals or groups who missed their goals. No worker deserves this type of treatment. Some managers think that singling out workers to chastise in front of their peers will motivate them (especially in sales), but such an approach intimidates all the workers, not just the ones who are singled out. Once again, the manager is creating hostility that will eventually result in turnover and may result in a lawsuit or even workplace violence. To some workers, it may suggest that such behavior is desirable, thus leading to bad interpersonal relations or even coworker bullying.

Show Favoritism

Managerial favoritism that is obvious to the workers is probably not totally oblivious to the manager. Rather, managers probably justify the different treatment as deserved or earned on the basis of a worker's behavior or for compassionate or humanitarian reasons. Many managers are overly sympathetic to some individuals who miss work to attend to family obligations and therefore increase the workload for others. They repeatedly expect other employees (especially single or childless workers) to stay late or pick up the work load of the absentee worker, schedule meetings around that worker's calendar, or excuse the preoccupied or lazy worker from meetings. Despite the fact that it is illegal, they may offer less pay to single or childless workers "because employees with dependents need more money" (even for doing the same work!). Medical insurance premiums may also reflect a similar bias by charging a family of two (husband and wife), for example, to pay the same insurance premium as a family of four or five. Such favoritism alienates single or childless workers and decreases their commitment to and performance for the organization. This is an organizational problem, not really the fault of the manager, of course.

Fail to Take Responsibility

Unlike the micromanagers, some managers practice a hands-off style of management that workers find equally frustrating and sometimes more counterproductive. These managers have too little involvement with their work and the workers. In many cases, they appear to lack the skills to communicate and otherwise deal with stressful encounters or decisions. Others lack the vision to plan properly so that workers can be content and productive. They don't see a problem even when an employee calls attention to it. For example, they don't notice or don't seem concerned about the fact that a couple of workers are "free riders"—people who avoid doing their share of the work.[14] When coworkers suggest a way of assigning work more evenly, those managers may be caught totally off-guard. "Why do we need to do that?" he may ask. "I don't think there's a problem, is there?"

Failure to take responsibility is especially evident when it concerns planning. Consider, for instance, a large technical firm that performs high-priced work, operates 24/7, and is totally dependent on having the latest, fastest, most stable computer-related equipment. Yet time after time they suffer breakdowns because someone has decided not to purchase additional equipment or an upgrade that they need. Or occasionally an individual worker has declined to have the latest version installed on his particular workstation, thus presenting a lot of problems due to incompatibility of software. Or when the equipment breaks down and Tech Support does not have replacement equipment in inventory, they try to patch it until they can get a replacement the next day. These downtimes are not only costly but also make it difficult to meet productivity expectations.

Terminate Improperly

Terminating an employee is one of the most important actions a manager can take. Unfortunately it is all too frequently done poorly. Some managers, too insecure to have a face-to-face encounter, use emails, letters, or phone calls to tell someone that they are fired. Other weak managers try to be nice and imply that the termination decision is not final. Other managers, assuming their superiority, fire individuals with no warning, do so with no documentation, or do so without having done due diligence. Some of these managers will feel the need to demonstrate their power and "set an example" for other employees by having security publically accompany the terminated employee while she cleans out her desk, then parading her in front of others as she is escorted from the building. Any time an employee is terminated, the fuse for potential workplace violence has been lit. All managers need to keep that in mind and take necessary steps to snuff out the fuse.

ARE INSECURE AND/OR INCOMPETENT

Managers need to be well informed and competent because these qualities help them also feel secure in their relations with their own managers as well as the workers they supervise. Nevertheless, managers are frequently chosen for their technical or job-related knowledge, seniority, or even personal favoritism with little or no thought given to their ability to manage people or relate to other persons inside or outside the organization. They may cover up their insecurity or incompetence by tossing decisions to someone else or by simply explaining with the phrase, "Because I'm the boss." You may have already reached that conclusion from your own experiences or from stories you have heard from friends and coworkers.

Most of us have also observed managers who are afraid that one or more of their employees might know something or have some level of skill or competence that the manager may not have. Workers respect managers who are secure enough to acknowledge their lack of information or skills and then to do something about it. Conversely, they lose respect for a manager who is too insecure or incompetent to make a decision. After all, decision-making is high on the list of the things that managers are paid to do. Nor do they respect managers who surround themselves with "yes" employees and refuse to accept blame or criticism. After all, managers should hire workers because the workers have knowledge, experience, or skills that the manager does not have.

Employees dislike jobs where they must answer to incompetent managers chosen as a result of the organization's use of improper criteria for hiring supervisors/managers. Sometimes this means that the organization will hire managers who are tough but incapable—they know how to crack the whip, but they are not technically competent and know little about managing people. These managers do not believe in making exceptions; they insist that "rules are rules not to be altered," which relieves them of having to make real decisions. These managers are insecure in their jobs or they are carrying out the wishes of upper management in a rigid culture. The incompetent managers may have been hired because they have, say, an MBA, yet they lack the knowledge and experience to manage others, especially when the lower-level managers and employees are older than the manager and have the skills and expectations that come with seniority on the job.

Insecure and incompetent managers badly need training but, unfortunately, many of them fail to respond to such efforts. Both types tend to be unable to accept criticism or blame.

Cover Up Their Insecurity or Incompetence

Workers don't seem to get bent out of shape if their manager doesn't know all the answers or how to perform some of the tasks that the workers perform. They know that everyone is human, especially managers! What they really dislike is a manager who tries to cover up the fact that he or she does not know the answer—a manager who is insecure and incompetent. Again, "Because I'm the boss" is not an acceptable response to workers' questions.

Although managers who are insecure and/or incompetent may also abuse their power or fail to control their anger publicly (topics we have discussed earlier), this is not necessarily the case. Instead, an insecure or incompetent manager may be a smiling, soft-spoken manager who tries to mask his insecurity or incompetence. As we have mentioned previously, he answers "why" questions from his workers with the words, "because I am the boss"—either because he does not know why or because he is afraid he cannot defend his reasoning. On the other hand, he may simply be an overbearing individual who is too arrogant to admit mistakes or lack of an answer to a question.

This type of manager may drive the workers "nuts" with his pacing, ranting, and asking for the status of the project. But an insecure or incompetent manager does not necessarily rant and rave when a project is still unfinished. Instead, he may sit quietly at his desk or leave the worksite to "run an errand" because he does not feel that he can be of help. He is a bad manager not because he rants and raves at the end but because he failed to keep on top of the project and assure its on-time completion.

A few insecure managers who are "on the edge" psychologically have been known to rig a project to "blow up" in their absence so it will appear that they are very much needed to insure the smooth running of operations. They can see to it that some of the parts or papers that are needed to complete a project are missing, thus delaying the completion of the project while they are away. Of course, competent individuals see this immediately as a sign that the manager is incompetent, as he or she should have been keeping tabs on such things all along and should not have left for vacation without checking on such details.

Workers may like but not respect a manager who refuses to "pitch in" because he feels that the work is beneath him or because he knows his incompetence will be evident. Managers who are incompetent and insecure can create considerable stress for the workers, who have no way of knowing whether details are being taken care of, whether deadlines are real, what are the norms of behavior or dress, and so on.

Avoid Making Decisions

Another type of manager who creates stress for workers is the one who avoids making decision. A competent, secure manager can assemble the facts, secure opinions if necessary, and then bite the bullet. It's what managers are paid to do. So avoiding decisions that could and should be made now is one of the surest ways of demonstrating incompetence or insecurity. Work gets interrupted and problems do not get solved in a timely manner when a manager avoids making decisions. Some of these reluctant managers could otherwise be considered as "nice managers" if only they did not have trouble "biting the bullet" because they are too friendly with some workers, too insecure, or too incompetent.

This problem is most frequently seen when managers need to make tough decisions that involve employee differences or that have legal implications. They may also be reluctant to resolve simple problems that could or will become major problems. Sometimes the decision may be relatively small and insignificant—the type of decision that another manager or a worker could make instantly, without further study or input. Sometimes the decision has a greater impact, such as whether to authorize workers to stay overtime to complete a project. Often the decisions have high impact on employee performance and stress, such as not deciding until 4:00 which items must be completed and shipped before FedEx closes at 5:30. Every day, then, 4:00 is crunch time, with incredible pressure, because the same manager would be irate if all the items did not get finished and shipped. Usually, the workers who are subjected to this indecisiveness have good ideas on how to prevent a rush like this, but their input is not wanted. So they leave in an angry, stressed-out mood almost every day.

Workers can be affected particularly when the manager refuses to get involved in disputes between workers, such as when one worker complains that he is doing his work plus some of the work that is or should be assigned to another employee. We also see managers who are so friendly with one or more employees that they cannot bring themselves to make a decision that those particular workers would disagree with. For example, if the manager has gone bowling with three guys every Wednesday night for 2 years, he may have difficulty denying a raise to one of those workers even if he knows that individual's performance is way below par. If the manager knows that an individual is a single mother/father who has a handicapped child who must be taken to a special daycare center, he or she also may have difficulty telling that worker that she is not performing well.

Cannot Accept Criticism or Blame

Acceptance of negative feedback or criticism is an important characteristic of effective managers who are secure in their positions and desire to improve. Without the knowledge of what others perceive as incorrect behavior, the manager probably won't change his behavior. Being open to criticism is, then, an important characteristic of good managers. None of us enjoys being criticized, but most individuals can accept constructive criticism that is presented appropriately. Regrettably, some managers simply cannot. They favor "yes" employees. They may even lie or terminate a worker to avoid criticism or blame.

It usually doesn't take long for a worker to learn that the manager cannot accept criticism or admit error regardless of how gently and positively it is presented. Even when asked a question that is not intended to be critical (e.g., "Has anybody tried packing these with bubble wrap instead of Styrofoam peanuts?"), the manager may hear the question as a criticism and react accordingly. Such managers prefer to surround themselves with "yes-men" so they do not hear criticism or blame.

WHAT NEXT?

This chapter has discussed characteristics of "bad managers," based primarily on reports of their peers and subordinates. Identifying bad managers is important because they are difficult for workers to survive, as we do not choose our managers, and they have a survival advantage over us because of their higher position. Workers choose jobs, but they quit bosses—bad managers, in particular. Bad is in the eye of the beholder, of course, so not all workers will agree as to how bad a particular manager is.

Chapter 3 discusses possible managerial solutions to bad managers—yourself or other managers. Chapter 4 presents ideas that nonmanagers or coworkers may find useful in coping with bad managers.

Appendage I at the end of this Section presents vivid real examples of many undesirable manager characteristics and behaviors that, if not corrected, could lead to violence in the workplace. Those examples have been drawn from material provided by consulting clients, students, family, or friends.

As you well know, not all problems that you may encounter in an organization revolve around a manager. Many times bad coworkers can make your life just as miserable or worse as can a bad manager. Chapters 5, 6, and 7 are devoted to bad nonmanagers (employees/coworkers).

NOTES

1. Litzky, B. E., Eddleston, K. A., & Kidder, D. L. (2006). The good, the bad, and the misguided: How managers inadvertently encourage deviant behaviors. *Academy of Management Perspectives, 20,* 91–103; Liu, D., Liao, H., & Loi, R. (2012). The dark side of leadership: A three-level investigation of the cascading effect of abusive supervision on employee creativity. *Academy of Management Journal, 55,* 1187–1212.

2. Working America. (2011). *"My bad boss contest" Grand prize winners announced.* Retrieved from www.workingamerica.org/press/releases/My-Bad-Boss-Contest-Grand-Prize-Winners-Announced

3. Kirschner, R., & Brinkman, R. (2012). *Dealing with people you can't stand* (Rev. & Exp. 3rd Ed.). New York, NY: McGraw-Hill; Pierce, J. L., & Newstrom, J. W. (2011). *The manager's bookshelf* (9th ed.). Upper Saddle River, NJ: Prentice Hall; Bramson, R. (1994). *Coping with difficult managers.* New York, NY: Fireside; Mr. X. (1995). *Fired? Fight back!* New York, NY: American Management Association.

4. We use the term "bad manager" to include managers at any and all levels who possess the negative characteristics described in this book. Those individuals have also been identified as abusive, destructive, dysfunctional, or similar terms. See, for example, Perrewé, P. I., Zellars, K. L., Rogers, L. M., Breaux, D. M., & Young, A. M. (2010). Mentors gone wild! When mentoring relationships become dysfunctional or abusive. In L. L. Neider & C. A. Schriesheim (Eds.), *The "dark" side of management* (pp. 1–25). Charlotte, NC: Information Age Publishing; Perryman, A. A., Sikora, D., & Ferris, G. R. (2010). One bad apple: The role of destructive executives in organizations. In L. L. Neider & C. A. Schriesheim. *op. cit.,* pp. 27–48.

5. Van Fleet, D. D., & Van Fleet, E. W. (2006). Internal terrorists: The terrorists inside organizations. *Journal of Managerial Psychology, 21*(8), 763–774.

6. Van Fleet, D. D., & Van Fleet, E. W. (2013). Future challenges and issues of bullying in the workplace. In L. M. Crothers & J. Lipinski (Eds.), *Bullying in the workplace: Causes, symptoms, and remedies* (pp. 550–577). New York, NY: Routledge/Taylor & Francis; Namie, G., &. Namie, R. (2000). *The bully at work: What you can do to stop the hurt and reclaim your dignity on the job.* Naperville, IL: Sourcebooks.

7. Van Fleet, D. D., & Van Fleet, E. W. (2012). Towards a behavioral description of managerial bullying. *Employee Responsibilities and Rights Journal, 24*(3), 197–215.

8. Carbo, J., & Hughes, A. (2010). Workplace bullying: Developing a human rights definition from the perspective and experiences of targets. *Working USA, 13,* 387–403.

9. Van Fleet & Van Fleet. (2013). *op. cit.*

10. Van Fleet, D. D., & Van Fleet, E. W. (2010). *The violence volcano: Reducing the threat of workplace violence.* Charlotte, NC: Information Age.

11. This section is based on Deutschman, A. (2005). Is your boss a psychopath?" *Fast Company, 96,* 44–51. Retrieved from www.fastcompany.com/53247/your-boss-psychopath

12. Chambers, H. (2004). *My way or the highway: The micromanagement survival guide.* San Francisco, CA: Berrett-Koehler.

13. Van Fleet, D. D., Peterson, T. O., & Van Fleet, E. W. (2005). Closing the performance feedback gap with expert systems. *Academy of Management Executive, 19*(3), 38–53.

14. For a more complete discussion of free riding see Albanese, R., & Van Fleet, D. D. (1985). Free-riding: Theory, research, and implications. *Academy of Management Review, 10*(2), 244–255; Albanese, R., & Van Fleet, D. D. (1985). The free riding tendency in organizations. *Scandinavian Journal of Management Studies, 2*(2), 121–136.

CHAPTER 3

BAD MANAGER BEHAVIOR

What Managers Can Do

Our most important task is to transform our consciousness so that violence is no longer an option for us in our personal lives.

—Deepak Chopra

In considering the implications of bad managerial characteristics, it is important to understand that a manager's effectiveness depends not only on ability and personality but also how others *perceive* that ability and personality. Bad is in the eye of the beholder, of course, so not all workers will agree as to how bad a particular manager is. Managers may indeed be bad, or they may simply be perceived by workers to be bad. Any number of reasons may account for why workers perceive a manager as bad, including a manager having a personality that workers don't appreciate, or workers failing to understand or appreciate the role of a manager. Regardless, managers must deal with what their workers and others perceive them to be, so to be effective they need to change the workers' perceptions. In this chapter we offer suggestions on how managers can make efforts to improve.

ANALYZE YOURSELF

Workers choose jobs, but they quit managers. With an understanding of the bad characteristics that workers attribute to their managers, managers who wish to survive and be successful will need first to look inward (preferably with input from others) to determine where there is need for improvement.

Self-Analysis

Think about what reasons anyone could possibly have for labeling you as a bad manager. For example, could someone feel that you treat them less like a professional than you do others? Do you sometimes lose your temper and yell at your subordinates? Have you gotten so upset with a subordinate that you threatened to fire him or her? Have you blamed someone else for a problem that you were a part of? Do you give unclear or inadequate instructions?

Using self-analysis to focus on your own behavior may enable you to improve the perceptions that others have about you. Some of the items in Exercise 3 at the end of this book may help you consider how others may see you and your behavior. Additionally, making sure that your behavior avoids the items noted in the exercise may well serve to reduce the propensity for violence in your organization.

Ask Others to Evaluate You

Because we never see ourselves as others see us, it is usually helpful to get the viewpoints of others—subordinates, peers, and superiors. Of course you need to be prepared for some criticism and take it as constructive and not become defensive. Be sure to ask for good points as well as for those areas in which you could improve. Again, you might use the items in the Exercise 3 to stimulate feedback.

POWER AND SELF-CONFIDENCE

Don't Abuse Power

As discussed in Chapter 2, abuse of power may take the form of threats against employees, taking unfair advantage of employees, or behaving heavy-handedly in other ways. Thinking back, can you recall having done these things? Can you recall anyone having tried to drop hints to you about overextending your power? In the future, watch the facial expressions and body language that may indicate your employees are thinking that you sound threatening, you are taking unfair advantage of them, or you are being heavy-handed in some other way. Listen for clues that employees perceive you as having improper motives and negative feelings or attitudes.

Eventually, depending on the type of workplace, you may observe signs of worker retaliation, ranging from cold shoulders to work slowdown and even various levels of sabotage or theft. For example, if you atypically begin to have difficulties meeting your own deadlines, the reason may be that the employees are causing the problem as a means to retaliate or to send a plea for help.

Another clue is an increasing level of absenteeism and turnover among employees, but you certainly do not want the abuse of power to reach that point before you see it happening. So before problems like these arise, observe the work environment for signs of discontent, lack of cooperation, and negative attitudes toward work. In particular, watch for problems with the areas that most directly affect the individual worker—determining what goes into the worker's personnel file, the size of salary increases, and whether the worker will be promoted, for instance. Organizational policies must be followed, especially regarding the use of performance appraisal and feedback. Managers must never justify their actions by saying, "Because I am the boss."

The best preventive is for you to serve as a positive role model. Use participative management as much as possible, and let your workers know that you want their suggestions and ideas. Treat them fairly and not dictatorially. Don't pretend that you care about the employees and then treat them poorly behind their backs. And, again, never use the fallback explanation of "Because I am the boss" to answer the people under you.

If you are accused of being a malicious person who abuses his power, for the sake of the organization you must either get out or begin to change your style or the workers' perceptions of your style immediately. Take advantage of the organization's resources for additional training, personal counseling, or a mentor. Don't wait for that abusive behavior to subject the organization to decreased productivity, sabotage, or legal action. Even if you are currently producing good results in the form of high productivity, those good results can be short-term and sure to create major problems for you and the organization as they lead to unacceptable long-term performance, employee turnover, grievances, false claims for workers' comp benefits, or legal suits.

Don't Bully or Harass

Tough, demanding managers are not necessarily bullies. If they are trying to get the best performance by setting high yet reasonable expectations for working safely and they are fair in their treatment of workers, they are not bullies. The distinction between bullying and legitimately tough management depends primarily on intent. Demanding managers don't just demand results. They also provide performance feedback along with coaching or counseling and opportunities to improve.

Develop a strong policy statement against bullying, harassment, and other forms of unacceptable behavior. Then walk the walk and talk the talk. You must show that you are serious by continuing to emphasize that everyone is expected to adhere to acceptable civil behaviors in the workplace. You should model acceptable behavior in your day-to-day activities. Managerial behavior is one of the most powerful ways in which a bully-free culture is established and provides a clear guide to others in the organization about what is acceptable, proper behavior in the organization. If managers act professionally and respectfully, others will do so, too. If not, deal with the problem quickly and decisively.

If inappropriate touching is a problem in your workplace, please consult your Human Resources department and avail yourself of the many books and articles that offer suggestions on how to respond. And remember that, if you do engage in bullying or harassing behavior, both you and your organization are subject to legal action.

Are You a Psychopath?

If you are a psychopath, in all likelihood you will not know or admit it. However, the self-analysis might yield some indications of how you are as a manager, and you could use the psychopathic characteristics in the Appendix for further self-analysis. Remember that some of the key characteristics of corporate psychopaths are failure to accept responsibility, lack of consideration for others, lying, excessive feelings of self-worth, and, of course, always looking out for "Number 1." And, if you dare, have a few other peers and/or subordinates share their views with you. If you feel that you are manifesting some of the characteristics of a corporate psychopath, by all means seek professional help.

Don't Micromanage

Another counterproductive behavior to watch for is the tendency to micromanage employees. Managers are sometimes hired specifically because they have the characteristics of a micromanager and are therefore likely to keep a tight rein on the workers. Is that true in your case? Were you already known as a person who keeps a very tight rein on the workers' day-to-day activities? If the organization hires competent workers, there is no need to have managers looking over their shoulders. Generally, managers who micromanage their employees will exhibit visible results of that counterproductive behavior—results such as an overworked manager, as he cannot let go of an assignment. Does that describe you? Eventually, signals will be sent by the workers, such as an unwillingness to do whatever it takes to finish an assignment properly, subquality work, an attitude of resignation, or some other sort of friction between the workers and their manager.

Managers who think or know that they have a tendency to micromanage should try to determine why. Perhaps they are insecure in their ability to lead, so they need to "stay on top of everything" to ensure that the work is done and done right. Almost certainly the manager who micromanages is not a bad employee or a slacker, but more likely is overly conscientious. Such managers are so concerned with getting the job done right that they cannot leave it to someone else. Maybe they feel that they are the only ones who can do the job right. They do not know or cannot accept the fact that they may be causing a larger problem than they are preventing or avoiding. They risk losing their most competent employees eventually, as those workers will seek jobs that offer greater opportunities and autonomy.

Learn to Accept Criticism

Competent or incompetent, no one likes to be criticized with harsh words or in the presence of others. Yet everyone, including managers, needs to learn to accept suggestions, constructive evaluation, or questions without regarding such feedback as challenges to their authority. Competent or incompetent, some managers may feel that they are above being criticized because no one else knows as much as they know. Incompetent managers may be so insecure that they cannot bear to hear critical comments about their performance. These managers prefer to surround themselves with incompetent individuals to whom they can feel superior or with "yes-men" (competent or incompetent) who know not to criticize. This is not smart; surround yourself instead with challenging individuals who will help you earn praise from your own managers. If you want loyalty from your employees, never expect them to accept blame or responsibility for something that you did not get done or for something that went wrong. Shifting the blame to an incompetent person or to a "yes" person may seem to be a low risk, but it will usually cost you the respect of your employees. In their eyes, if you will do that to one person, you will do it to any one of the others as well.

You can probably determine whether you are critical of or defensive toward the people working under you by thinking back on how much credit you give them when talking with them or other employees, your peer managers, or your own managers. Be honest with yourself as to whether you may be overly critical or blameful of your workers. Or better still, ask someone else if you are. And if you have a worker who offers criticisms only in a harsh, hurtful manner, you should be able to sit down with that worker and explain that you truly appreciate the feedback but he or she would be more effective if the message were delivered differently. Then spend the remainder of your meeting time exchanging ideas about what you can do differently. You may want to follow up on that exchange of ideas in due time by asking the person whether you are effectively addressing the problem.

DEVELOP PERSONAL AND INTERPERSONAL SKILLS

Become Competent and Secure

Ideally, an individual who is elevated to a supervisory level is competent and is secure in knowing that he or she is competent to do the job. However, inappropriate behaviors are often the result of a manager's incompetence and/or lack of security. Analyze yourself—do you feel competent to do your job, or do you feel ill at ease with the duties or the personnel?

Sometimes the insecure manager is a quiet, nonassertive individual who tends to avoid his or her subordinates. Such managers feel too insecure to judge, evaluate, or criticize their workers, although they may be able to accept criticism or blame themselves. On the other hand, attempts by managers to conceal feelings of insecurity more often result in a loud, overbearing personality or other signs of overconfidence. Verbal criticism, public or private humiliation, and assignment of blame to others is a frequent indicator of an individual who denies his or her own incompetence. The only way they can feel good about themselves is to tear down or belittle others.

Some insecure managers will attempt to attack virtually all of the competent people under and around them, while others tend to select only one or two individuals to harass. As a manager, take a closer look at the feedback you give to others. Do you have the knowledge and the confidence to give *constructive* criticism, not just criticism? If not, you should seek additional training in effective communications and interpersonal relationships, and also in the nuts and bolts of the business if you feel you lack that competence.

Find and Be an Effective Role Model

None of us is perfect; but even if we were, others might not regard us as such. As indicated earlier in this chapter, perception does not always match reality. So if your organization has managerial appraisal as a part of its feedback system, you should already have received some suggested areas for improvement. Listening carefully to any and all criticisms and suggestions is important because you serve as a role model for others in your organization, whether or not you like it or agree to it. So do your job right and well. Behave in the same manner that you desire and expect of your workers.

Perhaps the best way to start being an effective role model is by learning from the best. Find a role model for yourself. Observe how good managers in your organization perform. Read about good managers in other organizations. Avoid doing what the anecdotes presented in Appendage I show.

Control Anger

If you have a habit of "losing your cool" or not controlling your anger, you need to determine whether you indeed cannot control it or are choosing not to. Some people yell or display angry outbursts because they have learned that this is a shortcut to getting their way. Managers who have learned to use anger as a tool can be helped, but only if they choose to give up this negative tool for achieving results.

Those persons who cannot control their anger may or may not be able to change their style while functioning in a managerial role, depending on how deep-seated the problem is. Consider whether you may be under some particularly heavy stress or need some time off. Be honest with yourself—do you like being a manager, or is it too stressful for you at this point in your life? Managers who have consistently shown an inability to control anger should consider whether their job is destroying their quality of life and whether their other skills and abilities could function better in a non-supervisory role. Whatever the outcome, you can usually find assistance for counseling, anger management, career planning, or whatever through the organization's Human Resources department.

Communicate

Communicate, communicate, and communicate. The best way to get your employees to understand the importance of their contributions to the big picture is to share information. Communicate your vision. Communicate goals and your expectations about achieving those goals. Talk with (not to) your subordinates. And remember that yelling and using offensive language is not communicating, or at least is not communicating what should be. Likewise, touching others improperly communicates the wrong message and could lead to legal action as well as violent responses.

Also, remember that communication is a two-way process. Listen to your people, and take the appropriate action to show that you are listening and that you care. Pay attention to ideas, suggestions, and potential solutions to problems of which you were or were not aware. Seek ideas from others as to how to improve performance. Be open to criticism and responsive to change. An open organization is a better organization in the long term. Share feedback about goal accomplishment. Help others do their jobs better and reward them when they do. Tell people what they're doing right. And always remember to praise in public but criticize in private.

Don't Show Favoritism

Bending over backward to help a single employee or one group of employees is almost always likely to upset other employees. Giving one worker a higher raise that is not justified by performance is exercising extremely poor management ability, and under some circumstances could be illegal. On the other hand, giving all workers the same rewards is usually not good management. Whether the result of an effort to be kind, the fear of losing a particular worker, or the result of reverse discrimination, favoritism is a bad thing in an organization. It alienates workers and decreases commitment and performance. Simply stated, don't do it! Even though it is not easy to enjoy and treat everyone equally!

Take Responsibility

Taking responsibility, especially for failure, requires integrity. When individuals fail to take responsibility for their own actions, they destroy their integrity and lose the trust and respect of others. So it is important for you as a manager to take responsibility for your decisions, actions, and performance, including the way you interact with others. This means that you don't spend time and energy assigning blame but rather you accept responsibility and focus on correction and prevention.

Taking responsibility also requires listening to others who are in a position to observe from a viewpoint that is different from the manager's. Included here in particular are the individuals who actually perform the tasks. When workers offer suggestions regarding the tasks that they perform, a bad manager may be caught totally off-guard because he or she had never perceived that a problem exists. "Why do we need to do that?" he may ask. "I don't think there's a problem, is there?" Or he may even state, "Yes, but there's nothing that WE can do about it." And, so, another problem remains unfixed and may affect other future relationships between the manager and the nonmanager employees. At one company, the workers said they wanted to shout, "Ask us!! We know what to do!" So now they either resentfully continue as usual or just go ahead on their own and initiate a solution. In the latter case, workers have learned how to survive a bad boss by doing his work themselves! Listen with an open mind to what others are saying. Even better, seek open and honest input. Do not shirk responsibility by walking away from a problem just because *you* personally do not have a solution.

DEVELOP NEW MANAGEMENT SKILLS AND COMPETENCY

Managers may lack important management skills or competencies even though they have other strong qualities that led to their being named manager. Such deficiencies can usually be corrected easily through training, mentoring, or self-study.

Learn New Management Skills

As with other problems, you have a better chance of changing your behavior if you understand yourself. For example, do you erroneously think that the best way to motivate a worker is to correct and humiliate him in the presence of his peers? Do you think that employees can't be trusted to do their job unless you, the manager, are standing over them, intimidating or humiliating them? Do you not understand what constitutes harassment? Do you tend to discriminate against those who don't fit your personal concept of what a good employee should be, how they should groom or dress, or what the proper attitude should be? Even worse, do you think that you have the right to invade the privacy or disregard the legal rights of employees because you are the manager? Attitudes like these are especially dangerous to organizations because they jeopardize productivity and put their organizations at risk of potentially costly legal action.

In such cases, it may be easy to acquire new or different skills. You can always try to talk openly with your employees to make certain that you are not being perceived incorrectly. For example, tell them, "If I sound curt on occasion, please let me know as I don't mean to be." You can try to change yourself through reading books on effective management and leadership.

And, of course, you can avail yourself of management-development programs at your organization or those sponsored by industry, government, or universities.

Provide Timely Performance Feedback

Make certain that there are ways in which you can find out what subordinates think. A 360-degree feedback system of performance appraisal can help with this, as can simpler anonymous suggestion systems, the use of ombudspersons, and exit interviews. A 360-degree feedback system refers to performance appraisal in which multiple sources of evaluation (superior, peers, subordinates) are involved to provide a more complete view of your performance "from all angles." Engage your personnel in conversations that provide an opportunity for them to tell you about their problems and ideas and for you to ask questions in an informal setting. Without such feedback, it is difficult or impossible to make improvements; with the feedback, areas for improvement can be identified and addressed.

Providing performance feedback should be an organizational policy that results in appropriate information being added to the workers' files and inappropriate information kept out of the files. Hence, this obligation should never be omitted "because you forgot," especially if Human Resources is given the authority to notify appropriate authority figures when such feedback has not been performed by the specified time. It does not, however, ensure that the feedback is done properly. As a manager, you need at least some level of training in how to evaluate and how to perform feedback. If you have not had enough training to feel comfortable in giving effective feedback, talk to your manager and to your organization's human resources department.

Never use the feedback session to humiliate and instill fear in the worker. That is misusing the technique and showing a lack of management skills. The same is true also of giving low evaluations with the intent to use those against the worker in the future—often to justify withholding raises or promotions, or even to fire the worker.

Bad managers frequently don't have a clue about what their subordinates are doing or how well they are doing it. Listen for grapevine complaints about performance feedback, and look for clues such as negative attitudes, lower productivity, higher turnover, and friction among workers as well as between workers and you. To prevent problems from evolving to these levels, however, you may need to consult informally with other more experienced managers in your organization. Review the evaluations that you did previously, paying particular attention to your written justifications and recommendations for pay or position adjustments—increases, transfers, promotions, and terminations. In some cases, you may not be totally happy with what you did and could therefore benefit from sitting down with your own manager or other experienced managers to discuss how to handle difficult cases in particular. Also, it is important to note that there arc various training programs, software, and web-based sites to help managers provide this important function. Given the short- and long-range problems associated with inferior performance feedback, such sources of assistance are highly recommended for managers who lack experience in performance feedback.

Use Meetings Appropriately

Managers should be sensitive enough to observe employee reactions or body language to see when they are using staff meetings inappropriately. Never be so insensitive as to use meetings as the place to embarrass, humiliate, or berate a worker. That is not the way an effective manager behaves. Managers who do use staff meetings in this manner may be imitating managers under whom they have worked, without thinking whether the practice is good or bad. That style needs to be changed. Negative feedback to an individual is for private meetings. If the negative feedback applies to all or most, a staff meeting may be appropriate for discussing the matter, but without singling out any one person.

Finally, on the subject of meetings, most workers resent their managers calling unnecessary meetings or failing to make efficient use of meeting time. Always prepare thoroughly for the meeting, have an agenda, and follow it unless you have good reason to deviate. Respect everyone's use of time. That includes starting promptly and having a firm stopping time as well. Adhere to that schedule so your attendees can schedule their other commitments. Encourage participation, but insist that participants stay on the topic so the meeting can be completed by the expected time. When a discussion gets too far off-course, the manager is responsible for steering everyone back on-course. Rather than allowing meetings to get out of hand and run overtime, additional meetings can be scheduled for runaway topics or issues that concern select individuals rather than the entire group.

Learn to Make Decisions

Managers who avoid making managerial decisions have an intolerable effect on their own managers as well as the people under their control. These managers need to determine whether their indecisiveness stems from a lack of understanding as to their job duties, a lack of confidence, or a lack of competence. They may need additional training or someone to serve as a mentor or at least a sounding board until they get better established in the managerial role. Another potential solution is to use more participative management. Workers who are subjected to managerial indecisiveness often have good ideas for solving problems and aiding in decision-making. Rather than considering their manager incompetent and indecisive, workers who are critical of the manager's indecisiveness most always are willing to pool their ideas on solving problems, for example, that otherwise result in their being overstressed at work and carrying negative feelings with them at the end of the workday. Give them opportunities to provide feedback to you.

Some managers are so friendly with one or more employees that they cannot bring themselves to make decisions that affect those select individuals. This is especially common when a manager has been promoted from within the group, thus putting him or her into a position of making hard decisions that affect the people who have been considered their equals. "New manager on the block" can be a tough role. Start by putting some distance between yourself and the individuals you supervise. Try to spend time with your own manager or your own level of managers so that you are viewed as having less time to socialize with the employees. Sometimes the organization can provide managerial training programs that will help new managers bridge this transition period. By learning to communicate openly and fairly with employees, the manager can be both a supervisor and a friend.

HIRE AND FIRE PROPERLY

Firing, terminating, or laying off employees is perhaps the most difficult, gut-wrenching decision and potentially violence-causing action required of a manager. Consider the impact of an employee resigning because he or she cannot function under a bad manager or surrounded by bad workers. The costs will include recruitment-related expenses associated with preparing the necessary forms to fill the job, advertising the job, interviewing costs and time, orientation and training costs for the new worker, and doing the job of the employee who resigned until a replacement is hired and able to function at a satisfactory level. Turnover under this type of circumstance can decrease employee satisfaction, which in turn may lead to decreases in quality and productivity. Customer service can be affected and the organization's image damaged. These potential consequences simply cannot be ignored. With more good people to begin with, there is less chance of problems developing later on.

Hiring

So the first consideration is to hire the right people from the start. Then you don't have to worry about dealing with bad managers or bad employees—or, more realistically, dealing with bad managers will be something with which you will have to be concerned only occasionally. Of course, that is easier to say than to do. A good rule of thumb is to be as careful in selecting your employees as you should in selecting someone with whom you are going to live—a spouse, significant other, roommate, or the like. You should carefully consider the person's "history" and the feedback you can obtain from others. When checking references regarding a potential new-hire, be aware that references are usually guarded in their responses, as they are aware of the legal problems that could result from giving out negative information. Also, follow the company policy and governmental regulations relative to reference checking.

In the hiring process, you must not only assess the job candidate's ability and "fit" but also explain the job, the culture, the expectations, and such to that individual so they can more accurately assess their own fit with your organization. And be totally honest with the applicant. Misrepresenting the job or intentionally misleading the individual regarding its future or the company's future can lead to legal action if the job is eliminated or the company goes under. The job ad or posting must also contain accurate and complete information. Too often the real job requirements are either missing or simply imbedded among other "desirable qualifications." List them clearly; don't try to terminate someone later because they don't meet the job requirements.

Firing Issues to Consider

The first consideration in terminating a worker starts well before the actual firing process. Managers must document performance, behavior, evaluations, feedback, and poor interpersonal relationships. Don't "play nice" when noting problems; avoiding the ugliness or seriousness of an employee's behavior will come back to bite you when required to defend the termination decision. The absence or presence of documentation makes all the difference in defending a termination decision or challenge. The only thing worse than no documentation is unduly complimentary remarks, which some managers seem to feel they should place in everyone's files.

In some cases, terminating an employee is a risky move for the organization, as the worker may file a lawsuit or, worse still, attempt to retaliate against the manager or the entire organization. Even at the moment we are writing this paragraph on a Saturday afternoon, news bulletins are flashing reports of a fired employee who just shot his boss and three former coworkers, two of whom died. You, the manager, and your company should have ample motivation for trying to minimize the trauma of the firing act. The loss of one's job may trigger a seemingly uncontrollable rage. The results are compounded when the employee has medical issues or relationship problems within the family, is in an age bracket that vastly reduces the probability of finding another job, or lives in an area where the unemployment rate is already high. It is a severely traumatic event that evokes the fight-or-flight reaction that calls for "getting even" or seems to the terminated worker as the only way out. Also, when the job market is tight, employees will fight harder to keep their jobs—which means they may be more willing to use more desperate measures "to right a wrong."

Many acts of workplace violence have been attributed to employee termination, especially when the act of firing has further embarrassed the individual or insulted his ego. If the termination process is not done carefully, even the nonviolent person may make a claim in any number of ways, using contract issues, company policy, state laws, or federal regulations such as OSHA (Occupational Safety and Health Administration), Title VII, the Age Discrimination in Employment Act, the Americans With Disabilities Act, ERISA (Employee Retirement Income Security Act), the Fair Labor Standards Act, or the Family and Medical Leave Act.

Firing Alternatives to Consider

If you as a manager become aware that you have employees who fit the descriptions of bad workers, you should act immediately. Be sure you follow all company policies and procedures, observe all legal procedures and government regulations, and document the behaviors and actions leading to your identifying that worker as "bad." In many cases, you will also need to contact your Human Resource department in advance. You should first inform the individual that you are dissatisfied and are looking into the problem. This should provide the worker with an opportunity to correct the problem and hence avoid termination. It is imperative that you document every step, including *who* participated in whatever contact you have, *what* was said and done by whom, *where* (specifically) the problem or the meeting occurred, *when* (date and time), and whatever plan of action was suggested and/or agreed upon by whom.

There are other alternatives that you as a manager may need to consider, depending on company policy and the legal advice of company attorneys. If appropriate, provide education and training that will give the individual an opportunity to change the undesirable behavior. Again, your organization's human resources department may assume an important role in this endeavor. Formal and informal training and development programs can be extremely useful in communicating effective behavior for employees. Finally, if the individual cannot or does not change, you should assist the individual firmly and courteously in leaving your organization. The assistance may include providing a severance package that includes a job placement service as well as counseling.

Mediation or arbitration are other possibilities that may be more desirable than litigation. Alternative Dispute Resolution (ADR) involves a binding agreement between the employee and the organization to resolve employment disputes through binding arbitration. If your organization does not sanction ADR, it could use a system of progressive discipline. If the employee has been given the chance to correct performance or behavioral problems before being discharged, a jury is more likely to decide for the company. Also, the company could use a disciplinary suspension system, which means that the employee is "removed" from the premises but kept on payroll while the company ensures that the manager's documentation supports the decision, investigates the employee's conduct, and reviews the handling of equivalent problems in the past.

Firing Procedures

How you conduct the final step—informing the person of his termination—is extremely important. It can be the determining factor in how the individual handles the pain and anger of being fired.

First, the employee should have some type of warning and should be told in a face-to-face meeting, in the presence of a witness (often an HR representative). Firing a person via electronic mail, telephone, or texting is a cowardly act and shows a lack of respect for the individual.

Similarly, try to manage the firing logistics to avoid embarrassing the person in front of his peers. This can be somewhat difficult, as you do not want to allow the employee to access information systems, his work area, or his coworkers after being terminated. Nor do you allow the individual to leave with company property in his possession. Arrangements must be made to allow the person to take possession of his own personal property, however. All employees—regardless of their stature in the company—are infuriated by actions that suggest they are not to be trusted or that embarrass them in the presence of other employees. Even worse is the practice of having a Security Officer escort them from the building, denying them the opportunity to even wave goodbye to coworkers in the same area. While the company must protect itself, which may dictate that computer access be denied, seldom if ever is there a need to march an employee into HR or the manager's office while you pack his personal things and hand them to him (or worse still, tell him you will mail his personal items), deny him the opportunity to say a word to anyone as Security escorts him out of the building and off the premises. Such callous treatment practically begs a "troubled" worker to retaliate by filing a lawsuit or exploding in some form of workplace violence.

In situations where there is reason to suspect that the worker may respond in a disturbing or violent manner, Security can be asked to stand nearby but out of sight while the manager delivers the unwelcome news. Ideally, a representative from HR or other witness will also be present even if not required by company policy.

Provide the employee with a coherent, precise explanation—not inconsistent explanations—why he or she is being terminated. Don't supply lengthy rationale and examples; in other words, avoid giving too much information. If the person requests to see his personnel file, follow your state's statutes. Usually, you will suggest that he address his request to the HR department. Or, if a representative from your Human Resources department is present, you could ask that person to address this question now.

Before the meeting ends, the former employee should understand that the firing decision is final and how the communication of the person's departure will be handled internally and externally. Try very hard to end the meeting on a more positive note. One way is to make the person's final check available to him at this very moment. Or it may mean telling him when to expect a check or how to submit requests for references. Paying severance is also a positive action and can sometimes reduce the risks for the company.

WHAT NEXT?

This chapter has made numerous suggestions about how you might act to reduce the incidence of "bad managers" among others in your organization, or how you may analyze and modify your own managerial behaviors so you are not perceived as a "bad boss."

But others in the organization—the nonmanagers—can also act to reduce the number of bad managers in the organization. That is the subject of the next chapter.

CHAPTER 4

MANAGER BEHAVIOR

What Nonmanagers Can Do

Violence is a tool of the ignorant.

—Flip Wilson

In the previous chapter we recognized that a manager's effectiveness depends not only on his or her ability and personality but also how others *perceive* that ability and personality. We acknowledged that managers may indeed be bad or they simply be perceived by others to be bad, and we offered suggestions on how managers can make efforts to improve their actual and/or perceived behavior. But because not all managers will make such efforts, we need to consider what nonmanager employees may do to cope with or overcome what they perceive as a bad manager.

Bad managers are difficult for workers to survive. We do not choose our managers, and they have a survival advantage over us as a result of their higher position and greater power in the organization. As a capable worker who happens to be working for a bad manager, at some point you reach the conclusion that you cannot continue in your job unless your manager changes his or her ways or is removed from the job. Before choosing your course of action, take plenty of time to think through the situation by analyzing yourself and the problem with your manager. Realistically, you have only four options: (a) stay and adapt to the manager's style; (b) try to

---

Violence at Work: What Everyone Should Know, pp. 57–68
Copyright © 2014 by Information Age Publishing
All rights of reproduction in any form reserved.

change your manager's behavior by talking with him or her; (c) report the problem to the manager's manager or someone else in the organization— the Human Resources department if one exists or an ombudsperson if one exists; or (d) find another job. Admittedly, none of these is an easy option.

ANALYZE YOURSELF

Evaluate Your Own Performance

Remember that "people in glass houses should not throw stones." So first of all, make sure that your own job performance is unassailable. Be honest with yourself and do a careful self-examination.

Think about what reasons your manager could possibly have for saying or doing whatever causes you to brand him or her as a bad manager. Try to put yourself in your manager's shoes and critically examine your own behavior. For example, if the manager treats you less like a professional than he does others, what is it about you that may make him think you are less professional or that you don't seem committed to your job? Maybe— just maybe—you will see something that you did or didn't do that may explain some of the manager's reaction to you.

Are you missing deadlines because the manager says "no later than," which you interpret as a deadline whereas he interprets it as a date that has already granted you an extension of several hours? Are you preparing reports that look great but are too expensive to print? Do you return late from lunch? When the manager sees you return from lunch 15 minutes "late," he may be upset because he does not know that you left nearly 30 minutes late and took only 45 minutes for lunch. Do you enter meetings late because you believe that you should answer the phone when it rings whereas the manager thinks that you should stop answering the phone in order to get to meetings on time? Do you spend so much time talking about personal problems or family activities that you appear to be uncommitted as a professional? Make a list of the possible things your manager might misinterpret, put it aside for a while (preferably several days but at least sleep on it), and then revisit it to see if you feel that you have been open and honest with yourself.

Ask Coworkers to Evaluate You

Whether it be the good or the bad points, we almost never see ourselves as others see us. For that reason, it is usually helpful to get coworkers' viewpoints—but only if you truly want constructive criticism and will not be offended. Ask coworkers to tell you what they think you do well and where they could recommend changes. During performance feedback sessions, ask your supervisor to tell you the strengths that you should build on and any areas where you can do better. If given only general comments, ask for more specific feedback. Even if you disagree with what a coworker or your supervisor says, ask yourself why the person said that—what actions on your part prompted that observation? You may even want to ask the person that same question, but do so in a nondefensive, nonargumentative manner. For example, you can show your genuine interest in learning more by saying something like the following: "Hmmm, I had no idea that I came across in that manner. That's not good. Can you give me some idea of what I do or say that has the effect you described?" Then consider how you would go about changing that person's perception of your performance.

Focusing on your own performance may distract you from the manager's actions and actually improve your perceptions about the job and your performance. Additionally, making sure that your performance is good may serve to "protect" you from retaliation when (if) you decide to report your manager to upper management or agencies outside the organization. It is difficult for a manager to fire an employee if records show that the employee was given high marks or rewards for a job well done before he or she reported the manager's behavior or became a whistle-blower.

ANALYZE YOUR PROBLEM

After analyzing yourself, turn to what you perceive as the problem: the manager and his or her behavior. (NOTE: For your convenience, the following exercise is included in a different format in Exercise 1 at the end of this book.)

First, write down all of the manager's characteristics, behaviors, and actions that have been bothering or upsetting you. Pay particular attention to the signals (subtle or overt) he or she sends. This means remembering all the times that you have been angered, insulted, embarrassed, or humiliated; all the times you have been improperly corrected; and such things as feedback given to you in those morning meetings, the days you were asked to work late or come in on a weekend with only an hour's notice, and anything else you can recall as upsetting or stressful. Don't write paragraphs; write simple sentences.

Second, divide these characteristics, behaviors, and actions into three categories similar to the following:

For example, you would probably put the manager's "indecisiveness" in a different category from "goes into a rage when I'm two minutes late" or "often expects me to stay overtime to clean up others' mistakes." Likewise

Behaviors I Dislike	*Behaviors I Hate*	*Behaviors I Absolutely* *Cannot Tolerate*
1.	1.	1.
2.	2.	2.
3.	3.	3.
etc.	etc.	etc.

you might put "showed favoritism" in a different category from "not doing real due diligence in investigating complaints." Think about each behavior or action and assign it to one of these categories.

Third, revise your groupings as necessary. Think about what the manager's words and body language suggests. What is your manager's personal agenda, that is, what is the manager really trying to accomplish for himself or herself? Understanding your manager better will help you to refine those initial three groups to focus more clearly on the issues that concern you. Look at the first group, "Behaviors I Dislike" and mark off the ones you could probably live with, provided other changes were forthcoming. If you find an item in this group that you just could not live with, move it to the second group, "Behaviors I Hate." Then look at the third group, "Behaviors I Cannot Tolerate," and decide if each of these items really is bad enough to cause you to leave if it is not corrected. If any item is not so bad that it would cause you to leave, move it to the "Behaviors I Hate" group. Now you have a revised grouping that tells you how deeply you feel about various complaints that you have about the manager or the organization.

Fourth, reevaluate the "Behaviors I Cannot Tolerate" group. Ask yourself if any one of these is really bad enough to make you leave this organization. Then ask whether these same complaints may likely occur at other organizations where you might work if you left this one. In this case, it's a good idea to get someone else's input as well, just in case you naïvely think that some problems exist only in your current work environment.

We have seen individuals discover at this point that they should change career fields because seemingly all the managers in their field were untrained managers and thus the worker would most likely find the same caliber of managers in any organization that employs this type of worker. One example was a woman who at this point discovered that, in her field, all the managers were strong macho types who tended to behave in a manner similar to that of her current manager. She felt that, while she did not respect such behavior, she could tolerate it by not taking it personally. So she "undertook an attitude change" and stayed with her career choice, but ruling out any ambition to become a manager herself.

Another example was a worker who was considering asking for a transfer to a different division because he wanted far more direction and input from his manager than he was getting. When he realized that his organization operates in an entrepreneurial atmosphere where the worker is given great latitude and little direction, he decided not to transfer within the organization but rather to resign and move elsewhere.

On the other hand, you may decide at this point that you could cope with the 20 other things you wrote down if only the manager would do or not do the *one* particular thing that makes your workday miserable. We recommend giving more thought and getting more input before scheduling a meeting to discuss your concern with the manager. Before you do anything more, continue through this book and do the exercises that are presented. You can now discuss the final problem with others whom you can trust, or with a manager or coworker, without sounding like you are a miserable complainer who hates the manager.

GET OTHERS' PERCEPTIONS OF THE MANAGER

Discuss the manager and your options with others whom you can trust. However, you should be careful in talking with those inside the organization, as such discussions have a way of getting back to the individual concerned. Be sure the discussions are positive and constructive, not gripe sessions or efforts to sabotage the manager. On the other hand, if you have a mentor or can develop a mentored relationship with a more experienced senior employee, that individual might be an excellent person with whom to discuss the situation. Such a person typically provides career advice, but also can be an excellent sounding board about your situation and provide a different perspective on events.

Perhaps you will find that you are misunderstanding or misinterpreting the manager or the manager's style. For example, you may find that the manager treats everyone else the same way—it's nothing personal about you—so maybe you can learn to live with this idiosyncrasy. Or perhaps your discussions will reveal that everyone has the same problem with your manager and that several other workers would be willing to sit down and talk with him. You may even find that while no one admires his personality, almost everyone thinks he is actually a good manager otherwise, so no one can be counted on to back you up if the manager asks for their input.

A word of warning: It is often difficult to determine whether your peers truly agree with you that the manager is bad or whether they are simply placating you by sympathizing with your problem. What you learn from talking with coworkers should have a strong bearing on the action that you ultimately decide to take. We usually advise clients not to make a decision that will require the backing of other individuals as, when it hits the fan, you will seldom find the support you previously thought you had. After doing all of this, you should be ready to meet with the manager and calmly address the problem and its possible solution.

CONSIDER YOUR OPTIONS

As mentioned earlier, only four options are available when we have a bad manager: (a1) stay and adapt; (b) talk with the manager; (c) report the problem to the manager's manager, Human Resources, or an ombudsperson; or (d) find another job. Clearly, none of these is an easy option.

Option 1: Stay, Adapt, and Learn

Lots of employees stay in their job even when the manager is bad, difficult, or incompetent. Usually, that decision is derived from necessity, not desire. Family, friends, and confidants tend to give advice as to how to handle the problem—including quit the job. But seldom do they suggest that we stay steady and treat the situation as an opportunity to grow by learning what mistakes managers make, how they react to feedback, and how coworkers make the best of these difficult predicaments.

Although we often think of manager-worker incompatibility as an undesirable situation, with the proper attitude you can turn it into an invaluable course in learning workplace diplomacy. You can learn how to communicate and compromise with others who disagree with your point of view. Working with a bad or difficult manager is not an ideal situation to be in, but it can be fruitful for you if you turn it into a learning situation—at least while you consider your option of finding another job. In other words, you can use this as an opportunity to learn how *not* to behave, what not to do—which is at least as important as learning good managerial practices.

For example, when the manager fails to give enough instructions or assistance, accept this as a challenge to solve a problem on your own. You can also learn where and how to get necessary information so you can become more self-reliant and work more independently. You will have opportunities to enlist the assistance of coworkers, a step toward learning about team building. One of the most important lessons we can learn is to prioritize our complaints and decide which ones are significant enough to expend our time, energy, and any goodwill that may remain. If your manager has problems controlling his emotions, you can learn to choose your battles and when to back off or let the discussion drop. You can learn to accept some of the differences with your manager rather than trying always to defend yourself or your ideas, or to change his mind. And, of course, in any exchange with your manager, be diplomatic. Challenging and being overly aggressive could only make matters worse.

Option 2: Talk With Your Manager

Before trying to change your manager, remember that "no good deed goes unpunished." You are likely to be seen as a hindrance or, worse, as a threat. Seldom will trying to change your manager advance your career. Rather than changing your manager, which makes you an antagonist, a better approach may be first to try being your manager's supporter, to help your manager and in so doing, help yourself. Remember, too, that your manager may not even be aware of the behavior that you see as making him or her a bad manager, so your job will be to divulge this to him in the correct manner.

Prepare By Listing Complaints

Assuming that you are going to try to do something about your manager after "getting your own house in order," make a list that you can use in a meeting with your manager. Carefully observe your manager. Itemize those aspects of your manager's behavior that you see as contributing to his or her being a bad manager. Of course, you will not use that label except within your own mind. Be sure to focus on behavior and not personality in making up your list. What message is he or she sending to you through spoken and body language?

Wait a week or two (it is important to let some time go by and emotions settle a bit) and then go over the list again, making certain that it is complete and professional. Avoid sarcasm, anger, finger pointing, and the like. Check again to see that your items pertain to your manager's behavior rather than personality. Then arrange the list from the worst behavior or characteristic to the least. You might ask your spouse, a friend, or your mentor to look over the list to assure that it is as factual and unemotional as possible. Try to put yourself in your manager's shoes to see if you can understand why some of the items on your list might exist no matter who the manager is. In some cases, making the list and examining it closely, particularly trying to see things from the manager's point of view, can prove cathartic. You may conclude at that point that you can live with the situation after all. Understanding your manager will help you make up such a list. Then talk to others about the items on the list.

Ask Others

Ask yourself whether everyone else seems to feel the same way about your manager or whether it is just you. Perhaps your needs and wants are different from those of your coworkers and therefore your manager's style fits them but not you. If everyone feels the same way you do, your suggestions for the manager are likely to be different than if you are the only one having difficulties. If you are relatively new, for instance, you may want a fair amount of direction from your manager. If everyone else is experienced, they won't want or need that direction. Your manager may simply not be aware that he should treat you differently while you are learning the ins and outs of your new job.

Consider Your Manager's Lack of Experience

Is your manager new? Sometimes new supervisors are not well prepared or trained for the supervisory parts of their jobs, especially if they are promoted on the basis of seniority or their technical skills rather than their managerial skills. Careful, constructive (and gentle) feedback from you and your coworkers may greatly improve the situation as your manager learns to be a better manager. Understanding the situation can go a long way toward improving it. Working with and supporting your manager is clearly a better alternative than confronting and fighting with him or her. We do recognize, however, that some managers (especially those who are enamored with their power) do not want anyone's help, no matter how constructive.

Consider Your Manager's Personality

While you are being introspective, consider some tactics that you might use, depending upon the particular characteristics of your bad manager. If your manager just doesn't seem to care or doesn't do what you feel to be a fair share of the job, consider doing it on your own rather than talking with the manager first. It may be easier to ask forgiveness than to get permission. However, taking the initiative to do it on your own could be dangerous to your longevity if your manager is the insecure type who will feel threatened by your assertiveness. If your manager is incompetent, take the initiative. Decide what you need and try to get it; decide what needs to be done and do it. If your manager avoids confrontations and difficult decisions, try to work with your coworkers instead to resolve problems and decisions. If your manager is insecure about trying new procedures or ways of doing something, reassure him or her that you have anticipated all contingencies, document everything, and secure the cooperation of your coworkers if possible. If your manager has an ego the size of the moon, try to make him or her look good in ways that will help you do your job as well, and be prepared for the manager to take all or most of the credit. Workers have a better possibility of winning over their manager if they can make him feel like the change was his idea, or allow him to make others feel like it was his idea.

Of course, it is not always possible to get your manager on the same page with you. To illustrate how managers and workers can misinterpret each other, we can tell you of our own such incident, when one of us once had a manager who always seemed to resent and mistrust me. The manager treated me bad in general, including trying to assign projects outside my area of interest, ate lunch with the other workers but never with me, would not look me in the eye usually, and often asked me, "What can I do to make you happy?" I was quite happy in my job except for his treatment. So eventually, when I could no longer tolerate the treatment, I decided that a good way to approach him was to wait until he asked his question, then answer with, "Nothing—I am so happy here. I love my job and I believe that I am performing even beyond your expectations. Why do you ask me this question?" Although the surprised manager wanted to run, he finally said, "I know you want my job." I had no idea how he came up with that idea, as I had no interest whatsoever in becoming the manager, would not have taken the job for twice my salary. I was planning, in fact, to leave the organization and that part of the country! I did leave, but he never believed that I had not been lusting for his job. Later, I learned that he suffered from Avoidant Personality Disorder.

Narrow Your List

If you decide that you can't live with the situation as it is, narrow your list to those one or two points that absolutely make it impossible for you to continue working in this environment. Some workers mistakenly think that they will have more success if they go into a meeting with several complaints, which would illustrate that they have plenty of reasons to be upset. This so-called shotgun approach usually does not work. It identifies you instantly as an unreasonable complainer who would require changing everything. Instead, prepare to give the manager only one or two points (preferably one) that you would like to see changed.

Schedule a Meeting

When you think you are prepared to stand up for yourself, schedule a time to clear the air and seek improved conditions. Usually, it is advisable to schedule the meeting late in the day so that it can continue past the closing hour, if needed. You might want the meeting to take place on more neutral ground rather than your manager's office or at your workplace. Usually, it is not wise to request the meeting at your own work space, as the manager will resent being in your territory. It is in the best interest of all parties for the door to the meeting room to remain open unless there is a clear view into the room through interior windows. Either the manager or the employee may request that the door remain open, and you need to respect the manager's desire to keep the door open. Admittedly, that may create a privacy problem for the two individuals. However, we know of cases where a female worker has ripped off her own clothing and run from the room, falsely pretending that her male manager had attacked or sexually harassed her. We know of male employees who have run from the meeting room, falsely accusing the manager of sexual or homosexual advances.

Workers and managers sometimes wish to secretly tape-record their meetings. We personally know of cases where tape-recording was quite beneficial to the worker's case, as upper management would never have taken the worker's word for the manager's threatening and unbecoming behavior that constituted verbal abuse—yelling, accusing, threatening, taunting, making false statements, or the like. Before taping someone, though, check your state law to determine whether you are required to divulge to the person that you are taping him or her.

Meet With the Manager

Remember, individuals are not likely to change their behavior unless they know what behavior needs to be changed and how it might be changed. Having a carefully prepared and documented list will keep you professionally focused on behavior rather than making accusatory statements about his or her personality. Because trying to change a bad manager is so difficult, it is a good idea to try to ease the situation ahead of time. How? One way is to compliment your manager or express your appreciation for something he or she has done, where appropriate. Then when you have the talk with your manager, it won't simply be one more negative conversation.

You should be able to forestall a natural defensive reaction by using phrases such as "I know that this is not what you intend, but ..."; "I'm sure that you aren't aware of this, but ..."; or "You probably don't realize that ..." In addition, it would be good to have some suggestions for alternative behaviors that could be employed: "Would you be upset if I told you something that you could do to make everyone work harder at their jobs?" You should be prepared, however, that your bad manager will live up to his or her reputation of reacting very negatively, defensively, and perhaps even vengefully.

Option 3: Report the Situation

What if the discussion with your manager goes badly or seems to have little or no effect on the bad manager? Now your options have changed. Option 1 (try to live with your bad manager) may be far more difficult after such a discussion. Option 2 (changing your manager's behavior) also is now probably out of your hands and achievable only by someone higher in the organization. So you can move on to Option 3, report your manager to his or her superior, to your Human Resources department, to an ombudsperson if your organization has one, to a union or guild representative if you have one, or perhaps even to an appropriate outside agency (the EEO, for instance).

When reporting a situation, follow the same rules as we've mentioned for talking with the bad manager, for example, state facts rather than making judgmental comments, focus on behaviors rather than personality, and temper your observations with phrases such as "the way I see it" or "it seems to me" instead of making harsh accusations. Phrase your request to say what specifically you would like to see changed—not what the manager's manager must do to resolve the problem.

You should be prepared, though, for all higher levels to side with your manager and even to label you as a whiner at best and a dangerous trouble-maker at worst. Unfortunately, many of these groups side with the manager, sometimes even in cases where the manager is blatantly wrong. Should that occur, you'd best move to your fourth and final option: start looking for another job, as the organization will begin to gather evidence to use in "building a file" for the purpose of terminating you "with just cause."

Option 4: Get Another Job

Even while evaluating yourself and your manager, start assessing the job market where you live or would be willing to live. This head start can be of great value to you if you try the other options and end up leaving anyway.

If you feel that your manager is a managerial psychopath, getting another job is probably your best option. While you are preparing to exercise this option, "watch your back." Keep a diary/journal to record specific incidents. Password your computer and don't put any personal information on it. Lock your desk or secure your work area as best you can. Expect that your emails, Web searches, and even phone calls may be monitored. You also might want to increase your mobility by taking evening or online classes to bolster your credentials.

Your physical and mental health are more important than any particular job. Even if your boss is not a managerial psychopath, trying to stay and ignore or fight the manager is not worth it if it causes you physical or mental health problems. If you find yourself having symptoms of depression—trouble sleeping, gaining or losing weight, crying for no apparent reason, no longer caring about your appearance, or experiencing any other sudden change in your attitude or behavior—you should look for another job. A transfer might work if you like the organization; but if the organization supported your bad manager, chances are that another manager in the same organization could also be a bad manager. The new manager could be bad simply because that is the type of managers that this organization hires and supports, or he could be bad for you because he has been given information that immediately creates a bias against you. Get help for your-self. Get out of the organization. Take with you all that you have learned as you choose that next job. Chapter 12 contains advice that should help you apply what you have learned from your current job and from this book as you search for a new and better job situation.

WHAT NEXT?

Managerial personnel are sometimes reticent even to talk with managers about changing their behavior, and it's probably safe to say that most non-manager employees fear expressing a critical or judgmental statement to their boss. This chapter has made numerous suggestions, though, about how you might take actions to reduce the propensity for violence resulting from managers in your organization.

But because an organization's vulnerability for violence results not just from managers, we next turn to nonmanagers who may be involved as well.

APPENDAGE I

Anecdotes of Bad Managerial Behavior

The following anecdotes are real examples of bad manager behaviors that have been provided by consulting clients, students, family, and friends. They are arranged in the order discussed in the chapter. We have tried to leave them in the words of their writers, but have removed identifying information and offensive language.

BOSSES ABUSE THEIR POWER

Threaten Employees

Threaten difficult job assignment to keep employee in line

"I saw a warehouse manager using fear of job assignment as a command tool with his group. This was bad—everyone in this organization was aware of certain difficulties in warehouse tasks. The guy was using this practice to get commitment from the guys (100% males). He was also using overtime allocation as another incentive to get through to these persons. In fact, the guy himself was limited in terms of knowledge on how to deal with organized work involving manpower."

Threaten job if employee makes mistake

"I have worked in a place where management would use fear of losing your job to motivate. They would threaten to fire the next person to make a mistake, no matter what it was. This made us worry all the time about our jobs, every employee."

Threaten to withhold raise unless employee follows questionable directions

"My boss threatens me that I will not get a raise if I do not follow his directions exactly. I think that if I followed what he told me to do, I would be breaking labor laws or minimally not doing what is ethically correct to do. I am still working for the same company, but choose what is right to do instead of following his direction although that means that I get chewed out on occasion."

Threaten employee to accept work assignment beyond job description

"My boss wanted me to babysit his child. Needless to say, babysitting the boss's kids was not in my job description. He told me if I didn't, he would fire me. Being new to the country and not understanding employment practices or law, since I needed my job, I babysat his kid."

Threaten employee for wanting justifiable medical leave

"My boss once was threatening to fire me because I got breast cancer and couldn't come back to work right away to assist him because I was so sick from my chemo. I know it was not correct for him to treat me like that, so I quit. I am now looking for a new job."

Use unenforceable contract to threaten less educated employee

"In a company I once worked at, the manager advised the employee if she did not sign a contract that stated she could not work for any other company on days she did not work, or in a 3-mile radius after she quit working for this company, she would be terminated. This was after she was employed for the company for 4 years and they cut her hours and did not give her any pay raise for 3 years. She was scared of being fired but knew if she signed the contract and got a new job within 3 miles she would have to hire a lawyer and risk paying a legal fee. She did not sign the contract and was not fired, but the company was not very pleased with her. Feeble threat was only a threat."

Threaten termination for failure to meet sales goals

"One of the bosses I worked for used a bad strategy for motivating the sales force. He constantly threatened people with termination. Sometimes he would send us in for a talk with his boss (sales manager), but seldom was anyone actually terminated. Yet the remaining sales force lived in fear, because we were all young guys who were trying not so much to stay in this job but rather to impress the boss so we could get a good reference for future jobs. And getting fired certainly could not be expected to get one a good reference.

"The company's method of motivating salespeople may have produced bottom-line results in the short run (while employees were new to the job), but in the long run it hurt them. There was no natural enthusiasm on the part of the salespeople and no feeling of dedication to the firm. The stress showed on our faces and no doubt made us appear to our customers as too eager to sell. It was clearly the worst work experience of my life. I might add that those of us that I've kept in touch with have had a successful sales careers since then, and that that company is no longer in business."

Threatening employee for socializing with "higher-ups"

"I had a manager that always accused me of going behind his back. He'd often see me socializing with Vice Presidents in the building, and then he'd call me to say, 'What were you talking to them about? Don't you be throwing me under the bus.' It was as if he was implying that I was conspiring with these Vice Presidents. About what, I have no idea. At one point, someone complained about him to HR (Human Resources). He thought that someone was me, and called ME to yell about it. This is a big no-no. If HR is investigating a complaint against you, you can't retaliate in any way. He was let go for that reason."

Take Undue or Unfair Advantage

Defend their actions with "because i am the boss"

"Our company has cubicles rather than private offices. Conversations, therefore, can easily be overheard by those around you. As a result, we have learned to talk quietly on the phone or with others and to use the small conference room for conversations that are particularly confidential. Actually, this made for a really nice working atmosphere. It was quiet and pleasant and people were considerate of one another so we got a lot of work done with a minimum of interruptions.

"However, after several months, a new manager was hired who does not seem to get it. He is loud, crude, and rude. When he is on the phone everyone can hear every word he says and those words are often bordering on downright filthy. This loud behavior disrupts our conversations with each other as well as those with clients. Increasingly we have to use the conference room in order to carry on normal conversations. We wonder how many clients he is going to cost us before someone notices and does something about his behavior. If one of us says anything to him, he simply reminds that person that he is a manager and that he or she is a worker—end of conversation! When bosses take advantage of their positions rather than leading by example, it is always detrimental to the performance of the organization."

Set poor example for employees

"The manager of our department expects everyone to be on time and maintain full working hours. Yet that same manager is frequently late (I had to take the kids to school today) and also frequently leaves early (my daughter has music lessons today; this is my son's soccer day). We can't take our time that way, but she can. In addition, she frequently makes personal calls on company time, which is expressly forbidden for employees to do (her workspace is next to that of employees and so she can readily be overheard). This is not just setting a poor example, it just isn't fair!"

Force workers to work overtime

"The problem I observed was within a manufacturing organization, more precisely in a production unit. The supervisor was using fear to boost his output. He was listing those persons who were not willing to work overtime during their days off. He was threatening indirectly to reduce their bonus the day of merit review for cause of lack of collaboration. This technique worked for a long time because the operators in this unit were practically all senior operators, with a low skill to train on other more complicated tasks."

Threaten to relocate employee

"My boss practiced fear management by threatening us with a relocation. He didn't have to threaten all of us—just a few persons, so that word would get around that we could be sent to another subsidiary. The other locations were not as desirable as the one where we were, plus we would have to uproot our families for the move. Especially those workers with school-age children would do almost anything to keep from having to move their children to new schools in some other town or city. The threat worked well against most of us, but it caused many new, well-trained engineers to leave before they had much vested in the company or the community. Those of us who had too many years vested in the job suffered a decline in motivation. We protected our own jobs by suggesting to new interviewees that they should read their contracts (regarding relocation) before signing on, which made it more difficult for the company to reassign any of us who had been there for awhile."

Reassign Workers to Undesirable Workstations

"I observed a situation where a supervisor was using fear to motivate a subordinate to meet the output goal. The way this person induced fear was by changing workers' assignments. The targeted worker would be assigned to a workstation that is known for its harsh working conditions (heat) and heavy workload (bottleneck) in the process. This manager got away with the practice until the company introduced a highly automated process. At that point, the supervisor had a more difficult time managing more skillful, better-educated operators who were not willing to follow his fear techniques. He was later assigned to a position outside the production lines and replaced with a more competent manager."

Force unreasonable decision: Take promotion or get out

"The owner of the company offered me a promotion to a position I did not particularly feel I was qualified for nor interested in. As I hedged, he stated, 'You will quickly learn that in business, when you are offered a promotion, you take it ... whether you want it or not, as you will never have the opportunity again (at least as long as I am here).' This message was conveyed as the owner slowly narrowed the distance and personal space between us until I was facing him, and backed against a wall. I politely accepted the promotion and later resigned after one year (of misery)."

Use knowledge and connections to coerce employees

"History: The General Manager (GM) worked for this individual who had been a director of a subdivision for a Fortune 500 company. At the previous company, the GM brought in this person as the Director to head up a department of 150 employees. The Director used the 'bully' tactic to manage. The Director micromanaged each and every process from a clerk level to an exempt level. He often used the history between him and the GM to influence a decision or to ensure the staff understood his weight in each decision.

"The Director is a brilliant businessman, although he manages by fear and control. He was able to intimidate others based on his wealth of knowledge and reputation in the industry. If you did not agree with his decision, he would not ask for your opinion, but ensured everyone was asked their opinion in a staff meeting. He would verbally abuse his staff by inappropriate remarks, such as, 'You don't look too happy—you should be happy you're alive.' 'I will put you in a cage in my office,' 'Say I love my job 10 times to change your mind.' These comments were often heard, and no one talked about the issue due to the GM was his confidant. The business is a Fortune 500 company that was run as an individual enterprise for two partners. He would single out whom he wanted to leave the company—he was later accused of verbal abuse and inappropriate remarks in the business place."

Heavy-Handed in Other Ways

Apply HR policies inappropriately

"I witnessed an HR manager who was new to his job in this particular company. The company had big problems of the HR kind, and this man tried to use fear as a solution to these problems as well as a way to establish his power. So, for really insignificant behaviors (such as not displaying your badge or displaying it incorrectly, for example), he fired some people. This practice worked well with some few persons who needed discipline, but the huge majority that was in line with the work policies and have other sources of frustration, see this move as an additional and unwarranted punishment. He also was using some marginal interpretations of the company's policies to threaten workers. The worst thing he did is when he started cutting some benefits to the workers in a move to show that he can be worse. This was the drop that collapsed the system; an avalanche of resignations from a number of skilled technicians and engineers sent the turnover to levels never before reached.

"The motivation in this company was hit very hard in a few months. A regular company's survey driven by an independent organization for labor satisfaction, pointed out the serious level this situation reached with this HR manager, and the danger of turnover level at skilled and stable workers. A corporate audit of HR policies followed a few months after. This HR manager was fired by end 2001. I knew that from some friends because I was among those who left before the corporate audit came in. It was too late, after the damage was done, but still, a correction is better than keeping a bad situation going too far."

Try to prohibit socializing

"A new manager was trying to get people in the organization to comply with a new directive, which prohibited management and employees from socializing on or off the job. The first tool that he used was to threaten supervisors and employees with a written reprimand if they failed to follow the new policy. This was received with much less than a positive reaction! It instilled resentment because most everyone thought that the manager had crossed the line concerning his ability to dictate the lives of individuals off the job. That led to an increase in turnover, but the worst part was the change in attitude of the employees who felt that they could not leave the job. As you can imagine, these workers became less motivated and spent a fair amount of time concocting stratagems to secretly get back at the boss one way or another."

Refuse to recommend promotion in order to hold down boss' competition

"I observed one situation where a manager was using the refusal to recommend promotion as a fear practice to manage his part of the organization. If you challenged this supervisor, you would never get recommended to move up, where you might be more of a challenge to him. One example was a person who was known to oppose some of the manager's strategies (but usually for good reasons). Although he had all the competencies required, this employee never got to have the responsibility of a group head. Everybody in this organization knew that it was because of the manager's refusal to recommend him to the position. This manager was using his ability to withhold a promotion recommendation to keep in line those who may want to challenge him. Since then, I left this company and I do not regret having taken this decision."

Demand personal work on company time

"I know what personal assistants are, and I was not one. But a former manager treated each of her employees as if they all were personal assistants. She expected us to take her cat to the vet's, pick up her cleaning, return stuff to stores, chauffeur her around, and do all sorts of other personal favors for her. She also got upset if we did not buy her holiday gifts, even though everywhere else I have worked the rule was 'give down, not up.'"

Change job requirements with no notice or appeal

"I had a director tell me that working only 1 hour and 15 minutes of overtime was not good enough. The Vice President of our group requested two hours. I told the director that we were never told that overtime was mandatory. He made a series of comments such as 'Don't let (Vice President) hear you say that' and 'Well, I for one wouldn't want to have that conversation with (Vice President).' I felt he was trying to scare me into compliance. I told him I'd gladly have the conversation with the Vice President about how he didn't clearly state that overtime was mandatory."

Lie and exaggerate to inflame

"My district supervisor (with whom I often did not see eye-to-eye, as her management style was very abrupt and rude) called me to say that someone had told her that I said something really awful about her. I searched my memory and could not come up with anything I had ever said that would be worthy of her very angry response. I, of course, asked her who said this and what I supposedly said, but she told me 'I can't tell you that, because it's SO bad that you will have no choice but to deny it.' Also, she refused to tell me who made these allegations against me. She went on to deliver a very thinly veiled threat against my job, that if I continued to say negative things about her, she would 'be forced to take disciplinary steps.' I was at a total loss, not knowing what she had heard (but being confident that it was, at best, a significant exaggeration of the truth or at worst, a bald-faced lie) and having no idea how to defend myself.

"This occurrence was not unusual with this supervisor. I understood from talking to my peers that she had done this to several of them, until one man finally threatened to sue for breach of the right of free speech. That tempered her behavior somewhat, but she single-handedly drove away many of the district's best employees, including me. Eventually the company asked her to step down from management, but much damage had been done by then."

Punish employee for seeking another job

"About 6 years ago I worked for a supervisor who was continually experiencing many physical ailments. It was very typical for him to work 3 or 4 months of the year and take up to 6 months off using sick leave. During the periods of time that he was not working, it would become my responsibility to assume his duties as well as perform my own tasks. This went on for many years and I had finally endured this situation for too long.

"In an effort to excuse myself from this situation, I interviewed for a job at the local zone office as a 'tech advisor.' I proceeded through the process without my direct supervisor's knowledge, as he was out on sick leave. However, my area manager was fully aware of my request to leave my current job position. Although my area manager was not happy that I was trying to find a new job, he did support my decision to interview for the new position.

"I had a start date arranged for the new job, but the position was unexpectedly put on an indefinite hiring freeze. In fact, the job never was filled as the manpower requirement was reduced from 3 positions to 2. My supervisor finally came back to work and confronted me with what happened while he was gone. I confronted him in an angry manner about how I felt he was taking advantage of sick leave and leaving me with the responsibilities of his job and mine! He shook my hand and congratulated me on the new job, knowing all the time that the job no longer existed.

"He said that I did have a new job. He would require me to become the 'mobile diesel training instructor.' I was told to pack a 1,300 lb engine in the back of a truck and hit the road. This turned into roughly a one-year assignment where I traveled California going from dealership to dealership training technicians on how to work on diesel fuel injection systems and overhaul processes.

"Many miles on the road, traffic congestion, and weather-related issues made it a very difficult time in my life. My supervisor explained that he was going to teach me a lesson and remove the control that I once had. This was my reward for doing a good job in his absence. I know what 'fear of retribution' means. The fear that was induced taught me to worry about myself and keep my mouth shut. This situation ruined a good working relationship that I had once enjoyed."

Rely on the "whip" rather than the "carrot"

"I once had a boss that subscribed to the old way on managing people: berating them and using the whip instead of the carrot to try to get people to perform. Our industry was in a particularly sharp downturn because technology (pagers) was getting the better of us. The sales teams were worn to a frazzle and became immune to the tongue-lashings that more sales were needed to save the company from bankruptcy, etc. My boss was located in another city, but I shared an office location with the Regional Vice President who was just down the hall. On occasion, I would copy the Regional Vice President with the emails I received from my boss, asking us why were doing so poorly (but in much more colorful language).

"Eventually, I confronted my boss and told him that if things couldn't get to a more professional level, I would have to 'take that walk' down the hallway and ask for the Vice President's time. My boss flew out to my location at his own expense to tell me I had better watch myself or he would fire me on the spot. Since I was the only District Manager left (two others had quit, one without even having another job lined up), it didn't seem to be much of a threat … plus, I hated the job because it was so depressing.

I used his threat as a reason to approach the Regional Vice President and discuss the working conditions. My complaint wasn't the first he had heard, and within 6 weeks my boss was relieved of his duties. The company went into Chapter 11 anyway, and that's when I left."

Abuse employee to get him to quit

"The individual that was attempting to 'get her way' was a manager of 20 people. The majority of the people she managed were female. However, one of her staff members was a male. It was widely known that she did not like him and wanted to replace him—most people assuming that it was just because he was a male. The problem that she was to overcome is this individual had been in the organization for several years with a good professional record. I witnessed the following behavior from her to this staff member: she was manipulative, nasty, talked down to him in front of others, used unprofessional language, questioned his ability to complete the work, embarrassed him every moment she could, and continuously questioned his communication skills.

"This manager was very mean to him. She continued this manipulative behavior for several years. This manager was not a very nice person, professionally or personally."

Mislead/overstate problem to motivate employee

"The owner of a small company hired an operations manager to run what was presented to the new hire as an 'established firm.' Within a couple weeks of hire, the new manager was told that there was a change in the direction of the business, that it would now be more of an entrepreneurial entity, and that the manager would now have to develop new business ideas and make them operable.

"The manager performed this task, including launching a new business segment for the company and the corporation: development of, and sales of, interactive CD ROM disks for marketing software tools. The first of these sales resulted in a difficult task for the manager and his small staff, who did their best to develop a working tool on time. Bugs appeared, and the staff ended up contracting out the difficult work of debugging the operating system interface. When the owner found out that the product had not been delivered, he stated to the new manager, 'You get that fixed or I'll find someone who can.'

"The manager, having always been a conscientious employee no matter what, the company had never been threatened like this before. He got the bugs fixed and delivered the product to the customer (who was ultimately satisfied with the product, to my knowledge). He tendered his resignation within a couple weeks—even without a new job to go to—having been supremely insulted by the threat by the owner of the company."

Act inappropriately or illegally

"My first professional job was for an abused woman's clinic. My boss was doing 'inappropriate things' in the workplace. For example, she was taking donated items and keeping them to give out to her own family, giving money to certain clients, bringing her sons on the premises, knowing that they had been convicted of assault and battery, etc. When I found out about it, I tried to confront her about it. My subsequent reviews were affected and I was rated very poor. A time later, she brought one of her sons on the premises when I was working and she threatened me with him. Periodically, throughout the remainder of my time at this organization, she would make comments 'reminding me' that she was my boss and that she had the power to fire me at anytime."

BOSSES DO NOT CONTROL THEIR ANGER

Yell At Employees

Yell and humiliate to hide insecurity

"When I was 24 years old, I was transferred to work for a woman who was known company wide for humiliating her assistants. She had lost three assistants due to her yelling, bullying, and threatening their jobs if they did not do things exactly how she wanted it done—not because they had not performed well but because they hadn't done everything exactly the way she would have done. I could tolerate her bad style because my attitude was that I was there to learn, and I knew that I would leave for something better after I added new skills to my résumé. But most other workers, especially young people, would not tolerate this woman's way. Some of my coworkers thought that I was crazy for putting up with her, but I just refused to let it upset me. At times, her yelling and threatening actually seemed humorous to me because I could see that she felt very insecure and didn't know any other way to show her authority."

Yell and pound to motivate sales force

"I was a District Sales Manager for a large corporation in the Southwest. At the time, we were struggling to sell our available production to dealers. We spent a lot of time in the boiler room calling dealers repeatedly to sell them vehicles. Our supervisor, who had recently been promoted to the position, used a lot of threats and intimidation to keep the team focused. He would pound on the top of our cubicles with a mini baseball bat and scream at us to get on the phones and sell cars. He would also accuse us of screwing around and always assumed we could not be trusted. As a result, the team lost its respect for the supervisor and his effectiveness. The poorer we did, the more the threats and intimidation we incurred, so we basically became nonproductive. At a particularly low point, I stood up to the supervisor and told him he did not appreciate his team and I wasn't going to take it anymore. The reason for our ineffectiveness was due to his lack of respect, and he owned the results more than any other team member did. I would like to say that he took my comments to heart, but in reality he just got angry and although I remained reasonably productive, I took more of his wrath than usual. He was eventually reassigned and the new supervisor quickly turned the team around and we survived the ordeal."

Yell and berate both employees and outsiders

"I once worked very briefly for a small construction company where one of the main partners (who I'll call 'Bob') had a strong belief that intimidation (yelling, etc.) was the best means of getting someone to perform like he wanted them to. His excuse for mistreating people was that: (a) he was 'old and cranky' (he was in his mid-70s) and (b) 'I work in construction, and that's how we do things!' I'm not sure why being in construction necessitated berating people that work for you, but I digress....

"At any rate, there were many instances of Bob using threats, yelling, and harsh language to 'make his point' with everyone from outside contractors to office employees. However, there is one instance that stands out in my mind because it's the one that caused me to leave this particular job. Ironically, it was over something as ridiculous as an unsigned check. I had left a pile of checks for Bob to sign, and he managed to skip the signature on one of them ... so I put it back on his desk with a note asking him to please sign that one as well.

"The next morning, he came dashing into my office, red-faced and waving the check I'd left him, screaming, 'Why the f**k did you give me this today? I signed all the g*ddamned, f**king checks yesterday! You should've given me this yesterday!' After I picked my jaw up off the floor and collected myself, I explained that I had given it to him to sign yesterday ... he just overlooked it in the pile, and it still needed his signature. At that point, he stopped screaming, although he was still red in the face and he still insisted it was somehow my fault that he failed to sign it, and huffed away.

"While I didn't necessarily feel that I was in any real physical danger, it was still a little scary to work for someone that used anger and intimidation as a means of management. I don't respond well to that kind of environment and left within a month for another position. However, I noticed that others who worked there (employees and independent contractors) simply accepted this treatment from Bob ... mostly out of fear of losing their jobs (one admin was a single mom) or not being able to find something that paid as well. Bob was fond of bragging that he 'paid better than anyone else in construction' ... and I suspect that he felt this entitled him to treat his employees any way he wanted to."

Yell and belittle people who disagree

"At a previous employer, there was a Vice President who attempted to exert power by inducing fear by yelling at and belittling his employees (actually anyone who he came in contact with). In almost every situation when someone disagreed with his perspective/opinion or had an idea or opinion that differed from his own, the VP would become very angry and aggressive in an attempt to intimidate people, usually by raising his voice (screaming mostly) and using curse words when expressing his discontent that anyone would have an opinion other than his."

Yell and rant to control workers

"At a former employer, I had a boss, the owner of the company, who would rant and yell at the top of his lungs to get his point across. After the explosion, fellow coworkers would cower and act as if we were walking on eggshells, not wanting to do anything to set him off. It was all we could do to survive until 5:00 p.m. and get out of the store."

Yell and mock to single out an individual

"The bad boss that I worked with was inducing fear by using bullying techniques like yelling at this one person in a group. She also would roll her eyes and mock this other person every time the 'victim' made her point. She would encourage other people in the group to engage in the mocking, which made the singled-out person feel low, crawl into a shell, and therefore not participate in the discussions. The bully got her way!"

Display Angry Outbursts and Tantrums

Raise voice and use gestures instead of conversing calmly

"I observed a director of a division threatening a group of employees to change the way that they go about performing their work. He wanted them to relax their quality check of construction drawings. He was upset and angry and raised his voice at the employees. It would have been very easy for any other supervisor to approach their work unit and converse with the employees in a discussion of the cons and pros of doing work in a certain way, and then to explain to them what the better method was, and to give the employees new direction. The director I observed was not polite. He did not ask—he gave the employees a very lengthy lecture, warned them that if he heard of this happening again he would write them up; and with his body language, tone of voice, hand gestures, and spoken words, used fear and intimidation to threaten the employees."

"Go ballistic" and fire people to set examples

"In my last job where I worked for 3 years as the Director of Research and Development at a small online marketing company, I experienced fear in an organization first hand. The company employed about 30 to 49 people. First, everyone was always afraid they would be fired as the CEO had a tendency of firing 5 to 10 people at a time and it seemed like no one was safe from it. Second, you never knew when the CEO would go ballistic. Here are some incidents that I remember.

"I remember him punching his fist into walls and kicking walls and furniture when I first started. It was my first real job out of college and it did indeed motivate me to make sure I was not the one that was going to set him off. Later, I would witness him angry about low sales or something not directed at me. Throw a monitor down the hall. One time some people were eating cake in the back room and he came back there, threw the cake at the ceiling, and told everyone to get back to work.

"The scariest incident for me was when he threw a cup of coffee against the wall of my office because I was joking around with a sales guy. I also got yelled at for being depressed. Though this was scary, I was to the point where his antics were laughable. I was highly unmotivated to work and make money for a person that I really didn't like. They had fired so many people that I had liked over the years without thinking twice that I had lost all respect for them and the company. I think this type of fear works for the short run only. Then people get sick of it and usually quit, but everyone is eventually fired anyways. I actually lasted much longer than average. Three years. But the day I was fired was the best day of my life. For some reason there are a lot of people who work there that are afraid they cannot do better. I think this CEO somehow lowers everyone's self-esteem and says such great things about the company that people become afraid to leave."

Throw tantrums to express disappointment over sales figures

"This man got furiously angry because (as was often the case) the 'stats' were not good enough. He proceeded to throw his papers on the floor, shout, pick certain of the group present at the meeting to humiliate and then stormed out of the room. He never apologized and did this so frequently that even though it always made us nervous and angry, we learned to largely ignore it."

Throw tantrums and objects to express anger

"I once worked for a dentist who was a terrible mean person. When he would get angry for whatever reason, he would throw the instruments at me, which would cause me to be very fearful of him. I left that office very quickly and became an assistant at a dental office with a nice friendly dentist who never uses fear to get her way."

Use Offensive Language

Use foul language habitually

"A supervisor in a department close to the one in which I work is referred to as 'the sailor.' While that is probably an insult to sailors, it refers to the fact that he 'swears like a sailor.' I don't think that he can speak a sentence without using a cuss word of some sort, but he is really profane when he is chewing out one of this employees. They are all terrified of him and embarrassed by his language, particularly as he chews them out in front of everyone. His department has the highest turnover of any department in the firm, but it also has high productivity since the workers have a better chance of moving to another department if they have a record of being a high producer."

Cuss and threaten the bearer of bad news

"In a position with a company no longer in business, I observed the CEO (Chief Executive Officer) repeatedly abuse employees by yelling, cussing, and threatening them with termination. Whenever any message considered unpleasant was delivered to the CEO, the employee delivering the message was ripped to shreds. Comments like 'You are the demise of this company' and 'Pull your head out of your *?*' were often heard from the CEO. The location was irrelevant; meaning an employee could be on a conference call, in a meeting in his office or in the hallway."

Use foul language to intimidate

"I was chair of a committee which had a Vice President serving as ex-officio, who had make it known by making snide remarks that it wasn't appropriate for a woman to be chair. During one lengthy discussion on an issue that he wanted resolved one way, and the majority of the committee was opposed to (there were 12 committee members present), he told me, not once, but twice, to 'shut the f**k up.' Needless to say the room got very quiet, and the rest of the committee members had looks of fear on their faces. I remained calm and stated we would table the discussion for now and that I'd like to meet with Mr. Vice President after the meeting ended. After the meeting, several committee members came to my office to thank me for defusing a volatile situation with someone that intimidated them on a regular basis. To make a very long story short, the Vice President not only apologized to me personally, he apologized to me and the entire committee at the next meeting. Approximately 6 months after this happened, Mr. Vice President was asked to leave the institution."

Belittle, Demean, or Degrade Employees

Demean through emails

"One of the older managers in our company used emails the way some bosses use their voices to put down employees. He used words that were sarcastic or belittling to me and others. This made me feel he had terrible management skills and could not communicate effectively. Either one of two things. Either he didn't have the nerve to say these things face-to-face but could write them to a person not looking him in the eye, or this type of communication had always been his style and he was not technically savvy enough to know that those same words in email messages could be saved and used to build a case against him."

Treat employees as if they were children

"Two groups of employees were involved in a situation that ended up being blown out of proportion. One employee made a comment about the other work group, and one of the other employees ended up telling the other work group, thus causing bad feelings between the groups. When the manager heard of it, he called a meeting with the employees of both work groups and insulted them by talking down to them and talking to them as if they were children and not adults at work. His tone of voice and body language only intensified the situation and created worse feelings between the employees of the work groups. In the meeting, he forced each employee to indicate their participation in the incident, bringing to the open that this was really a problem with the rumor mill. But he intensified the situation and made it worse. He threatened all employees with writing them up if they were ever caught gossiping. He went as far as not allowing them to whisper in the office or to have private conversations unless it was done outside the office on their own time, which he could not control."

Belittle an individual in a group setting

"I was attending a meeting for a self-help organization and observed the leader of the group belittle a member who had not followed some of the guidelines that had been issued. The leader of this group verbally belittled the member, and the member was visibly hurt and angry. I, as an observer, felt sympathy towards the member and disgust for the group leader. Unfortunately, I said nothing, choosing not to create a scene."

Bully verbally to instill fear

"The individual attempted to induce fear in the workplace with unprofessional behavior and disrespectful or degrading remarks to her colleagues. That verbal bullying instilled a sense of fear in not only those who worked directly with her but also those around her. She was also capable of unprofessional passive-aggressive behavior, which also caused a negative work environment for many people over many years. My personal experience with this individual involved her emailing a false portrayal of my work performance on a specific deliverable to my manager, her manager, and the director without first discussing the issue with me.

"Fortunately, I kept good records of my work so I was able to correct her unsubstantiated remarks about my work's validity and quality. The attempt to induce fear failed in this instance because I quickly escalated the situation and pulled together the managers/directors involved to clear up the issue. I also took the opportunity to communicate my distaste and disapproval for this individual's unprofessional and disrespectful behavior. They assured me that I was not the only one who had experienced such issues with this individual. I then commented that our organization should not be harboring such an individual for this long, especially when they created such a negative work environment. One bad apple can ruin it for the rest."

Use "label" to embarrass employee

"I observed an executive insult a person by labeling him as a 'linear thinker' for the purpose of discrediting that person's response to a strategic question. The implication was that the accused could not constructively handle the multiple factors to a complex problem, but the reality was that the boss couldn't defend his own ideas when compared with the response of the so-labeled 'linear thinker.' I thought it adversely affected the accused's participation for the rest of that meeting and reflected poorly on the accuser's leadership. It certainly did not have the boss' desired effect of getting the remainder of us to 'buy into' his way."

Tease and haze the manager's "outcast"

"A friend of mine works for a prominent supplier of copiers, scanners, and fax machines, which has a sales team that embraces the good 'ol boy mentality of hazing others that aren't a part of their clique. The woman whose role was to support sales was often the target of their teasing, which would be as harmless as moving things around on her desk while she was gone to openly deriding her appearance and her age (she was 40-ish).

"Oftentimes she would be reduced to tears and would leave work with the desire to never go back to the office … ever. There was an occasion where someone pulled her chair out from under her while sitting down in a crowded meeting room, and she landed on her tailbone hard enough to knock the wind out of her and place her on bed rest for 3 days. Management, as well as everyone else, was aware of the teasing and the fact that it often got carried way out of hand. There seemed to be a silent approval by management that the weak would be driven off through the process of teasing and hazing.

"Once, the woman attempted to reach out to her few friends over a weekend because she was despondent about having to go into work on Monday morning. Unable to reach anyone, there was some surprise when she didn't show up early to work as she had earned a reputation for doing. Three hours later they found her in her bed after an apparent suicide involving a large number of sleeping pills and an empty bottle of alcohol. To this day, everyone acts like nothing happened."

Touch improperly to intimidate person of different race or culture

"A White male production manager working in a Native American-owned defense contracting manufacturing company belly-bumped a Native American production worker. He did it as an intimidation tactic in order to get the Native American worker as well as his coworker to comply with verbal instructions.

"The production manager's attempt at intimidation was successful as the workers immediately complied, but with resentment. No protest was lodged, but I observed and reported the incident. The White production manager was relieved of his duty immediately and thereafter terminated after due process of investigation and appeal within one week.

"Physical acts of intimidation, including threatening posture, inappropriate physical contact, and other gestures and speech are prohibited in the workplace. This production manager had previously been warned about intimidating Native American workers and denigrating them with derogatory comments such as 'You leave your Indian heritage when you come through the door and work for me. Forget you are an Indian when you work here.'"

BOSSES EXHIBIT POOR MANAGEMENT SKILLS

Micromanage

Focus on activity instead of results

"I witnessed a supervisor who was so hung up on people staying busy, as opposed to what they were accomplishing, that she had all of her subordinates email her reports at the end of each day about what they had done that day and what they have planned for the next day. Everyone spent about an hour each day composing these email reports to put themselves in a good light and to make sure that they were correct. Thus, over ten percent of everyone's time was nonproductive reporting time."

New-manager syndrome—micromanage to show power

"A manager quit and was being replaced by someone from outside the company. During the transition, the employees of the department took over some of the manager's tasks. The new manager arrived and proceeded to inform those employees that while their efforts were appreciated, they were to have nothing to do with those tasks ever again. When questions arose about events that happened during that period of transition, they were told not to get involved because they were not competent enough to deal with it and very much out of their realm. The people in the department feared speaking up and giving an opinion as they were degraded when they did. Three of them quit within months."

Constantly check up on employees

"I had a manager who would constantly check up on all of his employees. He insisted on having cell phone numbers for his employees so he could call them if they were not at their desks to find out what they were doing. He would call his employees between 4:45 and 5:00 on Fridays to make sure that they were still at work."

Dictate employee response to surveys

"When we got our employee surveys, a boss advised the business unit that we must answer survey questions favorably or there was a high probability that the unit would not receive any monetary increases during the yearly salary dissemination. He frequently told us how to fill out surveys, especially if they were from outside the organization."

Command unjustifiable adherence to boss' method

"The supervisor constantly watched her staff, continuing to criticize in great detail what the individuals were doing wrong and what the consequences would be if change did not occur. However, the performances were not wrong (the staff were just not doing it her way or style). She was removed from her position after a long period of staff reporting difficulties to her superior."

Provide Poor Performance Appraisal

Performance feedback to humiliate and instill fear

"I once had to deal with a supervisor who was a real bully. This guy was a real tool. He would come to town looking for someone to fire. Fear of losing your job was his way of motivating people. It did not matter who you were—when he came to town, someone's head would roll. I watched sales guys put in 80-hour weeks to make sure that their sales volumes were high on the week prior to a visit from him. Usually, he would come in and say, 'Gee Bob, your numbers last week were tremendous! Too bad the week before was so low ... hit the bricks.'

"I busted my butt week in and week out because I really needed that job and I did not want to be the next example. This intimidation factor was all about fear of job loss, but his tactics were to humiliate the person for several hours in meetings before firing the guy on his way out the door. It was his favorite thing to do, and it was very effective. I have never feared anyone in my life more than this guy.

"As it turns out, he called me out of the blue when his current company needed a pump in their sales volume. He complimented me on my career progress and that he had heard great things about me and my company. When he asked me if I could give him pricing on doing some lead generation for him, I told him to 'hit the bricks' and hung up on him. Justice is always served!"

Has misplaced goal emphasis

"I used to work in phone sales. I had a boss who insisted that each one of us should make 200 calls per day—or else. We were paid on commission, and my sales style was such that I liked taking my time with a client. It worked for me; I was selling and making commissions. However, my tactic rarely allowed me to squeeze 200 calls into a shift. I tried to argue with my boss, to explain that I can bring more sales with less dialing and more talk time, but he did not want to listen. 'Dial and smile' was his favorite saying. If you did not, you were fired.

"I tried it, and it did not work for me. I couldn't close a sale in the few minutes that his temper demanded. I was forced to go back to what I knew worked for me, and started making 'dummy calls' to fool the counter—dial a number, wait until it rings, hang up, and go to the next. This was the only way for me to make 200 calls and still have time to sell enough to make my commission. Not very efficient, but I was not fired before I quit in a few months. I moved to a company that measured my success in sales volume rather than number of phone calls."

Give low evaluations that can be used against employee in the future

"Several years ago, when I finished my MBA, I thought that I knew it all about the organizations and firms where I wanted to look for a job. I was fortunate to begin work as a financial analyst for one of the Big Four professional services firms. The organization was excellent and I was extremely happy with my job. I was trying my best, staying late nights and working on weekends. Every project I worked on was well received by our clients. Oddly enough, after a year of work, the performance evaluation from my supervisor put me at a below average performance level.

"I talked to some of my colleagues, and it turned out that our supervisor never gave high evaluations because she liked to have a reason to fire anyone at any point. They advised me not to confront her and to lay low. In my opinion, that was wrong, so I scheduled a time to talk to her about my evaluation. After our conversation, I realized that she actually didn't have a clue as to what I did in my job—she only knew that I wasn't doing it well enough. She criticized my 'technical' skills, but could not give me an example of something that I did wrong or something that I couldn't do. After talking to others in the firm, I realized that it is easier not to confront this supervisor.

"She had been at her position for over 20 years and knew the political games better than anyone else. She never got promoted—probably because even the partners thought it would be a hustle to confront her incompetence and fire her. After all, she is the loud, obnoxious type that would take them to court if they got rid of her, so they just did what was easier—nothing. Everyone in the firm had the fear of confronting her. Unfortunately for me, she was my direct supervisor and I was the one who had to constantly deal with her nonsense.

"Two weeks later I had 521 hits on my résumé on Monster.com and a few interviews lined up. However, this time I wasn't looking only for an organization that I liked. I was also looking at every person I had to be in contact with, because I never again wanted to work for the best firm and the worst supervisor."

Make false accusations to support low performance ratings

"A manager made false accusations pertaining to my work performance. The accusations were in a written memo that also outlined future expectations. The memo also stated that failure on my part to comply with the future expectations would result in immediate dismissal. The write-up later was dismissed after I provided evidence to the contrary of the accusations. It certainly didn't improve my productivity or the boss' to waste time like this. Also, it destroyed all trust between the boss and me, so that also was not good for us or the company."

Use Meetings Inappropriately

Use meetings to ridicule those who failed to meet goals

"In a sales environment, I had a manager who would ridicule sales associates who did not make their quotas. The setting would be a morning sales meeting, and I can recall one episode where a female in the office had poor results for a given month. This individual normally had very good numbers, but this month wasn't so good to her. The manager would make an example out of her in front of all of her associates. This included childish name-calling and much belittling. The associate was brought to tears after the meeting."

Use meetings to intimidate by pointing out individuals' errors

"I worked for a woman who frequently held staff meetings where the only agenda item was to go around the room and point out everyone's flaws, mistakes, etc. She managed our team by intimidation and would target individuals who rarely stood up for themselves. She often harassed team members to the point they were reduced to tears. It seemed she gained satisfaction by making others feel bad and would go so far as to threaten termination if people didn't perform to her standards. It created a volatile work environment, but pulled our team closer together. Those that were able to stand up for themselves often stepped in on behalf of those that were not as strong in their ability to push back."

Use meetings to humiliate publicly those who missed their goals

"I worked for an organization that had weekly staff meetings at which performance was evaluated. On a weekly basis, anyone who had a 'weak' performance for that week would be challenged and called out by the group and the leader. As part of the group, I felt fear attending the meeting and even fear throughout the week in anticipation of the meeting. Each week someone would be humiliated. Though performance at times was out of your control, there was always something wrong with you. You could not disagree with a challenge, and if you did, you were making excuses, in denial, or not teachable. I came to hate the job because of those meetings. Everyone in the group was happy when they were not the person on the 'hot seat.' It was an insecure and yet competitive atmosphere and very unhealthy."

Fail to Take Responsibility

Lets others do his job

"Many of us chose not to be a manager because we did not want that responsibility, but we find ourselves taking on our boss's duties in order to survive. He doesn't notice or seem concerned about the fact that a couple of workers avoid doing their share of the work. When we coworkers suggest a way of assigning work more evenly, he will say something like, "Why do we need to do that? I don't think there's a problem, is there?" Like, ask us!! So now we just go ahead on our own and initiate a solution, to which he replies: "Hmm, why didn't I think of that?" Why? Because you lack management skills! I guess we've learned how to survive a bad boss by doing his work ourselves!"

Fail to plan strategically

"I work for a very large technical firm that performs high-priced work, operates 24/7, and is totally dependent on having the latest, fastest, most stable computer-related equipment. Yet time after time we suffer breakdowns because someone has decided not to purchase an upgrade that we need, or an individual worker has declined to have it installed on his particular workstation. This presents a lot of problems due to incompatibility of software. But there's another problem, too. Tech Support does not keep replacement equipment in inventory, so when our equipment breaks down, they try to patch it until they can get a replacement the next day. These downtimes are not only costly but also makes it difficult for us to meet our productivity expectations

"It's upsetting because we spend a lot of time trying to solve the problems ourselves rather than wait for the replacements."

Terminate Improperly

Fire by email

"A friend of mine got an email that said, in effect, 'You're fired.' It 'explained' that increased competition and poor sales meant that 'his services' and that of others were no longer needed. Nothing about his performance; nothing about 'due process;' nothing about any possible appeal or recourse—just 'you don't work here anymore.' That sucks Big Time!"

Fire while on vacation

"My company had been having some ups and downs during a rough economic period but seemed to have stabilized recently. Because things had settled down, I decided to use a week of my accrued vacation time to get some personal projects completed. At the end of the week, I got a phone call from HR telling me not to come back as I was terminated. The woman told me that a final check would be mailed to me and any personal items at my work station would be boxed and sent to me as well.

"I had always received satisfactory or higher evaluations and not gotten any 'signals' from my boss that this might occur. Indeed, if I thought it likely, I would have never taken the vacation and made it easy for them to fire me without telling me to my face!"

Congratulations! You're fired

"My company (a major Fortune 500 firm) contracted with our major state university to have an MBA program offered on our premises and available at no cost to us. We had to meet the school's admission requirements and attend classes year round for 2 years. It was grueling but provided us with useful information and 'expanded our horizon' as most of us were engineers with little or no business training.

"Rather than have us go through the university's large commencement exercise, the school arranged for us to have a graduation ceremony for just our cohort. The ceremony would involve the graduates walking across the stage to receive congratulations from the faculty and would be followed by a reception. Family and friends were invited as this was deemed a major accomplishment for all of us students.

"The kicker was that as our boss congratulated us, he handed several of us an envelope. Inside the envelopes were termination notices. A couple of us 'pushed' the boss about this and his response was that since we now had MBA degrees, it should be easy for us to find new jobs! So instead of enjoying the reception, we were left with a bad taste in our mouths."

No notice

"I was working for a city government in its main office doing a variety of communication and PR assignments. While I always met deadlines (in fact, frequently early), my supervisor would occasionally rewrite my material (and as likely as not, she would make grammatical errors in her rewrites). I had been on the job approaching a year and my quarterly reviews were 'good' or better as I was learning the ins and outs of city government and organizational politics.

"Then one day my supervisor, accompanied by a security officer (in uniform with a sidearm), walked up, handed me a box, and told me to pack up my things. I asked what was going on and got no explanation, just a repetition of the instructions to pack my things. When I finished, they marched me (one on each side or one in front and one behind) past everyone else in the office and out to the parking lot. They removed my parking permit and told me to leave the premises. In response to my further inquiry about what was going on, I was told that my final check would be mailed to me. My supervisor then left and the security guard indicated that I should leave, which I did.

"I still have no clue why I was fired nor did any coworkers that I later talked to, although they all said, 'You must have done something really bad to have require a guard to make you leave!' So not only was I fired with no notice, my reputation was damaged as well."

BOSSES ARE INSECURE AND/OR INCOMPETENT

Cover Up Their Insecurity or Incompetence

Because "I'm the boss"

"A former (thank goodness) manager for whom I worked refused to listen to any criticism of his decisions. Anytime anyone started to question his decisions or actions, he would interrupt with 'Look, I'm the boss. It's my way or the highway, so that's all there is to it. End of discussion!' Know what that does to a business? Pretty soon we stop telling the boss if we know something is wrong of if we have found a better way to do something. Probably if the building were on fire, we'd all just run out quietly and tell him nothing! He's the boss; let him find it out on his own."

Refuse to "pitch in"

"Our work frequently necessitates 'emergency' levels of activity, where everyone has to work overtime or on weekends (for no extra pay). While other managers in the organization usually (almost always) lend a hand during these times, our manager refuses to do so, stating that it is our job—not hers—to do this 'menial' work. She will sit in her office and read while we work overtime, or maybe leave for awhile to run errands but then come back to check on us. You can bet that if we had any way out of this (and we constantly make up excuses to do so), we would not do it and leave her hanging! Eventually we'll figure out some way to get her, in the eyes of her bosses."

Rig problems to "blow up" in boss's absence to prove boss's value

"I have witnessed my Executive Director deliberately sabotaging deliverables so that they 'blow up' when she is away. Then she can come back and 'save the day' so she can demonstrate to our Board how invaluable she is. They've bought into this and now are afraid to get rid of her, even though they know she is destroying morale and has the highest turnover in the unit."

Scare workers

"Lots of people suffered from this operations manager who used fear tactics to cover up his own incompetence. This guy was a severe person, covering his lack of competence with a high level of severity and fear. He would sometimes say that some downsizing is on the horizon, and he would supply a list of the least performing persons to HR. The workers were scared to death that they would show up on this list, so they were never ready to report any problems to this manager. Everything he said met with 100% agreement.

"I was one of the first to tell him the truth face to face. I was young, with no heavy obligations and unwilling to continue working in this condition. He didn't appreciate that at the moment. But later on he was very respectful of me. He was even willing to consult with me on major decisions. The other colleagues felt it as a huge relief, and outside the manager's office they were congratulating me for this act of courage and integrity. I was surprised, because no heroism was in fact linked to this reaction. It was just stating the facts that cannot be ignored in an organization seeking performance. This move helped install a new climate of collaboration. I think the manager did appreciate it also, as since that time, a lot of energy got liberated and freed competencies that were blocked by this boss's fear practice. So now he looks better to his bosses, and the list that used to scare everyone to death is gone."

Avoid Making Decisions

Refuse to get involved with employee differences

"I work in the employee assistance group of the Human Resources department of a local telecommunications company. Our group interfaces with several others, including legal, payroll, training, and benefits. Our benefits group has a bully in it. She is a backstabber, gossip, and liar. Why she hasn't been fired long ago is a mystery to everyone. She tries to shoot down people and has now turned her attention to me, probably because I am new. She has sent emails to my group coordinator filled with lies about me and my performance, which thankfully have been relatively easy to refute (although they disrupted work and took time). She has tried to poison my relations with others in the department with vicious gossip but, thanks to her reputation, this has not worked either. My group coordinator tells me that it is a 'personality problem' and not the company's business. The department supervisor does not want to get involved either! What a lousy situation to be in."

Too friendly

"A former supervisor could not seem to forget that he was now the boss and not another coworker. He would go for a beer after work with those of us in his work group. He tried hard to be our friend and was constantly trying to listen to our problems, even those involving our spouses or dates. The result was that when it came time to do performance appraisals, he couldn't give any negative feedback, even when it was merited. And when he tried, naturally we would give him the 'I thought we were friends' routine. So he became a poorer and poorer supervisor over time."

Fail to resolve simple problem

"An employee was overlooked for a shift change—a simple oversight that could have been corrected with a phone call to scheduling. The employee brought the situation to her manager's attention via email and in person. Nothing was done to correct the situation. The employee then went to the next highest manager, who resolved the situation immediately. However, her first-level manager informed her that, if she *ever* questioned his decision again, he would see that she was fired."

Doesn't recognize a problem exists

"I have one of those bosses who does not recognize that her duties and responsibilities changed when she was promoted to a managerial position. She is a nice person, a wonderful coworker, but a lousy boss. She still thinks of herself as just another one of the workers, which means she does nothing to correct bad employee behavior such as not carrying their own weight. In her defense, I will credit this boss for acknowledging and thanking us when we initiate corrective action, but it is her job—not ours—to manage the workers. In other words she is willing to let us serve as her surrogate managers!

Cannot Accept Criticism

Use only "yes" employees

"A direct supervisor stated to an employee, 'If you cannot agree with me on this, I will find another employee for your position who will.' The employee went against his own belief/opinion and sided with the supervisor for an allocation of expenses that was not aligned with divisions' approved plan. This supervisor was a bad boss. He might have learned a lot if instead he had asked the employee to explain his thoughts, his resistance. This is also a good example of 'winning the battle but not the war.' The supervisor got what he wanted this time, but you can bet it will cost him in the future."

Take extra decision-making authority because of technical competence

"I was new to this design unit, where the boss in this organization (a vice president position) was known to not allow anyone to criticize his opinions. Sure, the guy was experienced, but this was reaching a limit of a dictatorship situation. The engineers and managers in this structure were suffering from a situation limiting their creativity. The fear practice this manager was using got power from his position as a research and development specialist with lot of years of experience, and nobody was willing to get in trouble with him—especially a person in such a critical position where usually nobody in the top management is technically able to challenge him in his area of practice. Therefore, decisions he made about people were welcomed without criticism, even those that were not in the best interest of the company. Many engineers left the organization, including some who had very high and rare skills.

"This manager was recently fired by the CEO in a diplomatic way (personal reasons). Everybody thinks that top management was finally aware of the problem this organization was facing and the limitations incurred. They finally realized the amount of improvement the company may have earned if more positive management was applied, especially in this area of creativity where flexibility in managing HR must be the key factor."

Refuse to accept criticism

"While in the service, I had a supervisor who could not be told he was wrong. On many occasions he would be working on an aircraft and perform a task wrong. The result of this wrong task could put the aircraft in peril or cause numerous deaths if the aircraft crashed. When he was confronted by a subordinate, he would shift the blame to someone else. On certain occasions, he would throw a temper tantrum, curse out the individual, and then start throwing tools at the individual. After he was done, he would threaten all the individuals present with bodily harm or bad efficiency ratings if anything was ever said about the incident. This went on for 2 years and was very successful at keeping all his people in line. After a couple of years, the individual threw a wrench, hit a person in the head, and almost killed him. This brought the military authorities into the picture, we all testified, and he was discharged and spent 6 months in jail."

Refuse to accept blame

"My current boss seems to want to have one or two poor employees around so that anytime anything goes wrong he can blame them. Even things that clearly are the result of his poor decisions, he blames on them. While he may be fooling his bosses with this, he isn't fooling any of his employees. We are looking for jobs before we become the objects of his blame."

Success leads to failure

"Our division got a new head who used his newness to enact some much-needed but rather harsh reforms. Within two years, the division was strong in terms of both profits and growth and so everyone seemed happy. The problem was that there were still issues to be resolved, particularly with regard to a changing customer base. But because the division head was so successful, he became rather incapable of being disturbed by bad news or criticism. The deference of people to him simply made it worse. By his third year, he was a virtual dictator and would listen to no one."

BOSSES BACKED BY WEAK/POOR UPPER MANAGEMENT

Ignore Bad Boss Behavior

Do not correct bullying boss

"My supervisor at my previous job was a controller who would bully people constantly He had a brusque manner and angered easily. He liked to stand by my desk and turn red in the face while pointing out minute errors. His style was to criticize, repeat the criticism, and then summarize the criticism once more. He applied the same tactics directly to my staff. I took the issue up with his manager (Chief Financial Officer) when she brought up the problem. However, she did nothing in response to my suggestion that people might begin leaving the company. She was retiring very shortly and needed him to provide some continuity after she left. When my staff looked to me for help, I replied that the controller lacked management skills. One other person and I left the company shortly after this since it was clear that no one was going to correct the behavior of our supervisor."

Do not deal with boss' animosity

"It all began when I got a promotion/raise at my work. The Operations Manager (let's call her 'Sue') took it upon herself to make sure I would be miserable and therefore eventually quit my job. A series of events followed.

"Sue started by telling me that 'people who get on my bad side, I can be a real big bitch with.' When I indicated that my name was misspelled on our new business cards, her response was, 'Pardon my ignorance, but does it really matter?' She would change meeting schedules without telling me, withhold travel details that I needed, asked me to take home all personal items such as my framed diplomas. Sue accelerated the problem by nitpicking my time sheet and requesting more details, 'losing' information that I had supplied via email, suggesting that I had not given her proper information for phone calls and meetings, and similar things.

"All of this conflict was handled by her superiors in a cowardly way. For example, they assigned the timecard oversight to another individual, asked me to copy them in on emails that I sent upward, and similar actions that were not effective in resolving conflicts. The final result was that higher management did nothing to reduce the individual's animosity toward me. And other employees learned that this manager could do whatever she wanted to anyone, with no fear of reprimand from her superiors."

Choose to keep "scarce" managers

"When I was in high school I worked part time in a restaurant as a busboy. I reported to work after school each day and worked until after the dinner hour (usually around 8 o'clock). My job was simple—I cleaned everything off a table when customers left and took the dishes to the kitchen where I put them in racks for the dishwashing machine. I got along well with the waitresses who sort of treated me like one of their kids, but my supervisor was something else. He would make racial comments about me and was constantly screwing up my timecard and then blaming it on me. I even got waitresses to witness my time to prove that I had reported things correctly on several occasions, but he changed my hours anyway. After a few months, I got fed up and went to the restaurant manager about him. I was told that while busboys were 'a dime a dozen,' kitchen supervisors were hard to find and that I 'could take it or leave it.' I left it."

Use boss's illness as excuse

"I am a professional with advanced degrees and a reputation of being highly capable in my field. Unfortunately, one of my bosses, 5' 5" maybe, liked to fill his division only with professionals to whom he felt superior (short man syndrome?). So he constantly picked at me because I was a threat in his mind. He decided, for whatever the reason, that I wanted his job—which was absolutely not the case. He would ask me to take assignments outside of my area of expertise, but did permit me to turn them down. He threatened to fire me if I ever made an error—surprising, since I had a reputation for competence far and above most, if not all, my coworkers. He tried doing everything he could think of to convince me to leave, which I just could not understand at first, since I was doing outstanding work and in my mind had never felt in conflict with him.

"After many months of harassment, I went to the next level of management and pleaded my case—asking only that they talk with him to see if they could find out 'why me.' I was listened to with sympathy, then told that 'we don't kick a man while he's down.' The boss had had cancer in the past and was basically promised he could stay on until he died. So his bosses chose not to even talk to him about complaints as long as he was 'terminally ill.' Problem was that he was now cured, but he knew he was safe as long as he kept that information to himself."

Uphold Bad Boss Behavior

Does check facts when workers complain

"In a meeting with Director X for the purpose of discussing conflict with my current manager, Manager Z, I asked Director X if he had a few minutes. I had been running into several issues with my current manager, Manager Z, who directly reported to Director X. I would ask Manager Z questions about my job and he wouldn't know the answers. He would brush me off or give me a response that didn't answer my questions. As people would go on vacations and maternity leave, the workloads did not get divided up.

"Manager Z did not give any direction on who was to take over other people's workloads and territories, which has always been decided by management since they know the amount of work each employee has. We all know some people can handle more than others and this is why management has always made the backup decisions. My group was getting several calls from our sales team complaining about turnaround due to people being gone. I, as well as a few other coworkers, brought this to Manager Z's attention. His response to our concerns was the same as always, brush the problem off. So the group decided to pull together and divide up the workload so we had coverage for the complete country in our technology. I became very frustrated and felt that I was not just doing my work, but the work of my manager as well.

"When I got into Director X's office, he asked what he could help me with. I told him I was having some issues with my manager and I am very frustrated. He then said, 'Manager Z has 30 years of experience, you have only 7. If you are asking for my support, my support is with Manager Z and any decision he has made.' He obviously didn't have his facts right, because I had been out of college for only 3 years at that time with this being my first job out of college in the real world, you do the math. I guess he doesn't really read his employee reviews too closely, does he. I was not in his office but 5 minutes before I walked out of there more frustrated then when I entered. I tried to explain why I was frustrated and the issues we were all facing as a team, but he wouldn't listen to what I was saying. He didn't even comprehend what the problem was. I left and decided that we will just have to be a stronger team with a weaker manager and director. We will have to pull together, work together to get through these rough unsupported times.

"Months later, I was moved to sit by my manager. I didn't ask why I was seated there, but I took it as a challenge to try and learn something from my manager and give him another chance. I quickly learned the reason he kept brushing us off from our previous questions and issues was due to him not knowing how to do our job. He didn't know how to do the job below him, yet he had a higher position than what he currently held before a round of layoffs occurred. I moved departments after a year of sitting next to my manager. Shortly after I left that group, I was called into HR to discuss some concerns about Manager Z and how he is as a manager. You could only imagine how I felt when I left the office of HR. I couldn't help from thinking, 'If only Director X would have listened to some of the issues I was discussing, perhaps it would have never got this far.' I couldn't help but laugh and say I told you so!"

Uphold boss who is less competent than workers

"After the service, I took a job in a cabinet shop because I had learned how to use wood-working tools in high school and in the service. The job paid well and never required overtime, so everything was pretty good for about a year. About that time, I started going to college at night and got a new supervisor. I don't know if those two changes were somehow related or not, but they did happen at the same time. School wasn't bad and I was studying business management, so maybe that's why I began to notice all sorts of things about my new boss. He was not really a good craftsman and so would make errors when trying to tell us how to do our jobs. We learned not to argue with him as that just set him off, so usually we just nodded and waited until he was busy doing something else and then did it our way anyway. Most of the time he never knew.

"But one day we had a special order that required some very precise measurements for the cabinets so that they would fit in the customer's house. Trying to be careful to get everything correct, as you can understand, was slowing us down. So the boss told us that he would do the measurements so that we could speed up. He was doing them wrong and we told him so. He got angry and said that he was the boss so we should let him do his job. We went to the shop manager and told him about it. But the shop manager backed up the supervisor with the same line—he's the boss so listen to him and get the job done; you're behind anyway! The consolation was that the cabinets did not fit and the shop had to redo them at its own expense."

Always take boss' side

"I used to work in a large state agency. It was a great place to work—good boss, good coworkers, pleasant environment, challenging and changing tasks. But then things changed. My boss's boss retired, and his replacement was the Wicked Witch of the West. She immediately got rid of my boss (a long-time employee, well-liked by other managers and coworkers) and gave herself that position also (temporarily). She belittled employees, called us names, yelled at us, changed our customary way of doing things with no discussions, assigned us clerical tasks instead of our professional duties, and generally ruined all of our lives. Yet she was totally lacking both managerially and technically in our field.

"The woman decided to next go after our level of professionals. We spoke with a senior manager in another department and he suggested that we file a complaint. Some people did, and were told 'Thank you'—in other words, take it or leave it. They left but I stayed on, thinking that surely top management would not let this unqualified person ruin a whole division. In fact, she was affecting the entire agency because other employees were worried when they saw that top management was upholding this new manager's behavior.

"Eventually, I did file a complaint with top management because I realized, like those who had already quit, that either this woman or I had to go before the job stress ruined my health. Management said it was just a personality conflict that frequently happens when new bosses come in with new ways of doing things, and that we should work it out through HR and learn to live with the new person's ways. I then filed a complaint with our Human Resources department. Same story, as the head of HR was afraid to go against the woman manager or the top administrator to whom she reported for fear of losing her job. The HR director also used this as an opportunity to 'kiss up.'

"Some really senior people came to our aid by telling top administration what was going on, but were given the cold shoulder. That's as far as they could go, as no one wanted to get on the bad side of the top administrator. But they did start looking for other jobs or taking early retirement. Meanwhile, even though this was the field I had chosen for my career, I left the agency and started over in order to protect my physical and mental health. The female supervisor continued her destructive ways for a couple more years. Eventually, this great new boss locked horns with the wrong person at the top and was asked to resign immediately. Meanwhile, most of the other highly qualified people who loved their work had already left."

Contribute to Bad Boss Behavior

Fail to train managers sufficiently

"At a previous employer that produced cosmetics, it was customary that the senior site leadership would make a tour of the production floor to review daily productivity metrics in each of the major areas. The main group consisted of 7 to 10 senior leaders who spoke with line management.

"Because of the dynamics of production, production lines were constantly changing between products, and there was a lot of emphasis placed on changeover times, downtimes, quality, and throughput. The use of older equipment, less costly components, and bilingual workforce presented challenges on a daily basis to line supervisors. Most of the site management transferred from the East Coast of the U.S. that used an outspoken, confrontational style of problem solving. The lower management and line production were mostly local with a quiet, relaxed style of communication.

"The two cultures typically clashed during these daily production tours. It was common for one or two senior leaders to argue passionately and uncensored over production problems, while the rest of the group and the production operators who were close by observed the exchange. This behavior at times carried into conference room discussions where resolution was typically gained by one point of view would eventually give way.

"This created a stressful environment for those people who chose to take supervisory positions and resulted in a high turnover in the management level. It intimidated individuals and drove out employees who were more analytical and had a quiet communication style. There was a very high level of turnover in production line personnel and kept Human Resources constantly addressing employee complaints. The facility was successful in achieving its goals; however, very few innovative ideas came from the production floor and seldom were production people promoted into senior levels. Typically, employee surveys were not very good."

Criticize boss to others but do nothing

"A manager on a new team has many challenges. There have been numerous situations that have caused significant risk to the company. The person in an upper management position has made remarks regarding the performance of the manager, stating things like, when the old manager was running this team, we didn't have these issues or, as the manager of this team, you need to know what is going on. It appears that the manager is not doing his job. Or that because the person in a leadership position feels that the manager is not doing the job that is expected, they may lose it. There are several factors that are involved with this perception. There have never been any audits on this team to prevent work being misplaced or misdirected. The manager in place has never been coached or even trained on what this team function is; however, past job experience has helped to determine the specific nature of what goes on. My concern is that the person in a leadership position feels inadequate in his or her own job knowledge, so that blaming someone else is much easier than admitting they don't know either. Causing fear and insecurity in another gives them the control they need to feel secure in their own position."

Reward wrong behavior

"I thought I had seen it all until I went to work for the local school system. Even though they didn't get paid extra for it, teachers put in time at night and weekends to grade papers and prepare lesson plans. They also bought supplies out of their own pockets because the district was too cheap to furnish them. In fact, if a department head or assistant principal were to be able to shave his (they are virtually all males) expenses, he would likely get the next promotion that came up because he 'ran a tight, efficient ship'—even if teachers were overworked and student performance levels were only average. Promoting these bosses whose objective for saving money overrode the objective to educate students was what the system was all about. Meanwhile, of course the superintendent and his assistants would get pay raises every year. What a joke."

Act without checking the facts

"I witnessed a situation where an employee was being sexually harassed by a coworker (manager) by extreme derogatory remarks. This employee was told that if she were to tell anyone, the manager would make sure no advancement opportunities would be available. When the employee went to HR about the issue, they informed her that the manager already claimed he was being harassed by the employee! Upper management fired the employee but took no action against the manager."

SECTION II

NONMANAGER BEHAVIOR AND VIOLENCE

CHAPTER 5

BAD NONMANAGER BEHAVIOR

How It Can Contribute to Violence

Earlier we looked at characteristics of managers that may contribute toward violence; now we look at characteristics of nonmanagers that can also cause problems for other workers. These coworkers, and sometimes even the customers/clientele, play a role in other workers' perceptions and in the stress they experience. They may compete for attention and rewards of any kind, and they may intentionally target others in the workplace.

The cooperation and camaraderie of workers, or the lack thereof, has a tremendous influence on how an individual views his or her job. The demands and behaviors of customers or clientele also play a role in the worker's job assessment. Descriptions and criteria vary as to how these individuals earn the condemnation of a particular worker or workers. The so-called bad nonmanagers that organizations need to address include (a) those employees whose performance or productivity is unsatisfactory, (b) those coworkers whose behavior or attitude may serve as the catalyst for workplace violence, and (c) those fragile or impaired individuals who are likely to allow their feelings to erupt in violence. In this chapter, we attempt to broaden the reader's understanding of the complexities of dysfunctional behavior in organizations—to see that behavioral issues exist in all organizations and not just business firms.

Violence at Work: What Everyone Should Know, pp. 97–122
Copyright © 2014 by Information Age Publishing
All rights of reproduction in any form reserved.

INFLUENCES OF NONMANAGERS TOWARD VIOLENCE

Nonmanager employees are not infrequently the target of workplace violence by other nonmanagers or coworkers.[1] Managers and supervisors need to be able to recognize these "antagonizing" individuals in order to try to change their behavior or attitude and then to terminate them if the employee cannot or will not change. Other employees need to be able to recognize bad nonmanagers or coworkers in order to avoid them or to "walk carefully" around them. Job seekers need to be able to recognize them (although they will find it more difficult to identify the bad nonmanagers ahead of time) so that they can evaluate whether to accept a position that requires working with a particularly bad coworker.

Bad nonmanagers adversely affect other coworkers when they become poor performers or are allowed to display bad behavior toward other employees, sabotage others' efforts or subject them to unnecessary risk, miss work unjustifiably, steal from the organization, and so on. They cause good employees to become overworked and more stressed from taking up the slack caused by troublesome workers. Good nonmanagers feel underappreciated when bad coworkers are rewarded, not punished for the mistreatment of coworkers, underperformance or and uncooperative behavior. These conditions can in turn cause good nonmanagers to lose respect for the management of the organization and lead to poor morale, decreased productivity, a decline in quality, and higher turnover. Some disillusioned workers may decrease their own performance or discourage sales by complaining to customers. They may try to "get even" by stealing money, supplies, or equipment; by developing or participating in websites that "bad mouth" the organization; or even by sabotaging products, projects, or personnel.

Of course, "good" coworkers are more important on some jobs than they are on other jobs and also more important to some individuals than to others. For jobs that involve teamwork such as many in nursing or health care in general, it is particularly important that members of the team be able to work cooperatively together. But having coworkers you can trust and interact with in a pleasant manner always makes any job more bearable, less stressful, and easier to perform. On the other hand, bad coworkers— dishonest, confrontational, unpleasant, snobbish, immoral, unethical, or whatever—make the job less bearable, less pleasant, and more difficult to be highly productive.

Let's examine some of the characteristics shown in Figure 5.1 that individuals have identified as needing the organization's attention.

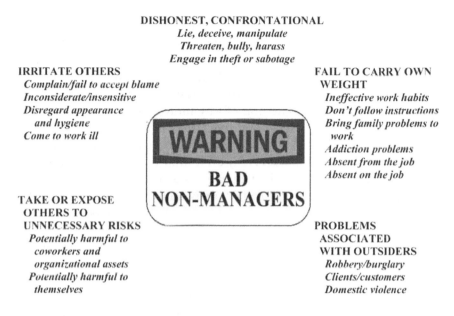

Figure 5.1.   Nonmanager characteristics or behaviors that increase an organization's propensity for workplace violence.

DISHONEST, CONFRONTATIONAL

Lie, Deceive, Manipulate

The "average" workplace has its share of nonmanager employees who lie, deceive, and manipulate.[2] All such behaviors can do great harm, sometimes in a relatively short time. Coworkers do not like working with individuals whom they cannot trust or whom they fear in some way, and productivity tends to be low under these conditions. Many such workers are abusing their authority. Although some people find it relatively easy to stand up to a coworker who attempts to dictate to them, others of different gender, race, cultures, and organizational tenure may not. Even authoritarian approaches that are directed toward outsiders rather than coworkers are resented by coworkers as they reflect negatively on the organization and are also an indication of the type of persons that those coworkers tend to be.

Most of us have known workers who lie or manipulate as a means of improving their own situation or getting their own way. Sometimes they lie even before they get the job—they falsify their résumé or overstate their credentials in the employment interview. Coworkers assume that these individuals will also lie about other important things. Also, if employees lie about their qualifications for the job, they may not be competent enough to carry their weight and will therefore have an adverse effect on group productivity. Furthermore, if they lack the necessary knowledge or skill, they could pose a safety threat to other workers. Always at the heart of the problem with liars is the question of why individuals feel the need to be less than honest with those around them; and as with most things in life, uncertainty about the individuals' dishonest actions makes their coworkers most uncomfortable. Coworkers may even draw invalid conclusions about a dishonest worker's potential threat to the organization's security. In some cases, these bad workers start rumors or commit other types of deceit in order to lower a coworker's evaluation in the eyes of the boss and other coworkers.

Manipulating through exaggeration is common, such as overstating family or health problems to make managers and coworkers feel sorry for the employee. In recent years particularly, applicants for jobs at all levels and pay grades have been especially overstating education or experience on their résumés. Others, particularly if they are members of a protected minority, may exaggerate about poor treatment by their coworkers or their manager because they know they can manipulate the system in this way. Some workers may lie or exaggerate in an attempt to cover for their own substandard performance by convincing the manager that another employee is responsible. Others may lie or at least exaggerate their accomplishments at the expense of their coworkers to convince their managers that they are so superior that the organization really can't function without them. No wonder, then, that employees hold in contempt those coworkers whom they see as brownnosers or bootlickers as well as coworkers who elicit undue sympathy to get preferential treatment.

Unfortunately, as discussed below under sabotage, some workers have a more sinister motive for lying or manipulating—to do harm or to cause harm to another person. They may believe, for instance, that in order to get a promotion, they need to reduce their competition by appearing superior to another worker or by causing him to lose his job. Perhaps they are biased racially or otherwise, or maybe they are jealous of or simply dislike the other worker.

Some workers are dishonest in the amount of work they perform. This deceit may include falsifying time cards, merely avoiding work, or taking undue credit for performance. "Free riders," for example, intentionally do just enough to stay on a project while letting their coworkers bear primary responsibility. Such workers then become overcompensated in comparison to the more honest and diligent workers.

Threaten

Some workers use threats to coerce or get what they want from coworkers and managers and nonmanagers. The threats may be relatively low-level mutterings or child-like temper tantrums, such as threatening to quit, to refuse overtime work, to initiate legal action, or to refuse teaming with select individuals on certain projects. Nevertheless, giving in even to simple threats simply reinforces the behavior so that additional or even more sinister behavior can be expected in the future.

More extreme threats include angry warnings of damaging action against an individual; the organization; its products, software, or records; or even the physical plant itself. Often, threats are a way of coping with a less-than-satisfactory job. The individual is trying to convince himself that he still has at least some control over his own situation.

Threats to litigate, including the filing of discrimination charges, are indicative of much dissatisfaction and should also be taken seriously, even if they do not appear to present a safety risk. In our work, we have seen many instances of minority workers getting preferential treatment by threatening to accuse coworkers—falsely, we believe—of discrimination. It takes only one such case to seriously divide the coworkers and have a long-term effect on morale, as workers do tend to choose sides in these cases, and the divisions are not necessarily along the gender, racial, or social lines that one might expect.

When the level of threat reaches the stage of threatened harm to the organization, bosses, or other workers, a more serious game is being played. Management and coworkers have reason to take note. Such threats may be serving as relief valves, and there is always the danger that the pressure could rise high enough to blow the safety valve. As incidents of workplace violence have taught us, threats to retaliate are often acted upon. Also, repeated incidents from the same individual may indicate that the individual is what has been termed a terrorist within the organization or a psychological terrorist—someone inside the organization trying to use fear to achieve his or her own personal goals.

Bully

Although bullying is a common behavior at work, it is not always given that label.[3] Nonmanagers who use ridicule, overt and covert threats, and either verbal or physical abuse are merely a grown-up version of the schoolyard bully. Psychologists suggest that they are insecure individuals who have unresolved personal problems of one kind or another. When these bullies pick on and threaten others, they are "acting out" their own feelings of worthlessness. For that reason, they often try to demonstrate their worth by attacking the most vulnerable—the coworker who is least likely to fight back, or least likely to win.

On the other hand, some bullies attack the most competent—the ones against whom they fear they cannot compete successfully on the basis of workplace performance. The idea is to get the overachiever to slow down or quit so that he is no longer a threat to the bully. Jealousy of another's competence or popularity is a similar reason for resorting to bullying tactics. In this case, the negative behavior probably is the bully's way of showing that, while you may be successful or popular, you are less powerful and more vulnerable than the bully is.

Other bullies intimidate anyone whenever they please as a means of getting their way or to compensate for their feeling of low self-esteem. They need to prove their self-worth to themselves. They do not feel that they are capable of winning others over to their side by stating their positions or depending on their ability to compete intellectually. Finally, there are individuals who are so mentally unfit that they simply enjoy humiliating, embarrassing, or degrading their coworkers. Even at the risk of alienating other coworkers, they savor the moments of control over the targeted person's sense of well-being.

Whatever the reasons or motivations for bullying behavior, the damaging effect on other personnel is serious and pervasive. Such behavior does not just cease if ignored. It continues to follow the individual, just as it has done since childhood.

Harass

When we speak of harassment, overt sexual harassment most often comes to mind because of the extensive coverage given to this problem in recent years.[4] Some examples other than sexual harassment include deliberate, insensitive acts like eating a smelly snack at one's desk near others who object, intentionally wearing too much perfume when it is known to make another person uncomfortable, smoking near a door or window so that the smoke drifts back inside where it will offend others, or using off-color words or swear words in the presence of someone who is known to abhor such language. In other cases, a worker may harass others because he is angry at his own partner outside the office, a boss, the organization, or the world in general. Occasionally, a worker will use harassment as a form of retaliation against a coworker, to encourage that person to leave. After all the press coverage, books, and employee training sessions, it would seem that no one in today's workplace would inadvertently or unknowingly harass a member of the opposite sex. Yet it does happen, both overtly and subtly.

Whether words or actions are considered to be harassing is determined by whether the person at the receiving end considers them to be unwelcome. Thus, some coworkers may have personality traits that are normal for them but unwelcome and therefore harassing to a coworker of the opposite sex or belonging to a different religion, culture, or socioeconomic background. On the other hand, some workers are perhaps overly sensitive, almost as though they are looking for something they can be defensive about, rather than something that genuinely offends them. Even if it is the result of a personality or cultural clash, harassment is unacceptable. And remember, harassment is defined by the subject or intended recipient, not the initiator.

Engage in Theft or Sabotage

Workers may engage in theft by rationalizing that their action amounts to nothing more than getting what they deserve or what the organization owes them. They reason that pilfering is "not a big deal—only a few cents worth" and that "everyone else does it." After all, even the boss occasionally takes pencils home or makes personal copies on the organization's copying machine. Some organizations are not opposed to "helping" their employees in such a manner occasionally. In fact, a few manufacturers are quite generous in giving their products—most notably food—to their employees. Others, however, consider it as theft. Workers know the rules; hence, by their actions they show coworkers whether they can be trusted to obey the rules.

Other types of theft are generally more serious, more damaging, and unquestionably illegal; for example, embezzling funds or altering records for personal gain or at the boss' request. Included here also is stealing by deception, such as faking an accident to collect insurance money, to avoid work, to obtain a transfer, or whatever reason. And we should mention that theft may consist of stealing from a coworker, not just from the company. Purses and electronic items are popular items with others in the workplace.

Some nonmanager employees who would never steal directly will nevertheless engage in sabotage against a coworker or against the organization that often goes unmentioned when tallying the cost of theft. Most of us have heard the stories about nonmanagers getting even with their managers or organization by engaging in assembly-line sabotage; for example, dropping a few rock gravels inside the door of automobiles to cause warranty costs and customer relations problems later for the manufacturer; and putting metal, glass, bugs, or animal parts in food products during the canning process or even in restaurants. Delaying important information or intentionally sending it to the wrong person has also been used. Walt Disney Creative Entertainment had an employee insert an obscene scene in a children's movie that required them to recall millions of videos, and Lockheed Martin had an employee crash its email system for 6 hours.[5]

A growing problem in many workplaces, sabotage will likely affect coworkers more directly than theft. For example, a saboteur can permanently damage a coworker's reputation by writing anonymous or "sock puppet" memos that misrepresent situations and sending them up the channel or within the same office. "Sock puppets" are aliases used to hide a person's identity, particularly when the effort is intended to damage the reputation of someone else. These messages may contain lies or rumors, or they may be in the form of titillating questions or statements that imply negative things about the coworker. One of the oldest forms of sabotage is manipulating information for the purpose of taking credit for work that was done by another worker. This act may be done in a sly, quiet, underhanded manner so as not to alert the worker who actually performed the work that the saboteur is taking the credit.

Another form of sabotage that can be hard to prove is intentional disruption of another person's work. Various sly methods are used, such as tampering with a coworker's computer, withholding or "misplacing" information that the coworker needs, providing incorrect information, changing information in a database, to name a few. Such cases may be difficult to prove, especially when they are not immediately obvious. We have seen cases where a saboteur would falsely claim that he needed a high-performing coworker's help on another project when his real purpose was to prevent her from having enough time to perform her own tasks at the superior level that had been her norm.

Related to these saboteurs are the "trolls" who "steal time" by failing to participate earnestly in meaningful discussions or meetings about organizational problems. These "trolls" make comments and interject statements to show that they are involved, but their "contributions" are jokes or insults that push discussions off track rather than helping to solve the problem at hand. Another form of unacceptable behavior is "flaming," which refers to bringing up topics for the express purpose of attacking, criticizing, or insulting others or their ideas.

IRRITATE OTHERS

Most of the nonmanager behaviors that we mentioned above are intentional acts that hurt other individuals or help the perpetrator. Other behaviors may be caused not so much by specific intentions as by egocentricity or self-centeredness.

Complain and Fail to Accept Blame

Employees with negative attitudes toward work, management, customers, or the organization are not pleasant to interact with or to work with, even if there is some basis for their criticisms or contrariness. Most likely they are not trying intentionally to irritate someone. Complainers are difficult to endure, overzealous critics can be threatening even when you are not the subject of the complaint, and coworkers who think that their way is the only way are especially threatening and difficult to tolerate. The uncomfortable relationships have an impact on employee morale and the organization's culture. These effects can, in turn, lead to lower productivity and higher turnover for coworkers. If the attitude problem results in a worker's doing things his way rather than following organizational procedures, workplace safety and product quality also may be affected, as well as relationships with customers and vendors.

Internal emails have become one of the most prevalent methods of revealing one's attitudes toward coworkers. Even individuals who would never make unwelcome remarks face-to-face seem to feel free to say or send material via email—as though they are virtually anonymous. For example, workers who would insist that they accept other groups as their equals may reveal a different attitude by sending emails containing jokes, photos, or other materials that are offensive to coworkers of the opposite sex, different religions, other races or cultures, and so on.

Among the least popular coworkers are those who blame others for their errors or oversights. After spending considerable time reading and correcting a coworker's report, for example, we resent that the lazy or distrusting writer fails to make the changes or credit us for our contribution. We may even feel indignation toward the worker who takes credit when the boss shows positive support for work that has been done but passes the blame to others when the boss reacts unfavorably.

Inconsiderate or Insensitive

An otherwise good job can become a terrible job when workers are in close proximity to inconsiderate workers, especially if there are also constant interactions with those workers. They often must try to think and to talk above the telephone and person-to-person conversations in the normal conduct of business as well as the other nonessential chatter and noise that goes on during work hours. They smell each other's perfume or cologne, and perhaps the tuna or sardine sandwich that the guy two rows over brought in his lunch bag today. On the assembly line, they may have to put up with the jabbering of the braggart or the competitor they never asked for. And in many cases, they are indeed in competition with each other in the eyes of their bosses.

Some workers are intelligent, hard-working, honest, and committed, yet unpleasant to be around because they are inconsiderate. One may say, "Good Morning," for example, in the same tone of voice used for saying, "Get out of my life." Another may cause embarrassment or anger by making fun of a coworker's blunder, whether a mispronounced word, a spoken grammatical error, or some other faux pas. They may demand extra concessions such as schedule changes to accommodate their family obligations without considering that others have the same constraints to deal with. They may intentionally refuse to cooperate and compromise, or they may be insensitive to others' opinions and thoughts—it's "all about me," my way or no way.

Inconsideration also is manifested by workers who disregard personal appearance or hygiene. Aroma overload is an awkward problem for both managers and coworkers. Who wouldn't like to put an unwelcome sign at their cubicle or erect an imaginary fence around their personal space when certain coworkers come near? We're speaking of those workers who expect us to conduct business as usual while tolerating their body odor, including bad breath or the stench of tobacco smoke on their clothes or from their mouths. Tobacco smoke is a frequent complaint, as smokers transfer the offensive odors to papers if they smoke in their offices or take home organizational work at night. Equally offensive to some people is the worker who reeks of excessive perfume or aftershave lotion (even expensive brands, but more so if it's cheap), fabric softeners, hairspray, perfumed soaps, and the like. "Layers" of these odors can build up, polluting the workspace even more.

Some employees have not learned that proper grooming is more than wearing expensive clothes. Some females, in particular, seem to need a dress code to remind them that proper work attire is not synonymous with after-hours "club wear." Their appearance tends to disrupt male workers and alienate other women. Frequent complaints about male workers include a need to trim the hair, mustache, or beard. Other workers smack their gum (even while on the phone), blow bubbles, or cough in your face. A few may stand near a door or window where they are not prohibited from smoking, letting the smoke from their cigarettes pollute the air of coworkers, although this has become far less problematic with new antismoking regulations.

In other work-related settings, coworkers complain about having to eat near persons who display poor manners, even when they are eating from lunchboxes or brownbags. We generally do not like to watch someone talk with a mouthful of food or chew with their mouth open, or listen to the guzzling or slurping of a drink. While some may not consider it a matter of etiquette, workers are quick to criticize coworkers who eat offensive-smelling foods in workplace areas outside the lunchroom; for example, fish (including tuna fish) sandwiches and popcorn. Popcorn eaters in particular appear to be unaware that many others dislike the smell of popcorn (especially burned popcorn!) in the office. Workers of different ethnic groups also seem not to realize that many workers despise the odors of some ethnically popular foods. The problem can intensify or extend to other areas of interaction because communication about the problem does not occur, as workers are reluctant to criticize individuals from another ethnic group.

Lack Interpersonal Skills

For whatever their reason, some workers are inconsiderate and disruptive in other ways. They rant when they're angry; complain incessantly when things go bad; and sing, hum, whistle, or chatter when things go right. Their loud talking or laughing is disruptive. They may interrupt your in-person or telephone conversations for no good reason, or talk so loud that they disrupt your concentration. Some individuals "smack" their chewing gum, blow and burst bubbles, slurp a drink, or eat while talking to someone in person or on the phone. They may be oblivious to statements or ask questions that insult the person to whom they are speaking or writing.

Inconsiderate workers often feel free to ask coworkers for favors, such as covering their phones or taking responsibility for a project when they leave their desks to deal with their "problems" or other interests. When they return, they may show no sign of being grateful for the help, which causes coworkers to feel even greater resentment and no future obligation to repeat their kindness. They frequently borrow lunch money and forget to repay it without being reminded. To such workers, "it's all about me."

Another major complaint that we hear from office personnel concerns coworkers who are obsessed with scheduling office parties or other types of "extracurricular" activities. Or they may invite some colleagues to lunch or to an after-hours get-together while ignoring another coworker who is standing with the same group. They may make no attempt to include a particular worker in discussions at meetings, mealtime chat, or water-cooler conversations. They may not even realize they are scheduling out-of-office activities that some workers cannot attend because of family obligations or religious affiliations. Mostly these complaints pertain to female employees, especially those who plan potluck lunches during the workday or disrupt the office by decorating and celebrating where others are trying to work. These inconsiderate individuals make it difficult for others to conclude team projects or even their own work assignments and often require coworkers' time outside the office for cooking, purchasing items needed for the get-together, or whatever. Frowning on or missing such activities can result in a person's being labeled as uncooperative, unsociable, or worse. Yet participating in such functions can result in an employee's being viewed by management as something less than professional and career oriented. Similar pressures on male coworkers tend to require their participation on nights and weekends, and usually involve a heavier outlay of cash—both of which can create problems at home.

Come to Work Ill

Managers and nonmanagers alike object to jobs that allow employees to come to work when they are ill, spreading germs and viruses when they should stay at home.[6] Those who are not ill do not wish to become ill, miss work, or carry germs and viruses home to their families. Furthermore, the ill worker probably will not achieve maximum productivity anyway. Ultimately, everybody suffers more from the worker's attendance than they would suffer from his absence.

Why do individuals come to work when ill? Some individuals think they are doing a big favor for coworkers, bosses, and the organization by showing up at work even when they feel terrible—but the opposite is true. In some cases, individuals don't want to miss work because they cannot afford to lose a day's pay or because they want to save their "sick leave" days in case they have a more serious illness in the future. In some cases, the idea of "sacrificing" by not staying home while ill may stem from previous experience with schools where staying because of illness is treated as a contrived excuse, otherwise called "a lie." Also, the school is paid according to the number of students in attendance each day, so they tend to push students to come to school unless suffering from a more serious illness such as the flu or chickenpox. Recent graduates and parents who currently have children enrolled in schools are already mindful of such a way of thinking and may be especially concerned that "sick excuses" could hurt their opportunities for advancement.

FAIL TO CARRY THEIR OWN WEIGHT

Other workers can be relatively sure that a coworker is not carrying his own weight when he is absent from the job, and they aren't fooled for long by the worker who is absent *on* the job. Shirking workers do not earn their paychecks. At best, this results in friction among workers; at worst, it creates resentment, anger, and stress. This is true especially when the underproductive person is of the same or higher rank and pay

Poor or Inefficient Work Habits

Conscientious workers can tell when a coworker has poor or inefficient work habits that interfere with the productivity of themselves or those around them. Some of these inefficient workers are not trained or qualified to carry out the job duties for which they were hired, others are lazy, and still others seem to think that the organization owes them a job and a paycheck even if they are not performing. A few workers come to work when they are ill and cannot perform at an optimum level. Surprisingly perhaps, some employees shirk their jobs because they enjoy playing what they regard as a simple game of "breaking the rules"—getting paid without doing the work. In some cases, it is their way of "sticking it" to other workers, to the boss, or to the organization.

Failure to Focus

A frequent cause of underproducing is the inability to focus on task completion. The worker's attention is often focused instead on personal problems, interests, or needs. Alcohol or drugs (both illegal and prescribed) can also affect a person's ability to concentrate on the tasks at hand. And some workers care so little about their job that they either cannot or choose not to focus on the job. These irresponsible individuals may be motivated only by the wages, without feeling a responsibility to perform like their coworkers.

Laziness

Failure to carry their weight is often the result of laziness. The interdependence of jobs can cause workers to dislike their jobs by creating negative feelings among workers when communication does not go smoothly or when one worker does not carry his or her weight on a project. Lazy workers are resented because they are paid for hours of work they do not perform. Furthermore, they make the job bad for others when they fail to meet their deadlines or contribute the quality and the share that is expected of them. Rude workers affect morale because they use verbal assaults that other workers feel should not be tolerated by management. That, in turn, can lead to poor relationships between workers and managers, or managers and executives. So can the antics of manipulative workers. They are insulting since the message they send is that they are too good or too important to do the work themselves.

Language or Culture Barrier

Some workers use the language barrier as their excuse for not carrying their weight in the workplace. They can pretend, for instance, that they didn't understand the assignment or the due date. Of course, continual miscommunication should be reason for dismissal for nonperformance, but the employee is usually given "more time to learn the language." Some successfully hold over the manager's head the threat of discrimination lawsuits, even though they may not even be a protected minority and even though the manager could easily document their performance failures. Again, employees who hide behind such an excuse can create interpersonal problems within the work group, which ultimately affect morale and productivity.

Habits and Attitudes

Every organization also has coworkers who are slow and wasteful of not only time but also office or inventory supplies. Some are just naturally slow-moving persons, some move unacceptably slow in order to avoid mistakes, and some are lazy or spiteful. In the view of dependable workers, we're paid to work for a certain number of hours, so there seems no logical reason to avoid work during that time. Unfortunately, a few others perceive it as a game of seeing how little work they can do relative to others and still receive the same pay. Their opponent, however, is not necessarily the other workers but rather management. The challenge may be to see how far they can push the boss without suffering the consequences. We have seen this intentional slowdown especially when workers felt well protected by their union membership and/or their minority status. In one large automobile company, employees and management referred to these "nonparticipating workers" as the "dare" workers, as in "I dare you to try doing anything about it."

On the other hand, coworkers with poor or inefficient work habits often seem oblivious to their failure to live up to the productivity expectations of others. Workers may not be aware that they spend excessive time chatting with coworkers, talking on the phone about business or nonbusiness matters, or sending blanket emails asking someone to contact them on some topic. For instance, they may have difficulty ending a face-to-face conversation or a telephone call. They may find it easier to call someone else rather than attempting to solve their own problem, extend a business call into a personal call, or use a legitimate call to segue into a "cry on your shoulder" opportunity. They may attempt to carry on conversations while faxing or copying and end up wasting supplies when they discover that their inattention led to errors. Other inefficient workers may go to great lengths to please their boss and coworkers in other ways so that they are not held accountable for their inefficiency. You probably have seen, for example, coworkers for whom someone is always willing to cover because, well, "You just can't not like them and forgive them"; for example, the office flirt (male or female), the comedian or clown who breaks the tension especially in "unrelaxed" settings, the former athlete who organizes sports activities outside the office, or the coworker who assumes a mothering role.

Fail to Carry Out Instructions Properly

Many of us may have been gripped by momentary paralysis when assigned a task with minimum guidance and what appears to be an insanely short deadline. If this happens repeatedly, though, and a worker always seems unable to carry out instructions or handle assignments on his own, problems arise within the work group, especially when those assignments interrelate or overlap. The manager and coworkers of such individuals usually know when an individual is just too lazy to try to figure out the assignment or will wait for help as their way of procrastinating. They will eventually determine whether the worker is technically incompetent also. Coworkers are not always aware, however, when an individual has difficulty because he lacks reading or listening skills, has a fear of failure, or has been given poor instructions. Right or wrong, the coworkers will make their own judgment as to whether the person should or should not have been hired.

Workers who don't carry out routine instructions properly or promptly can place unnecessary burdens on their coworkers who are facing their own production quotas, deadlines, and quality-control standards. For example, when the problem is language, technical know-how, reading or listening skills, coworkers are often asked to use their time to explain the task or show the individual how to carry out the assignment. When the individual is simply too lazy to do the job, a different type of problem is created—coworker resentment.

Some individuals have difficulty carrying out assignments because they are afraid they will make a mistake. Even workers who are capable of carrying out routine instructions and are not attempting to avoid work may have difficulty handling complex assignments if they are paralyzed by fear of failure. They may experience difficulty especially in getting started and/or wrapping up a project. Because of uncertainty regarding their own ability, some coworkers will consume excessive time and attention by asking dozens of questions of their manager or coworkers, requesting that coworkers read and critique drafts, or just talking about their stress to anyone who will listen. Eventually, even sympathetic coworkers tire of helping these hesitant, indecisiveness employees.

Unless the organization's mission is to hire mentally challenged individuals who cannot succeed in a regular work environment, coworkers tend to feel that workers who are not capable of carrying out instructions either should never have been hired, should be trained immediately or let go if they cannot perform, or should not be given the same title and pay as those who discharge their responsibilities more competently.

Bring Family Problems to Work

Workers who let family obligations interfere with work are also not favored by their coworkers. Most employees are sympathetic when a problem arises, but they think it unfair for some employees (often with management's consent) to expect others to do their work while they attend to family obligations. The problem sometimes involves a spouse's business or the worker's elderly parents but most often concerns school-age children. In addition to arriving late and spending too much time on telephone calls after 3 o'clock, all too frequently the coworkers are unable to schedule meetings during the early morning hours or after school hours. When parents are worried about their children in daycare, at summer camp, or at home alone, they often cannot concentrate properly on their work, which in turn affects their performance and often impacts the work of others as well. In the more extreme cases, parents bring children to work sometimes when school is not in session or the child is ill because the family has not made adequate arrangements for childcare.

Managers and coworkers have reason to be concerned about individuals who have family-relations problems, as these domestic problems frequently carry over to the workplace. For example, nearly a third of women killed in U.S. workplaces between 2003 and 2008 were killed by a current or former intimate partner.[7] The U.S. Department of Labor has reported that 75% of domestic violence victims face harassment from domestic partners while at work.[8] Another study reports that this problem caused 56% of them to be late for work at least five times a month, 28% to leave early at least five days a month, and 54% to miss three or more full days of work every month. In addition, almost one half of these women reported difficulty concentrating at work, with almost 20% reporting a workplace accident or "near miss."[9]

Family obligations as discussed above can become a large problem indeed because of other inequalities. For instance, because the work must get done, managers frequently ask single or childless workers to stay late or take on additional work when another worker is preoccupied with family obligations. Single or childless workers may be aware that they are paid less by the organization, whose argument has been that the person who is married and or has dependents needs more money (yes, even for doing the same work!). More recently, in many companies, medical insurance premiums also reflect a bias toward dependents. For example, a family of two (husband and wife) often pay the same insurance premium as a family of four or five. With such favorable biases toward the worker with family obligations, it is easy to see why single or childless workers resent being expected to cover for workers who let family obligations interfere with their work.

Addiction Problems

Workers who are hindered by alcohol or drug problems cause special concern among coworkers. Although most workers are sympathetic to coworkers who have alcohol or drug problems, they still do not like the idea of performing that person's work without extra pay or without that person being docked for nonperformance. In some settings, the coworkers of individuals with alcohol or drug problems also see and feel a potential safety issue. Even if the worker does not show up totally intoxicated or smashed, there can be a problem of concentration—the inability to focus on job completion or quality. The fairness issue most likely arises again, as someone else ends up taking responsibility for job performance.

Coworkers with drug or alcohol problems can affect the cohesiveness and the performance of the work group not only by their behavior on the job but also by their excessive absences. Workers in some workplaces know that on many Mondays—especially Mondays following Friday paydays—they will be expected to function without the entire team. Where worker performance depends on the input/output of others, most likely the workers who are present will feel they are being taken unfair advantage of, interpersonal relationships and group unity will suffer, and the organization's productivity will decline.

Absent From the Job

Bad things happen and people need personal time, so coworkers become accustomed to covering for one another—unless, that is, the absences are excessive or seemingly unnecessary. Workers whose tasks overlap are affected most when one of them is absent, but even when tasks are independent, habitual absences can be disrupting and demoralizing.

Chronic absenteeism is frequently associated with alcohol or drug problems and is most noticeable on the next workday following the distribution of payroll. Complicating matters further, these individuals may not be totally fit for work when they do return. But sometimes absenteeism is simply a matter of laziness or indifference. Even though they are paid well and not required to work hard, some workers simply do not have the self-discipline required to get out of bed, get dressed, take care of family obligations, and go to work. In a few companies, you will find workers who know that their jobs are secure, so they simply enjoy manipulating the system by being absent—as though it is a demonstration of their power that they can come to work when and if they want to without fear of repercussion. Workers who are overstressed either at work or in their personal lives may also be no-shows, but they are generally not resented as much as the previously mentioned absentees. After a respectable amount of time, coworkers tire of hearing others' problems and sympathizing with them if those ill or troubled workers fail to take advantage of the assistance that is available through health insurance plans or Human Resources.

Some workers report to work every day, but they either start late, leave early, or disappear for long periods during the day. This type of habitually absent employee may annoy their coworkers even more than the ones who miss a full day's work. They are viewed as irresponsible workers who cheat the system by staying at work only long enough to maintain an image of being responsible and concerned. We all recognize these individuals—they arrive mid-morning and declare that they were working from home or that they always make up the time by working late, after other employees are gone. Or they claim that they arrive an hour or two before other workers, which justifies their leaving work early. Although it would be easy for the boss to arrive early or stay late and check such claims, that does not appear to happen often—maybe because the boss prefers to avoid confrontations or is playing the same game at least part of the time. Employees who take excessive time for lunches and breaks also make undesirable coworkers, especially when the absences stem from procrastination. They tend to be unavailable when you need them and most likely will not meet deadlines that affect others. If they stay away from the office because they lack the commitment to perform as expected, then the quality of the work they do will also tend to suffer. Workers who must clock in are at least penalized for the time they are absent from the job. They justify their absence by saying that it hurts only them as they are unpaid for the time away, but in fact this type of absence or lateness also affects interpersonal relations and group morale as well as productivity.

Absent on the Job

Some workers can't do their fair share because they are absent from work; others are what we'd call "absent on the job," as they are physically there but cannot or do not fully perform their jobs. We all know workers who are seldom or never absent, arrive at work on time, and do not leave early, yet do not give the organization a full day's work. In other words, they are absent on the job. One of the most obvious is the employee who spends too much time chatting with coworkers in person or with whomever on the phone. The newest addition to these shirkers are the coworkers who use the organization's computer to surf the Internet, chat via email or instant messaging regarding nonwork-related items, play Solitaire, check stock market prices, search real-estate listings, and so on. Such excessive behavior usually results in additional organizational rules that place restrictions on everyone but then are frequently ignored by the very workers who abused the system in the first place.

Rather than avoiding work, some employees find other work they would rather do while on the job. For example, they may give priority to planning and carrying out social activities to be held at work (e.g., birthday celebrations, Over-the-Hump Wednesdays, Thank-God-for-Jobs Thursdays, Friday-the-13th luncheons) or after-hours (office softball team and tournament, Fourth of July picnic, etc.). Some workers have personal projects that they give priority over the work for which they are being paid. This may include a "hobby job" such as designing their neighbor's kitchen, work related to their membership in a nonjob-related organization such as a church or charity fund drive, projects related to their spouse or children such as designing fliers for the PTO or planning the family vacation, and such. They seem to feel justified especially in doing charity work on company time.

Some jobs do not require a lot of concentration or focus while others require a great deal. Nevertheless, all jobs require the jobholder to pay attention to what he or she is doing. A failure to do so can affect performance through lessened productivity, increased accidents, or mistakes. Attention problems frequently occur when the work requires greater effort than usual or takes more time. Under these circumstances, individuals may have difficulty in focusing on task completion. Typically, these individuals also have difficulty recalling their own mistakes and so careful documentation is required before attempting to do anything about their behavior. In some cases, poor concentration may result from a medical condition such as ADD (attention deficit disorder), lack of proper sleep due to a medical condition known as sleep apnea, from taking prescription drugs, or from drug or alcohol abuse.

Other workers may appear not to be concentrating on their jobs because they are engaged in other activities. It is important not to assume, though, that employees who are talking (even about nonwork matters) or listening to a radio are bad employees and that all such behavior should cease. Employee interaction can help build the esprit de corps of the organization, which is vital to effective performance in the long term. A problem arises when such behavior is excessive. In those cases, these individuals require constant or close supervision and therefore are more expensive for organizations.

TAKE OR EXPOSE OTHERS TO UNNECESSARY RISKS

Some employees are potentially harmful to their coworkers, other organizational assets, or themselves. Such workers include individuals who have not been properly trained by the organization, but others are what we sometimes regard as "forgetful" or "accident prone." Safety and health are so important that virtually all organizations conduct training programs periodically about accidents and safety. In addition, there are many organizations devoted to creating and maintaining safer work environments. The National Safety Council and the Occupation Safety and Health Administration are two such organizations, but almost every industry group has an organization or committee devoted to health and safety issues.[10] So if an organization pays attention to and uses these resources, employees are likely also to pay attention to the matter of safety and health.

Potentially Harmful to Coworkers and Other Organizational Assets

Employees have good reason to be concerned about coworkers who are potentially harmful to others and to other organizational assets. Those "others" may be inconsiderate, or perhaps they are not accustomed to being held accountable for their actions. They are the ones who forget to secure the doors, fail to follow correct procedures on the assembly line, forget to turn off the electric hotplate in the lunchroom, light a cigarette too close to flammable materials, or block emergency exits. In some cases, they may expose others to unnecessary risks by failing to remain alert on the job. This can include daydreaming, experiencing dull reactions due to medications, or falling asleep because of sleep apnea or sleep deprivation at home. Operating vehicles or machinery irresponsibly is another workplace activity that can put coworkers at risk.

Still others have mental problems or attitude problems about work that result in choices that subject their coworkers to unnecessary risks. Included here are workers who, consciously or not, want to "get back at" a coworker or the organization. They can represent security risks; for example, intentionally leave doors unsecured, sabotage computer data or equipment, jam machines, give information to competitors, participate in espionage, and so on. These individuals may fit the profile of someone who could potentially commit workplace violence in the future.

Potentially Harmful to Themselves

In many or most cases, workers who are potentially harmful to coworkers are also potentially harmful to themselves. For example, if they fail to follow assembly line procedures, it may be their own hand that they sever. If they disregard safety devices or safety instructions, such as lighting a cigarette too close to flammable materials, they are likely to get burned worse than their coworkers.

Other actions, though, are potentially harmful to themselves only; for example, lifting loads that are too heavy, attempting to work at too great a speed, operating equipment as toys rather than potentially dangerous machines, or goofing off as though the workplace were a playground. Workers seem especially inclined to treat warehouses without proper respect unless they have been thoroughly trained and are held strictly accountable. Although some pieces of office equipment (e.g., paper cutters and shredders) are also treated too nonchalantly, equipment used in production, construction, and mining usually has greater consequences. Of special concern is power equipment, including hoists, air hammers and wrenches, jacks, winches, transmission jacks, and some others.

PROBLEMS ASSOCIATED WITH OUTSIDERS

While most books and articles on workplace violence seem to concentrate on individuals in the workplace, the reality is that the truly violent forms come from the outside. In the four year period 2005–2009, about 70% of workplace homicides were committed by outsiders—robbers or other assailants. Other outsiders—customers and clients—accounted for about

10%. Members or former members of the organization accounted for 11% of workplace homicides. And finally, another group of outsiders, spouses or other relatives, accounted for about 4%, with the rest being committed by personal acquaintances of the victim.[11]

Robbery/Burglary

In the United States during 2009, those 12 or older experienced an estimated 20 million criminal victimizations, including 4.3 million violent crimes, 15.6 million property crimes, and 133,000 personal thefts. Violent crimes include rape, sexual assault, robbery, aggravated assault, and simple assault. Property crimes include household burglary, motor vehicle theft, and theft. Personal theft includes pickpocketing and purse snatching.[12] Even so, the crime rate in the United States is declining.[13]

But to clarify (and oversimplify a bit), let's examine a few terms. Theft and larceny are synonymous, and they refer to taking of something of value intending to keep it or to sell or exchange it for money, drugs, or whatever. Taking something from the organization would be theft but not workplace violence unless more occurred. Burglary involves unlawful entry (also known as breaking and entering) to commit a crime—theft for example. Robbery, on the other hand, is a forcible stealing from a person. So, people are robbed (usually by force or threat), places (buildings, vehicles, etc.) are burglarized by breaking and entering, and things (personal property or services) are the intended items of larceny or theft.

While most robberies occur "on the street" (strong-arm robberies), a great many do occur at banks or at late-night retail establishments like gas stations or convenience stores. Where weapons are used, firearms predominate, with knives or cutting instruments second.[14] This may help to explain why so many homicides occur during robberies.

During robberies and burglaries, the assailant(s) uses force to obtain money and/or goods, and the confrontation frequently results in very bad outcomes. As just indicated, these assaults are the most prevalent form of homicides during workplace violence. These outsiders, then, are criminals whose motive is usually theft. However, the criminal frequently carries a weapon and that substantially increases the likelihood that someone will be killed or at least injured in some way. Certain workplaces and jobs are more vulnerable to this type of workplace violence; for example, those that involve working at night, those who handle cash, taxicab drivers, and those who work in dangerous or isolated areas.[15] Chapter 6 will discuss these and other workplaces in more detail.

Clients/Customers

Some managers and workers assume that they have to please only the individuals who are employed by the organization—especially the individuals they work alongside. But customers or clients with whom you deal outside your organization can also make a job seem bad. Some individuals feel that, as a customer, they have the right to be very demanding. Unfortunately, many are not just demanding but also rude, inconsiderate, and insulting—perhaps because they think such behavior will ensure that their request will be granted. When workers who are a little thin-skinned meet up with outsiders who are quite assertive or even aggressive, the interactions that occur can make the worker hate his job badly enough to quit.

Jobs that are made bad by customer or supplier contacts can create extraordinary stress because the worker has no authority over the contact person and the organization has no control over individuals who are not on its payroll. Problems with outside contacts may include listening to their insulting or very unkind remarks, trying to meet deadlines without all the necessary information from the contact, or declining to accept or provide requested information or favors that are disallowed by your organization.

First of all, there are "rush hours"—times when numerous customers are wanting to check out at the same time so the worker is under a lot of pressure to work fast. That pressure can lead to mistakes, which can slow things down even more or be costly and come out of your pay. And, of course, there are customers or clientele who are rude, critical, angry, bossy, and sometimes even cuss you out. Others are never satisfied; these complainers haggle over everything. Customers or clients who have difficulty making decisions can also create problems for the worker. They can consume an unreasonable amount of time, whether it be on an off-site sales call or at closing time at your worksite. And then there are the irate clients/customers who insist on blaming the contact person, who has no control over the problem or the solution. Their unprotected accessibility by a disgruntled individual makes them extremely vulnerable to an act of violence, especially if they unintentionally provoke rather than appease the individual.

Domestic Violence

As discussed earlier in the section on bringing family problems to work, problems experienced by workers with their families often carry over to the workplace. Indeed, many of the homicides occurring to women at work are perpetrated by intimate partners, and the incidents often occur in parking lots.[16] When domestic violence moves to the workplace, it can lead to homicide. While women are more likely to experience domestic violence than men, it is a concern for both genders.

Even if something as dire as homicide doesn't occur, domestic violence takes a toll on workplaces. Productivity suffers when victims can't effectively concentrate on their performance. Victims tend to be absent or late to work. It has been estimated that as many as 85% of victims report being absent from work and over half late to work or leaving early due to the abuse. The victim may be blocked or delayed from going to work, worn out from the abuse, have injuries, feel shame or depression, or be afraid for the safety of her children. And, of course, the target may have appointments with doctors, lawyers, or law enforcement related to the abuse. Domestic violence also leads to employee turnover because they can't work while trying to deal with the abuse. In some cases, unfortunately, they may be terminated because their performance becomes unacceptable and the company can wait no longer.[17]

Regrettably, many organizations regard domestic violence as something that has little to do with them. However, increasingly, organizations are recognizing the effects just noted and are started to regard domestic violence as something that they can and should do something about.[18]

WHAT NEXT?

This chapter recognizes what many coworkers know all too well: that bad nonmanagers or coworkers can be as disruptive or offensive, if not more so, as bad managers. Numerous examples are given of behaviors or habits that appear "bad" to at least some of their peers.

The following chapter, Chapter 6, includes suggestions to managers for dealing with the kinds of nonmanager workers discussed in this chapter. Chapter 7 contains ideas to help coworkers deal with coworkers' undesirable behaviors. And again, Appendage II at the end of this Section provides vivid and real examples of many of the characteristics and behaviors discussed here. Those examples have been drawn from material provided by consulting clients, students, family, or friends.

NOTES

1. Haynes, M. (2013). Workplace violence: Why every state must adopt a comprehensive workplace violence prevention law. *Cornell HR Review*. Retrieved from www.cornellhrreview.org/workplace-violence-why-every-state-must-adopt-a-comprehensive-workplace-violence-prevention-law/

2. Greengard, S. (1997). 50% of your employees are lying, cheating & stealing. *Workforce Magazine, 76*(10), 44–53.

3. Keashly, L., & Neuman, J. H. (2004). Bullying in the workplace: Its impact and management. *Employee Rights and Employment Policy Journal, 8*(2), 335–373; Einarsen, S., & Mikkelsen, E. G. (2003). Individual effects of exposure to bullying at work. In S. Einarsen, H. Hoel, D. Zapf, & C. L. Cooper (Eds.), *Bullying and emotional abuse in the workplace: International perspectives in research and practice* (pp. 127–144). London, UK: Taylor & Francis.

4. O'Leary-Kelly, A. M., Bowes-Sperry, L., Arens-Bates, C., & Lean, E. R. (2009, June). Sexual harassment at work: A decade (plus) of progress. *Journal of Management, 35*(3), 503–536; Bates, C. A., Bowes-Sperry, L., & O'Leary-Kelly, A. M. (2006). Sexual harassment in the workplace: A look back and a look ahead. In E. K. Kelloway, J. Barling, & J. J. Hurrell (Eds.), *Handbook of workplace violence* (pp. 381–416). Thousand Oaks, CA: Sage; Berdahl, J. L. (2007). Harassment based on sex: Protecting social status in the context of gender hierarchy. *Academy of Management Review, 32*, 641–658.

5. Hafner, J. C., & Gresham, G. (2012). Managers' and senior executives' perceptions of frequency and type of employee-perpetrated information sabotage and their attitudes toward it—The results of a pilot study. *Journal of Behavioral and Applied Management, 13*(3), 151–167.

6. Hemp, P. (2004). Presenteeism: At work—but out of it. *Harvard Business Review, 82*(10), 49–57.

7. Tiesman, H., Gurka, K., Konda, S., Coben, J., & Amandus, H. E. (2012). Workplace homicides among U. S. women: The role of intimate partner violence. *Annals of Epidemiology, 22*, 277–284. Retrieved from http://www.annalsofepidemiology.org/article/S1047-2797(12)00024-5/abstract

8. Bondi, M. A., and Violence Prevention Committee. (2013). *Domestic violence and the workplace.* Washington, DC: Partnership for Prevention. Retrieved from www.caepv.org/membercenter/files/Partnership%20For%20Prevention%20briefing%20%28confidential%20document%29.pdf

9. Employers Against Domestic Violence. (2013). *Effects on the workplace.* Retrieved from employersagainstdomesticviolence.org/effects-on-workplace/workplace-dv-stats/

10. Information about each of these may be found on their websites: The National Safety Council (www.nsc.org/pages/home.aspx) and the Occupational Safety and Health Administration (www.osha.gov/).

11. Harrell, E. (2011). *Workplace violence: 1993–2009*. Washington, DC: Bureau of Justice Statistics, U.S. Department of Justice. Retrieved from www.bjs.gov/content/pub/pdf/wv09.pdf
12. Truman, J. L., & Rand, M. R. 2010. *Crime Victimization, 2009*. Washington, DC: Bureau of Justice Statistics.
13. Truman, J. L., & Rand, M. R. (2010). *Crime victimization, 2009*. Washington, DC: Bureau of Justice Statistics.
14. McGoey, C. E. (2013). *Robbery facts: Violent crime against persons*. Retrieved from www.crimedoctor.com/robbery1.htm
15. Federal Bureau of Investigation. (2004, March). *Workplace violence— Issues in response*, p. 13.
16. Corporate Alliance to End Partner Violence. (2013). *Workplace statistics*. Retrieved from www.caepv.org/getinfo/facts_stats.php?factsec=3
17. Hankwitz, H. (2013). Domestic violence statistics and your workplace. *Crisis Prevention Institute, Inc.* Retrieved from www.crisisprevention.com/Resources/Article-Library/Prepare-Training-Articles/Domestic-Violence-Statistics-and-Your-Workplace
18. Johnson, P. R., & Gardner, S. (1999). Domestic violence and the workplace: Developing a company response. *Journal of Management Development, 18*(7), 590–597.

CHAPTER 6

BAD NONMANAGER BEHAVIOR

What Managers Can Do

*... discrimination and violence in a culture cannot be
eliminated without changing culture.*

—Charlotte Bunch

As we discussed in the previous chapter, bad employees or "nonmanagers" impact everyone, including their coworkers, their supervisors, their organization, and contacts outside the organization as well as themselves. These nonmanagers consist of three groups: employees whose performance or productivity is unsatisfactory, coworkers whose behavior or attitude may serve as the catalyst for workplace violence, and fragile or impaired individuals who are likely to allow their feelings to erupt in violence.

The performance and behavior of bad nonmanagers can result in substantial costs. For the offending nonmanager, that bad behavior can ultimately escalate to acts of violence. For others, there are both direct and indirect costs. The direct costs include poor performance, lowered productivity and quality, inefficiency, increased absenteeism and turnover, and customer dissatisfaction and lost sales as well as possible damage

Violence at Work: What Everyone Should Know, pp. 123–138
Copyright © 2014 by Information Age Publishing
All rights of reproduction in any form reserved.

to the organization's reputation. Indirect costs include the "messages" unintentionally sent to others in the organization. For example, others may conclude that performance doesn't really matter. They lose confidence in the management of the organization, and morale begins to suffer. Productivity begins to fall as they, too, begin to let quality slip in a snowball effect that is difficult to stop.

Management is responsible for responding appropriately to lessen the risk of allowing inappropriate behavior to escalate. It is important that you, the manager, deal with bad employees as soon as possible to ensure the survival of yourself as well as the other workers. That responsibility is twofold: intervention or prevention before observable behavioral warning signs reach a critical point, and preparation for responding quickly and effectively to an unexpected situation that arises in the absence of observable warning signs. In this chapter we will discuss ways in which managers may address the undesirable behavior and inferior performance of nonmanagers.

ESTABLISH HIRING PROCEDURES

As talked about in Chapter 3, the best way to handle personnel problems—both managers and nonmanagers—is to hire right in the first place.

Obey the Law

From a legal standpoint, it is important to hire smart. The doctrine of negligent hiring provides that the employer may be held directly liable for negligence and breach of duty when an employee is injured as a result of the violent behavior of another employee. Negligent hiring may include, for example, failure to properly screen an applicant and thus overlooking his propensity for violence, which creates a risk of harm to other employees and managers. Many companies remove or reduce their negligence risk by hiring an outside background screening firm to perform this function.

Similarly, the doctrine of negligent retention applies after an employee is hired. The employer may be held directly liable for negligence and breach of duty when the employer does not take proper steps to alleviate the problem after becoming aware (or after he reasonably should have become aware) of unsuitable behavior for the workplace, particularly behavior that poses a threat or shows a propensity for violence.

Hire Right

If you hire the right employees, you won't have to worry later about dealing with bad employees—or, more realistically, dealing with bad employees will be something with which you will need to be concerned only occasionally. Spend enough time and energy on recruitment and selection to minimize later, more difficult and more costly problems. Organizations are obligated morally, ethically, and legally to hire and retain employees who will not present a danger to other employees.

Know What You Need

One of the most important keys to hiring the right people is to know what you really need to be seeking in a new employee so you can match the individuals and jobs. Each job necessitates not only particular skills and abilities but also certain levels of effort for the jobholder to perform effectively. What knowledge, skills, abilities, and experience should someone have to be successful on this particular job? Whether those skills and abilities are acquired through education or experience—that is, formally or informally—is not as important as whether the applicant has the stated qualifications. Matching individuals and jobs involves also considering the individual's values, needs, and expectations. Only with a appropriate match will jobholders have the "can do" necessary to perform successfully. As we say, "Give me the person with the right attitude and desire, and I can see that he gets the skills, whereas I cannot guarantee that I can develop the skilled worker's attitude and desire."

When recruiting and selecting, don't just rely on the kind of person that you had in the past. Perform a job analysis to determine what you need for any particular opening in your organization. Job analysis involves the systematic collection and recording of information about jobs. It results in job descriptions and specifications. A job description summarizes the duties encompassed by the job; the working conditions where the job is performed; and the tools, materials, and equipment used on the job. A job specification lists the skills, abilities, and other credentials necessary to perform the job. These documents, then, enable you to recruit and select applicants who fit the job. Figure 6.1 is a brief example combining the two documents.

Recruit the Right People

Once you know what you need, recruit individuals who will meet those requirements. Recruiting may be strictly internal—posting notices on bulletin boards, running an announcement in the organization's newsletter, having Human Resources post or announce it, and so on. Or recruiting may also involve the external job market. External recruiting involves placing

---

JOB DESCRIPTION AND SPECIFICATIONS

Job Title:

Data Entry Specialist

Job Purpose:

Maintains database by entering data.

Work environment is typical office cubicle.

Work involves use of PC computer and other office equipment

Job Duties:

Collects and enters data, processes information, and maintains files.

Transmits data to others as requested.

Tracks all files throughout the operating process.

Other duties as assigned.

Qualifications:

Two or more years of college preferred or additional relevant education and experience.

Skills:

• Proficient with all MS Office products

• Knowledge and experience using database software

• Ability to prioritize and manage time/projects effectively

• Self-starter, able to accomplish goals with minimal supervision

• Team player with strong customer service skills

• Detail focused

Figure 6.1.   An example of a job description and specifications.

announcements in local newspapers, the organization's website, local trade or civic organization's newsletters, online job boards, head-hunter companies, and so on. It also includes asking your other nonmanagers to recommend people they know and believe would be a good fit for the organization. In your recruiting, you need to be specific as to your needs so that those who do apply for the position are in fact more likely to have the credentials that you are seeking.

First and foremost, your organization should have an antiviolence, antibullying, antiharassment policy to which all existing and new members of the organization must agree. That policy, then should act as a starting point for hiring since any new employee would have to agree to it. Prior to starting any job search process, you should check with your HR office and possibly the legal staff to determine what preemployment screening techniques (such as interview questions, background and reference checks, driving records, and drug testing) are legal and appropriate for the job being considered. Figure 6.2 is an example of an organizational policy covering workplace violence, bullying, and harassment.

WORKPLACE VIOLENCE, ANTIBULLYING, ANTIHARASSMENT POLICY

Your organization is committed to providing a violence-free workplace.

POLICY:

Violence or threats of violence, either implied or direct, are prohibited on the organization's premises and at organizational events held elsewhere. Such conduct by an employee will not be tolerated. An employee who exhibits violent behavior shall be subject to disciplinary action up to and including dismissal and may be subject to criminal prosecution. Your organization will investigate all complaints and reported violations of this policy.

DEFINITIONS:

Workplace Violence: Behavior in which an employee, former employee or visitor to a workplace threatens to inflict or inflicts damage to property, harm, injury or death to others at the workplace. This includes making others afraid through intimidation.

Bullying: Bullying is unwanted offensive and malicious behavior which undermines an individual or group through persistently negative attacks. There is typically an element of vindictiveness and the behavior is calculated to undermine, patronize, humiliate, intimidate, or demean the recipient.

Harassment: Unwelcome verbal or physical behavior based on legally protected characteristics; e.g., race, color, religion, sex, national origin, age (for those 40-years-old and over), disability, sexual orientation, or retaliation.

Domestic Violence: Abuse committed against an adult or fully emancipated minor regardless of the marital status, age, race, or sexual orientation of the parties.

Workplace violence, bullying, and harassment may include, but are not limited to the following, whether such behaviors or actions are at or by a manager, nonmanager, or member of the public.

***

Assault

Attempting to intimidate or harass other individuals

Commission of a violent felony or misdemeanor on organizational property

Dangerous or threatening horseplay

(Figure 6.2 continues on next page)

WORKPLACE VIOLENCE, ANTIBULLYING, ANTIHARASSMENT POLICY
(Continued from previous page)

Direct threats or physical intimidation

Displaying an intense or obsessive romantic interest that exceeds the normal bounds of interpersonal interest

Displaying menacing gestures

Domestic violence

Intentional disregard for the safety or well-being of others

Loud, disruptive, or angry behavior or language not part of the typical work environment

Physical restraint, confinement

Retaliation against a person who makes a complaint

Stalking

Suggestions of violence

Throwing objects

Verbal threats to harm another individual or destroy property

REPORTING PROCEDURES:

[A description of how employees should go about reporting incidents.]

INVESTIGATION PROCEDURES:

[A description of how incidents will be investigated to provide both due diligence and privacy/confidentiality protection.]

VICTIM SUPPORT:

[A description of how the forms of support provided by your organization to victims of workplace violence.]

TRAINING:

[An indication that your organization provides training dealing with workplace violence.]

CONFIDENTIALITY:

[A statement of protection of individual privacy and confidentiality.]

NOTE: Considerable variation exists among what is included in such policies. We have indicated a few of the points that more complete policy statements might include.

Figure 6.2.   An example of a workplace violence policy.

Evaluate Applicants

Another part of your problem is determining whether applicants meet your criteria. You cannot rely on reference checks to determine some of the most important information about a potential employee, as former employers tend to avoid being candid for fear that they could be sued by the ex-employee. So you need to develop questions, tests, or brief cases that are designed to verify that individuals have the characteristics that your job and your organization's culture call for. For example, you can use simple scenarios during interviews to probe how potential employees might handle conflicts and interactions with coworkers.

Use the same tools as much as possible for all job candidates to assure fairness and comparability in the information that you obtain. If possible, have more than one person involved in the process so that the biases of any one person don't dominate. But one of the hardest points of all is to avoid hiring someone who is barely adequate because you need someone right away. Use temps or part-timers, but don't hire a full time employee until you are sure that he or she is the right person for the job.

Help the Applicant Evaluate Your Organization

As mentioned in Chapter 3, hiring individuals who are a "good fit" involves not only management's evaluation of applicants but also each applicant's evaluation of the job and the company. Define the job accurately and fully so applicants can decide whether they are qualified for, or capable of learning, the job. Also, discuss the company culture, expectations, and the like, and provide an opportunity to talk with other workers so applicants can ask questions that help them determine whether they would be happy in that workplace culture.

UNDERSTAND REINFORCEMENT

Remember, people tend to behave in ways that are reinforcing to them. That is, they behave in ways that get them attention, compliments, better assignments, easier work, more pay, or something that they value psychologically or economically. Therefore, the behavior of bad employees is behavior that is getting them something that they want. The key to effective management is to find out what is reinforcing the present unacceptable behavior and what would reinforce the desired behavior instead.

Perhaps the individual just wants attention, and getting feedback, even negative feedback, from his or her manager is satisfying that need. Perhaps the individual has a strong need for control or dominance and is trying to satisfy that need by what turns out to be abusive behavior toward others in the organization. Or it may be the satisfaction he feels from "messing with" another person. Repeated behavior is being reinforced in some way, otherwise, it would not continue to exist. A person who gets away with the bad behavior is likely to continue to exhibit that bad behavior. "Shaping him up" every now and then may get good short-term results that the manager wants, but the long-term impact can be disastrous. If you, the boss, can find out what is providing the reinforcement, then you can have an opportunity to eliminate it and thus change the behavior. Don't expect this to be a simple undertaking.

Managers sometimes unknowingly reinforce bad behavior by excusing some unacceptable behaviors that do not appear to be harmful to other members of the organization. Bad behaviors for some part of an individual's job (timeliness, attendance, completing paperwork) are sometimes overlooked or disregarded because other parts of that employee's performance are excellent (units produced, units passing inspection). In other words, good performers in selected areas frequently "get away with" things that others cannot (remember all those examples from high school?). This may send the wrong message to the other workers, though. If you become aware that a member of the organization fits the descriptions of a bad employee, then you should act in a timely manner. Act quickly enough so that the situation doesn't linger, but take enough time to make certain that you don't come up with a solution that you will later regret or for which you will later have to apologize.

Finally, we want to emphasize that the solution is not to reward one behavior (attendance, attitude, or attire, say) while hoping for another (good performance). That simply does not work. Employees respond to those things to which the organization pays attention.

Provide Feedback

Once an employee is made aware of the problem, he must be given an opportunity to correct it before anything else should be considered. For the organization, it is frequently less costly in both time and money to try to change the person than it is to terminate and replace the person. Recruiting, selecting, orienting, and training costs can be avoided if you can salvage an existing employee rather than having to hire a new one. So trying to change the behavior of bad employees ordinarily should be attempted before giving up on them.

First, all managers should always provide regular, informal feedback through day-to-day interaction with each of their subordinates. This informal feedback would be an ideal time to talk to employees about relatively simple problems such as appearance or hygiene. Perhaps simply being made aware of what is considered appropriate will suffice to alleviate problems in that area. This is also an opportune time to discuss any attendance problems to see if there is something going on that you as the person's manager should be aware of. The employee may be having some issues in his private life that are causing tardiness or attendance problems. By becoming aware of them, you may be able to suggest ways that the employee could address those issues.

Second, the organization should have a formal performance appraisal system that also provides written feedback at least once each year. Many managers are reluctant to provide feedback if it is negative. Most people resist communicating negative information, and managers describe giving negative feedback as one of the most difficult and unpleasant tasks they have to do. They perceive negative feedback sessions as confrontational and avoid them until the frequency and severity of a performance deficiency becomes intolerable. You must not avoid providing negative feedback when it is called for. Be careful, however, to insure that the negative feedback is not biting, sarcastic, or harsh because such feedback causes more harm than good.

Formal performance appraisal systems come in a variety of forms. Objective measures (quantifiable indicators of how well the employee is doing) may be used; for instance, units of a product an employee assembles adjusted for quality, or the number of sales dollars generated by a sales representative. Other common approaches use judgment. These methods typically involve having someone, usually the employee's immediate supervisor, subjectively evaluate that person's performance via a ranking or a rating procedure.

Ranking means that the supervisor ranks subordinates along a continuum from high to low performance. While it forces the supervisor to differentiate among high, moderate, and low performers, it also makes feedback more difficult to deliver as the last person on the list may still be a solid performer. Rating involves comparing each employee with one or more absolute standards and then assessing performance in relation to that standard. Two example rating scales are shown in Figure 6.3.

Rating scales are quite common because they are easy to use. However, they also suffer from a number of problems. Supervisors are sometimes inclined to give everyone the same relative rating, and they may be incorrectly influenced by an employee's most recent behavior rather than by the overall level of performance over the appraisal period.

To try to reduce these problems, some organizations develop more sophisticated and intricate appraisal instruments. Two examples of these are Behaviorally Anchored Rating Scales (BARS) and Behavior Observation Scales (BOS). In these, scales are divided into increments of observable job behavior determined through job analysis. Other organizations use multirater appraisals, the most popular of which is the 360-degree review whereby a manager is evaluated by her or his boss, peers, and subordinates. While they take time and effort to develop, these scales are an improvement over traditional rating scales.

```
      To what extent is this person dependable?

      ①———②———③———④———⑤

To a Minimal    To an Average    To a Great

   Extent          Extent          Extent




      To what extent does this person's performance meet expectations?

      ①———②———③———④———⑤

To a Minimal   To an Average    To a Great

   Extent          Extent          Extent
```

Figure 6.3. Examples of performance rating scales.

Regardless of the method of appraisal used, feedback is vital. A feedback performance review is the appropriate time to inform the person that his behavior is unacceptable and that he is being given an opportunity to provide explanations and/or to change for the better. When meeting with the individual, follow these guidelines:

- Make certain that you are dealing with facts rather than gossip or rumors.
- Focus on the problem, not the individual, and on performance, not personality. This will help you to be nonjudgmental in your discussion and perhaps to gain a better understanding of the employee's situation (on or off the job) that may explain his behavior.
- Describe the behaviors that you feel are bad or disruptive and what might be done to change those behaviors.
- Make a genuine effort to ensure that the individual understands how damaging his or her behavior is, not just in this job but also in his or her career.

Knowledge management systems should be used in performance appraisal since they provide a common frame of reference for dealing with both poor and good performers. Such systems should provide idiosyncratic suggestions for different employees and situations but also provide a common frame of reference when the employee and situation are similar across a set of managers. These idiosyncratic suggestions are the way in which such systems deal with both good and bad employees. A knowledge management system could be in the form of a handbook, a paper or computerized database, a website, a decision support system, or an expert system. The performance appraisal task has been greatly facilitated in recent years through the use of software and even Web-based systems. Such systems are particularly helpful in providing negative feedback in constructive ways.

RECOGNIZE PROBLEMS

Try as we might, sometimes we end up with an employee who needs to be removed from the payroll. This individual may have been fine initially but something happened since he first came aboard. Of course, the person may have always been potentially violent but was able to hide it successfully. Whatever the explanation, the first step in any change process is awareness of the problem and the need for change. Managers must recognize bad behavior, and they must communicate to those employees that their behavior is unacceptable. If neither of them is aware of the problem, then nothing will get done. Your organization should have written policies to deal with such situations.

Investigate Promptly

Sooner or later you will probably have to deal with a bad employee. Even when you thought you had fully investigated, analyzed, and evaluated the employee before hiring, you won't always be perfect. Some individuals will turn out to be disappointing employees or may become so over time. Or maybe you inherited the employee. All problems with bad employees necessitate a systematic approach to assure that the rights of all employees are protected, including the employees that you feel are bad and all others as well. That approach involves developing an awareness of the situation, understanding reinforcement, providing employees with feedback, providing remedial training, and assisting an exit by the problem employee if necessary. As a member of management, you should be aware that you are not a legal, medical, or psychological expert, so if you feel that such expertise is needed, don't hesitate to try to obtain it.

Upon recognizing one or more bad behaviors by an employee, take a look at the individual's history. Is there documentation of the bad behaviors?

Have there been any signs that you may have missed? Is the behavior new or has there been a pattern of behavior that is simply becoming evident now? Can you identify anything that might be causing the behavior that needs to be addressed? Is there a potential medical problem, for example, that could explain the behavior? Is the person from a different religious or cultural/sociological background that could affect on-the-job relationships?

Decide Type of Action Needed

You should also consider what type of unacceptable behavior is involved; for example, into which set of unacceptable characteristics described earlier does the individual's behavior fall? Many of the different types of bad employees would be dealt with in the same way and don't need particular attention. Some behaviors, however, are especially harmful to others or to the organization and therefore require immediate attention; for example, those who take or subject others to unnecessary risks and those who engage in theft or sabotage. The risks to personnel, equipment, finances, quality, and reputation may be so great that you must put a stop to the behavior without delay. You may simply have to remove the offending employee from the situation (e.g., administrative leave) until further investigation and possible action are performed. Threatening and sabotaging behaviors also require immediate attention. Employees who don't carry out instructions may require immediate attention, too, depending upon the nature of the instructions that they are failing to observe.

Some types of bad behaviors require more deliberate and documented attention. Harassing and bullying, for instance, should be documented by the targeted person and actions taken by appropriate members of management to bring it to a rapid halt. Hopefully, the organization has a written policy against such behavior. If your organization permits negative behavior such as bullying at the boss-employee and employee-employee levels, try to determine what, if anything, you can do to change the atmosphere around you. Bullying is not just a schoolboy tactic that will end soon; it is a dangerous behavior that can push another person over the edge. And it is not limited to males. As the manager over a bullying employee, or a manager who is being bullied by another manager or your own boss, you must make it known unequivocally that bullying will not be tolerated. Alert the Human Relations department to the problem and ask for assistance. Often, bullies are actually cowards in disguise and will "run" when confronted. However, they may merely keep a low profile for a short time and then select another person to bully. Absences on or off the job should be handled in a similar manner. Some of the other types of undesirable behavior—lack of interpersonal skills, attitude problems, and appearance or hygiene problems—may require counseling from HR or others within the organization.

Revisit Company Vision and Mission

Make sure that everyone understands and accepts the vision and mission of the organization. From there work with your people to translate those into goals and objectives that are clear, understandable, achievable, and measurable. Move this line of thinking all the way down to specific tasks and job requirements. Clarify (make sure everyone knows what they are supposed to do) and get "buy in"—if not active commitment, at least get acceptance and compliance. As goals are established and agreed upon, ensure that the focus is on positive expectations for jobholders.

PROVIDE REMEDIAL TRAINING

OSHA suggests that organizations should provide medical and psychological counseling for employees exposed to violent incidents. Some organizations train supervisors to recognize potential problems or by using postemployment Behavioral Observation Plans (BOPs). BOPs involve the supervisors' notations of job-related behavioral changes on specifically designed forms, which are then sent to an independent agency. Using an independent agency helps to reduce confrontations between supervisors and employee and leads to more effective referrals for counseling. That might be done by an Employee Assistance Program (EAP) counselor or through a Dangerousness Assessment program. Dangerousness Assessment is a formalized psychological evaluation to determine if a person represents a clear and imminent threat to those around him and should be done by a licensed psychologist or psychiatrist trained in such assessments.

You have time and money invested in your employees, so if problems develop, it makes sense to try to retrain and retain the employees involved rather than throwing them away. Offer the individuals appropriate education and training to help them modify unacceptable behavior. This may be the most appropriate way of dealing with employees with poor work habits or the inability to carry out instructions while still keeping safety and security processes and procedures current.

When you conduct a meeting with the employee to discuss training, do it in a positive way: "Here's how we can help you change that behavior(s) so that you will be a more successful employee in the future." Recognize—and help the worker to recognize—that a person can't change completely overnight. Instead, try to set specific goals and target time frames to assist the worker in becoming a more effective employee. Care should be taken not to trigger a sudden response on the part of the employee that is serious enough to result quickly in termination, quitting, or workplace violence. Remedial training may be conducted by the organization itself, a trade association, a government agency, a consulting firm, or a local college or university. While there would be costs associated with such training, in most cases it will cost less than searching, hiring, orienting, and training a new person.

Make it clear that the training is not punishment but rather that it is designed to help the individual to improve. Even the suggestion of training may make some individuals nervous, so help them understand that you are there to help them, not to punish them. If you are the one doing the training, explain the purpose of the training and what you are trying to accomplish. Then demonstrate correct behaviors and have the employees explain to you why the behaviors are correct. Next, have the employees practice the correct behaviors under different scenarios or situations. After the training, check periodically to be sure that the workers continue to behave correctly rather than reverting back to their old way of doing things.

Some pointers to keep in mind regarding training include the following:

- First, cover what you plan at a pace that the employee can handle. Don't go too fast or too slow. Periodically have the employee "play back" to you what you have covered to be sure that the pace is appropriate.
- Second, do the training at a time and place that assures that you won't be interrupted. Any interruption during the training can seriously interfere with the learning process.
- Third, keep the information at the employee's level. Don't talk over his head, and don't talk down to him.
- Finally, show the employee respect. If he seems to be having some difficulties "getting it," be patient. Rome wasn't built in a day, and bad employees won't be changed into good ones that fast either.

ASSIST THE EXIT

If the individual's bad behavior does not cease, that individual should be asked to leave the organization; or, depending on the problem, he or she could possibly be reassigned. Fix the problem or let the person go. Circumstances should not matter. That is, don't say, "The job market is such that we can't afford to let anyone go," or "Given all of the problems this person is having, we can't fire him now." Keeping a bad employee because the labor market is tight just means that you are building in low productivity and inefficiency, and it will be that much harder to terminate such individuals when the market changes because they will now have seniority. If you would terminate the person in other circumstances, terminate them now. How you terminate a person, however, is important as you most certainly do not want the termination to result in violence toward coworkers or the worker himself. Chapter 3 provided a more detailed discussion of how to conduct terminations. You should review that discussion at this point. Chapter 12 contains advice that you could suggest to the individual as he or she searches for a new and better job situation.

When individuals sense that they are "in the dog house," they may change their behavior to that which is acceptable, or they may retire on the job while they wait for the final axe to fall, or they may fight back. If their behavior becomes acceptable, that's the best possible outcome for everyone—breathe a sigh of relief because you just got lucky! If the individual just gives up, at least you will not have too difficult a time documenting the unsatisfactory behavior. Do it quickly to minimize the damage done by the lack of performance. But if the unsatisfactory worker elects to fight back, you may have problems. When an individual fights back, he or she tries to develop support among others (managers, HR, coworkers) that will cause you to back off and reconsider. The individual could spread gossip about you to try to make you look bad or vengeful or incompetent. He wants you to spend your time defending yourself instead of successfully documenting the behavior that would lead to termination. This is all the more reason to terminate quickly, for the longer the individual is around, the more damage he or she can do to you and to the organization.

One of the best approaches is to use progressive or sequential discipline in your organization, but in all discipline cases, and especially those that might result in termination, you should be sure to work with your Human Resources and legal departments to follow company policies and governmental regulations. Typically, progress discipline systems begin with meetings in which the manager verbally informs an employee about the unacceptable behavior and warns of the consequences if improvement does not occur. The next step is to provide written documentation that the employee has been informed (the behavior, when it occurred, and when the employee was warned) with a stronger warning and explanation of the consequences. This might be followed with counseling and advice and assistance for the individual to leave the organization voluntarily. After that, if all else fails, you go to the final step that involves furnishing the individual with a form that records all the details of the termination, including benefits and when and how the final paycheck is handled. An exit interview follows to assure that the process is as amicable as possible. Do not publicly humiliate the person by having an armed guard stand over them as they empty their desk and then march them in front of others to an exit and to their car. While in some extreme cases security may need to be involved, every effort should be made not to embarrass the individual. Individuals who are humiliated and embarrassed in the terminations process all too frequently return with weapons at some future time, so care should be taken at all times. Chapter 3 contains a more detailed discussion of the do's and don'ts of terminating properly.

WHAT NEXT?

Chapter 6 has made several suggestions about actions that managers might take to reduce the negative incidences of "bad nonmanagers" in your organization. However, nonmanagers themselves can also act to reduce the number of bad nonmanagers in the organization. That is the subject of the next chapter, Chapter 7.

CHAPTER 7

BAD NONMANAGER BEHAVIOR

What Nonmanagers Can Do

Education is the vaccine for violence.

—Edward James Olmos

Bad nonmanager employees are a major factor in the workplace survival of everyone else, including their coworkers and contacts outside the organization. They can result in substantial costs, both direct and indirect. The direct costs include poor performance, lowered productivity and quality, inefficiency, increased absenteeism and turnover, customer dissatisfaction, and lost sales as well as possible damage to the organization's reputation. Indirect costs include the "messages" unintentionally sent to others in the organization. Other workers see that performance doesn't really matter. They lose confidence in the management of the organization. Morale begins to suffer. They let quality and productivity slip. A snowball effect starts that is difficult to stop.

Beyond what has already been said, the most important issue for employees and coworkers is communication. You need to talk about bothersome situations. Avoid being a whiner or complainer while doing so, but keeping everything bottled up inside you will only lead to more problems over

---

Violence at Work: What Everyone Should Know, pp. 139–149
Copyright © 2014 by Information Age Publishing
All rights of reproduction in any form reserved.

time. Remember, you have only four options: (a) Accept and adapt to the coworker's style; (b) try to bring about a change in the coworker's behavior by talking directly with him or her; (c) try to encourage a change by reporting the problem to the manager, the Human Resources department if one exists, or an ombudsperson if one exists; or (d) find another job.

PREPARE TO COPE

All of us have aspects of behavior and personality that have been learned or developed over long periods of time. As a result, they are very difficult to change. Indeed, it may take as long to change the behavioral traits as it did to form them in the first place. Therefore, effecting a change in a coworker is not highly likely, although it is possible, and small changes are more likely than large ones. As a coworker, then, learning to live with someone's behaviors may be your most viable alternative for workplace survival.

Prepare Yourself

If you decide to try to cope with the situation, you need to first "get your own house in order" by making sure that your own performance is good. Keep yourself healthy by eating and sleeping right, drinking lots of water, exercising, and trying to maintain some positive relationships at work. Make sure that you have things to do off the job that you enjoy—a hobby, recreation, family, church, or whatever. You want to be sure that at least some part of your life is not miserable. Keep in mind, however, in the final analysis you should always be prepared to change jobs.

Ignoring the behavior of a bad nonmanager employee in hopes that it will go away is unrealistic. You can, however, decide to cope with it; but you need to exercise considerable caution about what you do. You don't want to sully your own situation by becoming the person who unnecessarily "cries wolf," a whiner that nobody wants to be around, or worse yet, the magnet for interpersonal conflict. Try always to take the "high ground" by handling the situation in a calm, professional manner. It is surprising how many times keeping to the "high ground" will strengthen your position and help to resolve the situation.

Identify Your Values

To the extent that a coworker interferes with you and your values, you must change either your values or your job—neither an easy choice! Thus, in coping with a bad coworker, you first need to develop a clear understanding of your own values—what really matters to you. This will enable you to "draw the line." Simply put, there are some things that you should or should not do because they will "eat at you" and eventually destroy your feelings of self-worth and respect. You need to learn to say "no" and to maintain your dignity and professionalism. Coping does not mean "giving in."

Your values represent what you think is important. There are no correct values, only those that are important to you and the society you live in. Values are of two types: terminal and instrumental. Terminal values represent what might be thought of lifetime goals—what you wish to accomplish in your life. Instrumental values represent behaviors or ways of achieving terminal values—how you would go about accomplishing your terminal values. To help you start thinking about what things are important to you, we have assembled the following examples of values from a variety of sources:

- Terminal Values:
    ◦ Happiness; satisfaction; joy; contentment
    ◦ Knowledge and wisdom
    ◦ Peace and harmony in the world; freedom from war
    ◦ Security; freedom from threat—personal and country
    ◦ Peace of mind; freedom from inner/personal conflict
    ◦ Pride in accomplishment
    ◦ Prosperity; wealth; material comfort
    ◦ Lasting friendships; companionship; trust
    ◦ Recognition; respect, admiration, fame, status
    ◦ Salvation; finding eternal life; Heaven; life after death
    ◦ Self-respect; pride; confidence
    ◦ Justice; fairness; honesty

- Instrumental Values:
    ◦ Assertiveness; standing up for yourself
    ◦ Service; being helpful; caring for others; giving to others
    ◦ Dependability; being counted upon by others
    ◦ Belonging; being accepted by others
    ◦ Education and intelligence
    ◦ Learning and growing as a person
    ◦ Hard work and achievement; contribution to society or organization
    ◦ Obedience; following others; followership

- ° Open-mindedness; receptivity to new ideas
- ° Self-sufficiency; independence
- ° Truthfulness; honesty
- ° Courtesy; being well mannered

There are, of course, many others—adventure, comfort, enjoyment, equality, freedom, love, pleasure, power, stability, and on and on. You need to decide which of these terminal and instrumental values are important to you and then concentrate on achieving them as much as possible on the job. One way to get a feel for what you really consider important would be to rank the values in each of these sets. Then select the top three values in each set and consider how well you are able to achieve them in this particular work situation. If you feel that you can adhere to your values under the present circumstances, maybe the job isn't so bad after all and you can justify staying. To the extent that your coworkers interfere with your realizing your values, however, you must change either the values or your job.

Be Polite and Professional

Always be polite and professional. Don't get drawn into arguments or shouting matches. Don't lower yourself to the level of a bad coworker. Managers and other coworkers are more likely to respect you if you remain calm and composed and try to perform your job even while problems exist around you. If someone is threatening, harassing, or bullying you, let them know that you recognize what they are doing and suggest that their behavior is inappropriate (more on this later). Don't threaten them, but do report them if it continues. Instances where people are subjected to unnecessary risks, however, should be reported promptly to management because of the potential damage to facilities, equipment, and personnel.

You also should be aware that different cultures and different age groups might well have different norms as to what is polite and professional. To U.S. citizens, some cultures seem to be overly polite while others seem blunt and brutal in their interpersonal interactions. Older employees may expect and give somewhat more deferential treatment than do younger ones. If your coworkers are from cultures or age groups different from yours, you should strive to determine the proper form of language (written, oral, and body), dress, and behavior for interacting successfully with those individuals.

Focus on Life Away From the Job

One of the most powerful tools in coping with bad coworkers is to focus more on your life outside or beyond the job rather than on the job and the organization. Don't make your job your life; make time for the things you enjoy doing outside the workplace, particularly with family and friends. Enjoy your nights and weekends. This will help you to forget the job and its problems and stresses for a while.

Define your self-worth more broadly than your job. Focusing on the bigger picture can improve your self-esteem and enable you to tolerate an otherwise intolerable coworker during the workday. Of course, this means that you need to develop activities and relationships beyond the organization. You may wish to involve some coworkers, but activities and relationships should take place off the job site and with a nonwork focus; for example, the organization's ball club or bowling team, a book club, or the like. Such activities not only help you broaden your horizons but also provide a social "safety net" if (when?) things go wrong at work or when significant changes occur there. Or more bluntly stated, you can lose or leave your job without also losing your personal life.

In developing these activities, you need to consider what you enjoy or what makes you feel good about yourself (remember your set of values). What is consistent with your self-image? Rather than joining the bowling team, for instance, you might prefer to help others by volunteering to work for a nonprofit or charitable organization. Many such volunteer opportunities will directly use your skills and abilities and may provide much stronger feelings of confidence and self-worth than you would ever get from your 9-to-5 job. Doing something that makes a positive contribution to someone else's life can greatly help you feel better about your own life.

Practice Avoidance

One common coping tactic is avoidance—not being around to interact with the person whom you see as a bad coworker. Closely related to that, try creating barriers—barriers of devices or space. For example, to shut out loud coworkers , try earphones. You don't have to actually be listening to anything; earphones can serve as earplugs to deaden sound. They can also act as a visual barrier to coworkers who would otherwise interrupt you. Again, you don't have to actually be listening—just appear to be engrossed in whatever might be playing. Also, when you see a habitually interrupting coworker approaching, you can quickly pick up the phone and pretend to be having a long and important conversation or appear in the process of making a phone call.

You may want to consider changing the arrangement of your work area if the organization will allow you to do that. Reposition your desk so that your back or side is toward the door or the cubicle entryway, thus preventing coworkers from easily distracting or interrupting you. You can also leave your work area to go elsewhere for a few minutes. If the bad coworker tries to follow, go to the restroom and enter a stall—it's less likely that you will be followed there.

TRY TO CHANGE THE BEHAVIOR

If you decide that you probably can and should try to change the coworker's behavior, pick your battles carefully. Many of these bad employees have personality problems that are difficult to change, particularly for a coworker. As a result, you need to be aware that the suggestions presented here to help you assist them may not work. A colleague once said, "It won't matter in a hundred years." While cynical, there is a kernel of good advice there. Is changing this person's habit or style really going to matter or make a difference to you personally or to your performance when all is said and done? If not, why risk everything for the battle? You may just make matters worse. And engaging in gossip about the coworker will undoubtedly make matters worse.

Analyze Your Feelings

If you decide to take on the task of convincing someone to modify his or her behavior, make sure you really want to improve the situation and not just "let off steam" or to retaliate by causing trouble for that person. Carefully examine the situation. Are you the only one who is in this situation? Exactly what is the source of your discomfort? How do you feel—angry, threatened, disappointed, childish, or like an outcast? Is there anything that you may have said or done that could have led to this situation? Are you and the individual(s) involved very different—in terms of gender, race, religion, education, socioeconomic upbringing, or other important background factors—that could make for difficult communications?

Decide What You Want

If you decide to speak with the coworker, you need to think carefully about what you want to accomplish. Do you want the person to change his or her behavior? Do you wish only to ask why the person behaves this way toward you? Do you want to change the nature of your communications? Do you want that coworker to understand you better or to see your side of things? Do you want the person to stop asking or telling other employees about you? Set your expectations for the meeting and keep them clear in your own mind. If you want several things, decide which is most important. That way you can be grateful even if you are able to achieve just that one thing only. Practice—think about what you will say, how you will say it, and how you will respond to what the other person says. And above all, keep your focus on the individual's behavior, not the individual personally.

Talk With the Individual

Now, pick the time and place for a conversation. You need to control when and where you will attempt to address the situation in a discussion with your coworker. Try to arrange a meeting at a time when both of you are calm and in a place that is private enough to avoid interruptions. Try to have documentation in hand or details in mind so that the discussion can focus on specific behaviors and not the individual himself or herself. Don't accuse the person but simply identify behaviors that need changing. It could be useful if you can suggest alternative behaviors. Don't be melodramatic—take the "high ground" by being soft-spoken and professional. Focus on listening to the coworker rather than trying to argue with him or her. If the coworker becomes loud, rude, and aggressive, quietly ask to meet again at another time and break off the discussion. In an initial discussion, you might try to get the coworker to agree to try to change one behavior (tiny steps for tiny-minded people). Be prepared for your coworker to identify your behaviors which that person finds objectionable. You should be ready to make some adjustments in your behavior, too.

Another strategy is to have the discussion in the presence of your common supervisor who can serve as a moderator. A problem with this approach is that both of you may try to appeal to the "boss" to "fix" the problem rather than working it out between the two of you. Also, how well this works is largely a function of the boss's personality and method of handling controversy. It may be more intimidating than meeting alone. On the plus side, usually it is good to have a neutral person witness the meeting but not actually participate.

Sometimes merely indicating, without an extended discussion, that you are aware of and/or bothered by an individual's behavior will bring about some changes. For instance, you could point out to a coworker that you've noticed that he or she frequently is absent, late, or lethargic while at work and ask if there is a problem that you might be able to help with since the person's behavior is impacting your work performance as well as theirs.

Similarly, when someone constantly interrupts your work for small talk, you could just say to them that you'd love to talk with them at break or after work, but just now you are busy and need to continue working. Those with poor appearance or hygiene (too much body odor or too much cologne) may just need to have it mentioned to them by you or by their manager or someone from Human Resources: "While we don't have a formal dress code here, you might want to consider how others are dressed in selecting your wardrobe." "I have some allergies to certain fragrances, and the amount you are using seems to trigger them. Could you perhaps cut back just a bit?" A similar statement could be made to those whose audio players are bothersome: "I have an ear problem such that I'm a bit sensitive to sound. Could you turn down the volume a bit? Thanks." The discussion gets more complicated, of course, for more sensitive topics. It's always difficult to talk with people who are behaving negatively toward you because they are competing against you or because they think you are competing against them.

Coworkers who can't seem to follow instructions may need more help than you can provide without decreasing your own performance. Offer to help and then suggest that they talk with supervisors to get more help as well. But what about those with attitude problems, especially the chronic complainers? Indicate that you, too, are aware that life isn't fair and that the organization and/or its management isn't perfect, but nevertheless you have a job do to and you find it easier and more pleasant to do if you focus on what is right rather than what is wrong. It may or may not help, but the complainer is likely to move on to someone else so at least you can get your work done.

SEEK HELP WHEN APPROPRIATE

You almost certainly will have to work with your boss if you are hoping to make changes in your job as a means of solving the problem you are experiencing with a coworker. This is not the type of change you can expect to achieve by going around your boss and directly to Human Resources. Managers also need to address problems with employees whose performance or productivity is unsatisfactory, coworkers whose behavior or attitude may serve as the catalyst for workplace violence, and fragile or impaired individuals who are likely to allow their feelings to erupt in violence.

Despite our having said that you should not ignore the problem, you should recognize that workers who engage in really bad behavior such as theft or sabotage are rightfully the concern of managers—not you, their coworker. Whether you and your coworkers decide to share with management the information you have regarding such behavior is a personal decision of your own conscience; but if you do, you must be absolutely certain that your information is correct. Some managers know that a worker is taking home company assets or cheating on his timecard; they just pretend otherwise, and they may not be open to bearers of bad news. But one thing is certain: Regardless of whether managers take the appropriate action, you need to think twice about trusting any coworker who lies or who steals by deception or otherwise, no matter how the person attempts to justify his or her actions.

Whatever problem with which you seek help from a manager, focus on what really matters to you—if you could make one and only one change, what would it be? Would that change be good enough, or just a good start?

Report Potentially Violent Coworker

There is another and more serious issue that also must be considered when you are debating whether to discuss a problem with the manager. Workplace violence is real, and confronting a bad employee could trigger an episode. If there seems to be any possibility of this, you should not do anything on your own. In other words, if the coworker appears to be highly defensive or aggressive, you probably should back off. Pushing them at that time may well just make matters worse. Instead, get the help of managers or other third parties in the organization (another coworker or someone from Human Resources)—individuals who are better trained to deal with such potentially dangerous situations.

Likewise, if you believe that laws have been broken, organizational policies have been violated, or ethical standards compromised, you should consider involving management or other appropriate authorities (Human Resources, legal affairs, union representatives, or others). Just be sure that you have documented details to back up your claims; do not rely on hearsay or your personal opinion.

Deal With Bully or Harasser

If you feel you are being harassed or bullied, you have a sensitive and legal problem to deal with. For that reason, you should keep a log of harassing or bullying acts, including what is said or done, the date, the time of day, who else may have witnessed, and what you said or did. The fact that so much has been said and written about harassment makes it simpler, we think, for you to get relief without creating major human relations problems within the department or organization. It's much easier now to explain quietly to a coworker: "I'm sure you are not aware of this, but (your flirting, the way you look at me when I walk by, the photos in your cubicle, or whatever) makes me uncomfortable. Could we please talk about this?" Even in the case of overt flirting or propositioning, it is possible to speak directly to the offender in a professional, nonjudgmental way: "I'm flattered by your attention, but I find it uncomfortable since I don't date married men/women (or I myself am married). I value your professional friendship a great deal, so I would really respect you more for keeping our relationship nonpersonal." Such an approach lets the harasser save face while still alerting him to a more severe handling of the problem if he does not respond. Whether or not the above approach works, be sure to make a note of this conversation in the log you are keeping.

Also try to observe whether others are treated similarly. Is this person singling you out, or is this just his personality? If you can totally trust other coworkers, you may choose to ask them if they have noticed this person's behavior toward you and/or others. Such behavior is unacceptable even if it is just that individual's personality, but you may deal with it in a different way. If others feel harassed or bullied, ask them if they are keeping a log. However, you should not threaten the harasser or bully or encourage someone else to speak to them on your behalf, as such actions usually end up making the situation worse. We do know of situations where another person, due to relationships that already exist, has been effective by saying something like this to the harasser: "You may need to back off Employee A—she doesn't seem to appreciate your jokes." Note there is no indication that Employee A has complained or has asked someone to intercede.

Occasionally, a worker will use harassment or bullying tactics against a coworker as a form of retaliation or maybe just in response to the organization or the world in general. In such cases of retaliatory actions, a low-key, professional discussion may not work if the coworker's psychological problems are too advanced. If you suspect psychological disorders or if you have had previous run-ins with this coworker, let your boss do the talking.

LEAVE OR REQUEST A TRANSFER

If coping won't work, take a leave or request a transfer. While a leave would only be for a relatively short time (a day, a week, a month, or maybe longer in some cases), it would get you away from the situation for a while. The time away might enable you to "recharge" so that you can return to your job with renewed interest and enthusiasm and thus be better prepared to cope with your coworkers. A transfer, on the other hand, would get you permanently out of the situation. However, if problems with others is endemic to your organization, you may just be "jumping from the frying pan into the fire." Be cautious with any such moves as your motives could be questioned, leading to a worsening of your situation.

Of course, if you feel that you can't cope and must leave the organization, start looking for another job but don't "jump ship." A "panic move" may result in a situation that is no better and may even be worse. And be sure that you don't "burn your bridges"—that you don't create enemies as you leave. You may need references, and careers last a lifetime.

Chapter 12 contains advice that should help you apply what you have learned from your current job and from this book as you search for a new and better job situation.

WHAT NEXT?

After reading Chapter 7, you should have some workable ideas for initiating behavior changes in coworkers that you think are more likely to cause larger problems within the organization. Also, this chapter addresses the distinct possibility that you cannot effect changes and may therefore need to consider other options. Appendage II at the end of this Section also provides a few examples that characterize bad coworkers, in the opinion of various types of workers.

As you may have already discovered, however, an organization's propensity for violence results not just from people. Therefore, we next turn to workplaces that may increase an organization's propensity for violence.

APPENDAGE II

Anecdotes of Bad Nonmanager Behavior

The following anecdotes are all real examples of bad nonmanager behaviors that have been provided by consulting clients, students, family, or friends. They are arranged in the order discussed in the chapter. We have tried to leave them in the words of their writers, but have removed identifying information and offensive language.

DISHONEST, CONFRONTATIONAL

Lie and Manipulate

Falsify résumés to work in high-security jobs

"I work for a state government agency charged with safety and security, but now I wonder just how safe and secure things really are. Recently, as a result of events in another state, all state employees had their files checked by an outside human resource-auditing firm. It was absolutely amazing how many inaccuracies were found. A couple of top officials were found to have bogus college degrees, including one who oversees security in higher education programs in our state. Others had degrees, but they were from 'diploma mills' that require little, if any, academic work. Still others had wrong and always inflated job titles or length of experience in their records. Are these people capable of doing the jobs they were hired to do in order to ensure our safety?"

Falsify résumé to inflate qualifications

"We once hired someone based mostly on a great résumé, although his interview was also pretty good. However, several months later a coworker happened to be visiting an area in which the new-hire had held a job with a solid title at Firm X. Our coworker noted that Firm X in this location was a very small branch, which was not likely to have had a position like the one that the new person had listed on his résumé. So he dropped in and casually asked if one of the two people there knew the person we had hired. They rolled their eyes and said, 'Do we ever! We know him and are glad to be rid of him. He was incompetent, a blowhard, and generally unpleasant to work with.' When asked about his fancy title, they laughed and said, 'That's just like him—make up a fictitious title when you think no one will bother checking up on you.' Finding out that he had falsified information on his résumé eventually cost him his job. As a coworker, I feel that if he would lie on his résumé, he would probably lie about other things, too. So he would be a bad employee in any company."

Get others to do their work

"Harry is an arrogant S.O.B. who manipulates his supervisor and gets others to do his work. One minute he can be all smiles and charming, like when he wants to persuade his supervisor that he is great. The next minute he can fly into a rage to threaten a coworker to get her to do something for him. He will say things like, 'If you can't do your job, why do you stay here?' or 'Why can you never finish anything without bothering me?' Yet, he is the one who is not doing his job. And if someone hasn't finished a project, it's usually because he didn't come through with the part that he is responsible for. Usually that's because he leaves early to play golf or take a long lunch hour. It seems like he really doesn't want to be at work, so he just puts off doing stuff, knowing that others on the team will do his part in order not to be called in by the boss.

"Harry takes credit for the work we do to keep the projects moving. But when something is wrong or is criticized by the boss, he (Harry) accepts no blame. Sometimes he will sit there shaking his head in agreement when the boss is saying how something should be redone, giving the appearance to the boss that he (Harry) knew that all along but just couldn't convince his coworkers! What an a**h***. He will probably be promoted to management because he seems to have no conscience, and he is an expert on getting others to do his work so he can loaf."

Elicit undue sympathy

"I have one coworker who is a horrible employee. She wraps our male supervisor around her little finger by doing the old pity-me routine. She'll plead, 'Oh, I can't work much today because I'm so upset because of my mother's ill health' or 'I'm so tired today because I didn't get much sleep last night.' She tries the same routine with us, but we've heard it so much that we just try to ignore her. She makes many trips to the ladies' room and the breakroom, often staying to lie on the couch and talk to anyone who comes in. Interestingly, she seems to feel much better when she is not doing her work!

"She even suggests that our company is cruel and unfair for expecting 'people in my situation' to have to perform at the same level as everyone else. If our supervisor pushes very hard, she tries to make him feel that any poor performance is his fault because he's driving her too hard. She knows she would never be fired—who could fire an older woman who has an ill elderly mother that is totally dependent on her?

"What we cannot understand is why the supervisor doesn't tell her to go see a physician or go to HR to get some help on obtaining assistance such as in-home nursing care for her mother. We are thinking of a way to have our boss divide up the work so that none of our projects are dependent on this woman being on the job and giving 100%."

Brownnose

"What I wouldn't give to get rid of brownnosers! Brownnosers, bootlickers, a** kissers, are unbelievable. They obviously think that the best way to get good performance appraisals, and hence raises and promotions, is by flattering managers. While just about all coworkers can see through them, I have been amazed at how few managers seem to be able to recognize them. One woman at our job even picks up the manager's preschoolers and drops them off with her kids at a daycare center, even though it requires her to start earlier and drive a few more miles every morning.

"Some of the brownnosers here don't see anything wrong with avoiding work and overstating their contributions to the organization. They don't respond well if you try to tell them the truth about their performance. Indeed, they are likely to report this to upper management and accuse you of trying to 'get them' or to discriminate against them. One of our male coworkers is a master at this. He will even twist what was said to use as an excuse to go to the boss and say, 'You have such a fantastic department, and you hire the greatest people. I love working here. But do you know any reason why _____ dislikes me so much that he would like to see me get fired?' The manager sees him as a positive, conscientious worker—not the worker who uses brownnosing to stir up trouble for others.

"Unhappily, a lot of managers actually encourage brownnosers because those managers like flattery (and they think that they deserve the lavish praise anyway). The result is that you can't do your job well knowing that it may not matter because what these people say is given more credence than what you do."

Abuse authority

"You want an example of a bad coworker or employee? Well how about the person who orders people around when they don't really have the authority to do so. Or the one who shows people how to do things but shows them the wrong way to do them. Or the one that alienates customers by making them wait while he or she does something else or insults them by word or manner. What's worse is that all of these are one person at my job!"

Lie about loyalty to get security clearance

"In a highly secure government installation, there was an employee who was a recent immigrant from a nearby country. He held a deep commitment to helping that country, even to the point that he seemed willing to talk about our work with his friends 'back home.' This posed a high security risk for the U.S. He had been told to hold his tongue, but when he was with those he regarded as his countrymen (as opposed to regarding U.S. citizens as his countrymen), he still just talked and talked. Soon he reached the point where he would also talk about our country. He criticized the President on down to the Governor. Sometimes he would be so critical that we would feel like shooting him. He seemed so angry that he was not in his country, yet he wanted to stay here. His loyalties most surely lay outside the U.S. The fact that he could not be trusted had an immeasurable effect on the work that could be done at this installation.

"As you can imagine, all his coworkers hated him. No one wanted to be assigned to a project with him. No matter if you were just starting a project or deep into working on it, you could count on him going on a tirade about the terrible United States and how they had mistreated his country. Not only that, we were afraid that this guy would someday just reach his boiling point and do major damage to the installation where we worked, or worse. As workers, we don't know the story behind why he was hired or why he was not let go sooner."

Threaten

Threaten to retaliate

"I work for a small nonprofit organization. Generally, everyone involved—volunteers, donors, clients, and especially employees—are caring individuals who are caught up in the mission of our organization. Every once in a while, though, an employee gets bent out of shape about something and threatens either physical harm, economic harm, or legal action against someone or the organization. They scream, 'I'll get you for this!' or 'You'll hear from my lawyer about this!'

"We have learned to keep records when such threats are made. We write down who said something, what they said, when they said it, and the context or why they said it. Most of the time nothing ever comes of it; and because we keep such careful notes, the few times when a lawyer has followed up, once he sees our notes that's the end of it. But every time we hear about someone going ballistic at work somewhere in the world, we all wonder if this will someday happen to us. Maybe that's why the bosses haven't fired these people already—maybe they're afraid they will come back and take out all of us."

Threaten litigation

"We hired a young guy from a small local college. Even though the college really didn't offer a major in our field, this guy had taken some courses and so seemed to be minimally qualified for what was a very low position in the company. After he was hired, he kept telling everyone how much he knew and how he could do things better than they could. However, he made mistakes on his assignments that others had to fix—but he contended that they weren't mistakes but rather improvements in the product.

"HR was contacted to begin termination procedures, but instead insisted that he be given a second chance since they were concerned because he had discussed legal action against the company. He was gay. Later HR changed a 'no raise' recommendation to a raise recommendation for the same reason. I quit, as I didn't want to work for a company that would reward poor performers to avoid unfounded litigation."

Threaten to file discrimination charges

"A bad employee? A bad employee is one who threatens to sue the company for discrimination rather than just doing the job like everybody else. We have one like that at work, and she even upsets other minorities because she gives all of them a bad name. She gives customers incorrect information that later has to be corrected by someone else, uses a company vehicle to take her kids places, fails to follow directions, doesn't complete her time card or does it incorrectly, doesn't fill out the forms correctly or at all when she uses equipment, and otherwise is just a poor performer. But if anyone in management says anything to her, she informs them that she is an officer in a local minority organization and that if they continue to pick on her, she will sue. Now no one even questions her. She gets her way.

"She also creates problems for others. If she thinks that someone will report her for her behavior or mistakes, she will jump the gun by going to HR, sometimes crying because she is so 'hurt,' and she will tell HR that this other employee is probably going to report her but that it is all lies. She will then tell her side of the story, which shows her doing nothing wrong. Sometimes the boss or HR will then call in the innocent employee and write them up for discriminating behavior toward the minority employee! So dishonest and bizarre that you can't hardly believe it, even if you work here and know it's true! That's a bad employee, and the type that do cause racial tensions."

Bully

Bully to eliminate personal competition

"Joe was a grown-up bully who had been with this company longer than most of the rest of us. Maybe the fact that he had some seniority is what made him a bully. He would single out a vulnerable person and talk about him behind his back, interrupt him, shout at him, or simply stare at him like he was crazy. He would send emails criticizing the individual's performance to coworkers and supervisors. In short, he would make that person's life miserable, which in turn would lead to poor performance from that person—and to which Joe would note, 'I told you so.'

"In the year I've been with this firm, Joe has always targeted the better performers. He apparently is trying to run off anyone who might make him look bad. And he generally succeeds, as two of our top people have left for better jobs after having been 'attacked' by Joe. My big concern is that I suspect that I am next on his 'hit list.'"

Bully to get one's own way

"I work for an organization in which virtually all of the work is performed by teams. While most of the time this approach seems to work pretty well, there are times when it doesn't. For instance, one individual always puts himself and his interests ahead of those of the team; it's 'his way or the highway.' And, of course, his way is always the best way, according to him. He is a 'legend in his own mind.' If things aren't going his way, he disrupts meetings by interrupting others, shouting at those who disagree with him, slamming things on the table, or even jumping up and leaving (turning over his chair as he does so). One time he even threw a book across the room at someone—then laughed because he thought it was so funny to see the surprised look on everyone's face.

"This guy bullies coworkers to try to get them to go along with him. He tries to go around the team to its supervisor to lobby for his way instead of what the team came up with. And that usually means that he criticizes one or more team members for the way they are suggesting things should be done. He lowers the productivity of every team when he is a member. Nobody wants to work with him individually or on a team anymore. You can predict the problems. You just don't know which of you will be his 'whipping boy' this time."

Bully because of jealousy

"Our work group has a back-stabbing, gossiping, lying bully. We interface with legal, payroll, training, and benefits personnel, and not one person in these groups can understand why this bully was not fired years ago for constantly trying to shoot down her coworkers. Now she has turned her attention to me—probably because I am new. She has sent emails to my group coordinator filled with lies about me and my performance. Fortunately, I have been able to refute these relatively easy, but that has taken otherwise productive time and has been disruptive to my thinking. She has tried to poison my relations with others in the department with vicious gossip, and this worried me more than anything because it's harder to prove yourself innocent than it is for someone to say you're guilty of something.

"Furthermore, you can never know when she has spread lies or inaccuracies about you unless the person who heard them decides to tell you. However, thanks to her reputation, she has not succeeded. My group coordinator tells me that it is a 'personality clash' and not the company's business. It's certainly not a clash on my part—I was fine with all my relationships in the division. So if she tends to clash with personalities (which apparently she has always done), the supervisors need to see that she improves before she runs off the best workers."

Bully to belittle, whatever the reason

"Joe, a coworker, is a classic bully. He loves to humiliate and degrade you in front of others, particularly at meetings or in emails where others are copied in. He misstates things you have said or repeats them out of context. He will say just about anything to make you look bad. Joe accuses everyone else as thinking only about themselves rather than other people in the organization. But everyone else would say he is the epitome of someone who thinks only about himself.

"So why not confront him to get him to stop? I've tried that. He says that I have misunderstood what he was trying to say or that I'm overly sensitive. His favorite expressions are 'You need to lighten up' and 'Why are you so defensive?' Note that even these statements tend to put the blame back on me. We don't need this sort of coworker, but there doesn't seem to be much we can do about it."

Harass

Harass sexually

"We had a male employee who said that he was a 'Southern gentleman' and that all true Southern gentlemen had an 'obligation' to proposition any females that they came into contact with. He certainly lived up to that! And it didn't seem to matter if he was turned down (as far as I know, he always was), he would just do it again later (and again and again). Since he was a very senior employee, nothing much was done about it. New female employees were warned and told that he was actually 'harmless'—'wouldn't know what to do if he was ever taken up on his offer.' Yet his presence had a disrupting influence on the female workers. Maybe it bothered males, too; I never knew. He was periodically given a 'slap on the wrist' (talked to by someone), but it continued for the several years I was there and probably is still going on if he's not retired by now."

Intimidate with "dirty" pictures

"I am a relatively attractive single woman. Despite having been warned on several occasions not to, several of my male coworkers nevertheless secretly leave lurid pictures on my desk, sometimes with phone numbers written on them. When I complain, the usual response of my supervisor and HR is that they don't know who is doing it so they can't do anything about it. A couple of times they have brought it up at meetings where people laugh about it and seem to think that the whole thing is my fault—that I 'can't take a joke' is the usual response. I am going to talk to the EEO office in town to see if there is anything that can be done to remedy this situation. If not, I guess I'll be looking for another job."

Harass with religious indoctrination

"Mary is driving me crazy. She is a coworker and constantly harasses me and others about religion. When she was first hired, she invited everyone to 'a little get-together' at her home. It was supposedly for the purpose of letting us get to know her better, and letting her get to know her coworkers better. So most of us went. It didn't take too long for us to figure out that this was not an office party—it was a recruiting meeting for her church. She wants to convert all of us to her religion and constantly sends us emails and pamphlets about it. She corners us in the breakroom and at lunch to push her views and has even called some of us at home. All of this is done at first as a pretext to something that's office related, but it always ends up with her turning the subject to her religion and how we need to experience what she experiences.

"Several of us recently approached our supervisor about this. What a shock that was! Our supervisor goes to the same church as Mary, and her response was that Mary is just trying to help her fellow man and that maybe we would all get along better if we did share the same faith. Now we wonder if we have just made things that much worse!"

Harass with smoke

"Our firm has a rule that smoking is not permitted within 30 feet of any entrance to our building. Joe, who is a chain smoker and needs lots of breaks to satisfy his habit, resents the rule. So what does Joe do? He goes outside the no-smoke zone, finds air conditioning inlets or open windows, and smokes near them so that the smoke gets into the building. He moves away after a bit, so he can't be caught unless management spends a lot of time/money monitoring just him. Nobody here will have much sympathy if this clown comes down with lung cancer."

Harass to retaliate

"We work in cubicles and sometimes there is a lot of personal noise—workers talking and laughing, radios playing, loud telephone conversations, etc.—in addition to the normal office noise such as file cabinets being opened and closed, normal telephone voices, and so on. I and several others find it very hard to concentrate on our work in such a noisy environment. I finally talked to my supervisor about it and even talked to her supervisor. A memo was sent to everyone in the unit, pointing out that the area sometimes got very noisy and that we should all work together to create a better working environment.

"Somehow, though, the word got out that I was responsible for this. Now I am apparently the common enemy. Dirty looks, talking behind my back, bumping me, 'accidentally' messing up my papers, and other things are now almost a daily occurrence. Whenever I am around, things seem to be done in a more noisy way—books are slammed on tables, file cabinet drawers are banged shut, carts are bumped into walls, anything to make more noise rather than less. It's clear that my coworkers are angry with me and won't let me alone. But I'm afraid to complain about this harassment for fear it will make my work situation even worse."

Engage in Theft or Sabotage

Sabotage through notes and work disruptions

"I once worked in an organization that had a work saboteur. I never knew who it was and, thankfully, he never got me, but the more senior workers felt sure that they knew who it was. Anonymous notes to managers was a favorite smear tactic because, even though the manager says that he doesn't pay attention to them, the information has a impact—a negative one.

"Occasionally, a person's computer would not work right. The printer cable would get 'accidentally' unplugged, a network connection would quit working, a Trojan or virus would get on the machine even though the organization had several layers of protection. Any one of these disrupts work, sometimes substantially.

"Others would discover that an important document that they were working on had become misplaced. It might be found later, but its absence at the very least delayed someone's work. Still others would find that information needed to complete a project was not being transmitted as promised. 'Oh, I understood that you didn't need that right away.' Try to find out why the misunderstanding occurred and you would get nowhere.

"We had some success in minimizing these disruptions by taking turns at coming to work early (before he arrived), staying until after he left at 5:00, and making sure that someone was in the area during the lunch break. We certainly made it harder for him. But once it would get stopped, we would pull back on our monitoring because it was extra trouble to us to get to work early, etc. And then it would start again. Some of us would wring that guy's neck if we weren't afraid of going to jail."

Sabotage through anonymous memos

"In our office, instead of 360-degree feedback performance evaluation, we have a peer evaluation system. The information from the peer evaluation is used to determine merit raises, job assignments, travel reimbursements to conferences, and possible promotions. Thus, these evaluations are very important to everyone involved. When Mike and Phil were being considered for special assignment or promotions, or when they seemed to have had great years and would be getting good raises, suddenly anonymous memos/letters would either be sent to the supervisor or circulated among all of us. These anonymous memos would either suggest or state explicitly that this individual (usually only one at a time was attacked) had done something unethical, illegal, or immoral.

"The memos contained phrases like 'I represent several members of the group who are afraid to speak up for themselves' or 'Several people have come to me about this' or 'You need to be aware of something that Mike (or Phil) did (or was involved in).' They did not represent several members of the group, of course; and I am not aware of anyone being afraid to speak up. Those were just lies.

"The writing style was highly consistent and easily identifiable as coming from a particular member of the group. Although it was common knowledge that this person was the memo writer, no one in authority ever examined her computer or investigated the memo writing in any way as this was a person who always threatened discrimination charges when anyone challenged her about anything. If they had, she would have yelled 'discrimination,' even though she was merely foreign-born and not a member of a protected minority."

Lie and spread rumors

"We have a very dangerous person in our office. She is a liar. She appears to be a wonderful person, cheerful, smiling, friendly, and volunteers for many little extra duties (United Way, coordinating a meeting, putting together mentors for new employees). But below the surface she is mean, vindictive, and intends to look good by making others look bad.

"She has been the source of many anonymous notes that libel another employee. If she can learn anything negative about someone, she will almost certainly embellish it and then leak it to whoever can do the most damage. If anyone ever makes a mistake, she will exaggerate it and see that everyone knows about it. But in the department, she is all sweet and wonderful—a real team player!

"She lies and spreads rumors, but she also steals credit. Interestingly, she sometimes steals the credit for herself, but at other times she gets the credit for someone else. She just sees to it that the person who really deserves the credit either gets no credit or has their role diminished in some way. Why? Because that person now owes the liar a big one. That's the way she keeps 'friends.' Perhaps, also, because the deserving person is a real performer and hence a threat to the liar."

Steal by deception

"I know one really bad employee, although I guess it doesn't affect me directly. John (not his real name) injured his back while working in his garage restacking the Christmas tree box and boxes of ornaments. He required brief hospitalization and was out of work for several weeks. Recently when he returned to work, he was bragging about how workers comp covered everything because he told the doctors that the injury had occurred while he was working on the loading dock.

"Now no one wants to have anything to do with him because he has proved himself to be dishonest. I believe that a person who will lie about something like that—especially when he knows that we all know he's lying—won't think twice about lying to any one of us. He's on my radar but not on my Christmas list!!"

Steal to compensate for being underpaid

"Stephen does not consider himself a thief, but he is. Because he feels that he is not paid what he should be paid, Stephen feels that he is entitled to 'extras' from the company. He uses the company phone and time for personal business. He takes supplies home—paper, stapler and staples, pens, pencils, scissors, cups and coffee from the lounge, and anything else he can get his hands on that will fit into his briefcase. Apparently, he also will lie on his timecard and on his expense report. I haven't personally observed that, but I did overhear him telling another worker how to do it and assuring him that everyone does that."

Alter computerized payroll records to get extra money

"I recently became aware of a tough situation regarding a guy in our payroll department. We're a midsize company that is owned by a man who also has several other businesses to run. Supposedly, Frank, this payroll guy, was diagnosed with some sort of weird disease that was not covered by our insurance plan. He was going to have to spend a lot of money for medications and it would have to come out of his own pocket.

"But Frank knew how our computerized payroll system worked. So he would create dummy employees (part-timers) and have them get paid just enough to cover his medical expenses for a few weeks. He would then pick up their paychecks and cash them to get the money. He would then delete the dummy's records so that no one could trace him, although an auditor would have known something was wrong. A few weeks later he would repeat the process. The word is that he never took more than he needed for medication and so when the company finally uncovered his actions, it did not prosecute. The company let him resign and supposedly even offered to help him get another job. What happened after that I don't know."

Alter employee records for bosses

"Sue works in our HR department helping to keep records. It's not so much that she is a bad employee as it is that she helps the bosses commit fraud. For example, we know that she alters records so that our worker's compensation insurance premiums are kept low. She will record workers who hold risky jobs like forklift operators as holding safe jobs like administrative assistants or file clerks. She also puts some employees on the payroll of fake companies so that our total employment figures are not as great. It's really the bosses who are bad, but she is also bad for going along with them. Someday, one of those workers may get hurt in a company accident and find that they are not covered for hospitalization. As for us coworkers, we wouldn't trust her to be honest with us if she is dishonest with the books."

WORKERS LACK INTERPERSONAL SKILLS

Attitude Problems

Negative attitude toward everything

"Marsha (not her real name) is a pain to work with. She has a bad attitude that poisons the air around her. She complains all the time, so no one wants to have to work with her or to interact with her in any way, yet in our organization, it is almost impossible for anyone to work totally alone. She expresses disapproval of everything and everybody. Nobody can do anything right; nothing ever goes right; and certainly the organization can do nothing right either. Thus, her presence hurts everyone and lowers our overall productivity."

Think their way is better than that of the organization

"We have one person who absolutely refuses to follow procedures. Our work is quite technical, and failure to follow procedures can result in substantial downtime or increased costs. Nevertheless, he claims that his education (certificate from a technical school) and experience (quite a few years but all very low-level jobs) makes him an 'expert' in this technical area. He feels that he knows better ways of doing things (even though they repeatedly don't work) and so always does things his own way. Thus far, he has not cost us a contract, but it has been close on at least two occasions."

Misuse internal emails

"It is common at our company for people to send email jokes or silly photos or songs to one another as a way to lighten tension and make our work atmosphere more pleasant. One person, however, began sending highly religious notes that all too often contained appeals to join his church. Even though he was asked not to send them or to send them only to those who agreed to receive them, he continued to send them to everyone. When this was brought to the attention of upper management, they simply banned any and all email that was not directly related to our work. The resulting decrease in an otherwise pleasant work environment has led to lower morale and some turnover. For instance, I am looking for another job as a result.

"Of course, misuse of email can occur from the top as well. Supervisors in another organization I worked for not only routinely read internal email of employees but also had some sort of spyware that let them secretly monitor all activity on company computers. What this meant was that if you checked your personal email from work, they would get your user id and your password and could then read your personal email, too. When people eventually found out about this and complained, the company said that anything done on its computers was 'fair game;' they had the right to view anything that involved the use of company equipment. Talk about turnover! After they found out, everyone changed their passwords and quit."

Blame others for errors

"An employee at an office where I used to work asked me to go over a report that he was doing. It was horrible! Every page had typos, misspelled words, and/or grammatical errors (often several per page). I marked several of them in red and told him what he was doing wrong. I then suggested that he should go back over the report carefully to correct all of the ones I had marked as well as others that I did not have time to mark. I also suggested that he use a grammar-checking program and a spell checker, too. I hoped that he would learn from this so that not only would this report be good when he submitted it but that his future work also would be better (without involving me).

"Several days later our supervisor asked me why I had given him wrong information if I didn't know any better. When I asked what he was talking about, he showed me the report, which still had lots of errors in it, and said that the other employee had told him that he had asked me to go over the report and that he had done the report exactly as I had told him to. It took a lot of talking, reminding him of the quality of my reports, and a good bit of time to convince my supervisor of what had really happened. Thankfully, he finally was convinced—a second report from that employee that was as bad as the first helped convince him. Needless to say, I have never helped that individual again!"

Inconsiderate Workers

Fail to cooperate

"The kind of employee I would call 'bad' is the kind that insists on having everything his or her way and won't cooperate with colleagues. They demand particular schedules (because of children or spouses or other personal reasons) and don't recognize that others also have such personal reasons. The self-centered, refusal-to-cooperate attitude of these employees makes other employees angry. If they get their way, it also makes other employees less likely to care much for or about the organization."

Insensitive to others' needs

"My example of a really bad employee is one that totally disregards others. For example, we have a person in our office who constantly hums and sings all day long. That might be okay if we had private offices, but we have cubicles with only 5-foot separations, so this person's voice carries for quite a distance. It disrupts everyone else's concentration and interferes with phone calls. When she is counseled about this, she tones it down for a day or so and then it begins all over again. If one of us says something, she cries and complains that 'everyone hates me,' causing the person who said something to feel guilty for having done so. Why can't she just keep quiet?"

Ungrateful, inconsiderate

"My partner on a major project suddenly had lots of personal/family problems that necessitated his taking a lot of time off (taking days off and/or cutting days short). I had to pick up the slack. While that meant working longer hours and an occasional weekend, I didn't mind too much because we had worked together for some time and he had always been hard working and dependable. I was bothered by the fact that sometimes he would just take off in the middle of something and go to the company stress reduction center (a gym) without telling me that he was leaving or when I might expect him back. But what really got to me was that, while this went on for months before things returned to normal, he never even thanked me."

Disregard others' opinions

"My office never dealt with the gift exchange idea. Birthdays and holidays were regarded as personal matters that had nothing to do with the business. Then along came Hilda (not her real name). Hilda was horrified that we didn't celebrate each other's birthdays and ALL holidays so she just started doing it—cheap gifts, chintzy decorations, and store bought (day-old, usually) cakes. Then, of course, she started informing us about her birthday, her anniversary, her children's birthdays, and any other 'holiday' that she could think of and not just hinting but also stating that she deserved gifts and a party for each of these.

"This continued for over a year until upper management began to notice that an awful lot of company time was being used for parties (planning them, decorating for them, having them, and cleaning up after them). A staff meeting was held to discuss the situation. The majority wanted to return to a 'no gifts, decorations, or parties' situation. Hilda fought vigorously for the opposite and had a few people trying to seek some sort of compromise. The meeting got extremely tense and personal with lots of angry words being said by both sides.

"Even though management did finally come up with a compromise, the atmosphere in the office was so poisoned that turnover shot up over the next year. I don't know what finally happened as I left about 10 months after the meeting."

Talk loudly in cubicles

"Our company has cubicles instead of private offices, so it is easy to be heard by anyone around you. As a result, we have learned to talk in a low voice on the phone and in private conversations with coworkers. The physical layout works fine for almost everyone, except this one young guy. He seems to think that you have to project your voice in order to be heard over the phone. He is so loud that those closest to his cubicle cannot concentrate or carry on a conversation on the phone. Clients on the phone sometimes comment to us about the loud voice in the background. Someone told him one day that he doesn't need to shout to be heard on the phone, and others have walked by his cubicle with their hands over their ears. When we remind him, he seems to recognize that he really projects his voice when on the phone, but it's such a habit that he will have to work hard to change it. Like maybe someone will have to remind him on every single call for weeks and weeks. It makes it difficult for us to concentrate on our work, and the longer this goes on the more agitated people are getting about it."

Complain about financial problems

"Mary seems to have constant financial problems. She gets calls from creditors at work, is always needing to borrow money for lunch, has had her pay garnished before, and has admitted to having to declare bankruptcy twice. Her constant financial troubles impact not only her work but that of others as well, as she talks about her problems and asks her coworkers for money all the time for lunch or snacks."

Smoke in the office

"I am extremely sensitive to cigarette smoke and so I carefully chose a job in an office in which no one smoked. My mistake was in thinking that because no one smoked that the office had a rule against smoking. A very senior person had been on assignment out of the country when I was hired but returned about 6 weeks later. He was a regular smoke stack—he smoked constantly, dropping ashes all over people's desks and even into their drinks. He not only smoked but also was inconsiderate and messy besides.

"Shortly after the return of this person, I had to see the doctor for bronchial problems. The doctor said that if I stayed around where the smoking was, I would be seriously endangering my health. When I raised this with upper management, I was told that I should quit because they weren't going to restrict the senior guy at all—'He's much too important to the firm to upset in any way.' I filed a health complaint against the company and got a nice severance package out of it but still had to find another job and incur the costs of relocation."

Disregard Appearance/Hygiene

Body odor

"At a university where I was in graduate school, graduate students used to work late at night (and early in the morning, too). One time several of us began noticing that something in the air was causing our eyes to water. We didn't detect any particular odor, but as most of us smoked at that time and ate pizzas in our offices, other odors would have to be real strong to permeate.

"When this continued for several days, though, we attempted to find the cause. We soon located the problem—a new custodian who had been hired for the graveyard shift smelled like he had come from a graveyard! He had body odor that was unbelievable. What was strange was that while the odor was overwhelming near him, it was simply acrid (and stayed that way for some time) away from him.

"We had to ask the university to either help him learn about bathing or fire him. He was replaced or reassigned soon thereafter, and we got a new custodian who seemed perfectly normal."

Grooming

"I wish some of my coworkers would learn that good grooming involves more than wearing nice clothes. Clean, combed hair and fingernails are important, too. Perfume or cologne needs to be kept to a minimum, and revealing or too tight clothing is unacceptable, too. There are days when I feel like I'm working in a brothel instead of a bank."

The need for a dress code

"In our work we have contact with the public. As a result, 'business attire' is the norm. Recently we hired a young woman to work in our office. On her first day at work, she came in with a bare midriff. She dressed that way every day until our supervisor counseled her about that being inappropriate dress for our office. She complained about the 'old fogies' in the office but did start wearing outfits that covered her middle.

"Now, on the other hand, she comes to work in sleeveless outfits and tank tops. This might not be a problem except that she has numerous tattoos on her upper arms and upper body. Our clients stare at her and seem distracted by the 'body art,' but so far only a few have said anything about it (they were all negative comments, needless to say). The way she dresses is not helping her make friends with the other women in our department or anywhere else in the company. You can see the whispering when she walks into the lunchroom. Our supervisor is starting to talk about establishing a dress code for the office and has sought our opinions and that of both HR and legal as well."

Aroma overload

"The kind of employee that I and many others cannot tolerate is the person who smells either like a bottle of perfume or the back room of a smoke shop. Some of us have allergies that are set off by one or both of these types of smells. But to anyone that has a nose that is still working, either type is an overload that we don't appreciate.

"Even when the perfume is expensive, too much is too much. You can smell those individuals 15 minutes after they leave. And then there are the ones who wear cheap perfume and think that more is better. Your nose shuts down when they pass through, but it stores that smell for hours. Apparently some of those perfumes don't come out in laundering or dry-cleaning, so then you get 'layers' of different perfumes!! Put that with some hairspray and deodorant smells and you have a room full of sweet reek!

"Even worse are those people who smoke in unfiltered rooms. They smell like ashtrays filled with stale cigarette butts. Some of us would like to strip those guys and gals and toss their clothes outside to air out—their naked bodies would be less disruptive than their cigarette odor. You dread ever to get papers from them that they took home at night to work on because they, too, will reek of cigarette smoke.

"It is annoying beyond belief to have to work alongside either of these 'nose killers.' Just having contact with them, like delivering papers to them in another office, is enough to make you run. It is amazing that they don't seem to get a cue from the body language (especially facial expressions) of those who come in contact with them."

WORKERS DON'T CARRY THEIR OWN WEIGHT

Poor or Inefficient Work Habits

Slow and wasteful

"We have one person in our group who is slow and often wastes materials and supplies. This person's poor performance lowers the efficiency of the whole group because we miss our deadlines unless we all pitch in and work extra hours to compensate for his slowness. Some weeks we do the extra work, but sometimes we just can't. This sort of weak link in the chain hampers everyone.

"Management has sent the person for additional training but it doesn't seem to have helped or doesn't for very long. One of our coworkers has suggested that we need to 'talk' to him in the parking lot since management's efforts didn't seem to do any good. I hope it doesn't come to that, as he is a nice person who just seems over his head on this job. And I don't think that bopping him over the head in the parking lot is going to help any!!"

Unacceptably slow in order to avoid mistakes

"At our firm, a lot of work is sequential in nature. Sequential means that Person A's job requires input or depends on the work of Person B. Person B's job, on the other hand, requires input from Person C, and so on. Each of us depends to some extent on the others. What this means is that one person can slow down or mess up the whole process. And we have that one person. He is slow but sure—in fact, his slowness seems to be because, for one thing, he is terrified of making a mistake. Apparently, he thinks a mistake would get him fired whereas being slow just gets him chewed out—and, unfortunately, he is right. He gets chewed out and nothing seems to change.

"He has a reason to be concerned about making mistakes. His mind seems to always be on something else, so he could easily make a mistake because he is distracted. Our jobs involve routine manual labor, so most of us can talk while working. But as you might have noticed, there are some people who can't do anything else when they are talking—sort of like the saying, 'can't walk and chew chewing gum at the same time.' Well, this man is that way. So he is slow because he doesn't want to make mistakes, but he is afraid of making mistakes because he is too busy talking."

Lets family obligations interfere with work time

"At my job the women who have families constantly arrive late or leave early (sometimes both) to take care of their children, and those of us who don't have children are expected to pick up the slack in the work. Male employees, and many single females as well, feel left out and discriminated against as a result of all of this—I wonder when one of them will file an EEO complaint or sue? We cannot talk with management about this, as most of them are also females with school-age children. Believe me, we have tried. One response we got was, 'I can't deny her leaving early for her kids, or she'd give up her job.' Our feeling was, 'Fine! Let her go and give her job to one of us who can work full time so we don't have to do her work and ours, too—and for the higher pay she's getting.'"

Hindered by alcohol problem

"We have one person (I'll call her Mary) who is an okay person and worker but she has a problem that requires almost constant supervision. Mary has told just about everyone that she goes to AA (alcoholic anonymous) meetings and is 'working' on her problem. It's no secret—in fact, she seems proud of it. However, at times she has appeared to be intoxicated at work, slurring her words, and almost falling down once or twice. Several of us suspect that she has a bottle hidden somewhere in the office, but we haven't found one. What's worse is that on two occasions she was found sleeping in the employee's lounge. We don't think that she is making much progress on her 'problem.' It seems to us (her coworkers) that the company should send her for medical and/or psychiatric help, as she certainly needs it."

Affected by health or drug problem

"Sam seems to be having some kind of health problems. He has been seen frequently taking pills of some sort. A coworker said that he went to the restroom shortly after Sam had used it and smelled something peculiar—not smoke but sort of like an aromatic smoke like maybe Sam has a breathing problem and needs some sort of vapor to open up his passages. Sam seems fine most of the time and as far as I know his work is also fine most of the time, but on occasion he gets extremely hyper and totally neglects his work—even leaving in the middle of the day or the middle of a project sometimes.

"We don't know what to make of this, but the up-and-down levels of his performance are taking their toll on the rest of us. Some of the workers are wondering if he has some type of disease that they could get. Most of us are just getting tired of having to pick up his work when he isn't getting it done. In a way, we feel sorry for him. In another way, we don't see why he isn't doing more to help himself. Our company has good health insurance."

Attitude and behavior changed by drugs

"We are all concerned about one person in our office. She has recently developed a bad attitude and changed in other ways, too. She seems rude and increasingly nervous and depressed and is neglecting her appearance. When we tried to talk to her about it, she cut us off and has since become isolated from us. Her work is suffering as she has become isolated and unmotivated, and our concern for her and her changed condition is starting to affect our work, too. We also think that she may be shooting up or sniffing something in the restroom at noon."

Cannot focus on task completion

"This is only my second full-time job. I didn't seem to have this problem or at least it wasn't as great on the first job I had, although at that time I was fresh out of school and 'rarin' to go.' Now, though it's another thing entirely.

"Most of the time it really doesn't much matter, but when there is a pressure deadline, which happens fairly often, I just can't seem to meet it because I can't keep my mind focused on the job. I talked to my supervisor and he recommended seeing a doctor because he thought that might involve some sort of physical problem. I did that and got medication but the pills just seem to make it worse and make me dizzy sometimes besides. I know that many or most of my coworkers think that I'm just making up excuses. And having them upset seems to make things even worse. I now think that maybe a different job would be better and so I have started looking around. I'm a bad worker and I know it. I just don't know what to do about it."

Uses language barrier as excuse

"My example of a bad employee is one who pleads 'language barrier' when challenged or reprimanded for doing something incorrectly or for not behaving professionally. When she doesn't do something right, she will say that she 'didn't understand' what was required because 'English is my second language.' When she is about to be called on the carpet for doing something unprofessional, like lying on her résumé, she pulls the same old trick—'Really? Ohmygod, I had no idea. I misunderstood what was wanted. Sometimes the language confuses me.' When she is trying to delay something or intentionally cause a problem, suddenly 'English is my second language' becomes her excuse for messing things up.

"What is most frustrating is that she seems to be able to con people into accepting that lame excuse over and over again, even though she is a middle-aged woman who has lived in this country all her adult life. All of her degrees (she has several) are from American universities; she has written several papers for projects (and even published a couple); she writes and reads memos, email, and the like all the time. She never seems to have a problem until she is reprimanded, challenged, or held responsible."

Don't Carry Out Instructions

Difficulty carrying out routine instructions

"The law firm where I work is organized by the type of activity involved. Most of the time this works well as everything and everybody involved with a particular client is together and so things get done quickly and accurately. However, once in a while there is something that cuts across our groups. Even then, so long as Jane is not involved, it's not a problem. But when Jane is involved, look out! Jane is incapable of following instructions correctly. She screws things up on the first try, usually on the second try, and sometimes even on the third try. Eventually everything does get done but the delays can be frustrating to everyone in the office and particularly to our clients. The partners do talk to Jane every now and then, but she is older and 'so sweet' that nothing really changes."

Difficulty carrying out any instructions

"George is a college graduate and around 40 years old, but he is a problem and should never have been hired for this job. He just can't seem to understand instructions, written or oral. If you give him a manual for operating the FAX machine, he will spend hours with it and then ask you to show him how to use the machine. Not once, but every time he has to use it in the future. If you tell him to do something, he will ask a million questions about how you want it done and why and why it isn't done some other way—so finally you quit asking and do it yourself. He's not dumb, but he seems bewildered about how things work in general and how to do his job in particular. Maybe he is just being super cautious and trying to do things right, but whatever the reason, it lowers the performance of others in our department as well as that of the organization itself. It would be humorous if only it didn't eat up our time."

Difficulty handling complex assignments even with supervision

"In a plant where I once worked, we frequently had trouble with one guy. The work was relatively complicated, and as a result, this guy was always unsure about what to do and when to do it. It seemed like he was not qualified for the job, but supposedly he was because he was hired to do the job.

"He would ask for the assignment to be explained again, and he'd ask a few questions before tackling the assignment. Then he would come back to the supervisor and ask more questions. His uncertainty about procedures and timing slowed everyone down and frustrated the supervisors because they had to go over instructions multiple times all the time in order to get any work out of him. That caused his productivity to be much lower than ours, even though we were assigned the same tasks and apparently were paid at or near the same amount. That doesn't earn him any sympathy from the rest of us."

Absent From the Job

Habitual absenteeism

"The most significant problem with productivity at my shop is absenteeism. Not the occasional missed day or part of a day that some people have, but rather the persistent absenteeism of one particular employee. He holds the record for absenteeism in our shop. He takes all of his sick days, all of his vacation days, and pushes the limit for unpaid absences. It's almost as if he can make enough money in a certain number of days and so he won't work more than that. I've talked with him and he improves for a short time afterwards. There are only eight people in my shop, so losing the productivity of one person is like suffering a drop of 12.5%. This, in turn, affects the morale of the other workers. It doesn't take many such days to make earning profits difficult.

"This began about 2 years ago. First he just started using up his vacation time, then his sick leave, and then he started calling in with all manner of excuses and finally with no excuse at all. I'd certainly like to fire him and get someone to replace him who was more dependable. However, my legal advisor says that he seems to know exactly where the line is where he could be fired and stays just barely short of it, so if I do fire him, I could end up spending a lot of time and money in litigation even though I would probably win given that we keep good records of attendance."

Regularly leaving work early

"I know one person who leaves work early so often that it affects not just his overall performance but also the performance of others in the office where he works since some of their work depends on him. Most of the time he shows up at work on time and performs reasonably well. But frequently he leaves early, probably two or three times a week. He leaves because he'd rather go to a ball game or fishing or to run errands instead of being at work.

"Apparently, he doesn't need the money as he is hourly, and every time he misses work, he doesn't get paid so he is docking himself by this behavior. Since many supervisors in the company leave early to pick up their kids from school or to take them to the doctors or whatever, he feels that he should be able to take off early whenever he feels like it, too. Monkey see, monkey do. I guess there is a lesson there for companies. It doesn't feel fair to the rest of us, but we're afraid to just take off work early, too. However, we don't work very hard when all of these people are gone! We work some and socialize a lot, probably our way of getting even."

Missing work because of stress

"A couple of my coworkers shared a 'tip' with me for getting absences paid by the company. They gave me the names of a couple of clinics and doctors (general practitioners) that are quite willing to sign off employees from work based on 'stress' even though they know that those individuals continue to pursue active hobbies. The physicians argue that their hobbies are stress relieving and so they can do them even though they can't work.

"It's a great way to be absent and not be penalized for it. How do you think that makes the rest of us feel? You bet we resent it. And we wouldn't trust these coworkers on anything they tell us in the future because they are cheats. Yet we are expected to pick up the slack. I'm sure one of us will pull up the nerve someday to rat on them."

Absent on the Job

Too many parties during work hours

"I work for an organization that employs mostly females. A few of them insist that everything be done in a 'cute,' 'happy' way. We have to have decorations and parties for everyone's birthday and holidays, and potluck lunches are the norm (even if we don't cook or have spouses, we feel compelled to bring something and to come 'solo'). Company time is wasted on these events and individual productivity suffers from all of the interruptions. When I was new in the organization, I tried to raise this issue with upper management (mostly females not trained in business). I was told that all of those things contributed to a spirit of 'family,' which in turn leads to greater morale and productivity. I spent some time gathering information about our operations and from academic literature on this, and nearly got fired when I shared it with those managers. I now keep my mouth shut and do my job with as little participation in those 'events' as possible without alienating anyone."

Cube chatting

"While I was in college, I was a student worker for a big department at a major university. While the regular staff were nice to me as well as to others and did their jobs, some of them did their jobs less efficiently than they could or should have. One of the most common things that interfered with their efficiency was what I came to call 'cube chatting.'

"Cube chatting consists of people in adjoining cubicles (ours were only about 4 feet high so you could see over them if you stood up) talking to each other across the cubicle partitions. They would talk to one another about families and family problems, health issues, the weather, sports on some occasions (especially about the university's teams), and, of course, about the faculty, administrators, and other staff. I guess this is the equivalent of the old 'gossiping across the backyard fence.' But whatever it is, it slowed work down and led to occasional mistakes when people got distracted.

"I don't know if taller partitions would have cut down on this chatting or not, but it seemed clear to me that the university administration should have done something to reduce it in order to get better performance from its staff."

Avoiding work while on the job

"There is a guy in our shop who is absolutely amazing. He comes to work on time and leaves on time. In between those times, he is constantly on the move. Not doing his job, mind you, but going from place to place to talk to people, to use the restroom, to get materials, to take long smoke breaks, to get a snack, to have lunch, to do this, to do that, to do anything but his job. Why this is amazing is that I have been here for three months and observed him doing this virtually every day, all day, but apparently his supervisor has never seen it (or doesn't care, which would be even worse). It makes me wonder if I am the only person who can see what this guy is up to."

Working on outside projects while on the job

"We have a bad employee in our art section. He just can't seem to keep his mind on his work. His work seems to take more time than he has or at least more than he is able to focus on. He has several projects going on the outside that he works on at nights and on weekends, and it appears that he spends more time thinking about them than he does his 'day job.' In addition, he has been known to use company equipment (but only on breaks and lunchtime) to work on these outside projects. Not only does he fail to meet deadlines and sometimes do sloppy work but also he keeps others from meeting their deadlines when their work depends on his doing his first, which is fairly common. He claims to have a medical problems associated with his blood sugar that causes him to not be able to focus on his job like he should, but we all know that he just has too much on his plate. He can't seem to say 'no' to any request for his skills."

Constantly quitting

"Where I once worked, 'Eric' (not his real name) was always saying he was going to quit. A lot of people mumble and grumble about their jobs and many of them talk about quitting. But Eric was the only one I have ever known that made a career out of 'going to quit.' 'Going to quit' was why he was late or didn't even show up for work on some days or missed deadlines on assignments—'I was late because I wasn't sure I was even going to come to work today. I'm really thinking about quitting.' 'I know we had a meeting, but since I'm planning to quit, I didn't think it was important for me to be there.' 'I missed yesterday because I was out looking for another job.' Eric never did quit, but he got away with that excuse the whole time that I was there—well over 3 months!"

Lazy

"Seems like every group where I have worked has at least one person who is downright lazy and has figured out a successful way of avoiding work. She constantly gripes about some aspect of the job in order to convince the boss to stay away or to "go easy" on her. Actually, I think she knows how good she has it, but she wants to keep it that way so she threatens to quit or to go up the organization chart and "tell all." Couple that with a weak boss, and the rest of the workers end up doing the complainer's share of work and still have to listen to the whining."

Taking unfair advantage of coworkers

"In Recovery where I work, nurses are assigned to the different beds. Sometimes we get a nurse who will hold down her own work by putting a patient into another nurse's area. Not only does that create an immediate overload for the hard-working nurse but also it spills over into the follow-up duties like calling patients at home the following day. Besides that, having the work divided unevenly results in the patient's being kept longer than necessary in Recovery, which is bad for PR."

WORKERS TAKE OR SUBJECT OTHERS TO UNNECESSARY RISKS

Potentially Harmful to Coworkers and Other Organizational Assets

Failure to secure doors

"Hank doesn't seem to get it when it comes to security. He frequently works in the warehouse at night when hardly anyone else is around, but he invites his friends to drop by to visit and have a beer with him on his break. Because he may be in the back of the warehouse when a friend comes by, he props a door open with a chair. This puts everyone working there at risk as well as the company since someone could rob the warehouse easily."

Careless with electric hotplate

"Mary is an airhead and puts us all in danger. She frequently brings food to work that requires using the hotplate in the employee lounge to cook. When she finishes she almost never turns the hotplate off. She has even left a pot sitting on the burner that was left on! It melted the pot, smoked up the area setting off the smoke alarm, and could have caught everything on fire if someone else hadn't come into the lounge at about that time. We resent having to look after her every time she goes on break."

Take stupid risks

"'Accident prone' really means 'stupid behavior.' At a warehouse where I worked, there was one person who constantly did dumb and unsafe things. He would go higher on ladders than was safe (they always have a step marked 'Do not climb higher than this'). Not only did he endanger himself, but many of his stupid actions endangered other employees and sometimes customers. He moved things from top locations without first shutting down the aisle endangering customers and other employees. He tossed glass bottles of soda to other employees frequently with no warning to them other than his hollering 'Catch!' He would cut lumber without wearing safety glasses. He loved to speed around the warehouse on the forklifts. And on and on.

"His supervisor would explain things to him and even had him go to a special safety class. He responded well and his behavior changed—for a while. Then it was right back to his old ways. Nobody wanted to work near him, and we all had to stay on guard when he was around. He was an accident waiting to happen, and it finally did. A large crate that he was trying to get from a top storage area fell on him, putting him in the hospital for a couple of weeks."

Block emergency exits

"Two of my coworkers are nice people but they subject all of us to a potentially serious situation. Our storage room has one of the exit doors that we might need to use if there was a problem in the front of the office. For example, if we had a fire or if a person with a gun walked through the front door, we would need to make a quick exit through the door in the storage room. These two coworkers frequently move boxes and other stored items around, but they leave them either in front of the door or in what would be our pathway if we had to exit. Their attitude is that we could still see our way around the stuff or move it, but not if we were running for our lives or if the place were filled with smoke. Our solution up to now has been to try to keep an eye on the room and clear the way if we see a blockage, but that means that we are taking time away from doing the work that we are paid to do."

Smoke around flammable materials

"A long-time employee with a history of performance problems was caught smoking in a restricted area where flammable chemicals were stored. This clearly endangered him, his coworkers, and the entire factory. He was terminated for unsafe behavior.

"The employee then filed suit against the organization alleging (1) age discrimination based on comments that his supervisor had made (e.g., 'You're too old to be doing this kind of work'), and (2) disability discrimination because the company refused to make accommodations for his high blood pressure (which was only slightly high according to the company's doctors and not high enough to represent a genuine disability). I left the organization before this had all been settled so I don't know how it turned out, but it seems to me that no form of discrimination can excuse such unsafe behavior that endangered the factory and everyone in it."

Sleep on the job

"Ron is a danger to everyone including himself but he doesn't seem to know it. His problem is sleep—or rather the lack thereof. Ron is single and fancies himself a 'real party animal.' He is out on the town almost every night, drinking and dancing and whatever. The result is that he comes to work tired and exhausted. We have tried to talk with him about it, but he always says, 'Man, I'm not tired. I'm just quiet.' But his fatigue does slow him down. Our supervisor has noticed that. But when he calls Ron's attention to it, Ron will then work extra hard to meet his quota.

"His lifestyle also makes him inattentive and clumsy. For instance, he drops the tools far more often than the rest of us. And sometimes when someone is trying to tell or ask him something, it's like he's off on another planet. We have to call his name a few time, or louder. We've muttered about that to him in a nice sort of way—like we would tell him to go get his ears tested or to wash the wax out of his ears, or something like that. He'll say something like, 'Sorry, man. I was just thinking about how many of these I had done today,' or 'I was trying to remember when I need to take my car in for an oil job.' Always some excuse, but the truth is that his mind is not on his job. He's in the twilight zone, half asleep. He perks up and acts alert enough when the supervisor is up close, but when the boss is not around, Ron turns back into a zombie.

" If given a choice, none of us would prefer to work around Ron. We've thought about pulling some trick on him when he's in his zombie state, like hide a couple of his tools. But it's really not a funny thing because being constantly tired on the job will lead to an accident."

Potentially Harmful to Themselves

Disregard safety devices

"We had a worker who constantly took risks by using dangerous equipment without using the safety devices—almost like he wanted to hurt himself. All of the power equipment in our shop had safety devices built in, but it was possible to disconnect or bypass many of those devices. This worker would almost always bypass the safety devices when he had to use the equipment. He was warned about his unsafe behavior, but his response was that safety devices were for 'sissies' and that they just slowed him down so he couldn't make as much money. He continued to break the rules but eventually the company started writing him up after a couple of really close calls. One time, for example, he left a handbrake off and that big dump truck rolled down the slight incline and narrowly missed hitting three workers who were having lunch at a table outside near the parking lot. After much documentation and many hearings and grievances, he was finally terminated."

Fail to take prescribed medication

"Sam is more of a danger to himself than to others, but if he were to keel over on the job it could be dangerous to several of us. We work on high-speed printing presses. We produce a newspaper and sizeable booklets for advertising companies on our huge presses. These have elevated 'decks' for reaching the tops of the machines. These 'decks' are used to reaching numerous areas of each press to service them when they are down and to adjust them when they are running. If anyone were to slip while a press is running, that person could get badly hurt and it might cause one or even two others to get hurt.

"The big danger, though, is to the person on a 'deck' making an adjustment—and that's where Sam comes in. He has some sort of medical problem for which he is supposed to take medicine a couple of times a day while at work. When he does not take the pills, he gets dizzy and disoriented and can stumble or fall down. He hates taking the pills because he thinks it makes him look weak and he prides himself on being so macho. The result is that frequently he does not take his meds and so he endangers himself."

Lift loads that are too heavy

"Our office is mostly staffed by women, and none of us is in outstanding physical condition! We usually are very careful, like we team up to move furniture and heavy boxes, use a dolly when appropriate, etc. Except for Emily. She is always in too much of a hurry to wait until she has the help she needs, like sometimes she will insist that only one of us help her instead of waiting until a third person can join in. She lifts boxes that are too heavy, and she doesn't pick them up in the correct manner so she risks damaging her back. I have also seen Emily carry a box that is so large (even if not too heavy) it blocks her view, so she risks running into something or tripping over something. In fact, she did trip and fall once. When a box or piece of furniture is too heavy to slide, Emily will sit down in the floor and use her whole body to press against the item, bracing her legs to get more pushing power. We told her about another woman who crushed her vertebrae by pushing that way, but Emily is too gung-ho to think about it—'not me, my back is very strong.'

"I suppose we could just throw up our hands and declare that it's her problem, not ours. But it is distracting and an accident could put her work in our laps for several weeks. We think she's a bad coworker for acting this way."

Treat work as playground recess

"I work in an automotive repair garage. We use a lot of power equipment including hoists, air hammers and wrenches, jacks, winches, transmission jacks, and some others. We also frequently employ high school kids to work in the shop to do clean up and some low-skill jobs. Therein lies the problem.

"Some of these kids don't seem to realize that power equipment can be very dangerous. For instance, I caught Danny playing with the electric hoist. He would hitch it to his belt and take himself for a ride, swinging around and going up and down. What he didn't seem to understand was that as he was swinging around the cable could have wrapped around his neck and choked him. Or that his belt could have broken and he could have sustained serious injuries from the resulting fall.

"We try to educate these kids about safety and how to properly use the equipment but many of them just seem to think that they are invincible. In that sense, they are not good employees."

Treat equipment as toys

"It seems like warehouses are filled with accidents just waiting to happen. Most everyone is aware that stuff stacked on shelves could fall on somebody but nobody thinks much about it.

But what's worse is that some of my coworkers don't seem to understand that the warehouse equipment can also be dangerous.

"Lifts are not elevators to be ridden up and down, for instance. Arthur is one of the ones who not only uses the lifts as elevators, but also will jump on a moving forklift for a 'free' ride around the warehouse. He doesn't seem to understand or care that he is endangering himself and others by his foolish practices.

"I asked him one day if he didn't have enough work to do or if he was bored. He say, 'No, I've got too much work to do, but I just enjoy having a little fun.'

"We tried to tell him that having a little fun at work isn't worth injuring or killing yourself. He said, 'Some of you guys want to smoke on your breaks, and that is killing you, and I don't do that. I just happen to want to take a free ride on my breaks. So you smoke on your breaks and I'll do what I want to on my breaks.'

"I guess you can't help somebody that refuses to be helped. We'll just try to stay out of his way when he decides to take his 'breaks.'"

SECTION III

JOBS/WORKPLACES AND VIOLENCE

CHAPTER 8

BAD JOB/WORKPLACE FACTORS THAT MAY LEAD TO VIOLENCE

Meanwhile, hardworking Americans are increasingly faced with workplace conditions in which critically important safeguards are watered down, emerging problems are ignored, and enforcement is scaled back.

—Tim Bishop

Good workplaces benefit employees and their organizations, and ultimately they benefit society as a whole. Conversely, bad workplaces do not serve anyone well. Bad workplaces can lead to mental and physical health problems for members of the organization, personal relationship problems, low productivity, higher costs, and sometimes even to violent acts of behavior.

But what is a "bad" workplace? As shown in Figure 8.1, what constitutes a bad workplace may depend on several factors, including personal factors such as a worker's physical and mental makeup; the nature of the job and its associated risks; the physical environment in which the job exists; the organization's culture; and, of course, the rewards and degree of security associated with the job. The quality of working conditions can make for a good job and hence long workplace survival. If unsatisfactory, these factors can lead to mental and physical health problems for members of the organization and sometimes to violent acts of behavior. This and the next two chapters are designed to assist workers, potential workers, and managers

---

in identifying the many and varied characteristics of such workplaces. But you should remember that it is each individual's perception of the workplace conditions, particularly the job itself but importantly including that person's conceptualization of fairness and justice, that determines whether a workplace is "bad."

CONFLICTING PERSONAL FACTORS
Changing perceptions and expectations
Physical and mental makeup
Remuneration expectations
Fringe benefits expected
Need for status and respect
Job security, advancement opportunities
Worker-job incompatibility

HAZARDOUS JOBS OR WORKPLACES
High injury occupation
Unsafe worksite
Vulnerable to outside attacks

WARNING

BAD WORKPLACES

UNFAVORABLE ENVIRONMENT
Undesirable location
Too physically demanding
Uncomfortable environment
Long hours or overtime
Duties not wanted or anticipated

POOR ORGANIZATIONAL CULTURE/CLIMATE
Threatening environment
Dishonest, unethical management
Bad attitudes
Incompetent management
Weak/poor upper management

Figure 8.1.   Characteristics of workplaces that contribute toward violence.

CONFLICTING PERSONAL FACTORS

Whether a job or a workplace is good or bad depends a great deal on personal factors. Managers and nonmanagers may define a bad job as an unsafe job or a low-paying job or a job with low status or one with little opportunity for advancement. Yet other workers seek those jobs. In other words, what seems bad to me may seem fine to you. Also, it is important to note that one's concept of what is good and what is bad can change over time. Abilities, tastes, and priorities of individuals change over time, and thus what constitutes a bad job at one age may be inconsistent with that same person's view at another age. Nevertheless, bad jobs take a toll on individuals and can be one more factor that pushes a person to behave in an unacceptable or violent manner.

Changing Perceptions and Expectations

Of course, needs, preferences, expectations, and perceptions often change over time, thus transforming a good job into a not-so-good job. Workers or managers who initially dislike being a manager may someday want to move up the ranks to get a higher salary when their family status changes from single to married-with-children. Pay increases may or may not be as important to workers who are approaching retirement age and not supporting children. Maintaining the status quo may become more important than moving up. Increased responsibility, status, and pay may become less important than the security of simply keeping the same job, especially because of the person's comfortable familiarity with the job. Adapting to new jobs is also more difficult. Also, age discrimination makes it difficult for the older worker to find another job. On the other hand, pay may still be very important to other older workers even though they may no longer be supporting a family. Besides the fact that we tend to equate importance with pay, retirement income (Social Security or otherwise) is largely a function of the salary that the worker is earning at the time of retirement. For that reason alone, the worker or the manager may seek a promotion so that his salary is as high as possible at the time his retirement benefits are calculated. The fringe benefit of health insurance also becomes extremely important because the older worker is certain to pay much higher premiums when that worker is not eligible for group insurance offered through the organization.

Physical and Mental Makeup

The perception of whether a job is good or bad can be a function of a person's physical size and condition. For instance, workers who are strong and healthy would view the attractiveness of many jobs quite differently from workers who cannot stand or sit for long periods of time. Construction jobs, for instance, are considered great jobs by some men but few women. Most individuals who normally work at indoor desk jobs would find construction jobs far too unappealing and too physically challenging, while construction workers would "go bananas" if they were "chained" to a desk in a quiet environment. Such jobs would include manager, cashier, waitperson, dispatcher, ticket agent, and receptionist—jobs that other people routinely seek.

How an individual deals with stress is an important factor. For many workers and managers, the amount of stress that they feel determines whether a job is bad, good, or something in between. Some individuals like to work in close proximity to others with whom they can interact freely and frequently; others find that unbearably stressful and prefer working alone in quiet surroundings. Some employees are unhappy unless they have coworkers with whom to share their breaks and lunch hours, while others do not and will not socialize or fraternize at work.

Some people dislike change; they find it stressful. Yet others are bored with sameness and instead embrace or even encourage change. Others apply the "bad" label to jobs that are frequently subject to abrupt and involuntary shifts and jarring transitions caused by reengineering, layoffs, downsizing, outsourcing, and wage cuts. Holders of those jobs typically have very limited choices in the job market and may simply move from one bad job to another. Some managers intensely dislike their highly stressful supervisory jobs but rationalize staying on the job because of the pay and status. Stepping down to a nonsupervisory job would be worse than the "bad job" they currently hold.

Remuneration Expectations

Even though some individuals may be reluctant to admit it, pay or compensation is one of the most powerful motivators of job performance, especially if pay is linked directly to performance. Seldom do we hear a person say that a job is good if he feels it underpays the worker. If the wages for a job are low, most workers will consider it as a bad job, regardless of their qualifications or lack thereof. This will likely be true even when the worker is actually being overpaid for his skills and future potential. Not only will there be difficulty in attracting qualified applicants for the job, but also there will be little or no incentive for jobholders to perform well or stay on the job any longer than they must. The same is true for fringe benefits; they usually go together.

It is true, though, that some relatively low-paying jobs do have some allure that partially offsets the low pay. These may include working for a not-for-profit or charitable organization where the meaningfulness of the job helps compensate for the low pay, or working in a creative job such as interior decorating, fashion designing, news reporting, filmmaking, and architecture. Some applicants will take jobs that have managerial job titles even though they are paid less than rank-and-file employees in another organization. Frequently cited examples can be found in banks (the Teller who has a Vice-President title) and janitors who are titled Sanitation Engineers. Conversely, there are a few jobs that pay well but have less allure—statisticians, CPAs, and actuaries come to mind.

According to the Bureau of Labor Statistics, among the occupations with the lowest annual incomes are personal and homecare aides, maids and housekeepers, custodial workers, childcare workers, parking lot attendants, food preparers and servers, fast-food and short-order cooks, recreational protective service workers (lifeguards, ski patrol, and the like), farmworkers, cashiers, counter attendants, amusement and recreation attendants, bartenders, dishwashers, and theater workers (ushers, lobby attendants, and ticket takers).[1] The highest paying occupations include just about any job with engineer or manager in the title or any medical, computer, or scientific job. In between are many jobs that require advanced skills, training, and in some cases licensure but still command only moderate pay: teachers, nurses, and first responders, for example.

Incidentally, what is "low pay"? Low is a relative term when discussing the pay level that makes a job seem bad. How much is enough? That, too, is a function of the individual worker's mindset—and that can change over time. We know that one consideration is the minimum amount of dollars it takes to pay for the necessities of life—food, shelter, and clothing. Of course, the definition of "necessities" differs from one individual to another. Also, most workers are trying to "move up" in life, so they need more than the bare necessities that they currently have. In addition, fairness comes into play as comparisons are made with the pay received by others. Feeling underpaid may lead to resentment that can eventually wind up with a violent response.

A seemingly objective characteristic such as pay may not mean much in and of itself. A low-paying job may be "bad" relative to a high-paying job, but not so bad relative to no job at all. A low-paying job with good coworkers and bosses may seem better than a higher paying job with bad bosses or bad coworkers. Also, a low-paying job that offers good fringe benefits (especially health insurance) or other perks (company car, housing allowance, uniform or wardrobe allowance) may be reclassified in the worker's mind as an OK job or even a good job. One additional point: the pay that a worker may consider as too low or as not too low is usually the function of other characteristics of the job. If the fringe benefits include, say, health insurance, we can get by on lower pay than we could if we had to buy our own health insurance. In contrast to accepting lower pay at a nearby jobsite, if the job is a long distance from home we may want more pay to compensate for the additional time that we are giving up and the greater out-of-pocket cost of transportation.

Fringe Benefits Expected

Wages and salaries are not the only way in which to motivate and reward employees so they can feel good about their jobs. Among those most commonly cited are the level of fringe benefits (which actually are another form of compensation), opportunities for advancement, job security, and the nature of the work itself. However, benefits (especially health coverage, which has skyrocketed in cost) and job security or longevity may be considered even more important when jobs are scarce or when a person is lacking in education or other qualifications.

Fringe benefits, especially health insurance, are of major importance in defining a job that is good enough to attract qualified applicants. Then, because the worker does not want to lose them, the fringes motivate continuing performance after individuals are hired. Jobs with low or no fringe benefits tend to attract and retain lesser-qualified people or those who see the job as a short-term "fix" to their employment situations. An exception to this is the employee whose spouse already has coverage for dependents and perhaps an individual who is covered by Medicare/Medicaid. Thus, jobs with low or no fringe benefits have impacts that are quite similar to jobs with low security, as shown in some of the examples of worker comments that we presented earlier.

Because of the burgeoning costs of healthcare, the future of fringe benefits does not look as bright as it has in the past. For example, some organizations are considering eliminating health coverage that has been available in the past to dependents and to retirees, and some are reducing medical coverage, thus requiring the individual worker to bear a larger share of the cost of medical coverage. Those companies who are totally eliminating health coverage as a fringe benefit are giving up one of their competitive factors for attracting and retaining the workers they need or desire, but the tight labor market may permit them to get away with it.

Companies that support continuing education through tuition reimbursement or pay increases for course credits are less likely to have their workers complain about their pay or their opportunity for advancement, as continuing education enables the worker to prepare for a better job while continuing to earn a living. Some organizations offer other ways to attract and keep employees, including letting them bring pets or children to work, offering a child- or pet-sitting service at work, providing a fleet of vehicles to facilitate carpooling or gyms to encourage fitness, and many other creative things.

Need for Status and Respect

Status is important to an individual's self-esteem and self-efficacy, and therefore helps to determine whether a job is good or bad. Status is relative to other considerations—the take-home pay of one person relative to what others are paid, the size and location of one office relative to others, having or not having windows in the office, invited to attend meetings or go to lunch. When the job is regarded as a low-status job, it is more difficult to get well-qualified workers to apply for the job, more difficult to persuade people to stay on the job, and more difficult to entice people to perform well when they are on the job.

But many workers do seek jobs that others may label as low status. As we all know, workers differ in the challenges they seek or avoid, in their interests, and in their training or skills. Some individuals, for example, would prefer lower-status "worker" jobs than higher-status managerial jobs because of the additional time and stress they perceive in supervisory jobs. The same is true for physically demanding jobs—a worker may prefer a lower status job to a physically challenging job.

Some relatively low-status jobs that workers consider "not so bad" include licensed practical nurse, insurance claims adjuster, bill collector, computer tutor, dispensing optician, emergency medical technician, fundraiser, locksmith, manufacturer's sales rep, and telecommunications installer or repairer. However, most low-status jobs are demotivating, dead-end, unsatisfying jobs. The quality of working conditions can make for a bad job and hence low workplace survival. For that reason, some workers will choose a lower-status job if they like the working conditions. Examples mentioned by many workers were attractiveness of surroundings inside or outside, low commute time, dress codes, state-of-the art machinery or tools, and such.

Jobs can become unsatisfactory when coworkers on different pay levels are thought to be more important than others. This can lead to a difference in job status among workers, which also may affect morale and work relationships. Nursing jobs are an excellent case in point. Nurses commonly complain about the inferior manner in which physicians treat them when they are supposedly working as a team. Another example is the different levels of nurses (RNs and LPNs) who report to the same manager but have distinctly different tasks to do, hierarchical titles, different amounts of education, and differences in pay rates. If the higher-paid RNs do not regard the LPNs as equal and vital working partners, the LPNs will resent the fact that they are not given the proper status. The consequent rift will be felt over and over again, and the LPNs will think that their job at this hospital is bad while the RNs will think that their job would be great if only it weren't for their griping coworkers, the LPNs.[2]

Many employees have a preconceived notion that any IT (information technology) job is undesirable because it brings high pressure and little gratitude or respect. This seems to be true especially for IT jobs with the word "maintenance" in the job title—web, database, systems, or computer maintenance. These jobs can be stressful, unrewarding, and involve long hours (often being on call 24/7). They require a tremendous amount of training and a high level of skill, yet users of those workers' skills do not always treat the jobholders with respect. Computer maintenance workers, in particular, interact with computer operators mostly when something is wrong, which means the operators are often in a bad mood. Although the users should express gratitude and respect to the person who has come to their assistance, most likely they are stressed or even irate because giving up their computer for repair may then require them to work late or miss deadlines. Programmers and other high-level computer personnel, on the other hand, are generally paid well, respected, and have a lot of control over the performance of their jobs. Those personnel and many computer "maintenance" personnel also, would probably not consider their higher-up jobs as bad.

Job Security, Advancement Opportunities

Frequently, bad jobs are defined as those with low pay or perhaps low pay with little job security or advancement opportunities. The major criterion regarding remuneration may be whether the job pays a fixed salary that can be confidently expected at the end of the pay period, whether the wage rate is based on sales commissions or piece-rate production, or a combination of the two. Other criteria include the opportunity for promotions, salary increases, and bonuses.

Job security—being able to count on holding a job as long as one's performance is acceptable—and the opportunities to advance are also important factors in developing loyalty and solid performance from jobholders. Jobs that do not provide those opportunities are usually considered as bad jobs. When there is little security in the job or it is only for a short duration, job holders obviously will not invest heavily in the job and will instead seek a job with a more reliable paycheck.

There was a time in the U.S. labor market that a worker would accept a job that he or she liked for a variety of reasons, and if the worker performed well he or she would stay there throughout their career. Workers felt that they could count on the organization to take care of them after they became too old or too ill to work. But that is not likely to be the case today. First of all, employees know that they are instantly dispensable—they could be laid off tomorrow, or later today! With this in mind, they have little or nothing to lose by constantly seeking another job that they think they'll like better, that will give them greater opportunities to grow, or that pays more money. Sometimes there is not much the organization can do to keep those workers, but the majority of workers do respond positively to well-thought-out plans and procedures for worker evaluation, performance feedback, and job advancement. In other words, they tend to stay if the organization removes some of the job uncertainty by communicating with them in an honest way about their performance and the organization's plans for them.

Job security may be less of a factor for younger workers who do not have dependents to support, are more mobile, are eager to get a variety of experience, or can reasonably expect to find another job in their wage/ salary category. As workers become older and take on more debts as a result of building a family, job security becomes of paramount importance. They are generally more eager to take advantage of promotional opportunities that give them additional security by making them more mobile. Jobs that do not provide what the worker considers as sufficient job security will be considered as bad jobs that do not warrant the worker's loyalty.

Of course, some jobs are contracted jobs—for instance, construction and remodeling jobs—that last only until a building or project is completed, yet they are not considered as bad jobs. The workers' only hope of job security within that organization is to be contracted by the same company to work on their next project. Otherwise, the workers may need to move elsewhere to contract with a different organization or to use their skills in a related job such as remodeling. In that way, working as a carpenter or electrician can still be a relatively secure way to earn a living. But suppose the individuals live in a very cold and/or very wet climate where they may be unable to work for days or weeks at a time (plant nursery and car wash employees in North Dakota and Washington State, for instance)? Since they are paid only for the hours worked, their jobs now may not look so good, as they still have the same bills to pay but fewer hours of paid work time. The organization does not control such variables; thus, it cannot offer total job security in contracted jobs. Workers accept this as the way that contracted jobs function, and they must prepare accordingly for periods of unemployment. Often these jobs pay higher hourly rates for the time that the workers are actually on the job.

Worker-Job Compatibility

Some workers find their jobs to be unsatisfactory because they are either over- or underqualified for the job; that is, job compatibility is lacking. Their organization apparently did not "hire smart" and/or has not trained the workers adequately. The workers are bored, unhappy, or unduly stressed. Poor performance in turn has an adverse effect on their morale and confidence as well as their productivity. Very quickly, then, theirs becomes a bad job, because the organization has not "hired smart" or has chosen to rush workers into new jobs before they have been adequately prepared—maybe because the organization pays wages that are too low or feels that training is unnecessary or that training costs are too high.

Jobs like cashier, waitperson, dispatcher, ticket agent, and receptionist are sought by millions who love their jobs because they provide an opportunity for the workers to interact with interesting people. Workers in jobs that require high levels of mental creativity or thought-processing may want little or no interaction with others. Individuals with conditions that limit their short-term memory or present difficulties in verbal and nonverbal communication and social interactions would not like jobs that have too many things to keep track of or too many people to deal with. Workers who might find these jobs too difficult for them to function well could include those individuals who experience degenerative or pervasive developmental disorders such as autism, Asperger's disorder, Childhood Disintegrative Disorder (CDD), Rett's disorder, Parkinson's disease, and even those with degenerating sight, hearing, or memory.[3]

Since classifying jobs as "bad" is highly subjective, no survey or published data captures all or even most of the bad jobs where you could end up working. Rather, jobs have a number of characteristics that should be taken into account in classifying them as "good" or "bad" or something in between. The nature and kind of supervision, the kind of coworkers and relationships involved, and the culture or climate of the work environment also need to be evaluated. The work itself—the physical environment and working conditions, safety considerations, location, hours, status, travel requirements, and similar characteristics—also needs to be considered. As stated earlier, what all of this means is that "bad" is in the eyes of the beholder. In your mind, is the job compatible with your expectations and needs?

HAZARDOUS JOBS OR WORKPLACES

No one really wants to work in an unsafe environment, and the government makes a considerable effort to see that such environments do not exist. However, there are workplaces, jobs, or occupations that consist of risky, safety-related tasks and are therefore inherently unsafe. Their associated risks can only be minimized, not eliminated. Other workplaces and jobs are made unsafe by worker attitude and conduct, and these may be the most difficult for coworkers to control. Unfortunately, there are also a few workplaces that are unnecessarily unsafe because of management attitude. Sometimes that means that the organization does not want to spend the necessary money to make the workplace safe. Generally, that's not true, though, as safety standards are rather closely monitored and tightly enforced by the U.S. Department of Labor through OSHA (Occupational Safety and Health Administration).[4]

High-Injury Occupation

Some jobs are considered bad because they require performing job duties that expose the worker to personal risk. Using U.S. Bureau of Labor Statistics (BLS) data, some broad job categories with higher than average nonfatal occupational injury and illness rates include "food and kindred products," "primary and fabricated metal industries," "lumber and wood products," "trucking and warehousing," "industrial machinery and equipment," "general building and special trade contractors," "heavy construction," and inherently unsafe jobs such as demolition and mining.[5] Some people would add law enforcement and fire department personnel to this group, especially in some cities or geographical areas. According to the same BLS figures, the lowest rates of nonfatal occupational injury and illness are among finance and insurance industries.[6] However, there is considerable variation within these broad categories of jobs. For instance, outdoor jobs that involve using heavy equipment are generally less safe than those that do not involve such equipment.

Unsafe Worksite

An often overlooked part of dealing with violence prevention is the worksite facility itself. Every workplace has personnel and physical assets—employees, power plant, computers, generators, and so on—that are most likely to be targeted by an angry employee or an outsider. The protection of assets means that such assets are identified, protected, and secured. Equally important is an understanding on the part of all workers as to the early warning system and proper security procedures to follow in case of an emergency, including but not limited to an act of violence.

A safe worksite would be environmentally designed to make the company and its employees as safe as possible. The worksite does not provide a worry-free area if employees do not have, or are not familiar with, who-to-call lists and evacuation procedures, or if the structure does not provide dependable door locks, automatic lockdown procedures, bulletproof glass, and such. Furthermore, the worksite is not worry-free if the exterior is not well lighted and does not offer protection from individuals hiding behind shrubbery or walls, from vehicle crashes through doors, or from the entry of people who are not authorized to come inside.

Another type of danger is acts of terror from within the organization, including threats to or sabotage of either an employee or the organization. There are numerous ways in which one individual can sabotage the organization's computer system, including low-level cyberattacks and setting up a Distributed Denial of Service (DDOS) attack on the organization's email that overloads the system and causes it to be shut down.[7] Individuals can also sabotage another employee's work because of resentment or in hopes of making oneself look better, threaten to sue the organization if they don't get their way, or spread untruths to discredit or even ruin another's reputation. More drastic, destructive acts include setting fire to the factory after being fired, slashing the tires of one's superior, and killing a supervisor or coworker. Organizations that rely on punishment-based discipline systems rather than positive reinforcement seem to be where many incidents of workplace violence have happened.

Organizations Vulnerable to Outside Attacks

Even occupations and workplaces that are traditionally considered to be safe can be vulnerable to violence, especially from unstable clients, outsider criminals, and fanatics. Charged with the responsibility of providing a safe place to work, organizations must recognize these potential hazards and take steps to prevent harm to their workers.

Organizations That Handle Cash

While indoor office jobs are generally safer than outdoor jobs, that is not necessarily true of indoor jobs that involve handling cash or working late at night. Robberies and attempted robberies account for a large amount of workplace violence. Banks have always been vulnerable to robberies, but nowadays professional bank robbers resort to cybercrime—taking the bank's assets by computer instead of in person. Other "amateur" robbers often prefer an easier "hit" than banks, such as convenience grocery stores, fast-food restaurants, check-cashing businesses, hotel/motel registration desks, and gasoline stations—where workers usually handle a large amount of cash and work alone during hours when fewer would-be witnesses are around. The fact that these organizations have on hand either cash or items easily convertible to cash makes them especially attractive to drug addicts, who generally will do whatever is necessary to get the cash to buy their drugs. It is not enough to post signs saying that cash is kept only in a safe that no one there can open, as many of these robbers cannot or do not read the signs. Furthermore, since they are desperate and irrational, they will kill for even the small amount of cash that needs to be kept in the register to make change. They also know that jewelry stores cannot operate their businesses without keeping their products in public view and taking pieces from their sealed cases to show interested customers. Jewelry is easily pawned or sold for drugs.

Organizations That Operate Long Hours or Around the Clock

We need also to be concerned about workplace safety where robbery may not always be the motive. Included here are attacks on employees who perform their job in relative isolation, including jobs where a few workers come to work early or remain at the worksite well after most other personnel have left for the day, or where workers finish their shift and depart after dark when witnesses are less likely to be around. Perhaps the most obvious examples are teachers and janitorial personnel who work alone in their buildings for a short time before or after hours, and employees of late-closing businesses such as bars. Any workplace that involves a single employee is vulnerable. In these cases, the attacker is intent on committing a crime such as rape or murder, not robbery.

Healthcare Organizations and Clinics

Nearly 60% of all nonfatal assaults and violent acts occurred in the healthcare and social assistance industry. Nearly three quarters of these were assaults by healthcare patients or residents of the healthcare facility, not workers or outsiders. The most common victims of assaults in 2007 were nursing aides, orderlies, and attendants.[8] In 2011, health care and social assistance reported more cases of nonfatal occupational injuries and illnesses than any other private industry sector.[9] Such violence includes (a) patients targeted by healthcare workers; (b) healthcare workers targeted by patients or coworkers; and (c) organizations or clinics that are attacked by outsiders. The types of violent actions vary across these three groups.

Patients in all kinds of health facilities are vulnerable to abuse by workers, other patients, and outsiders, particularly during the night shift. This is especially true of patients in nursing and retirement homes as well as mental institutions. These acts of violence include rape and even murder by injection or smothering as well as verbal abuse, theft, and milder forms of physical abuse such as slapping or neglect. The sexual drive and lack of sexual inhibition in many mentally disabled patients makes them especially vulnerable to sexual abuse by workers and by other patients. Some healthcare organizations are not eager to expose such conditions, and innocent coworkers are not likely to speak up.

On the other hand, because of their close contact, the healthcare workers also are vulnerable to both physical and verbal abuse by patients. Patients can experience behavior changes resulting from medications, pain, depression, or loss of memory; and they may strike out at the person closest to them or the person they think is not doing enough to help them: the healthcare worker. Many are not happy to be confined or they may have family problems to worry about. Workers in mental hospitals and prison hospitals are especially susceptible to patient abuse and must be trained thoroughly to protect themselves.

The safety of healthcare workers may also be jeopardized by other workers or visitors. This is particularly true of nightshift workers in hospitals, workers in the more isolated areas of a clinic or hospital, and workers in mental health facilities. This abuse may come from visitors or outsiders in emergency departments and mental health facilities—workplaces that are frequented by emotionally charged individuals and/or mentally unstable persons. Unlike hospital corridors at night, where unauthorized individuals are more suspect, emergency rooms are more at risk because they involve relatively unrestricted movement of the public. Overcrowded and uncomfortable waiting rooms, long waits for service, outsiders under the influence of drugs or alcohol, understaffed high-risk areas, and untrained personnel compound the problem. Pharmacies and similar healthcare organizations are vulnerable to addicts seeking drugs, especially when they are open around the clock but also during regular daytime hours.

Disliked Organizations

Political terrorism, one of the oldest types of terrorism, is another growing problem that affects the safety of the modern-day workplace. Some organizations are likely to be attacked by political terrorists or religious fanatics. Other vulnerable organizations include those that are perceived to damage the ecological environment or that are judged negatively by "animal rights" groups. Organizations that are more vulnerable include, for example, transportation hubs, oil refineries, federal buildings, electrical grids, abortion clinics or Planned Parenthood offices, churches and synagogues, bars and strip joints, and also the means of transportation to and from the workplace. Law enforcement agencies fit in this category when they are targeted by people who feel that the criminal justice system is failing. Large companies, especially international businesses, are in danger when they are considered to be "the root of all evil," even if no specific demands are made by the terrorist. Capitalism is a threat to those terrorists. They may use sabotage of an organization's computer system, destruction of its physical facilities, the kidnapping and/or murder of its managers or other employees, hijacking of its shipments, or even spreading false information that causes its stock to plunge. Some of these same techniques, plus pirating on the high seas, are used to collect ransom money to support political wars abroad.[10]

The Unabomber provides a memorable example of how vulnerable a low-profile organization can be, even if considered objectionable by a single individual. The bombing of the federal building in Oklahoma City and the events of 9/11 show us how innocent people and organizations like a childcare center suffer collateral damage from acts of terrorism simply because of their proximity to a targeted site.

PHYSICAL ENVIRONMENT

The physical environment is an important determinant of what may be regarded as a bad job or workplace. Seldom will you find a worker who says that he or she works in an undesirable workplace but his "job" is good. Rather, when the workplace environment is undesirable, the worker is more likely to say that the "job" is bad, or at least not good. Even in jobs that are considered inherently unsafe, workers often express a desire for a workplace that is clean, comfortable, and safe as can be expected, given the nature of the work itself. Conversely, put a worker with an undesirable job in a relatively desirable workplace and that worker may say that the job is not so bad after all, or "at least the company cares." A factory that is not kept clean or almost any job where equipment and furnishings are in need of replacement sends a signal to the workers that the company is not doing well, does not care about its workers, or may even be unsafe. Naturally, the definition of an undesirable workplace does vary among individuals according to how strongly they react to these various elements.

Undesirable Location

For many workers, the location of the workplace may determine whether it is good or bad. Similar to a bad physical environment, jobs in bad locations also tend to be less attractive, hence more stressful, to employees. Whether these locations are in a dangerous area, a distant area, or an unappealing area, employees of any rank who label these jobs as bad are saying that location matters. They don't want to work "on the wrong side of town" or a long commute from their homes or in an area where they don't feel safe. They weigh this against other factors such as the pay and fringe benefits, opportunities to succeed, the people with whom and for whom they work, and the like.

Having to work in high crime areas or areas subject to higher levels of pollution also make jobs unappealing. In addition, locations far removed from where the jobholder lives or from amenities such as restaurants, service stations, banks, and the like are considered less desirable. Even workplaces that are located near the worker's residence may be considered bad if the worker feels unsafe getting to and from that location. A good job can become a bad job due to location when other factors change for the worker. For example, initially the job location can be within acceptable driving distance of the worker's home; but if the worker's situation changes so that he first needs to go in the opposite direction in order to, say, chauffeur a child to school or daycare, the job then becomes inconveniently located. Also, in recent years a dramatic increase in the price of gasoline has made some otherwise good locations seem bad because of the long commute from the worker's home

Too Physically Demanding Job

Physically demanding jobs are considered bad by many workers, especially those who have health problems, lack muscular strength, or otherwise feel that the duties are too demanding. Continuous long hours or physically demanding duties, for example, lead to fatigue, poor decision making, slowed reflexes, muddled thinking, accidents, and less-than-optimum performance.

Jobs that are too physically demanding may also be unsafe if they are performed by individuals who have not been trained adequately or are not of adequate size or physical condition. Even getting to and from work can be unsafe if the organization or the worker does not take adequate safety precautions. Sometimes a job becomes less safe, unsafe, or even more unsafe because the workers are physically unfit, perhaps impaired by illegal or prescription drugs, alcohol, or over-the-counter medications. While this applies mostly to jobs that involve the operation of machinery, it would also be true of, say, impaired sales representatives who drive from one client's location to another.

Physically Uncomfortable Environment

Some individuals are willing to work in what others would consider as an "uncomfortable" environment because the job offers them other things of value, such as good compensation, opportunity for advancement, access to facilities and equipment that they could not afford to buy for personal use, or the ability to earn a living doing something they enjoy. Perhaps they like the outdoors, or the job allows them to have no or low supervision ("I'm my own boss"), or the pay more than compensates for the discomfort. Maybe it's the only type of job for which they are trained or which they enjoy. Workers who direct the parking of automobiles in dirt parking lots outside race tracks probably do not enjoy parking the cars while "eating dust" on a hot, humid day; but they love the excitement that surrounds automobile racing, the free tickets to view the races, and the relatively high pay for a few hours of work. Depending on the person and their background, they may not even perceive these jobs to be uncomfortable. But workers who do find themselves in what they consider as uncomfortable jobs know what they feel, and they are ultimately determined to leave if at all possible.

Working outdoors in the cold of winter in northern areas or in the heat of summer in southern or desert areas clearly does not constitute a good job in the eyes of many employees. They often will work for less compensation in order to have the amenities of jobs with heaters and air conditioners. Dirty, smelly, dusty, dark, and dank work places are also clearly not desirable either. In fact, such jobs could be deadly to workers with certain physical conditions. To be sure, workers can be found for such jobs; for example, coal miners. Some have even told us that the constant temperature below ground makes the mine a good place to work and that they enjoy the camaraderie that mine workers feel while working in the dark, dangerous underground. They usually add that it pays really well and that it's the only type of work they can find near their home. In other words, they give money, food, and shelter priority over the physical environment—and, for that matter, priority over the safety factor.

Restaurant and fast-food workers are subjected to very difficult working conditions: hot kitchens, slippery floors, aging equipment, low pay. The jobs generally are dead end, with little training that could lead to better jobs. They work long hours for low wages and frequently receive no health insurance benefits, no paid vacation, and no paid sick leave.[11] If workers miss time due to illness or family emergencies, they not only lose their pay but also may be subjected to disciplinary action. Most of us do not covet their jobs, but many people depend on the jobs because they need a job temporarily, they need schedule flexibility, they have the skills already, or other reasons.

Long Hours or Overtime

Working long hours can also make for a stressful job. Long hours that are constant or sustained for extended periods of time lead to fatigue, poor decision making, slowed reflexes, muddled thinking, accidents, resentment against the company, and less-than-optimum performance. These consequences can be disastrous and almost always lead to decrements in health and productivity, or to high turnover. Even when the workers are carrying out all the tasks while the supervisor does nothing but watch the workers, the supervisor also feels the stress of carrying the weight and the blame on her shoulders. An occasional "push" that involves longer hours to complete a project or meet a deadline has some of these same consequences, but the relatively rapid return to more normal hours may provide time for recuperation (rest and relaxation).

In some jobs—for example, shooting and editing feature films—long hours are typical and expected by the crew. The high cost of equipment rental and the amount of time it takes to set up for a shoot, to apply the actors' makeup, edit tapes, and so on necessitates extending the hours of operation. Potential and regular employees know this; and while they may still label the job as "bad" because of its long hours, these creative workers are willing to accept it because they view it as their only path to a career in filmmaking.

The same is probably not true for a construction worker or for a secretary or manager who has three small children at home. For physical reasons, the construction worker cannot work 18- to 24-hour shifts. Because of family responsibilities, the secretary or the manager dislikes spending those kinds of hours at the worksite. Workers who carpool may be unable to extend the 8-hour shift, at least not without advance notice. Also, if working longer hours would necessitate the worker returning home during the darkness of night, many individuals will likely consider the job as a bad one.

Duties Not Wanted or Expected

Not infrequently we hear workers talk about how their jobs are bad because they require duties that the workers had not expected to perform and do not want to perform. Sometimes this is a job that thousands of other workers perform daily, but the complaining worker was simply uninformed about the nature of the job and thus feels unjustly treated. For example, a person who goes to work for a pet store or a veterinarian's office will be disappointed if he or she does not know that this job requires cleaning the cages, not just feeding and petting the animals. A waiter or waitress will think theirs is a bad job if they come into the job mistakenly thinking that the restaurant has busboys for cleaning tables but then find that this task is performed by the waitperson. Some employers will intentionally misinform an applicant as to the job duties in order to get that person to sign on. Also, some workers or managers may take advantage of a new worker's status by relegating the tasks that are not a part of the new-hire's work, at least until the new worker figures out that he is being treated unfairly. Sometimes a rather simple problem like this can be the final straw that pushes an employee toward a violent act.

POOR ORGANIZATIONAL CULTURE/CLIMATE

Regardless of the job duties, physical conditions, location, coworkers, and supervisors, whether an individual considers a job as bad or as acceptable is also influenced or determined by the organization's culture/climate. An organization's culture consists of behavior and attitudinal norms, stories, beliefs, and actions that characterize the organization and affect every individual from the CEO to the maintenance personnel. As such, a bad organizational culture or climate refers to the atmosphere that permeates the whole organization, not just one department or workgroup that answers to one bad boss or contains one "bad apple" among its employees. Enough bad apples, though, will make the whole barrel rotten.

The history of the organization and its top managers are important shapers of an organization's culture. The culture, in turn, helps to shape or reshape the attitudes and behavior of people who are members of the organization. For example, the work ethic of top management sets the tone or serves as a model for others. If top managers come in early, work late, work hard, and genuinely care about the organization and its goals, that behavior and those attitudes tend to permeate the organization and be copied by others. If top management tends always to arrive late, leave early, and shift the blame for errors, supervisors farther down the chain will probably do likewise. The same is true for many other practices, such as attitude toward employee health and safety, bullying, customer satisfaction, and the like. "The culture of an organization will always trump policy when the two are not aligned.[12]

Individuals who work for an organization know of other very important factors that are related to the organizational culture/climate and that play an important role in determining whether their job is good or bad. The four things we often hear mentioned are dishonest or unethical management, management with an attitude, incompetent management, and a threatening environment created by management.

Threatening Environment

Undoubtedly some of the worst workplaces and jobs are in companies where there is a threatening environment. The threats may be explicit statements from executives to lower-level managers or to workers, including shouts of "I'll fire you if (or unless) … ;" or they may be indirect, as in quietly or enthusiastically firing a worker to show other employees what can be done to them.

Not only is there the stress of working in such an environment for eight or more hours per shift but also the residual stress that lingers after leaving work. Threats encountered at work tend to go home with the person—they weigh deep on the mind and therefore affect the person outside of the workday world. Lingering stress includes the apprehension of returning to the same stressful environment the next day and the fear of losing the job undeservedly in a tight labor market. That is especially true when the threats involve the family, as many do, such as threatening to relocate the person, reduce his or her pay, or even terminate him.

A threatening environment affects both the physical and mental well-being of workers and their families. For example, workers who are threatened with losing their jobs without true cause are constantly worried about paying their bills and possibly having to uproot their families. Such an environment has a tendency to cause further problems both at work and outside work, including mental instability ("going postal"), health problems, or excessive mistakes that could affect not only production but also the safety and well-being of other workers.

Sometimes the problem is caused by one or two "kick-ass" managers who create bad job situations for other managers under them and for workers. These managers may be new people who are lacking in experience and confidence and want to establish a reputation by playing tough, or management may have intentionally selected these managers for their toughness. Regardless, the blame still rests on the executives and their organizational culture, as top management either wants or permits these managers to use a threatening managerial style.

Dishonest and Unethical Management

When workers and supervisors observe dishonest or unethical management, their perception of the entire organization and their own job is usually affected. The honest, ethical behavior (or lack thereof) of top managers sends signals to everyone else in the organization regarding what is acceptable behavior and what is not. If top managers are principled, law-abiding, and fair, others in the organization will also tend to be that way, too. On the other hand, if top managers take undue advantage of others, operate in the "gray area" of ethics or the law, and seem to care only about themselves, other members of the organization are likely to behave similarly.

If members of the organization treat one manager or worker or client dishonestly or unethically, they likely will treat anyone else the same way. Everyone has a reason to feel vulnerable to being on the receiving end of a bad action or decision sometime, whether it be the customer who gets no adjustment for a bad product, the supervisor who is asked to forge a document or fire a worker for no reason, the worker who is terminated or not given the promised raise, or the new employee who does not get the job duties or the salary that was promised in the interview. Furthermore, when that supervisor or worker is asked or expected to do things that are not law abiding, they are being asked to torment their own conscience and perhaps risk everything they have worked for by getting caught for breaking the law.

Some of the examples we have observed include altering, forging, or destroying documents; altering time cards to favor or punish an employee; billing clients for an inflated number of hours; and printing fake receipts or otherwise padding expense accounts. In one division of a Fortune 500 company, midlevel managers would alter employee time cards to reduce the number of hours worked in order to make their departments look more profitable.[13] They had designed a payroll system that made it difficult for workers to check their shifting hours, varying rates of pay, and the like.

One of the stranger examples involved companies "hiring with intent to fire" or "low probability to retain." In one case, the organization in need of a highly competent individual for a nonroutine project would advertise for a full-time position, heavily recruit the applicant, inflate the salary offer in order to hasten the decision, and then retain the employee only until the project was completed (1–3 months). At that point another manager or his assistant would inform the new-hire that the company had decided not to fill the position just yet. Such actions are difficult to manage psychologically. First, the terminated worker wonders if he did something wrong or if they decided he was not qualified, even though they had raved about the work and indeed continued to use the project output. The mistreated worker then feels really angry that he had been pushed to accept the job quickly and therefore missed other opportunities in the meantime—especially since the company knew they would retain the employee only a month or so. And therein lies the explanation—they could afford to quote a high annual rate because they knew they would be paying for only 1 or 2 months, which would be a lot less than if they hired the expert as a consultant for a similar time period. To what extent do you think the current full-time employees trusted this organization?

In a similar case, a manager badly needed an additional employee but was not getting a positive response from his management. He hired the person anyway, thinking that "it's easier to apologize than to ask permission." His bosses overrode his decision and made him let the person go only about a month after the newly hired professional had moved her household belongings hundreds of miles, registered her personal vehicle in the new state, and signed a one-year lease on an apartment. The hiring supervisor subjected the employee to an expensive risk in an effort to satisfy his own needs—an action that was both dishonest and unethical.

Bad Attitudes

As discussed earlier in the book, management at all levels set the tone for workers' attitudes and behaviors. If top managers shirk their duties or break rules rather than following sound policies, others in the organization are likely to assume that they, too, can get by in the same manner. Managers who show a lack of trust in their employees may find that workers either live up to that low expectation or find other employment where they are appreciated and trusted. If management is rude to workers, then workers will tend either to be rude to coworkers and clients or to band together in defense against management. The environment created by management's poor attitude, where questions are discouraged and mistakes are not tolerated, frequently leads either to low productivity or to excessive mistakes.

In an organizational culture where top management has a judgmental attitude, workers (and sometimes their bosses) have good reason to think that their workplaces are bad. Workers don't want to have their bosses distrust them and think that they are potential cheaters or lazy slackers who must be constantly monitored or else they will not work every minute they are on the clock. Take, for example, the boss who arranges to have workers' computer monitors turned at angles that allow the boss always to see what the workers are doing.

Workers feel that they should not be required to ask permission to go to the bathroom or make a phone call when they are mature and honest enough not to abuse that work break. All workers should not be punished for the behavior of those few who abuse the system. Such a restrictive type of organizational climate does not motivate a worker to respect the organization and give 100% to the job. They also detest being treated as though they are stupid when they ask questions that are intended to help them perform their jobs. What is worse, perhaps, is having bosses act like they never make mistakes or blame their mistakes on others while sending the message that the employee who makes a mistake is stupid and should be fired. Sometimes it is not the words that are spoken but the body language, such as glaring or rolling eyes that communicate a "you-are-so-stupid" message. Workers also dislike a culture in which managers break the rules or take excessive privileges but are strict with workers, as in taking excessive breaks, arriving late, leaving early, or using the telephone for personal calls.

Bad attitudes at lower levels are often a reflection of the way those individuals are treated by management at one or more levels above. They feel underpaid and mistreated, then take it out on the persons they supervise. For example, the supervisor may refuse to support his workers for promotions and raises unless he, the supervisor, is similarly rewarded from the top.

Many times bad attitudes are a manifestation of the manager's incompetence. He criticizes the work of his people when they are rushed, even though he caused the rush by giving last-minute assignments with inadequate instructions. Or maybe he doesn't know what he wants beforehand—only when he sees it finished—then he'll suggest doing it a different way. He's a bad planner and scheduler, but ordinarily we find that his whole company functions in that same type of environment.

Incompetent Management

When workers complain about their jobs, invariably they will speak of "incompetent management." A boss may indeed be incompetent, or he may be inadequate in only one area, which prejudices the worker's judgment about the boss's overall competency. Either way, the job is considered bad, and the manager is viewed as the nucleus of the problem. Employees who must answer to incompetent managers blame the organization for having used improper criteria for choosing, hiring, and/or training supervisors/managers. The critical feelings become more intense when incompetent managers are retained even after higher management knows, or should know, about their incompetence.

Incompetent managers usually do not consciously make bad working conditions for employees. They simply are not sufficiently knowledgeable or experienced to perform their jobs effectively or efficiently. When employees know or sense that management's way is not the best way or is absolutely wrong, a condition of mistrust, resentment, or even fear is created. Workers come to disrespect management, which then leads them to characterize their job as bad.

Insecure, incompetent upper-level managers do not ordinarily allow input from those under their supervision. They are usually opposed to asking those below them whether they have a solution to a problem or know how to do a job better or faster. Often, these supervisors and their workers justifiably feel that they are more knowledgeable than are the upper-level managers about the job they are doing, so they resent the fact that they are not asked or allowed to make suggestions for improving the job. Feeling that management is too incompetent, the individuals may ultimately come to resent the entire organization.

Sometimes incompetent or inexperienced managers act tough because they are insecure in their jobs. Also, upper management may feel that the young, highly trained new-hire must be tough if he is to succeed. One example of this is the new-hire who has, say, an MBA, yet lacks the knowledge and experience to manage lower-level managers and employees who are not only older than their boss but also have the skills and expectations that come with seniority on the job. Incompetent managers are even less tolerable when they were hired because they are both incompetent and tough. Management knows they are neither technically competent nor experienced in managing people, but they want someone who will "crack the whip." In such cases, these incompetent managers are simply carrying out the wishes of upper management in a rigid culture.

Weak/Poor Upper Management

Bad managers are sometimes created—and always made worse—when top management permits bad-boss behavior to exist. In some instances higher levels of management don't know, don't care, or won't do anything about that bad boss's behavior or attitude. Rather than correcting bad bosses, upper management may ignore the behavior, uphold the behavior, or even contribute directly to the bad behavior of bosses. Often, members of higher management are reluctant to get rid of a bad manager because that would be an admission of their own failure to make a good hiring or promotion decision. While there may be many other reasons (none good enough to excuse it, though), upper management's support or tolerance—intentional or nonintentional—of bad bosses is always dysfunctional. Consider these examples.

Ignore Bad Boss Behavior

Ignoring the bad behavior of a child may be a way of diminishing that unacceptable behavior, provided the bad behavior isn't little Johnny locking little Suzy in a closet! But ignoring the bad behavior of a member of management is never a good approach. In that case, ignoring the behavior can have the same effect as endorsing it—it worked once for the bad manager, so it will work again.

Three types of bad boss behavior that should absolutely never be ignored are bullying, harassment, and discrimination. Many companies have made considerable progress in dealing with discrimination and harassment; bullying needs much more attention. Executives who ignore the behavior of a bad manager are, in effect, telling the bad boss that he or she may continue the behavior that the workers find unacceptable. A manager whose bad behavior is ignored has no motivation to change that behavior. Workplace bullies take this as a license to continue their ways.

The motives of upper executives for ignoring such problems may be that they don't want to get involved with what they consider "small problems," or they have information that makes them sympathize with the offending boss. In such cases, the behavior of offending bosses who are meeting the expectations, however slight, of their own managers may escape reprimands or punishment. Depending on the skill or educational level of the workers, executives may assume that the organization is better off losing the worker than the manager, especially if the manager meets their productivity expectations.

Unsatisfactory behavior by bosses who are known to be angered easily are sometimes ignored if they are doing a satisfactory job otherwise. It may be simpler for executives to let the worker leave than to fire or to deal with an angry boss. They rationalize that it is easier to replace a worker than a boss. Animosity in any form should not be accepted in the workplace as it not only interferes with productivity but also with the workers' attitudes toward the company. Unfortunately, some managers know that they can get by with virtually anything because of their relatively scarce skills or their personal contacts, friendships, or family relationships. Some know that upper management is too busy fighting fires or meeting budget constraints to bother with replacing someone already in place and trained. Occasionally, a boss will successfully use health problems to avoid being terminated for bad behavior.

Uphold Bad Boss Behavior

If upper management takes the boss's side by choosing not to reprimand him even when they know the boss is wrong and the employees are right, they are upholding his behavior. Likewise, if management takes the boss's side by punishing the worker, they are upholding the boss's behavior. The company and its employees are in even greater danger when management upholds bad boss behavior than when they simply ignore it.

It is not uncommon for upper management to "go on record" as upholding what the boss does. Even if management says that the boss's actions are not a good solution, the fact that they make excuses for the offending boss and take his or her side rather than attempting to remedy the situation is like adding fuel to a fire. Now the offending boss, the other bosses, and the workers all know that whatever a boss does, the employees have no recourse. They recognize that "Management" subscribes to the motto of "sticking together," even when the boss is less competent than the workers under his supervision.

Management may uphold bad decisions and behaviors because they think that to do otherwise would be seen as admitting they have made a poor hiring decision or that a member of management can be less than perfect. The important point is that, in taking the boss's side when the boss is clearly wrong, upper management is upholding that behavior; thus, an improvement in the boss's behavior is not likely to occur.

Contribute to Bad Boss Behavior

Unfortunately, upper management sometimes contributes to bad boss behavior in ways other than ignoring or upholding the bad behavior. For example, management may reward the wrong behavior, like allowing the boss to decide to increase production or decrease costs without considering the negative effects on workers. And when upper management ignores workers who complain about the boss's heavy-handed behavior and rewards their boss for meeting or exceeding productivity goals, they are reinforcing the bad boss's behavior. If upper management dismisses a complaint without checking the facts, they are effectively ignoring, upholding, and contributing to unacceptable boss behavior. Bad boss behavior is likely to grow when it is reinforced by higher organization officials.

Another example of contributing to bad boss behavior is making poor hiring decisions and failing to train or procure the necessary training to ensure that the bosses act competently and professionally. When upper management criticizes the boss's behavior but fails to take the necessary action to prevent its recurrence, they are contributing to continued bad behavior. Agreeing with a worker's criticism while doing nothing to prevent a repetition of the undesirable behavior is tantamount to ignoring the worker's complaint, and it contributes to future bad behavior.

Some of a bad manager's behavior is the result of upper management's failure to have its reward system carefully thought through and spelled out. Sometimes management purposely chooses bad bosses because they want "strong" (read that, "bully") supervisors. But even when a boss is not chosen for that reason, upper management contributes at least indirectly to bad boss behavior when they do nothing and therefore allow it to continue.

WHAT NEXT?

Bad workplaces and bad jobs can add to an organization's potential for violence just like bad managers and bad coworkers. This chapter has made it clear that not all problems that you might encounter in an organization revolve around managers or nonmanagers, though. Many times you will just have a "bad job" or a "bad workplace" regardless of who the managers and nonmanagers are.

Chapters 9 and 10 discuss suggestions for dealing with the kinds of bad workplaces talked about in this chapter. Following Chapter 10, an appendage presents real examples of many of the characteristics discussed here. Those examples have been drawn from material provided by consulting clients, students, family, and friends.

NOTES

1. U.S. Department of Labor, Bureau of Labor Statistics. (2013). *Labor force statistics from the current population survey, household data annual*

averages, Table 39. Median weekly earnings of full-time wage and salary workers by detailed occupation and sex. Retrieved from http://www.bls.gov/cps/cpsaat39.htm

2. Longo, J., & Sherman, R. O. (2007). Leveling horizontal violence. *Nursing Management, 38*(3), 34–37, 50–51; Jackson, D., Clare, J., & Mannix, J. (2002). Who would want to be a nurse? Violence in the workplace—A factor in recruitment and retention. *Journal of Nursing Management, 10*(1), 13–20.

3. American Psychiatric Association. (1994). *Diagnostic and statistical manual of mental disorders* (4th ed., pp. 70–71). Washington, DC: American Psychiatric Association.

4. Occupational Safety & Health Administration (OSHA). Information can be found at www.osha.gov/

5. Bureau of Labor Statistics (BLS). Information can be found at www.bls.gov/

6. *Ibid.*

7. Markoff, J. (2013, April 2). DDoS (Distributed Denial of Service). *The New York Times*, p. D7.

8. Janocha, J. A., & Smith, R. T. (2010, August 30). Workplace safety and health in the healthcare and social assistance industry, 2003–07. *Bureau of Labor Statistics.* Retrieved from www.bls.gov/opub/cwc/sh20100825ar01p1.htm

9. U.S. Bureau of Labor Statistics, U.S. Department of Labor. (2012, October).

10. Globe Risk International. (2013). *Kidnap & ransom.* Retrieved from www.globerisk.com/kidnap.php

11. Royle, T., & Towers, B. (2002). *Labour relations in the global fast-food industry.* New York, NY: Routledge.

12. O'Bryan, B. (2013, June 24). How "see something, say nothing" trumps policy and impacts workplace violence. *HR and Employment Law News.* Retrieved from http://hr.blr.com/HR-news/Health-Safety/Violence-in-Workplace/How-see-something-say-nothing-trumps-policy-and-im?goback=.gde_3876184_member_254572429

13. Personal correspondence, n.d.

CHAPTER 9

BAD JOBS/WORKPLACES

What Managers Can Do

*On paper, being good sounds great but a lot depends on the atmosphere of
the workplace or community we live in. We tend to become good or bad
depending on the cues sent out within a particular space.*

—Alain de Botton

Based on the experiences cited by members of a variety of organizations,
bad workplaces and bad jobs can be found in all types of organizations—
different sizes, public and private, for profit and not-for-profit. Just as with
bad managers and bad employees, bad workplaces and bad jobs require
immediate attention when a manager becomes aware that they exist. Eliminating these would be the simplest way to improve the attitudes, health,
and performance of workers in those organizations—if only that were possible! At least a large number of the cited workplaces or jobs could be
modified, but sometimes managers and workers will need to adjust to the
so-called bad factors.

The first thing, of course, is to determine what factors make the situation bad in the eyes of the person who performs that job or occupies that
workplace. Some problems should be easy to address; for example, giving
workers more input, providing more or better training, and disallowing
rude or intimidating supervisors and workers. In addition, regardless of

Violence at Work: What Everyone Should Know, pp. 203–224
Copyright © 2014 by Information Age Publishing
All rights of reproduction in any form reserved.

the size of the organization, other problems could be eliminated by redesigning some jobs, altering their bad characteristics to make them more acceptable. Other solutions may be more difficult, more costly, or more time-consuming. The organization could modify standards and procedures to facilitate the selection of acceptable workers and managers, to pay them more equitably, and to make their workplaces safer and more comfortable. Modifying the organizational culture or climate may be the most difficult of all as it has a long history that reflects the values and standards of people at the top. The following pages offer a few more potential solutions for bad workplaces and jobs.

PERSONAL FACTORS

Personal factors refer to those aspects of a job or workplace that an individual would find undesirable and hence would label as "bad." We need to recognize, in the first place, that what seems undesirable to one person may not necessarily be undesirable to another individual. On the other hand, some workplaces and jobs are undesirable to virtually all individuals— period—that's that. Still, even though no one may want to work there, some people will accept it or even learn to like it. Why? Because the pay makes it worthwhile, because the job involves low stress, because they cannot qualify for a better job, because they are desperate for any job, because it offers tuition reimbursement or other significant benefits, or whatever personal factors are given higher priority by a particular worker.

For employees at all levels, being paid fairly and having a feeling of job security as well as the opportunity to advance and further their careers are powerful and clearly desirable motivators. Where jobs lack one or more of these three components, something needs to be done. It may seem that low pay and lack of job security and advancement would be the easiest problems to resolve: simply "up" the wages, promise no layoffs, and promote those who work hard. Unfortunately, it is not that simple, usually. Job titles and promotions need to reflect contributions; job vacancies, downsizing, and layoffs can't always be avoided; and increases in compensation can affect the bottom line.

Low Pay

Seldom do you hear of an individual who says his job "pays too little" but he "loves his job." On the other hand, many individuals will remain with a job if "the pay is good." Low pay and good pay, as we mentioned much earlier, are relative terms. As the manager you should do everything within your power to see that employees are paid fairly, relative to other employees both within the organization and in the marketplace. If your company has a sound wage-and-salary system, follow it. If such a system does not exist, work with the HR department and higher levels of management to establish such a plan. Arbitrarily deciding what to pay individuals or setting their salary on the basis of how much you like or dislike them personally will virtually always lead to problems later on.

What is considered low pay or adequate pay also changes over time. The same pay that would make some young, inexperienced workers feel that a job is good, for instance, may make the same job appear bad in the eyes of an older, more experienced worker. If employees are expressing unhappiness regarding their pay, you need to request the organization to review its wage and salary system to see that it reflects the levels of skill that are necessary and then rewards the workers as they progress in experience. A manager who can show that an employee's pay does not reflect his level of skill, experience, and contributions will have a much better argument for a pay increase than the manager who says only that an employee needs more pay.

Low Job Security

There was a time when managers and workers did not need to give much thought to job security, as good employees had a job essentially for life. There was an "implied contract" between employer and employee: Do your job, keep your nose clean, and you will always have a job here. That is not the case today. Your job is made harder by the fact that the workers under a manager's control feel no sense of loyalty from the organization and hence feel no duty to pledge loyalty in return. You can, however, communicate with workers and learn what it takes to keep them content and productive—good pay, prestige, a feeling of power and being empowered, pleasant working conditions, compatible coworkers, for example. At the same time, you must be on the alert for conditions that could cause undesirable employee turnover, which could include several of the factors mentioned in this book regarding jobs, managers, and coworkers. (Since even you, the manager, cannot count on the security of your own job, you also need to continue updating your knowledge and skills so you are ready to reenter the job market at any time.)

The nature of some jobs is such that job security simply cannot exist—the job just ends. These include seasonal jobs, contract jobs, special-event or special-project jobs and even high-tech jobs. When there is little security or the job is only for a short duration, job holders will not invest heavily unless there is promise that their work will be seen and recognized sufficiently to get them hired for another similar or better job. In such cases, these workers will spend some of their time networking and job hunting while "on the clock." Indeed, some workers are likely to devote considerable energy toward improving their skills or finding other jobs, preferably ones with more security or longer contract periods. Thus, you may need to be more visible or see that contracts specify output rather than man-hours or days worked. In the case of uncontrollable variables such as weather conditions, the organization has little to offer in the way of job security. For example, few or no drivers bring their cars into a carwash on a rainy day, and some construction contractors cannot perform their jobs in inclement weather; so these organizations cannot justify keeping and paying the workers for those days, but workers should understand those situations.

Lack of Advancement Opportunity

It is often said that getting a job depends not on what you know but on whom you know—you need an inside contact to "champion" your résumé. True or not, once you are on the job you should expect to be treated fairly and equally. Employees have reason to be unhappy when they are passed over by individuals who are less qualified, are chosen for promotion based on factors that result in discrimination, or are selected because of "who they know" or "who they are related to." Such problems should be avoidable if managers follow the organization's policies and procedures for perfor-mance appraisal and feedback. When others with less experience or less skill are promoted, complaints may well be justified and both productivity and morale may suffer.

Depending on their education and skill levels, employees may consider their jobs as less than desirable because they perceive a lack of opportuni-ties for growth and advancement. Such opportunities are largely a function of the absence or scarcity of jobs to move into—a situation over which you as manager may have little or no control. Also, some jobs are actually dead-end jobs that provide no advancement opportunities—there are no higher jobs that require the same sets of skills. A call-center employee may be promoted to a supervisory level, but then what? This situation stems from a lack of career planning (unless the employee intentionally took the job only temporarily). The individual chose a job because he or she was already skilled in that area or enjoys doing that kind of work, not realizing that improving or even mastering that job will not prepare that individual to advance without additional training or education. As manager, you can suggest that the worker obtain career-planning assistance through the organization's human resources office or take advantage of the organiza-tion's support of continuing education through tuition reimbursement or pay increases for course credits. This could enable employees to continue to earn a living while training for a career move.

For some jobs, limited opportunities for advancement are simply "the nature of the beast." For one thing, higher-level jobs are fewer and generally have lower turnover than the jobs from which workers would be more readily promoted. To where or what, for example, can the HR Director be promoted? How many Head Cooks, Comptrollers, or CEOs can your organization use? And what kind of extra skills must the Head Cook or the Comptroller acquire in order to be promoted to a higher position? If possibilities are low for both upward and lateral moves, the employee will in many cases consider the job as unattractive and therefore leave the company. Depending on your managerial level, solving these problems to your employees' satisfaction may be beyond your control as their manager.

PHYSICAL FACTORS

The physical environment is frequently the cause of complaints about one's job. A common, widely expressed criticism is that the workplace is much too cold or much too warm, or the work areas are not evenly heated or cooled. Another complaint is the noise level and interruptions by colleagues, especially when open or cubicle workstations are used. Factory workers and other workers who occupy cubicles think the conditions would be more tolerable if they were permitted to listen to personal headphones or piped-in music, have a nice breakroom, hire someone to keep the floor and workspaces clean, or some other change to offset the problem. Office workers may like their jobs much better if they are given new chairs or new computers, or maybe if the walls are repainted and the floor is carpeted. In some situations, management can allow cubicle workers to wear earplugs or headphones without sound to muffle the noise and to make it more difficult for coworkers to interrupt them. An appropriate dress code could be allowed for workers in areas that are too cold or too warm; for example, allowing males to wear short sleeves and no coat.

If positive changes cannot be made to improve the workplace, perhaps the worker can be given other considerations such as higher pay or more fringe benefits to offset the unpleasant characteristics of the job (like "combat pay" in the military). One organization with which we are familiar allows workers to use the "green space" around their building to plant flowers, which they can tend before and after work. All employees who have window access can enjoy the gardens, and the company does not need to hire gardeners to trim and mow that area. Another organization provides similar privileges to one or two "green thumb" employees, who plant and tend vegetables and then share the harvest with the other workers. Workers also respond positively when the organization spruces up the physical plant with bright colors instead of the gray metal structural beams and air conditioning ducts that surround the worker all day every day.

Of course, management cannot always do a great deal to improve a bad physical environment. Cleaning a kennel or a sewer line, for example, is just not a pleasant job to do. Nevertheless, unpleasant jobs should still be reviewed with an open mind to see if they can be improved. Getting input from current job holders would be an excellent place to start. They frequently know better than anyone else how conditions could be improved. For instance, would it be helpful to issue a mask to the kennel cleaner? Would it make the job better if the poop were removed sooner or less often? Can a different type of litter be used? In some cases, uniforms and a uniform cleaning service can be provided at headquarters so that workers can avoid wearing messy or foul-smelling clothing to their homes. Rotating tasks so that one individual is not always responsible for the most undesirable task can also sometimes serve as a partial solution. True, paint rooms will always be smelly, spray-filled rooms that require the worker to wear a special suit and mask. But could a better air-filtering system be installed in paint rooms? And what provisions could possibly make an outdoor job more tolerable—offering readily available ice water and better portable toilets, or permitting workers to play radios, for example? These are the types of questions that need to be asked by managers. Again, the jobholders themselves should be asked for ideas on how to improve the job or workplace conditions. After all, they are the ones who see and feel the problem on a day-to-day basis.

Undesirable Location

As mentioned earlier, descriptors such as good, desirable, or convenient are in the eyes of the beholder. So managers usually cannot be concerned about the proximity of the organization to the home of any one individual. In some respects, that is also true of the safety of the location. Many companies have specific location needs, such as near a railway or a dock, near a supply source such as a forest or mining area, or in an area zoned for their type of manufacturing business; and these areas are often in the more blighted areas of a city or in a rural area far from neighborhoods with desired amenities. Depending on the nature of the job, management may be able to allow some flexibility that will partially compensate. For instance, a flexible shift schedule can enable workers to drive during lighter traffic or during daylight hours. A 10-hour/4-day schedule can also reduce total commute time significantly. They may also be able to facilitate car pools, which makes a drive less costly, less lonely, and somewhat safer since the worker is not alone.

Long Hours or Overtime

Some managers choose to schedule employees for overtime work rather than hire additional employees. Paying for overtime work can be more cost-effective in the short run because it avoids paying fringe benefits. And some employees like a job that allows them to earn extra money by working more hours, regularly or overtime.

Managers need to understand, however, that there can be a considerable downside to overwork, from mental-health problems to physical ailments and job injuries caused by fatigue and stress. Long hours can have a negative impact on both the employee and the employee's family. The health risks associated with working long hours are predominantly the result of the great amount of stress placed on employees who work long hours. Stress is likely to cause sleep deprivation, which in turn can lead to weakened immune systems. Then contagious viruses and colds are more likely to spread among employees and also taken home to families. The last thing that an employer wants is for employees to become ill and request time off from work, but that does not stop some companies from requesting or requiring their employees to work long hours on a sustained basis. So employers or employees who put their health at risk are putting not only themselves in danger but also those around them. Mandatory overtime, then, can be extremely costly as a result of stress- and fatigue-related problems. This is another important reason why managers need to consider carefully and explore alternatives to keeping workers on the job for long hours.

One more vital issue needs to be mentioned here: giving an hourly worker a job title that fraudulently classifies them as "management" or "independent contractors" in order to release the company from overtime, fringes, or potential unionization. Those actions are coming under increased scrutiny and should be done with great care as they may be illegal and certainly can create ill will among employees, particularly when they find that they are working more hours without an equivalent raise in pay.

Duties Not Wanted or Expected

Some jobs are unfairly labeled as bad because an employee accepted the job without a clear understanding as to the job duties or requirements. In some cases, the problem could have been avoided if the individual had researched or asked more questions during the hiring process. In other cases, a realistic job preview may not have been furnished. After the fact, the only alternative is to inform workers what you and the organization expect, and then let them decide whether to stay, request another job, or resign. This assumes, of course, that the job duties are standard and equitable, not discriminatory in any way. Finally, it assumes that the duties have not been changed substantially from the duties that were described when the worker was hired or given performance feedback, unless the worker (and the union, if appropriate) has agreed to the change. Both management and human relations may need to discuss the duties with the concerned employee. If the duties have been changed, the job should be reviewed officially to determine whether it should be redesigned and whether the remuneration should be changed. Management should clarify the job duties for all prospective employees. And, of course, before any such changes are made, employees should be consulted and informed.

Task and Job Redesign

One type of change that could and frequently should be made involves redesigning the job. Once the broader issues are resolved and the decision is made to implement a job redesign, several approaches are available. Sensitivity training and Management by Objectives (and Self-Control) frequently have been used to bring about change in organizations. Changing jobs, on the other hand, has involved job enlargement and job enrichment, neither of which has demonstrated long-term success. Task or job redesign has been used with more success.

Task redesign seems to be one of the best approaches to changing jobs so as to make them more productive and more acceptable to job holders. Task redesign involves combining tasks, forming natural work units, vertically loading the job (e.g., providing more control or decision-making to the jobholder), and/or opening feedback channels. Using these techniques increases the skill variety needed on the job, the identification of the tasks, the importance of the tasks to the organization and/or society, the autonomy or self-control of the jobholders, and the feedback to the jobholders. These lead, in turn, to greater fulfillment and responsibility by jobholders. In addition, the jobholders develop a better knowledge of how well or how poorly they are performing on the job. Ultimately, job holders should then become more satisfied with their jobs and more motivated to perform well.

Sometimes a bad job needs to be redesigned, thus allowing management to minimize the bad characteristics or justify pay increases to offset them. Redesigning should always start with the recognition that such a redesign will benefit not just the worker but also the organization. For example, productivity may increase; or turnover, absenteeism, or complaints may decrease. The health or well-being of jobholders may improve. In any event, you and other managers must recognize that the job redesign will benefit both the managers and the organization. Otherwise, you will not buy into whatever is necessary to redesign the job. On the other hand, redesigning a job will not correct broader problems such as a poor organizational environment or improper applications of technology. Those sorts of issues need to be corrected before tackling any redesign efforts.

If redesigning a job is not possible, eliminating it can be considered. Automation or outsourcing, for example, could eliminate especially boring jobs. On the other hand, if neither redesign nor elimination is possible or feasible, efforts should be made to offset the bad characteristics in some way—higher pay, more released time with pay, greater promotional opportunities, some form of rotating tasks, or something else to make up for at least some of the bad characteristics.

JOB SAFETY ISSUES

Some jobs are "bad" because of safety issues. They may be inherently unsafe as they involve tasks that are or can be dangerous. Public safety, nursing, hospitals, certain types of manufacturing and construction, crop and animal production, and mining come quickly to mind. Yet the U.S. Government, through OSHA, requires that companies provide for safety on the job. Organizations and their managers are responsible for learning and implementing the regulations and safety rules that OSHA has developed. Individual managers must strictly adhere to OSHA's demands but often can do little else to make the jobs better for the workers. Other jobs, however, may be made safe or safer by conscientious attention to the problems.

Even in jobs that are not inherently unsafe, managers must listen and report problems to the appropriate organizational officials when employees complain about perceived safety issues or that a job is too physically demanding. First of all, management should respect its workers enough to be concerned for their safety. Yet we know that this is often not the case. Second, OSHA safety rules absolutely must be followed, lest the organization face various penalties from the U.S. Department of Labor. Third, complaints about jobs that are said to be too physically demanding may result in future claims against the organization. The manager could request HR to question workers about their health—whether their complaints are the result of a change in health (e.g., a hernia, diabetes, high blood pressure)—and should offer to assign them to other jobs for which they are qualified. It may also be appropriate for managers to request that workers schedule medical release examinations before being allowed to return to the job. If the job itself (not the person) is the problem, it should be analyzed and changed as necessary.

Unsafe Facilities

Managers have full responsibility, of course, to report to the appropriate personnel any reported safety "problems" related to location. Management should perform, or preferably hire an outside consultant to perform, a worksite analysis to determine if there are things that could be done to make the location safer or make the employees feel safer. This "threat assessment team" should consist of representatives from senior management, HR, security, occupational safety, legal, and human resources or employee assistance. These same individuals or others should then use the findings to develop engineering controls, work practices, and administrative procedures and adaptations to remove or reduce the safety risks. The possibilities are many:

- New construction or physical changes, such as enclosed work stations, deep service counters, and bullet-resistant glass in reception and cash-handling areas
- Improved lighting and heat-AC control
- Alarm systems and other security devices (panic buttons, hand-held alarms or noise devices)
- Controlled access to facilities
- An updated list of "restricted visitors" at security checkpoints and visitor sign-in areas
- A sign-in procedure with passes for visitors and enforced visiting hours
- Cellular phones and private channel radios, especially for field employees
- Metal detectors
- Closed-circuit video recorders for high-risk areas on a 24-hour basis
- Curved mirrors at hallway intersections or concealed areas
- Employee "safe rooms" for use during emergencies
- Comfortable client/patient waiting rooms designed to minimize stress
- Two exits for some rooms
- Lockable doors (consider automatic locking exterior doors also)

- Signs that state clearly that violence is not permitted or tolerated
- Liaison with local police and state prosecutors, including providing physical layouts of facilities to law enforcement
- Evacuation plans
- A requirement that employees report all assaults or threats to a manager
- Properly trained and equipped security officers and written security procedures
- Measures to decrease waiting time for outsider visitors
- A policy that prohibits employees from working alone, particularly before or after regular work hours when assistance is unavailable
- Parking areas that are highly visible, well lit, and safely accessible to the building
- Security escorts for personnel to parking areas in evening or late hours
- Use of the "buddy system" when appropriate
- A daily work plan for field staff to keep a designated contact person informed about their whereabouts throughout the workday

The Occupational Safety and Health Administration of the U.S. Department of Labor has several publications that help organizations address safety problems. Included are the following, obtainable through https://www.osha.gov/pls/publications/publication.html

- *Workplace Violence: Guidelines for Preventing Workplace Violence for Health Care and Social Service Workers* (OSHA 3148 - 2004).
- *Workplace Violence: Preventing Violence against Taxi and For-Hire Drivers Fact Sheet* (2010).
- *Workplace Violence: Recommendations for Workplace Violence Prevention Programs in Late-Nite Retail Establishments (OSHA 3153 - 2009).*

Workplace Violence

A special safety area concerns the topic of this book—workplace violence. Managers today must be alert to signs of potential workplace violence that could place many workers at risk. Organizations and their employees must be concerned not only with violence involving insiders but also with domestic partner vs. worker and criminal outsider vs. worker. Indeed, worker vs. criminal outsider and worker vs. domestic partner account for most of the workplace violence and deaths. Several books, including those by the authors of this book, are available in libraries and bookstores on the prevention of workplace violence. Thus, in this book we will cover only a few major points, such as identifying signs or behaviors of potentially violent individuals.

Because we can almost never predict violence accurately, people need to be trained how to react to violent actions. Until recently, workers who were trapped by a violent person were trained to crawl under their desks or behind other equipment and pray that the police would arrive in time to save them. Now, training sessions are conducted by trained police officers and include fake weapons and videos that focus on running, hiding, and fighting, if necessary.

Employee vs. Employee

As indicated throughout this book, some organizations seem more prone than others to experiencing workplace violence. Management should check its own behavior to see if perhaps it is operating on a punishment-based system, which sometimes leads to violent behavior in workers, rather than a reward-based system. For employees who are already upset over matters at work or outside work, criticism or punishment may be all that is needed to push them over the edge. Instead, reward workers when they do something right or good—anything for which you can even provide a pat on the back or a happy-sounding "atta boy." At the very least, you must be cautious about how you approach or reprimand an employee who is overstressed or cannot take criticism.

Managers should also familiarize themselves with other signs or behaviors that suggest that a worker could potentially commit an act of workplace violence. Pay attention to workers' behaviors and interactions to determine if an individual appears to be having personal problems, is being harassed, or is having difficulty getting along with others. Consider this list of possible indicators:

- Has attendance problems
- Expresses disgruntled complaints
- Seems to have concentration problems
- Has inconsistent work habits
- Engages in malicious gossip, rumors
- Requires much supervision
- Was caught destroying or stealing company property
- Has threatened others

- Has had a decline in productivity or performance
- Has uncontrollable temper and emotional outbursts
- Has recently changed behavior or personal appearance at work
- Blames others for problems at work
- Shows indications of substance abuse
- Seems to be increasingly anxious/nervous
- Was recently disciplined and seems resentful about it
- Makes coworkers uncomfortable by expressing extremist views
- Makes coworkers uncomfortable by fascination with guns/weapons

While none of these in and of themselves would be a strong indicator of potential violence, the presence of several of them for the same individual would clearly merit precaution. In particular, you should give careful consideration also to the manner in which a worker is terminated or fired, as the psychological impact of such an action may put a person "over the edge," causing him or her to seemingly snap (see Chapter 3).

Significant Other vs. Employee

One particular form of workplace violence is often overlooked, neglected, or ignored because it involves relationships from outside the organization. Domestic violence impacts the workplace both directly and indirectly. Indirectly because an abused employee and her or his coworkers are distracted and may not be as productive as usual and, of course, they may have more claims against the organizations' healthcare system. Directly because organizational resources may be used in domestic disputes, attendance may drop as abusers hide car keys or engage in other actions to prevent the victim from working, or work may be interrupted by phone calls or personal contacts from an abuser.

Why would an organization ignore domestic violence? It endangers an important asset—their human resources. But they don't want to interfere in nonwork issues; they want to protect individual privacy; and they may be unsure what they can do. There also is the question of how much the organization can get involved in the private lives of their workers. Nevertheless, organizations need to protect their employees as well as providing support and assistance for victims. Managers and employees need to be trained to look for signs (see above) that trouble is brewing in another employee's personal life that may carry over to the worksite.

Internal Terrorists

Another form of workplace violence to which managers should be alert is internal terrorism. Terrorists are individuals or groups who attempt to achieve their goals by creating fear. Internal terrorists are people *inside* the organization who create fear as a means of getting whatever they want. These individuals are not necessarily bullies. They may appear, in fact, to be passive and detached while they plot behind the scenes to recruit another person to speak or act and take the potential blame for them. By identifying potentially destructive individuals, you may have some opportunity to forestall the act and help that individual solve his problems. These undesirable employees may be your subordinates, or they may be others in the organization who are targeting your subordinates. Books are available to help individuals identify potential internal terrorists; for example, employees who appear to be overly stressed, angry because they were passed over for promotion, overly unhappy with their own performance, or carrying a heavy resentment toward the organization.

Other Violence

There are numerous other forms of violence in organizations of which you as a manager need to be aware. As indicated in Chapter 5, bullying, especially by managers, must not be tolerated. Harassment, especially based on gender or gender preference, also must not be tolerated. These behaviors will become commonplace when they are accepted as commonplace, and the perpetrators know they will not be held accountable. Organizations need a culture of openness to encourage the active reporting of such acts. Antisnitching needs to be replaced with a "see it or experience it, report it" culture. This requires that the organization establish clear reporting lines—when, how, and to whom they should report—for its people to send their feedback confidentially.

ORGANIZATIONAL CULTURE/CLIMATE

Bad managers and nonmanagers have been discussed earlier in the book, yet when we gathered anecdotes about bad workplaces and jobs, they recurred. So considering what might be done about them in the context of bad workplaces and jobs is also important when weighing the impact and any possible changes to the organizational culture. Solving a bad job dilemma is more difficult for you, the manager, when the problem results from the organizational culture or climate. Advising how to change the culture of the organization is a topic beyond the scope of this book, but an organization's culture or climate influences and is influenced by its members.

Because the organization's culture stems from the top, is slow in developing, and equally slow in changing, there may be little that any individual manager can do. However, the first thing is to try to identify and analyze the cultural/climate characteristic that is affecting your workers' perceptions of their jobs. It may be that you can change some aspects of the culture at your level to alleviate the negative reaction to it. This may be particularly the case if you are perceived as contributing to a threatening environment or displaying a judgmental attitude. You may need to have a few "let's let our hair down" meetings to clear the air and eliminate misconceptions to deal with these problems. On the other hand, you should also look in the mirror—are you, in fact, the problem? Have you created or contributed to a threatening environment, or do you maintain a judgmental attitude? Managers should be able to look at the anecdotes reported in previous chapters and then analyze themselves as well as their own organizations. Most likely you will not perceive these negative features in yourself, so you will need to ask others to give you an honest evaluation. They should correct any personal deficiencies in their own behavior and recommend that top management adopt an attitude of no tolerance of supervisors who are dishonest, unethical, or threatening.

In some organizations, the problem may be rather easy to resolve or change (e.g., the way employees are recruited or trained), or it may require a major cultural adjustment like firing a top executive or a manager who is unbending on items that need to be modified, or putting in place the controls to prevent something like padding of expense accounts. Either way, when the organizational culture is the culprit, improving the characteristics that make a job bad will be more difficult than most other fixes as it involves changes that will affect and require the support of upper management.

Avoid Negligent Hiring and Retention

As discussed earlier in Chapter 5, organizations are obligated morally, ethically, and legally to hire and retain employees who will not present a danger to other employees. The organization should (really must) have written policies prohibiting violence and discrimination to guide its hiring practices. Many companies remove or reduce their negligence risk by hiring an outside background screening firm to reduce the risk of hiring a potentially violent employee.

The doctrine of negligent hiring provides that the employer may be held directly liable for negligence and breach of duty when an employee is injured as a result of the violent behavior of another employee. Negligent hiring may include, for example, failure to properly screen an applicant and thus overlooking his or her propensity for violence that created a risk of harm to other employees and managers.

Similarly, the doctrine of negligent retention applies after an employee is hired. The employer may be held directly liable for negligence and breach of duty when the employer does not take proper steps to alleviate the problem after becoming aware of (or after he reasonably should have become aware of) unsuitable behavior for the workplace, particularly behavior that poses a threat or shows a propensity for violence.

Retrain Incompetent Managers

Managers may be viewed as incompetent because they are doing or have done things that suggest a lack of competence or because either the managers or the workers lack a clear understanding of the nature of managerial or supervisory work. Truly incompetent managers cost their organizations in terms of quality, productivity, turnover, and morale, just to name some of the costs. These managers need to be trained or retrained, and they should be more carefully monitored by their superiors until their performance is judged to be acceptable. If training doesn't work, they should be relocated to jobs in which they will be competent; but if that, too, fails, they should be helped to secure employment elsewhere.

On the other hand, if the issue is perceived as incompetence because employees don't understand the job of managers, training/education for the employees can be beneficial at several levels. Employees develop a better understanding of not only what managers do but also what the organization is all about. They can get a feeling for whether they want to consider trying to move into management. And they may develop a more tolerant attitude for the varied and complex nature of the work and the coordination required to achieve it in the organization.

Train to Avoid Micromanagers

Managers who micromanage need someone to work with them, preferably on a daily basis, to help them develop a different outlook about work and their workers. They must be taught how to let go of a project and still maintain control. They have to learn to trust the workers under their control so that they do not insult them and so that they can perform their jobs. If the micromanaging managers wish to specify procedures, they should do so at that time and then let the employee proceed with the project. After that, they simply let go, telling the worker to check in with them if there is a problem or maybe to check in with them at particular points. Until they learn to fully trust the worker, the manager may want to ask occasionally, "How's it going? Any problems? Are we still on time?" In other words, the micromanager must learn that when assigning a project they can go over the details of the project with that person, ask how the worker plans to proceed, make suggestions if they wish, ask the person to check in with them occasionally, and then let go. Sometimes this change in attitude and behavior requires one small step at a time. Since micromanaging is caused by something more than mere habit, more than mere talk from higher level managers may be needed to change the style. Micromanaging managers may find that changing their management style will be a long, slow process at best.

Don't Tolerate Abusive Managers

No manager has a right to abuse those under his or her supervision. Clearly the organization has a responsibility to protect workers from the verbal abuse that can make for a bad job. Thus, managers must know that verbal or physical abuse will not be tolerated. And if such behavior is observed by other managers, they must call it to the attention of the appropriate person, who will suggest the proper behavior. The abusive manager may need to attend behavior modification classes; or in cases where the manager is not responsive, he should be relieved of his duties rather than allowed to upset workers or clients and interfere with productivity. If the abusive manager does not alter his behavior, the observing manager has a responsibility to report the behavior to HR or higher-level management as the organization's procedures dictate. Most employees will leave rather than attempt to change their managers, as they are aware that the odds are not in their favor. The abused who stay and the other workers who have observed a manager's abusive behavior will not respect the abusive manager, and this will adversely affect the work environment and most likely the productivity. In addition, it may cost the company future legal problems and bad publicity, which can in turn affect such important matters as sales volume and hiring opportunities.

Don't Tolerate Bothersome Workers

Good jobs can become bad jobs when coworkers have or develop unacceptable characteristics or behaviors. They may be lazy, jealous, or bitter. They may try to manipulate one another or managers. They may be incompatible, inconsiderate, practice unsafe work habits, or not be trained properly to handle dangerous situations. The best solution for you, the manager, is to hire properly in the first place, but conditions and people can change, so you need to pay attention to what is happening.

In situations where jobs are made bad by unpleasant interactions between coworkers, the problem may be relatively easy for the manager to resolve through employee seminars, sensitivity training, the use of mentors, and rewards for proper behavior, such as recognition in the form of "Employee of the Month." These approaches may help where coworkers are inconsiderate because they don't know how to dress or behave properly at work, or they fail to shift into the workday mode of dress and behavior. The same approaches may even be helpful in dealing with jealousy or envy issues or workers who are manipulative. Training may well be the answer for workers who are really unqualified for their jobs, too. Rather than sensitivity training, however, it would be job knowledge and skills training.

On the other hand, some employees may unwittingly present a problem by doing what they think is being considerate and conscientious but, instead, causing others to label them the opposite. For example, they come to work when they are ill so they do not shirk their responsibilities, but instead they expose others to their germs or viruses and fall short of performing their full workload. To prevent your employees from coming to work ill, you could request the Human Resources department to send an organizationwide reminder when a public health problem is eminent (e.g., flu, chickenpox, and measles). For new employees, the organization can address all of the "bad worker" characteristics during orientation, or through a printed handout from HR, so that workers know the organization's attitude toward reporting to work when ill. Young parents, in particular, may come to work when ill so they can take their official "sick days" when their children are sick at home.

The company is in no position to monitor a worker's health at home, and it has limited power to prevent workers from coming to work ill in order to save their "sick days" for future illnesses and more vacation days. If fringe benefits are negotiated by union representatives, you and the organization may have even less power. Some organizations are now combining "vacation" days and "sick" days into Personal Leave Time (PLT), but that still may not encourage the worker to stay home when ill. We know of organizations that send a companywide memo that forewarns employees that their immediate supervisor has the power to send them home if they come to work with what appears to be a contagious illness. That policy seems to have the greatest effect in keeping sick workers away from the office since the workers feel that they will be sent home anyway if they try to go to work.

Sometimes workers make a job unsafe, or more unsafe, because they are impaired by drugs, alcohol, or medications. While this applies mostly to jobs that involve the operation of machinery, it would also be true of, say, impaired sales representatives and workers who drive company vehicles, handle money, and work on night shifts. Management needs to maintain a tough organizational policy regarding drugs and alcohol, including both prehiring tests and random on-the-job drug tests of all employees. Some public school districts are installing ignition interlock devices (IID) in school buses to prevent alcohol-impaired drivers from operating a bus. Hopefully, your organization also will have policies in place for dealing with the rehabilitation of employees. Rehabilitating employees may well be more economical than having to recruit, select, hire, and train replacements. Typically, larger organizations have EAPs (Employee Assistance Programs) for dealing with just these sorts of issues.

In still other cases, jobs can be undesirable because workers are not trained properly. As mentioned previously, installing bullet-proof glass and training employees to give robbers whatever they want rather than trying to fight back may potentially save lives, even if it doesn't make the worker less likely to be confronted by a robber. In jobs involving potentially unsafe machinery or workplace design, one of your duties as a manager is to see that workers follow instructions from the equipment manufacturers and from OSHA.

OUTSIDE ISSUES

Not all workplace issues come from inside the organization; some come from outside. While you as a manager may initially think that there is little you can do about outside issues, there are certain actions and preventives that can be taken.

Teaching employees to give robbers whatever they want rather than trying to fight back is one solution that can save lives. However, some criminals "shoot first and ask questions later" so that the employee becomes a statistic just waiting to be counted from the moment that criminal walks through the door. To discourage criminals and to help the workers if a criminal does appear at the worksite, managers must persuade upper management to provide whatever types of preventive protection they can find, including both obvious and hidden camera surveillance, on-site guards if warranted, hidden alarm buttons, and a policy of not allowing employees to work alone. Another good safety measure is asking the local police or hiring a private security company to be present at closing time.

Vulnerable Workplaces

Some workplaces and jobs are inherently vulnerable to violence. Many in this classification are targets for criminals rather than sites where employees may engage in violent behavior. Jobs like convenience stores and service stations that involve handling cash and working late hours are especially attractive to criminals. Workplaces in health care where drugs are stored or sold, especially pharmacies, are obvious targets for those wishing to gain illegal access to those drugs. There are also organizations that because of their day-to-day activities are more vulnerable to violent attacks by outsiders. Organizations perceived as damaging the environment, X-rated movie theaters, bars, abortion clinics, law enforcement agencies, and organizations owned or operated by foreign governments or just "foreigners" are some of the more obvious ones. All of these are targets for acts of political terrorism.

Outsider vs. Employee

In a tight economy, incidents from all categories of workplace violence are likely to increase, but particularly those involving criminals. Typically, the most frequent form of workplace violence involves members of the organization; however, in those jobs involving frequent contact with outsiders, workplace violence may well involve those individuals. Jobs involving direct public contact along with available cash or items of high value have an increased risk of criminals engaged in robbery. Organizations that deal with large client populations such as hospitals, schools, and universities have an increased risk of violence from outsiders as well. As noted earlier in the chapter, there are numerous physical and safety actions that can be taken to reduce these risks.

Disliked Organizations

Potential acts of political terrorism are something that most managers can do little or nothing about as such individuals are not likely to be employed by the organization. Like all other Americans at work or elsewhere, though, managers can be alert to such things as unfamiliar workers without adequate identfication, unusual dress such as wearing a coat in hot weather, packages or briefcases left unattended anywhere, unsecured doors, behaviors of their own workers that might suggest they are not loyal to the United States, and so on. If an organization is particularly vulnerable to political terrorists, employees can theoretically avoid the problem by seeking employment in a less vulnerable organization. One of the fallacies of that approach is that, while your organization may not be the target of political terrorists, it can be subject to collateral damage if it occupies space near a vulnerable organization or is considered by terrorists to be associated in some way. Innocent workers at a hair salon or insurance company, for example, could be exposed to violent acts because they share a building in a strip mall with, say, an abortion clinic or Planned Parenthood office. Furthermore, in countries that experience suicide bombers, car bombs, and the like, no type of organization is safe.

Difficult Contacts

Jobs that are made bad by outsiders (customers, clients, suppliers, contractors) with whom the workers must deal can be difficult to change, depending on the attitude of your own workers. In most cases, you have little or no control over individuals outside your organization, so little or nothing can be done directly about the behavior of those individuals. The solution lies in having your workers treat outside contacts respectfully and avoid antagonizing them and preventing abusive or negative persons from hurting your own workers or the organization's bottom line. The organization cannot allow outside individuals, including customers, to harass its own employees.

The best place to start is hiring the right workers for jobs that involve dealing with outside contacts. Those workers should be mature enough and have enough self-confidence to interact with the bad outside contacts. They can be given additional training to learn how to handle abusive contacts so as to minimize their own stress and hopefully prevent agitating the contact person. Also, if an employee is having difficulty with an outside contact, consider having a different employee serve as your point person with that troublesome contact. Maybe the outside contact will, for whatever the reason, respond differently to the new person.

If an outside contact exhibits behavior that absolutely cannot be condoned, you may wish to communicate with the outside person yourself to determine what the problem is. Also, consider whether your organization's relationship with the customer or supplier is such that the problem could be resolved by a talk with the bad contact's superiors. When all else fails, you may need to request that your organization sever ties with the contact organization.

WHAT NEXT?

This chapter has suggested actions that you as a manager might take to reduce the incidence of bad workplaces or bad jobs in your organization. However, nonmanagers themselves can also act to reduce these. That is the subject of Chapter 10.

BAD JOBS/WORKPLACES

What Nonmanagers Can Do

To cure the violence, we must identify and heal the causes of hatred and violence. If we don't deal with the causes we will never be safe.

—Peter Yarrow

In an earlier chapter, we presented characteristics that workers say cause a workplace or job to be bad in their view. We noted that workers differ in their perceptions of what is desirable and undesirable. What is considered undesirable to one person may be tolerable to another person who perceives wages/salary, location, and job duties as more important than, say, the physical environment. But all of us can perhaps agree that no workplace and no job is perfect. So when an individual feels that he is in a bad work situation, the first question to answer is, "How bad is it?" To decide whether conditions in these situations are really bad enough to justify leaving the job or taking some other action, the worker should determine his own priorities regarding the characteristics of a workplace or a job. The following discussion contains some suggestions as to what nonmanager employees may do to improve a job situation—or to recognize that sufficient change is not likely to happen.

First, though, a word of caution. It's always easier to find a job while you already have a job. So if you think you want to move on, don't "jump ship"

Violence at Work: What Everyone Should Know, pp. 225–244

while you are looking for a better job—or as the saying goes, "Don't quit your day job." Instead, focus on the near term—getting through each day, one day at a time.

PERSONAL FACTORS

Workers realize that a body mechanic (physician) is paid more than an auto mechanic, but often they do not internalize that various similar jobs within society or within the organization vary not only according to the training and experience required but also to supply and demand and even the stress level of the job. Some workers seem not to recognize that advancement opportunity may not be related to their abilities but rather to the absence or scarcity of jobs to move into, because perhaps the higher-level jobs have low turnover or the lower-level job is a "dead-end" job.

Frequently, the problem is a lack of career planning—workers choose a job because they are skilled in that area or enjoy doing that kind of work, not realizing that improving or even mastering the job will not prepare them for another job without additional training or education. Sometimes, then, a Human Resources unit in the organization needs to give this type of information to the worker and, depending on the individual's education and abilities, suggest that he or she go back to college or trade school to prepare for a higher-paying job. Companies that support continuing education through tuition reimbursement or pay increases for course credits are less likely to have their workers complain about bad jobs for these reasons, as the worker can continue to earn a living while training for a career move.

Low Pay, Low Status

You may also have heard individuals say something similar to this: "I thought I had a pretty good job until I found out that (name of person) makes $500 more per month than I do." Or "I felt okay working here until (name of coworker) got promoted. I should have been the one who got promoted, as I have been here longer and know the job better than he does." In other words, "low" is a relative term—my salary compared to someone else's, someone else's promotion when I was passed over. You may have had nothing to complain about before since you had not known you were being paid unfairly low or that someone was getting promoted. Now, though, is when you need to go back and look at your job evaluations for clues. If you feel strongly that you are being underpaid or passed over unfairly, you can ask for a meeting with your supervisor and/or with your organization's

Human Resources unit, depending on your organization's rules for such things. How you approach the supervisor, though, is key to the results you can expect—or the surprises you may not want to expect. We agree that it is unprofessional to pay individuals according to their bargaining ability during the interview rather than according to the work they are hired to perform, but there is little you can do other than leave the organization if your appeal is not successful. Organizations without a defensible wage-and-salary system are not likely to care deeply about your feelings if they can continue hiring individuals below an equitable wage scale.

As with low pay and lack of advancement opportunities, low status is also relative to other people's jobs. Nurses know that they have less status than the doctors whom they assist. That is a function of the difference in training and in the public's view of the two different jobs. As a nurse, then, there is little or nothing you can do to give your job the higher status that a physician enjoys. Such status is a function of the career you have chosen. So to obtain the job status of a physician, the nurse would need to go to medical school and get an MD, DO, or other degree. If the LPN wants the status of the RN with whom she works, she will need to go back to school and get her RN degree. If the sales clerk wants the status of a nurse, she would need to go to nursing school and get her RN degree. The same type of career movement would apply to workers and supervisors in other jobs.

Since status pertains to your standing relative to another person or persons, it is also a function of the job you are in currently. Maybe you don't need additional training or a new career. Perhaps you can achieve the higher status you desire and still continue on the same career path if only you can get a promotion. Winning an award for your work may boost your status among your coworkers, too, but probably not to people outside that circle. So you will need to find out the requirements for a promotion and whether such an advancement is probable. Talking to your supervisor about how you can improve your performance could be helpful if your supervisor is a secure individual who seems to want his workers to succeed. However, some supervisors feel that their jobs are threatened by workers who appear to be go-getters. Other options would be to seek a transfer or look for a job in another organization. Your supervisor could be of help in either of these two options; on the other hand, they might regard you as a disloyal worker and then treat you in such a manner that you would feel it impossible to stay.

Stress

Stress is one of the big triggers for workplace violence. The workplace environment may be uncomfortable, thus causing you stress. You may find the physical demands of the job to be stressful. Or you may feel that your manager or the organization is making unreasonable demands on your time, energy, or skills. Regardless of the source of your stress, the first thing you should do is to clarify the situation—make sure that you understand all that is expected of you. Perhaps your information or your perception of what is required is not accurate; you may be trying to give far more than what is expected. Perhaps you are not really compatible for this job. Try to understand what your manager or the organization really wants and why, and then see if you can come up with different ways in which that might be accomplished. Go over your ideas with your manager to see if a less stressful alternative can be used.

You can always try giving your manager nonjudgmental feedback about the job. If you don't share the problems with your manager, it will only frustrate you and the problems will not get solved. Problems with coworkers can be particularly trying, and your manager might be able to help resolve them if he or she knows about them. Perhaps the manager can change things just enough so that the job isn't completely bad anymore. In communicating with your manager, however, don't try to get everything changed (and certainly not at once). Pick one or two of the most significant or important aspects of the job that bother you and focus on them. Do not be a chronic complainer.

Try to prepare for different situations on and off the job. If you have to wait for supplies or to see the doctor, get something done. Either use the time to relax, to read something, or to take notes that you may need for another assignment. Use the time; don't lose it. This means being prepared—having a book with you or something upon which you can take notes. However, being prepared goes beyond this. If you are aware (through the grapevine, for instance) that something bad or stressful is "in the works," get ready for it. Think about what its consequences for you are likely to be. Think about your emotional response to the event. Think about what it will do to or mean to others. Then try to develop ways in which you can handle the event so that its impact will be lessened. Even something like doing the laundry or grocery shopping on the weekend before a stressful week of overtime can help reduce the "crunch" that will otherwise be unavoidable.

Start a period of exercise shortly before going to work. Do some stretches or go for a short walk. Or rather than exercise listen to some music that you like, play a game of solitaire, work on a crossword puzzle, just do something to relax a bit before going to work. You will arrive at work more relaxed and better able to cope with the stress of the job. Exercise can help you release tensions and anger. Set up a dartboard and put pictures of the organization on it. Then throw the darts as hard as you can for several minutes. Use a punching bag, shoot some baskets, or run around the block, anything to burn off some of the steam that you have built up while at work.

Closely related to relaxation are diet and sleep. Healthy individuals can handle more stress or handle it better than those who are not healthy. Avoid junk food. Eat a sensible diet. Search the Internet for help with diet, or ask your insurance company about covering an appointment with a dietician. Do what you can to keep healthy. Keeping healthy also involves getting enough sleep. Surviving a bad job is difficult enough, but trying to do so when you are sleepy or exhausted is virtually impossible.

PHYSICAL FACTORS

You can also make suggestions and try to convince management to improve the environment of some jobs. Whenever there are duties that you had not expected or that you don't want, you should talk to your supervisor to see if more satisfactory arrangements can be made. While some jobs can be changed, other jobs are "love it or leave it" jobs—they simply exist in a bad physical environment and not much can be done to improve those conditions. If an undesirable physical environment is simply inherent to the job, you can request a different assignment or leave that job. For example, you probably will have to accept the fact that a paint room will always have air fogged with sprayed paint, that most auto mechanic jobs will be dirty and greasy, and that coal mines will be cold, wet, dark, and filled with airborne coal dust. Nevertheless, from time to time you and other workers may have ideas for improving conditions even in these jobs. Management can be reasonably expected to provide acceptable filtering, proper clothing and other protective gear, and so on. Workers can make these suggestions to the appropriate management or union leaders. Of course, when conditions are unsafe, workers should report these conditions and follow up if necessary, including contacting OSHA (Occupational Safety and Health Administration).

Undesirable Location

Like a bad physical environment, a bad location is a function of the worker's priorities and viewpoint. Those who move to the countryside because they despise the city may not be happy in a job that requires them to drive much farther to work. Yet, a scientist at the National Institutes of Health in Bethesda, Maryland, is willing to commute 3 hours in order to raise his family in a more rural, less populated area. Likewise, a Wall Street broker accepts the long commute from a Connecticut suburb because it enables her to do what she wants to do and to be paid well for it. This would not necessarily be true of a public school teacher, nurse, or even an office manager, who could probably find a similar job with similar pay and similar prestige closer to home.

Again, you must determine what is best for you, considering the experience and skills that you have. Some employees have reduced their dissatisfaction by requesting and receiving permission to avoid driving during rush hours, telecommuting or working at home part of the time, or joining carpools that are organized or even operated by the company. Since we cannot expect the organization to move its location for us, the alternatives are clear: either dwell on the good things about the job and stay at that location, ask for a transfer if the organization has locations that are better for you, or find another job in a location that better matches your preferences.

Long Hours or Overtime

Because the U.S. Department of Labor regulates conditions such as work hours, for most workers, long hours mean overtime hours for which they are paid 1.5 times their regular hourly wage. Some workers like the long hours because of the extra money they earn; others need or prefer that extra time for other activities. Ideally, you should be able to decide if you will work overtime, but we know that some companies insist on regular overtime work and usually specify this in your contract or other papers issued by the organization. You may find this more frequently within organizations that have extensive dealing internationally or coast to coast because of time differences. If long hours are making your job intolerable, your choices are rather clear: try to reach an understanding with your supervisor or your organization's Human Resources unit about how many hours you can work, refuse overtime and risk being fired, apply for a different job at the same organization, or find a different job elsewhere. Unfortunately, in tight job markets, many workers will feel too insecure in their jobs to protest the long hours, and in any labor market, some supervisors are too intimidating to approach.

Many jobs that pay a monthly salary are exempt from overtime regulations. Managers, for example, may need to work 50–60 hours every week to perform their jobs, and their increased pay supposedly reflects these expectations. One option in many companies is to accrue what is called "comp time"—for every hour you work beyond the standard 40-hour week, you are allowed in the future one hour of paid time off to compensate for the hour already worked. Comp time is customary for salaried workers who are occasionally asked to stay overtime—often at the last minute—because of a rush job or a temporary surge in workload. Managers probably knew when they took their job that they would be working long hours, so they do not expect to have 20 hours of comp time every week. But they would feel free to take a day off or even a week off sometime when their workload permits them to do so. If you seek a position at this level, you will probably have no choice but to work the longer hours without extra pay—unless you can convince the right organization officials perhaps to hire additional personnel (maybe another assistant). At the time you are hired, the organization should tell you the level of overtime work to expect.

In some cases, these sudden overtimes are absolutely necessary and unpreventable, but often they are the result of poor planning by someone. In that case, try to determine how things could have been done differently to avoid the problem and then sit down with the supervisor and suggest these changes. Even if you have no suggestions, sometimes a calm, face-to-face talk with the supervisor will encourage him to analyze the problem and make changes to minimize the longer hours.

Unfortunately, there are some jobs that always require extraordinarily long hours and are not compensated as well as the managerial jobs we mentioned earlier. The movie industry, for example, often plays by its own rules. These organizations must maximize the usage of expensive equipment during its rental period and the long preparation time (for setups and makeup). They don't stop shooting after 8 hours, for example, after actors, makeup artists, and prop workers have spent hours in preparation and on location, plus several additional hours applying and removing makeup. They don't turn off expensive editing equipment and close the doors at 5:00 when they have a tight deadline to meet or are renting the equipment for hundreds or thousands of dollars per day. Some personnel—for example, actors and actresses, the director, cinematographer, editor—know they will work very long hours during a "shoot," but they negotiate a salary that compensates for that short-term sacrifice. Low-level personnel work the same or even longer hours at minimum wage without overtime—and even for no pay, as in the case of some production assistants, for example. In those lower-level jobs where personnel are not scarce, you can ask for a little more money but your odds of success are quite low. Mostly, it's a "take it or leave it" situation. Does the opportunity outweigh all the other factors such as long hours and bad pay? If not, maybe it is time to move on.

Still, telling management that we don't want to stay late or work overtime can be a difficult decision. Will that preference be respected, or will management interpret it as unprofessional or a lack of commitment? Will the desire not to work long hours or overtime be used consciously or unconsciously as the basis of discriminating against you for future assignments, pay raises, or promotions?

SAFETY ISSUES

High-Injury Occupations

First, every worker should become familiar with the protection they have through the U.S. Department of Labor, especially OSHA (Occupational Safety and Health Administration). If you think your workplace may not be safe, you can first speak with your supervisor or your union leader. But you may need to contact OSHA first if you do not have a union leader or if you have any reason whatsoever to think that the organization is already aware of this condition but has chosen not to correct it.

If having a relatively safe job is important to you, take time to research the statistics on work safety. You will need to consider carefully the source of that information. The National Safety Council, the Occupational Safety and Health Administration, and industry safety associations have been quite successful in improving workplace safety through a variety of approaches, including establishing safety rules, advising companies, inspecting premises, and assessing penalties for violations of safety rules or conditions. These organizations try to arrive at comparable data on safety so that managers and workers (current or prospective) can be reasonably informed. So as long as you are careful as to sources and do not regard any source as absolutely correct, you should be able to make reasonable comparisons.

Workplace Violence

OSHA's concerns are primarily with the safety of the physical environment, but workers today need to be alert also to signs of other safety issues such as potential workplace violence and acts of workplace terrorism (intentional—not accidental—acts of person-to-person violence). You should pay attention to your coworkers' behaviors and interactions to determine if someone seems to be having personal problems, is being harassed or bullied, or is having difficulty getting along with others. Pay particular attention to abrupt changes in behavior, attitudes, or appearance.

Some behaviors, like refusing to cooperate with supervisors or arguing with coworkers, may not seem so bad unless they are repeated or are extremely intensive. On the other hand, spreading rumors and gossip, telling lies, being belligerent toward customers/clients, swearing, or making sexual comments are always inappropriate and may be early warning signs of problems that could lead to violence. More severe signs may include stealing property or sabotaging equipment to "get even" with the organization for perceived injustices. Telling a coworker or manager that they "will get theirs" or some other form of threat would also be a strong warning sign. You must immediately report to management if an individual frequently erupts in rages, especially if this leads to threats, physical fights, destruction of property, or criminal acts such as the use of weapons or rape or arson.

Bullying and Harassment

As noted in the previous chapter, bullying and harassment absolutely must not be tolerated. Bullying and harassment were discussed in more detail in Chapter 5, but occur so frequently that repetition here is worthwhile. If you experience these or other issues, such as someone sending anonymous memos about you to others in the organization, you need to report the problem immediately. Of course you must be careful not to accuse someone without good evidence as that could result only in even more problems for you.

Bullying and harassment constitute a hostile work environment, which is illegal and therefore subjects the organization as well as individuals to legal action. It is therefore absolutely essential that management develop a zero-tolerance policy, distribute it to all employees, and post it appropriately on company premises. Generally, the company will include a copy of such important policies in the packet of newly hired employees and, preferably, require each employee to sign a statement that they have read and understand the policy. But such a policy will not be effective unless clear reporting lines are established and emphasized and the policy is enforced. All employees need training and periodic retraining on what constitutes bullying and harassing and on the warning signs for workplace violence. They need to understand that, when they observe or experience such aberrant behavior, they are expected to document and report it immediately through proper channels.

After documenting and reporting the incident, let management and Human Resources deal with the problem. The target of the bullying or harassment should continue to maintain self-confidence and refrain from retaliating or behaving in a way that might make matters worse. So that you are not caught off-guard, decide ahead of time how you will respond to the next incident. Don't argue, exchange negative words, or lash out—some bullies and harassers love that kind of reaction. Instead, be as pleasant and positive as possible while management works on the problem.

ORGANIZATIONAL CULTURE/CLIMATE

As we acknowledged in Chapter 8, sometimes the organization itself—not a manager, a coworker, or the job—is the cause of a poor job, especially a threatening environment. Keep in mind that the activities and behaviors at the top level, where the organizational culture or climate is determined, filter down to the lowest level of the organization. Supervisors and employees at lower levels see what they must do to keep their jobs, and they modify their own behavior accordingly.

Don't try to change things that are beyond your power to change, and don't expect your manager to change things that are beyond her or his power to change either. Nowhere does this apply more than when the problem is caused by the organizational culture or climate. But as noted in the previous chapter, an organization's culture or climate influences and is influenced by it members. So the context of bad workplaces and jobs involves consideration of your managers and coworkers.

Your Compatibility With the Culture/Climate

Before you place all the blame on your manager or higher management, take a look inward to see if perhaps your own personality and body language may potentially cause others to treat you differently from what you think is appropriate or fair. Perhaps you have heard or read that when many abused women leave their man, they gravitate toward the same type of personality the next time and the next time because the signals they send tend to attract that type of abusive person. Why? Could this also be true of you in regard to coworkers or managers? It is definitely worthwhile to take time out to assess your own appearance, personality, or habits to see if you may be sending signals that are different from what you have previously thought. Since self-examination is rather undependable for this type of analysis, you should probably ask a neutral person, perhaps someone in HR or at least someone who is not a close friend, if there is something about you that could be altered to make you less vulnerable.

For example, dressing to look more mature or more professional could be helpful for younger employees. Looking your manager in the eye rather than looking away is another possibility. Other factors could include changing the tone of your voice, decreasing your complaining, or participating more or participating less in workplace activities. If you have any indication or suspicion that you are in need of improvement to avoid such treatment as described above, search the Internet or ask a librarian for a self-help book that would give you ideas of what to look for in yourself, and what to do about it. Do not, however, automatically accept the blame for negative, judgmental treatment.

Incompetent, Insecure Managers

Understandingly, we resent managers or supervisors "overobserving" us and perhaps "cracking the whip" as though we are unmotivated workers or "slackers," or we are too stupid to perform the job. We dislike managers who act as though they never make mistakes and consider us stupid when we ask questions. We abhor managers who penalize us for being a moment late when they abuse their 40-hour week by leaving early, abusing breaks, and the like. Although some workers ignore or adapt to being treated in such ways, those who are offended and cannot adapt may have a difficult time if they choose to stay. Some will become overloaded with stress, adversely affecting their personality and eventually their health.

Workers often think that they would like their jobs if only they had a different manager. In those cases, it may seem like the problem could be solved if only the worker talked with the manager about changes that would make the job better. We think it is important for workers to understand that, when he goes up against his manager, the worker should always be prepared to lose—even if he or she is morally and legally right and the manager is morally or legally wrong. Many managers will react negatively to any criticisms, no matter how tactfully you try to present your ideas. Even if the worker ultimately "wins" the case, he or she must still be prepared to leave the job and perhaps sever ties with the organization. The worker most likely will be unable to function in the job under the same manager, and the organization is more prone to move workers than supervisors. In other words, you can win the battle but still lose the war.

Here are some ideas to help you if you do decide to approach your manager about his or her behaviors. Just as you should never be given bad news in front of others, so, too, you should not confront your manager in the presence of others. To the extent possible, try to phrase your communication in a manner that allows your manager not to have to take personal responsibility—"I'm not certain that I understand … ," "I need help understanding … ," or "I need to check that my information is correct about …" Remember that your goal is not to "win" or "put the manager down." Rather, it is to improve the situation, and that is most likely to be accomplished by cooperative endeavors rather than antagonistic ones.

Workers are rather helpless to change incompetent and insecure managers, but they should not have to work under abusive managers. However, unless the manager is believed to be immediately dangerous, the worker should first try to tell the manager in an unemotional tone that what he is doing is not appreciated. If that does not solve the problem, the manager should be told again that this behavior will not be tolerated. Before and after these conversations, the worker must keep a diary of what is happening, the date, time of day, and the names of anyone who may have witnessed the abuse, harassment, or conversations. Always keep the diary with you, just in case you may be unable to go back to your office to retrieve it. The Human Relations (HR) department should be told about the individual and the events. They will likely call the supervisor to their offices to inform him of his rights and the worker's rights. They may reprimand the supervisor immediately or inform him that he will be reprimanded if the behavior is repeated.

Supervisors can help make a bad job good, or a good job bad. However, the organization's culture will likely determine whether the manager or the worker will be given the benefit of the doubt when a worker complains. Theoretically, if the worker "wins," after the manager apologizes and changes the behavior, the manager and the worker could then have a comfortable relationship. However, almost any time a worker has a bad encounter with a superior, the worker will likely suffer consequences of some type. At the very least, the relationship between the two individuals will probably be awkward, not comfortable. It may be so tense that both individuals' performances are affected. The worker's performance may be criticized unfairly and unjustly. The worker may eventually be fired or made so miserable that he chooses to quit. Such workers likely will find themselves alienated from other workers because those workers do not want the manager to think they are friends of his "enemy." We have seen other workers brownnose the manager by siding with him even though they knew that the manager was the one who was wrong and was mistreating their fellow worker.

Dishonest or Unethical Management

If you find yourself working in an organization with dishonest or unethical management, your choices are few: either find another place to work or stay at the organization but keep your nose clean and watch your backside. You are usually safe to assume that individuals or companies that will deceive or defraud one person or in one type of transaction can be expected to do the same to another individual or in another type of activity. Nowhere is this more obvious than in small businesses, where workers have more opportunity to observe the behavior of top management.

Don't try to change the members of management—you cannot—but do avoid being made a part of anything dishonest or unethical. Resign from your job rather than follow orders to do something dishonest or unethical. And although reporting such incidents may be the ethical thing to do, keep in mind that you will probably be the one who loses most. The whistle-blower pays a big price, even if he or she "wins." Perhaps you have watched enough nightly news and law-and-order television shows to know that those at the top can usually find a way out by blaming someone else.

Negative, Judgmental Management

Top management that has a negative, judgmental attitude will likely affect workers all the way down the organization. When you hear others being bad-mouthed or criticized in unacceptable settings, realize that the same kind of thing is probably happening to you when you are not around to hear it. Low-level supervisors and some workers will see and imitate this "normal" behavior in the same way that children tend to imitate their parents or other adults. Do not take part in such conversations. Avoid even being in the presence of such negative discussions. When asked to give your views, try something innocuous like "Sorry, I don't know the person," or "I don't feel comfortable discussing another person." It's usually NOT a good idea to make implied judgmental statements like, "We shouldn't be talking behind his back," or "Judge not, lest you also be judged."

Perhaps you have seen individuals who are treated so negatively at work that they become "different persons" outside of work, too, because their egos or self-esteem have been damaged. This is especially true when workers are made to feel stupid because they make mistakes, ask questions, lack social skills, or are simply not the manager's favorites. Others will fight back in whatever way they can, or that they can justify—sometimes stealing from the organization, sabotaging a project, brownnosing the manager, or lying. Avoiding interaction with judgmental management and workers may be an option; but be aware that, while another department or division in this same organization may be better than the one you are in, you cannot expect it to be significantly different. Behaviors begin at, or are sanctioned by, the top. Don't expect one department or division to be different from another unless the problem is originating at the department or division level and has not yet been corrected by upper management. Your best option is to seek employment in a different organization.

Threatening Environment

When supervisors learn—or maybe are even told by top management—that negative motivation and reinforcement are permitted or even encouraged, those who stay and grow with the organization will most likely use those methods. Those who don't buy into that threatening style probably won't be chosen or permitted to move up in the organization. In a poor organizational climate, you can expect to have a threatening environment, and you may even experience such an atmosphere (temporarily, we hope) within some departments or divisions of organizations that are not considered as having a poor overall organizational climates. All it takes is one yelling, cursing supervisor who threatens employee jobs, pay, or promotions. The difference is that, when top managers in a bad climate become aware of the bad supervisor, they do not intervene. Indeed, management has been known to promote the supervisor, which places him another step away from the worker and now in a position to affect other supervisors!

If you feel that your manager or the organization is making unreasonable demands on your time, energy, or skills, check carefully and objectively before you criticize the situation. Perhaps your information or your perception of what is required was not accurate. Try to understand what your manager or the organization really wants and why, and then see if you can come up with different ways in which that might be accomplished. Go over your ideas with your manager to see if a less stressful alternative can be used. The threat of losing one's job is a big burden to carry, and it must be removed either by the organization or by you. Assigning major priority to your health and the well-being of your family will permit you to consider more options for changing jobs, such as relocating even when you would not ordinarily choose to do so.

Demands are often unreasonable when they involve after-work and off-site activities. For example, the organization may ask workers not to see a movie they object to (usually on religious grounds), try to get workers to boycott some product or organization, try to influence their political choices, dictate to workers how to vote or how much to contribute to non-profit drives such as United Way, or demand that workers and managers not reveal their pay to their spouses or anyone else. An organization that tells its employees not to reveal their salaries probably fears that, if managers or workers learn what they are paid relative to each other, there will be a major upheaval because the organization pays as little as they think they can get by with, without regard to equity. In all these cases, the workers and their supervisors feel threatened if they do not follow the organization directive. Your alternatives depend on such things as the job pool for your type of work, offsetting compensations that your job provides, and whether you have a union.

Micromanagers

Micromanagers are more than just a pain—they actually inhibit high performance and creativity. Try to do as much as you can without the involvement of your manager, but be sure to keep your manager fully informed. Sometimes managers micromanage because they fear not knowing what's going on, so keeping them informed can lead to an eventual "pull back" on their part.

Managers, and especially micromanagers, also hate being surprised, so keep your manager informed about things that matter so he or she does not feel a need to look over your shoulder. Also, don't try to get your manager to make decisions for you. If you are the one who should make the decision, do so. If you need help making a decision or you fear that your manager will not like your decision, try discussing the situation with her and perhaps with others. Then make the decision yourself. If your manager is the person who will make a decision, provide her with the necessary backup information, including some background and alternatives. Give her all the necessary information, bad and good. Of course, telling your manager something that is negative requires sensitivity. You need to be able to tell your manager about it in such a way that it is not threatening to him or her. The person being micromanaged can help the situation by voluntarily checking in with the manager to answer these questions before they are asked.

Inconsiderate Coworkers

If at all possible, keep inconsiderate coworkers at a distance. Whether they are lazy, noisy, manipulative, creating or dealing with relationship problems, or otherwise just unpleasant, try to keep your distance. But this is especially difficult in areas where workspaces consist of cubicles or totally open workstations. Their behavior disrupts your thinking and hence your ability to perform.

Noisy

As mentioned in Chapter 7, one way to handle noisy workers is to create barriers or interruptions when these coworkers are around. Try using headphones to block out their noise. They might even take a hint and "tone it down." If your office has a door, make a point to close it but do so quietly, not by slamming it. In some workplaces, it would be advisable to ask your supervisor to make an appearance when things get noisy. Depending on your relationship with the noisy individuals, you may be successful in approaching them yourself to ask if they can tone it down. Light humor is often the best way to handle a not-too-serious problem, as in "I'm bringing some dirty socks tomorrow to stuff in your mouths if you stand here yelling at each other!" Some individuals are just naturally loud, whether by habit or because they have a hearing problem. They're the ones whose conversations you can hear at the back of a commercial jet when they're seated in the first or second row—so whether you like it or not, you can monitor their conversations, especially on the telephone, when their office is 14 cubicles away. They are not likely ever to remember to hold down the volume, so your best bet is to ask whether you can be moved farther away because the loudness interferes with your work, especially when you are trying to talk on the phone.

Time Wasters

If you have a coworker who hangs out at your desk to talk, excuse yourself to make a phone call or ask a coworker who can see your desk to telephone you when they see this person loitering at your station. Perhaps they will leave when they see you are really busy. Or use the coworker's interruption as an excuse to go to the restroom, presuming that the coworker will not follow you to the restroom or remain at your desk until you return. If the coworker does not take these hints, you should try to explain politely that you have a large workload with many deadlines and cannot take time out to talk except during breaks or lunchtime.

Sick

Workers and managers dislike being exposed to other workers or managers who come to work sick. In some companies, managers may have the authority to send the person home. Depending on the individual's personality, you may be able to talk with the individual regarding not wishing to be exposed to his or her illness. Both workers and managers can use body language—that is, stop outside the door instead of going in, call on the phone rather than walking to the cubicle—to convey their feeling of wanting not to be close to the worker. Often there is an opportunity to say something like, "Let's postpone that meeting (or lunch, or whatever) until you are well."

One tactic that seldom works is telling a coworker that he or she should go home because you are worried about their health. Such a comment can reinforce some workers to continue coming to work ill because that's what martyrs do—sacrifice themselves. It can motivate some employees to work harder to prove they are not too ill to come to work, and it can satisfy the attention needs of insecure workers and thus increase the probability that they will come to work sick just to get the attention they crave. For the employee who does come to work sick, the solution is simple: Don't! It is important to your coworkers that you not share your germs or viruses. If the organization cannot function without you, try giving them the information they need by phone or email.

Other Issues

As you may already know, working with bad coworkers or supervisors can be the most stressful part of a worker's day. No one wants to spend the greatest part of their day alongside or interacting with someone with whom they are having relationship problems whether at home or work. If you complain or report the problem, even if you are right, you never know whether other workers or the supervisors will believe your story. You face the possibility that the difficult person could sabotage your work or your relationship with other workers by giving a different account of the problem (see the discussion under "Other Violence" in the preceding chapter).

Another thing to remember is not to ruin relationships with others at work. You may well need the support of coworkers, so don't antagonize them by constantly complaining and criticizing (no matter how well deserved). Bringing problems from home to work can also be problematic. Sometimes talking them over with coworkers can relieve your stress, or they may even provide helpful suggestions. However, constantly complaining about how bad things are at home is never appreciated by anyone. One way to keep good relations at work is by maintaining a sense of humor. It may well be "gallows humor," but an occasional joke (keep it clean) or discussion of Dave's "Top Ten List" can go a long way to keep spirits up. Also, changing the subject can be helpful, even if what you are doing is a bit obvious.

OUTSIDE ISSUES

As noted in the previous chapter, not all workplace issues come from inside the organization; some come from outside. While you as a nonmanager employee may initially think that there is little you can do about outside issues, there are certain actions and preventives that can be taken.

Customers/Clients

Jobs that are made bad by customer/client or supplier contacts with whom the workers must deal require patience and diplomacy since the organization has virtually no control over individuals who are not on its payroll. Workers must not upset or alienate outside contacts, act angry, or become irate, lest they cause the customer/client or supplier to cease doing business with the organization. Instead, remain calm and try to determine what is causing contacts to behave as they are. Listen to what the contacts say, but do not necessarily believe that the problem is what they say it is.

Use what we call the LADDNOS approach: Listen, Apologize, Dig Deeper, Neutralize, Offer Something—an explanation, alternative, or adjustment. For example, if a contact complains about the slowness of a shipment, Listen carefully, Apologize, and then ask what you can do to help the person. If the contact's rudeness continues, Dig Deeper: How many days did it take for the shipment to arrive? Is this unusually long? Check to see if the shipment left on time. During the momentary delay while you are checking your computer to see if the shipment left on time, try to Neutralize the hostility by getting the contact to talk, preferably with you leading the conversation. Depending on whether the individual is calling from another city or standing in your office, you could ask a neutral question such as, "How hot (cold) is it today in (his city)?" or "Is the traffic still crawling?" or "Were you slowed down by the construction or did you find a way around that?" If the contact totally ignores your question, ask something closely related to the problem; for example, "Was this shipment the same size that you usually order?" If the answer is affirmative, you can comment, "Well, then that's not the problem, so let me check a little further on this" (Dig Deeper). If the answer is negative, you can respond, "Perhaps that is part of the problem. Let's check a little further on that." Hopefully, this short time delay and your active determination to solve his problem will begin to neutralize his hostility so that he is more open to your explanations or Offer of Some assistance. Depending on what you have found or what you need time to check further, you could then suggest that, if the carrier has become less efficient, perhaps the contact would like to change the method of shipment.

If the LADDNOS approach doesn't work, the problem is likely due to something else. Perhaps the outside contact has an ill-tempered personality and is always difficult to deal with. Maybe he or she is an unhappy person, is not well, or is working in a bad workplace. Perhaps the contact hates the job, so dealing with anyone is a problem. Maybe the contact hates his mother-in-law, and your voice or your hairstyle reminds him of that person. Perhaps she harbors a negative feeling about your organization because she once applied for a job there but was not hired (in fact, maybe you are currently performing the job that that person applied for!). If an outside contact is repeatedly bad to deal with, you, the worker, can ask for advice from managers and other workers who may have weathered similar experiences. If you have done all you think you can do to appease the contact and your job is intolerable because of this contact, suggest to your manager that someone else try dealing with this contrary person at the next opportunity. A change in contacts on your side will at least help determine if the outside contact, for whatever reason, does not like dealing with the original worker. If the outside contact remains hostile, management must either find someone who can tolerate the abusive contact or elect to sever ties with that customer/client or supplier. On the other hand, you, the worker, must not behave in such a manner that causes the customer or supplier organization to sever ties with your organization. That's a risk for managers, not you, to take.

Vulnerable Workplaces

As indicated in the preceding chapter, some workplaces and jobs are inherently vulnerable to violence. Those include convenience stores and service stations that involve handling cash and working late hours, and healthcare organizations where drugs are stored or sold. In addition, organizations because of their activities are more vulnerable to violent attacks by outsiders. Such organizations include those perceived to be damaging the environment, X-rated movie theaters, bars, abortion clinics, law enforcement agencies, and organizations owned or operated by "foreigners."

If your workplace is in one of these organizations, you need to be extra careful. Ask that your organization provide reasonable physical protection. These might include extra strength door locks, automatic lockdown procedures, bulletproof glass enclosures, metal detectors, hidden camera surveillance, on-site guards if warranted, hidden alarm buttons, and a policy of not allowing employees to work alone. But it should also include well-lighted parking lots, walkways, stairwells, and corridors with automatic backup generators in case of electrical interruptions. You could also ask your organization to arrange for local police or private security to be present at closing time.

You should not try to fight with robbers. Give them whatever they want and protect your life and those of others rather than putting everyone at risk trying to be a hero. If you feel that you cannot handle the stress associated with working in one of these organizations, you should seek employment in a less vulnerable organization.

WHAT NEXT?

Even if you are not a manager, you may be able to help change a bad job or bad worksite so that you can continue working in your current position. Toward that purpose, this chapter has suggested actions you as a nonmanager might take to make the workplace safer and more desirable.

An appendage following this chapter contains real examples of many of the characteristics and behaviors described by consulting clients, students, family, or friends.

APPENDAGE III

Anecdotal Descriptions of
Bad Jobs/Workplaces

The following anecdotes are all real examples of bad jobs/workplaces behaviors that have been provided by consulting clients, students, family, or friends. They are arranged in the order discussed in the chapter. We have tried to leave them in the words of their writers, but have removed identifying information and offensive language.

PHYSICAL ENVIRONMENT

Uncomfortable Work Environment

Outdoor job can drive you indoors

"I am a fresh air freak. I love hiking, sunbathing, sitting outside at cafés, anything to get outside. So naturally I wanted a job that was outdoors at least most of the time. I found it—working for a lawncare and sprinkler company. Virtually all of my time would be spent outdoors. I was so happy that I didn't worry about pay or fringe benefits, which, as it turns out, weren't too bad anyway.

"I soon learned though that hiking and sunbathing aren't the same as mowing lawns, raking grass and leaves, trimming trees and bushes, replacing sprinkler heads and other parts, digging in the dirt and mud, and doing all of the other tasks involved in this job. I started work in the spring and that wasn't bad. But summer in Phoenix almost did me in. Even though we tried to start work as early as possible, many clients did not want us around until 8 or 9 o'clock and by then the temperature was already climbing. By the end of the day, we were sunburned and suffering from heat exhaustion and dehydration (even though we carried water on our truck and tried to drink all day). It was brutal.

"But then call fall and things gradually cooled down again. Fall, though, is followed by winter. Winter in Phoenix isn't much—but at 7 or 8 o'clock in the morning, digging in wet mud to repair sprinklers can be downright cold. So you get filthy, wet, and cold, and you have to keep on the same clothes for the whole day. It shouldn't have surprised me to learn that virtually all of us would get multiple colds and sometimes infections in cuts on our hands.

"Maybe outdoor jobs are not what I should be looking for after all!! So I'm looking for something indoors and will spend my free time outdoors, like on weekends and some evenings."

Boring indoor job can drive you back to school

"I graduated from high school and then went to the service. After that I returned home and got a job in an assembly plant. It paid pretty well but it was so noisy that we wore earplugs and can't talk to one another until lunchtime and we made sure not to talk about work then. The job had been engineered so that I was supposed to fasten two parts together every minute. If one or the other was not right so that they didn't fit properly, I could either let them go and somebody else would fix it, or I could take a bit of extra time and get them to work, but then I had to speed it up on the next few to keep everything on schedule. At first this didn't seem to be bad work, especially when compared to being in the Armed Forces. It was steady and the pay was OK, but after a few years the boredom started building up. I was taking more and more sick leave to break the monotony until I started going to college at night. After a while I took out a student loan, quit the job, and went full time to get my degree. Now I've got a college degree and a much better job."

Paint room not a pretty place

"My bad job was working in a paint room. Parts came in on overhead conveyors, and we painted them with spray nozzles attached to coiled hoses. Paint got everywhere, but we had suits that covered everything (including our feet) but our faces and hands. For the hands, we wore gloves. For our faces, we had masks that were like gas masks. The plastic eyepieces had to be frequently cleaned and sometimes even replaced, and the filters changed several times a day. While the filters kept the paint out of your nose and mouth, they did not block the odor, which was so strong that you could hardly breathe at times.

"There were no windows and little ventilation of any kind in the paint room as that would have stirred up the paint in the air. The result was that it was hot, smelly, and hard to breathe. The heat sometimes got almost unbearable, particularly inside the paint suits—pools of sweat in your feet (the suits had covers for the feet) was common. I already mentioned the smell. It certainly felt good at the end of a shift to get out of the smelly paint suit and take a hot shower. The smell tended to stay in your nose for several hours, though."

Food industry not always tasteful place to be

"Restaurant and fast-food workers frequently receive no health insurance benefits, no paid vacation, nor paid sick leave. The jobs generally are dead end, with little training that could lead to better jobs. In addition to long hours, low wages, and limited benefits, many of these workers are subjected to very difficult working conditions: hot kitchens, slippery floors, aging equipment. If workers miss time due to illness or family emergencies, they may be subjected to disciplinary action. As a result, turnover tends to be quite high."

Janitorial job too filthy

"When I was in high school, I took a job at a garage to earn some spending money. I knew that I would be a gofer—doing odd jobs to help the mechanics, but I didn't know what all that would entail. I emptied the garbage, swept the garage, washed cars, and cleaned up spilled oil or other lubricants. In addition, I was supposed to keep the waiting room clean, chairs lined up, and magazines neat and orderly. Even though temperatures in south Texas frequently reached into the upper 90s, most of this wasn't too bad, even though it was exhausting.

"What was bad was cleaning the restrooms. The employees' restroom wasn't so bad, but the one used by the public was unbelievable. The toilet was almost never flushed. Urine and fecal material was frequently on the toilet and the floor. The sink would have dirt and hair in it. Paper towels and toilet paper would be all over the place. Cleaning this mess in 90-degree heat was enough to make you sick."

Emptying septic tanks not a pleasant job

"I helped my uncle one summer emptying septic tanks. You drive up to a house or a mobile home and locate the tank. Of course tanks are frequently located in the most inaccessible part of the property for houses but relatively close-by for trailers. Our pumping truck has 150 feet of hose, though, so we can usually get to any tank from a driveway without having to tear up a yard. Our truck pumps or vacuums out the tank and then uses water from the truck to wash the tank. Sometime there is 'spillage' that we have

to clean up, too. No matter how much technology is involved, and no matter how you try to describe this job, it is a sh*tty job—a smelly, dirty, very unpleasant way to earn a living, no matter what the pay!"

Abusing workers to provide customer service

"It's hard to believe that it's called customer service. There are nearly a hundred of us crammed into a room so that we literally are sitting elbow-to-elbow in front of computer monitors with telephone headsets on. We are supposed to answer calls, look up accounts, and 'help' customers.

"In reality, we put off customers or just take down information to be passed along to someone else who decides if the customer will really get some kind of help. If a customer gets totally irate and demands to speak to a supervisor, we merely transfer the call to another person in the room (and we tell that person that he is at this moment a supervisor).

"We are so packed together that it is hot and smelly and then having to lie and deceive customers just makes the job worse. I mean, if you tried to pack prison inmates or schoolchildren together like this even for an hour, the whole world would attack you for physical abuse and knowingly endangering the life of a person. But it's apparently okay to put noncriminals into this situation if it's outside an institution.

"I am looking forward to finding another job and getting out of this one—so my ears can stop ringing and my elbows can heal."

No party for party animal

"For a short time that seemed much longer, I was a mascot. Well actually not a mascot but a party 'animal.' I wore a big, heavy costume to kids' birthday parties. While I sweated profusely inside, the kids would pull, pinch, hit, hug, kick, and kiss me from the outside. I'm supposed to move very slowly so that I don't knock a kid down (I can't see well at all in the costume, and it is big and heavy). Talking is also limited to 'Have a nice day,' 'We're glad you came,' or other innocuous lines. Thankfully I don't have to be there in costume for the whole party—but the 20 minutes or so in costume is the worst job I've had."

Unsafe or too physically demanding

No one really wants to work in an unsafe environment, and the government makes a considerable effort to see that such environments do not exist. However, there are jobs that are inherently unsafe (demolition, mining), and the risks associated with the job can only be minimized, not eliminated. Other jobs are made unsafe by worker attitude and conduct, and these may be the hardest for coworkers to control. Unfortunately, there are also a few jobs that are unnecessarily unsafe because of management attitude. Sometimes that means that the organization does not want to spend the necessary money to make the job safe. Generally, that's not true, though, as safety standards are rather closely monitored and tightly enforced by the United States Department of Labor through OSHA (Occupational Safety and Health Administration).

Jobs that are too physically demanding may also be unsafe if they are performed by individuals who have not been trained adequately or are not of adequate size or physical condition. Even getting to and from work can be unsafe if the organization or the worker does not take adequate safety precautions.

Demolition too dangerous

"One hot summer I learned about construction—or perhaps I should say the opposite of construction—since a couple of us were hired to help demolish some buildings. We needed to save everything though as that was how the boss made his money. He sold everything for scrap—nails, boards, busted-up concrete, sheet metal, insulation. Everything had some value, and he wanted it all. While it was hot, physical work, we were teenagers and so we felt good flexing our muscles and getting tanned. Having a beer (illegal but furnished by the boss) at the end of the day was wonderful, too.

"Needless to say, though, we weren't really trained. We were hired for our hands, backs, and muscles, not our skills nor brains. So we frequently had lots of accidents. Thankfully, virtually all small ones—hitting a finger with a hammer, getting dust in your eyes, having a pile of stuff shift and fall against you, getting itchy from improper contact with the insulation, and lots and lots of scratches and bruises (some pretty good ones). We also got burned a few times on one project as we were taking off a sheet metal roof and the sun got it so hot that, if you got your bare skin against it, you could get a rather severe burn.

"But one day we had gotten the roof off a building and were working on the sides. We dismantled them by removing the nails, insulation, and wood sheeting and then finally took out the studs. The problem was that we didn't know much, if anything, about how buildings are put together. That meant that we didn't know about things like load-bearing studs or how braces worked or whatever (I really still don't know much because I was an accounting major in college). So when we removed the last part of the wall we were working on, all of the other walls started to collapse. I ran to get away but my buddy tried to grab a stud to stop it. He didn't succeed and spent a couple of days in the hospital for his efforts. The only redeeming thing about it was that the boss covered the hospital costs and it was our last building anyway."

Up on the roof

"One summer I took a job putting roofs on houses. Being on top of houses in the summer in Arizona is not something you want to do. We started work at 6:00 in the morning so that we could be on the job by 7:00, but by the time we quit, temperatures would routinely be above 120 degrees. We had to rip off the old roofing material and clean the area before we could haul up the new material (shingles or tiles) and put it in place. You could easily get cut on the material or by a tool. You could suffer from heat stroke or exhaustion. There was always the danger that you might slip and fall off the roof. It was physically demanding and nerve wracking."

Roustabout work too physically demanding

"The worst job I ever had was a roustabout in the Giddings (Texas) area. Roustabouts are manual laborers for the oil industry. I dug ditches, loaded and unloaded trucks, helped assemble rigs, and worked with a lot of hot, smelly, noisy power equipment of one kind or another. Not only is this hot, sweaty work in south Texas, but it is genuinely hard work and frequently involved long hours, sometimes at night or on weekends. At the end of each day, it was all I could do to eat a fast-food sandwich with a beer, take a quick shower, and collapse in bed. I frequently got cut or burned or scraped pretty bad—nothing serious enough to go to the clinic, but I used a lot of first-aid cream and bandages while I held that job. Obviously, I was not in good enough physical condition for such hard work, so I should never have been hired. I sure learned why they pay roustabouts pretty well, but I don't think my work life would have been very long if I had stayed in that job."

Loading produce not a mellow job

"A bad job? How about unloading pumpkins, cantaloupes, watermelons that could weigh as much as 50 pounds or more, and other heavy fruits and vegetables and doing it for minimum wage? Try doing that day in and day out during the hottest part of summer. The only good thing was we got to eat them if one dropped, which would happen every now and then—sometimes on purpose."

Lumberyard work has undesirable dimensions

"While putting myself through technical school, I took a job in a nearby lumberyard. It was hard, dirty, dusty, smelly work and outdoors most of the time, but it paid pretty well and I was in good shape. My training was meager to say the most. On my first day, an experienced employee took me around, showed me several different jobs and very briefly what each involved, and that was it. My second day, my supervisor took me to one of those again, briefly showed me what was involved, and then left. The job was stacking loose cut lumber into neat stacks that could be picked up by a forklift and moved somewhere.

"The problem was that some of the cut lumber had warped from lying out in the weather so that when you tried to stack it into a pile, the pile would fall over. This was not a big deal until the stack was several feet high when it fell. Then unless you were very quick, the pile would fall on your legs. The scrapes and bruises would be sore for days and sometimes required Band-Aids to stop the bleeding. And even though I wore gloves, I would get splinters and pinched fingers all too frequently.

"After several days of this, I was moved to another job. This one involved unbundling stacks of lumber. The stacks would be delivered to us tightly bound with metal straps. The forklift operator would place them in bins where customers could get the number of pieces that they wanted. But the metal straps had to be cut so that customers could pick through the stack to find just the pieces that they wanted. I quickly learned that while cutting the straps was simple, getting out of the way as the stack then nearly exploded apart was not so simple. The number of cuts, bruises, pinched fingers, and flattened toes on this job was a lot more than the other. And after I cut the straps and the stack came all apart, I had to restack it neatly for customers.

"Finally, I got to use the saw. Actually there were several saws—some horizontal, some vertical, and some that you used by hand. Again, I received minimal instructions on the use of the saws and safety wasn't even mentioned. It didn't take long. I cut myself several times the first few days while changing blades, but as I grew comfortable using the saws, I also grew careless. About the end of the first week, I cut my thumb pretty badly. I had to go to the emergency room and got a bunch of stitches.

"When I came to work the next day, I found out that my hourly pay would be reduced since I was relegated to doing very simple tasks because of my injury. Only when the doctor said I was well enough to 'go back to work' was I put back on the jobs that I was doing before and at the pay rate that I had originally been hired at.

"The next time I was assigned to work the saws, I was a lot more careful. But then the supervisor started criticizing me for how slow I was and pushing me to speed up all the time. Eventually I did and eventually I had another accident. This finally caused me to start wondering about keeping the job. I looked around and found that I could work in a movie rental place—indoors, comfortable, clean, and especially safe—for only about a cut of 20% in my pay. I jumped at it and was a lot happier."

Inconvenient or Unsafe Location

A far-out job

"When I joined the U.S. Forest Service, I had an office job in town. While the working conditions were nice, it was boring work. So I requested a field assignment and got it. The new job was just about 60 miles from where I lived—it usually took well over an hour each way to drive there. Not only was it far away, but it was also in the boonies. There was nothing around—no stores, no fast food, no service stations, nothing! I had to bring my lunch and make sure my car had a full tank of gas every day or risk getting very hungry or stranded or both.

"When I requested a new job, I had assumed that I would be able to move close to wherever my field assignment might be. But, as luck would have it, there were no towns closer than about 35 miles from my new assignment. Given that, I elected not to sell and move, but going to the boonies every day got very old after a few years. I kept requesting another field assignment closer to a town, but none was available. So I ended up leaving the Forest Service rather than spend over 2 hours a day alone in my car and 8 hours a day alone in the boonies."

Home is where the job is not

"My job wouldn't be so bad if it weren't for the location. It is downtown, so parking is a major problem or very expensive. Finding a place to grab a bite to eat is the same—a problem or very expensive. In fact, if I paid for parking and food on a regular basis, I'd probably barely break even on this job. But to make it worse, I live in a rather distant suburb. I could get a bus into downtown but that involves taking Bus A and then transferring to Bus B and having to walk several blocks to Bus A from home and then from Bus B to the job. While cheaper, this is less convenient, especially when its raining or snowing, and involves so much time that I have to get up about an hour earlier and don't get home until way after dark. I can't afford to move downtown, so I guess I'll just keep looking for a job closer to home."

Can't get there from here

"I was happy in my retail job until the company moved from downtown to a regional mall several miles away. Not that I mind working at the mall—if I could get there conveniently. I don't have a car, so I rely on mass transportation, and the busses didn't change their schedules just because my company moved. Before, I could walk to work, or if the weather was bad I might take a bus up the street to the store. Now, I have to walk to that same bus stop and then change buses three times to get to work. That means I get up earlier and get home later, so I don't have much time to take care of my house and family. We spend more on food, too, since I get home too late to cook regular meals. Plus, the bus fare is higher. Not much each way, but it adds up when you figure it's two ways each day, 5 to 6 days a week."

On the wrong side of town

"Once I had a job for a nonprofit organization that, in order to save money, had located in a rather poor, run-down part of town. The offices themselves were relatively clean and nice, but parking was on the street, and in the several months I was there, at least three people had their cars broken into. What got me though was that, as a woman, I had to drive through this rough neighborhood to get to and from work every day. And sometimes I was unable to leave until after dark at night. I constantly worried about my car breaking down and stranding me on these streets, particularly at night. That worry interfered with my concentration on the job and caused me to have to find another job."

Out walking after midnight

"While an undergraduate, I got a job at a movie theater. It seemed like a neat job—I got passes to the theater (although they were good only for off-peak showings) and the work was indoors where it was air conditioned. The worst part was cleaning a screen room after a showing. It would be dimly lit and you had to sweep every row and aisle as well as check each seat for spills and candy or chewing gum stuck to the seats. But still, several of us worked together, and when the customers were out of the room, we could talk to each other and socialize a bit.

"But one day I was asked to work the night shift. I didn't think that I had much choice and so agreed. The last movie did not end until after 1:00 a.m. and so we (there were only three of us on that shift) could not leave until around 1:30. I had to walk back to my dorm through a pretty bad part of the campus. For a young girl, this was extremely harrowing, and I vowed never to work the night shift again."

Duties Not Wanted or Expected

"New kid on the block" gets the worst duties

"Maybe if I had stayed it might have changed to where it was not so bad, but as the 'new kid on the block' I was so mistreated that I soon quit. Because I was new, I was given all of the jobs that no one else wants to do. I never got to weld anything. What I did was prep work and clean-up work. Prep work might involve washing cow dung off equipment so that it could be welded or using acid to get oil off the metals so that welds would hold. Clean-up work involved collecting any metal droppings from the welders work, sanding welds smooth with sandpaper or steel wool, sweeping the area, or whatever. While the welders usually worked indoors, most of my work was outdoors in the heat."

No work is not good

"Believe it or not, my worst job was one where I didn't have to work. I got an office job for a major manufacturing company one summer while in college. I was looking forward to learning about how the business worked and gaining experience that would help me in my courses (I was a business management major) and in getting a good job (possibly with this company) upon graduation. What I found was that there really wasn't much for me to do. I wondered why a company would hire someone and then not use them. The job didn't generate much enthusiasm or contentment on my part. Instead, I felt unappreciated. I also wondered if there was something wrong with me so that they didn't want to fire me but were reluctant to give me much to do either. The job was a waste of my time and the company's money, and it really hurt my self-esteem. If a company overworks you, at least it tells you that they think you are capable of doing something."

Zookeeper job has bad ending

"Being a zookeeper isn't all bad. Sometimes we get to talk to the public, children especially, and that's nice. That's one of the things that attracted me to this career. We also have to keep lots of records about observations about the animals, feeding schedules, counting and checking them, etc., and that's not so bad either. But it isn't all good either. The paperwork, which I had not anticipated having to do, can become quite boring.

"We also feed the animals—which I thought would be the best part of the job. But it turns out that feeding can sometimes mean lifting and carrying heavy containers of food or bales of hay or straw. Feeding also can be dirty, smelly work and either too hot or too cold, depending on the time of the year. Even indoors, since cages don't have heaters or air conditioners!!

"But the worst part is that we have to clean the pens and enclosures and even sometimes collect samples of feces or urine for lab analysis. That's the worst part of all because the animals don't always cooperate and you get 'it' all over you! You get the smell 'locked in your nose,' and that sometimes makes it hard to eat your lunch or dinner because the food doesn't smell good. I never thought about this end of the job when I committed to being a zookeeper, and sometimes it makes me think about quitting the job."

POOR ORGANIZATIONAL CULTURE/CLIMATE

Threatening Environment

Intimidate workers to produce, then fire them to avoid giving pay raises

"I worked for a mutual fund company, whose strategy for motivating the sales force was to threaten people with termination. These were not idle threats. They were of real concern because the company would terminate a salesperson every 2 weeks or so just to make their point. The remaining sales force lived in fear of losing their livelihood, and the stress showed on their faces. To accentuate the atmosphere of fear, the senior salespeople were routinely marched into the CEO's office, without notice, to answer a barrage of questions about their top prospects. If you did not know all the answers, you were summarily dismissed on the spot.

"The company's method of motivating salespeople produced bottom-line results in the short run but came back to bite them in the long run. There was no natural enthusiasm on the part of the salespeople and no feeling of dedication as the workers did not feel that they would have a long-time relationship with the firm. And at least in the long run, the bottom line is affected by this attitude, the high turnover, and the reaction of potential clients to the hard-sell tactics of the new salespeople. On the other hand, the company did get really hard workers at a relatively low commission for a few weeks, and the turnover assured that the company never had to give raises. It was clearly the worst work experience of my life. The company was eventually bought out by a larger company."

Motivate by threatening relocation

"In an office area (headquarters), I saw supervisors practicing fear management by threatening to punish subordinates with an undesirable reassignment if they did not meet management's sales goals. The company's policy, in fact, spells out during the hiring process that the associate/worker can be reassigned during his work period with the company to any of its subsidiaries around the country. So the managers used this policy as punishment or a threat to 'motivate' workers. They would threaten to rotate the workers to other subsidiaries of the company, far from the city where this office is located so that they would have to move, change their kid's schools, and have lots of hassle in relocating. The worst is that managers used the policy openly. This threat worked well, but over time, a lot of skillful engineers left the company as the job market improved. Only those with children at school and who did invest in that city were reluctant to leave, but they were all at very low motivation and morale. This company has a monopoly in this business area and is government held, so high performance was not a very critical aspect for its management. It probably won't change significantly unless it is unionized—which is not likely."

No unionizing talk allowed

"My job could be a lot better and would be, too, if we had a union. But our supervisors are determined that no union will ever get its foot in the door of our plant. We are threatened with our jobs if we are ever caught talking about joining a union, and I do know for a fact that a couple of hotheads were fired for just that. We have frequent anti-union meetings that we must attend (careful records are kept about who attends and who doesn't)—these are usually labeled as supervisory training programs. And about every other week we get anti-union leaflets or brochures mailed to our homes. Of course, there is never any indication that they come from the plant.

"It really seems unfair that the company won't allow us to even talk about a union, but they apparently can propagandize any way they want against unionizing."

Management censors movies

"I work for ____. Recently a 'documentary' about ____ has appeared. It has played at some theaters around the country but not here. But recently it was announced that a local 'art' theater was going to show the film. Almost immediately we got a memo from the store manager telling us that we should not go see the film. Rumor has it that the company has hired private detectives to keep track of who goes to the film. While I'm very curious about the film, I probably won't risk my job by going to see it. Maybe it will be out on video and I can rent it then. But I'm surprised that management can act in such a repressive manner today. No wonder workers founded unions to protect themselves."

New "kick-ass" manager

"I'm with a major manufacturing company (Fortune 500) that has numerous divisions, several of which are housed here locally. A few years ago we got a new CEO who wanted to 'kick ass' to show rapid improvements in our financials. He asked each division head to set targets for the next year, and then he raised each of those by 10%. All divisions did better than they ever had before, but a few (four I think) did not hit their targets. Those division VPs were fired immediately—no second chance! After that, fear spread through the organization like wildfire, and people began sending out their résumés as fast as possible."

Dishonest or Unethical Management

Alter timecards and lie about pay rate and benefits

"The bad job that I had was in what I came to regard as a very dishonest company. I needed a part-time job just to help make ends meet. A major insurance company told me that they could use me for 30 to 35 hours a week if I was available. While I had to adjust schedules a bit, I made myself available because they said the pay would be for $X.00/hour and that I would accrue vacation and sick time. The pay was not great, but the vacation and sick time made it seem worthwhile.

"When I got my first paycheck, it was for less money per hour than I had been promised, and the stub did not indicate any vacation or sick time. When I asked about it, my supervisor said that I must have misunderstood the people in HR because they don't pay anybody that high an amount. He also said that as a part-time employee, I would not get any vacation days but that I would start earning some sick hours (hours not days) after I had accumulated 100 hours at the company. I was sure it was the supervisor and not HR that had told me those things. But I didn't have anything in writing, and I figured that challenging him would only get me fired. I needed the job, so I let it slide.

"The next week my paycheck was for fewer hours than I had worked. When I asked my supervisor about this, he said to contact payroll as there must have been an error. Payroll showed me my time card, and it had the hours changed one day. They didn't know who might have changed it but said that they couldn't do anything except pay me for what was on the card. That happened again a few weeks later and again about a month after that when I finally got more than 100 hours. Then when I asked how much sick leave I was entitled to, I was told that they didn't need me anymore.

"So it's back to looking for another part-time job. And this time I'll get things in writing before taking the job."

Ask workers to pad expense accounts and destroy evidence

"The law firm that employed me as an administrative assistant for a while was unbelievable. The first thing I learned was that people got billed for totally trivial things. The firm charged its clients in 15-minute intervals no matter how little time was actually involved *(Editor's note: This is not uncommon practice)*. In fact, if a client called for a lawyer but did not get him because he was on another line or in a meeting or something, the client was still billed for a 15-minute segment. When I expressed dismay over this practice, I was assured that (1) every law firm operates this way [I have since learned that is not the case], and (2) that the clients understand and accept the practice [I have also learned that is true only for the big corporate clients who just pass the costs along to their customers].

"In addition, the lawyers padded their expense accounts (they are billed to clients, too). I was asked to make up taxi bills, bills for local stenographic services, and other 'small' bills so that the lawyers could 'prove' to clients that they had actually incurred the expenses. When I balked at doing this, I was told that they had incurred the expenses but then lost the receipts so that nothing illegal was going on. They were simply replacing lost receipts with the ones I would compose.

"What finally got me though was when one of the lawyers asked me to change a figure on a document and then copy it and destroy the original so that the change could not be discovered. I was absolutely flabbergasted. So I went to one of the senior members of the firm and told him about it. His response was, 'Well if you don't want to do it, that's fine—you don't have to do it. We'll just get one of the other girls to do it.'

"I quit and have never trusted lawyers since, although I did end up working at another law firm a few years later where it was virtually the exact opposite of the previous one."

Hire and fire

"The shortest job that I ever had was in an engineering consulting company that was dishonest in such a way that now, several years later, I will not even consider working for an engineering firm. In essence, here's the way they functioned. When they needed to hire a nonengineering consultant, they would instead advertise for a full-time position. They would rush the applicant's decision, saying they really were desperate to fill this job because they have a very pressing deadline for some of the work; and they could even be persuaded to up the annual salary figure to get the person onboard. Then when the initial assignment is completed (mine required about a month), the person who wooed you to the company would be absent for the afternoon, and another manager or his assistant would tell you that the company had decided not to fill the position just yet.

"Such behavior really hits hard both monetarily and psychologically. First, you wonder if you did something wrong or if they thought you were not qualified—but they had raved about the work and you find out that they are indeed using the assistance that you had given. Then you feel really angry that they pushed you to work for them, which caused you to miss other opportunities that were in the making—and they knew at the time that they weren't going to employ you for more than a month. And therein lies the explanation—they could afford to quote you a high annual rate because they knew they would be paying you for only one month, which would be a lot less than if they hired you as a consultant for one month.

"I haven't yet figured out how to spot a company that is managed in this way. I'm sure if I asked a potential employer to issue an employment contract for at least a year, they'd wonder why I was so insecure and they'd walk away from me."

Cheat one, cheat all

"I once worked at a resort hotel. The manager was completely dishonest, which made me lose all respect for her. She would demand credit card numbers from people inquiring about accommodations and then intentionally book them for rooms that did not meet their requests. When the people would cancel, she billed them for 'administrative overhead fees' associated with her time and effort. That way she made money without renting the rooms, which she would then rent to someone else anyway.

"I left the job because my feeling is that, if a person treats one individual dishonestly, he will have no qualms about treating me the same way. I don't want to be around that kind of person, and I certainly am not motivated to help them look good in their jobs or make more money."

Forge documents

"A person can learn a lot by working in the controller's office. For instance, I learned that one way to falsify documents is to cut and paste from the original and then make a copy. You sometimes have to take white-out and clean up the copy to get rid of some shadows and lines and then make another clean copy. That clean copy is then put in the files to document the information.

"Another approach is to scan the original, edit the scanned document, and then print it on paper like that of the original. A little folding and wrinkling and it will fool just about any auditor—they are not trained to detect forgeries, after all.

"But even though I learned a lot and would have learned even more, I chose to leave because I didn't want to be their pawn when they get caught. I figured that any company that operated this way would hide behind an honest worker like me if they ever got caught."

Management With an Attitude

Treat everyone as potential cheaters and lazy slackers

"I worked in a research group where no one was allowed to speak to anyone else unless it was through our supervisor. If you were one minute late, you would be told about it and have it deducted from your timesheet. This was true before work, at lunch, and at the end of the day. The place was like a morgue or an empty church an hour before the services— eerily quiet. Every Friday, about half the day was spent in preparing detailed reports about everything we did during the week (it had better match your timesheet!). I can't recall anyone ever being questioned seriously about specific items in the report, so I don't know why the company would lose the half-day productivity from all of us, week in and week out. Maybe because our supervisor was too busy reading our email to make sure we weren't using it for personal reasons. We had no phones, but because we used computers, we did have email. Looking back, I am surprised that we didn't have to ask permission to go to the bathroom. Maybe that was because we didn't dare go to the bathroom often or stay long. This job was a bad place to spend one's time! We were treated like prisoners, not professionals, so I would not want to work there again."

Require workers to ask permission to use bathroom

"I worked for a major supplier of chicken parts to grocery stores. My job consisted of separating parts and tossing them into the proper boxes as fast as I could. I had to learn to identify the chicken parts, which was not a big deal except that no one trained me. What was really bad was that breaks were all taken at the same time when a whistle would blow. If I needed to use the restroom at some other time, I had to shout, 'restroom,' until a supervisor heard me and granted me permission to take a bathroom break. I had no idea that situations like this existed, and I got out of there as quickly as I could. One good thing about the job, though: it was a real motivator for me to get a college degree so I would never have to work again in that kind of place."

Workers are stupid and make mistakes

"This midsize company where I work has an attitude that starts with the president and goes down to the bottom level of supervisors. They act like they are perfect even on first try: 'Why can't you do this like I do?' They act like they never make mistakes: 'Why do you always f*ck up?' Or they say nothing but look at you with eyes that say, 'I hate you,' or 'You are so totally stupid.'

"We don't even have to do something wrong—just asking a question to avoid doing wrong gets the same type of response, like 'I can't believe you asked that?' or 'Can't you figure out something that is so simple?' When you humbly point out that 'You did the same thing last Tuesday, didn't you?' the response is a glare and a snappy 'I have a right to ask questions or make mistakes—I'm the boss.' They seem to become defensive when we ask questions, like they are afraid they don't know the answer. But also it seems like some of the supervisors just use mistakes or questions as opportunities to belittle us workers in order to stroke their own egos.

"Believe me, they do make mistakes—bigger ones, usually, since they are management related—and they cover up for each other. And a lot of times their mistakes could have been avoided if only they had asked the workers how something is done. You don't hear them put each other down when they screw up or when they ask questions that even us workers could answer.'

"Taking extra privileges and breaking rules, though, are what really upset us workers. Like they almost never return from lunch on time, but if they think that we are a minute late, they get furious, and some of the supervisors even dock the workers' time for 15 minutes. But they don't offer us overtime when they catch us at 5:00 just to 'ask a quick question' that ends up taking 10–20 minutes about something they had forgotten to do earlier. That infuriates me when they excuse themselves from all wrong by using that old 'I'm the boss' line. I don't think I will ever be like that if I work my way up to a supervisory or upper management job."

Unhappy supervisors

"Our supervisor makes our jobs hell because of his attitude, which seems to reflect his managers' method of operation. He seems to have low self-esteem and little self-respect. He dresses sloppily and seems to think that being crude is a macho thing to do. Our department's performance under him has been consistently poor (it was better some years ago under a different supervisory).

"He bitches about being underpaid and mistreated by his bosses and then takes it out on us. For example, he refuses to support us for promotions and raises (we get them only if they come automatically from the top). He criticizes our work when we have to rush because he gave it to us as a last-minute assignment with too little instructions.

"He can't tell us what he wants beforehand—only when he sees it finished, then he'll suggest doing it a different way. He's a bad planner, but that also seems to be the environment in which the whole company functions."

Incompetent Management

Train workers inadequately for job rotation

"I worked for a local airline operation. The managers there thought that job rotation and cross-training were wonderful ideas—they didn't have to live with the results! We were supposed to work at Job A (customer service rep) for half a week, then Job B (ticket counter). The next week it would be Job C (phone reservations) and Job D (office assistant), to Job E (baggage claims) and Job F (clerk), and finally back to Job A the week after that. No employee does any job well. While this approach certainly kept me from being bored, it also kept me from being particularly effective. I was always learning and rarely producing. I couldn't get one job right before it was time to move on. Even when I came back to the job I had before, I couldn't remember some details and would make mistakes and have to learn all over again. I did not function well under these conditions because I was never proud of my performance. And I always wondered what the flying customer must be thinking about the quality of the workers. The big thing I learned was that these approaches don't make much sense unless you allow time for the workers to learn each job well enough so that they can feel good about their job performance."

Avoid input from those who perform the work

"My example of a bad job was one I had some years ago in a defense plant. I can't tell you about what we did, but it's how we did it that matters anyway. I would come to work before 8:00 a.m. so that I could be at my workstation precisely at 8:00 a.m. My daily instructions would be printed out waiting for me. Those instructions would tell me exactly what I was to do and how long it should take for me to do every task that day. I was not permitted to discuss the instructions with anyone, including my supervisor. Nor was I permitted to ask questions or make suggestions—'ours is not to reason why, ours but to do and die' seemed to be the motto of the company. I could have made a lot of suggestions about how to do things better or faster but was not permitted to do so—so I quit. To me, it seemed insane that a business would not want to implement changes to make the work more efficient or faster. And also it told me that management did not respect me as a worker when they did not permit me to ask questions or make suggestions."

Hire the loudest, not the finest, supervisors

"I once worked for a small manufacturing plant in a remote east Tennessee location. The key to getting promoted to supervision was to yell loudly—preferably in a deep, menacing tone. It didn't matter much what you yelled about. The key was getting heard by upper management. Then once you got in supervision, your job was to yell and threaten your workers. That would get you into management.

"The plant paid very well for the area and so workers would put up with a lot. What's so strange about this is that those are hard workers who believe in working for their pay, so nobody should ever need to yell at them."

Rules rule

"A local entrepreneur started an Asian restaurant and was pretty successful. In fact he was so successful that he opened a second and then a third. At that point, he decided to franchise his operations. He soon had about a dozen restaurants around the area. In trying to control operations, he would drop in unannounced to check on things. He also had comment cards for customers to fill out. The problem was that his solution to any problem, real or perceived, was to write a rule that all locations had to follow. He soon had nearly 100 such rules, many of which proved to be disastrous. The tension that employees felt was reflected in their dealings with customers. The workers weren't rude, but they were stone-faced and obviously unhappy.

"One rule was that everything had to be cleaned up before the evening rush—the rule said by 5:00 p.m. This meant sweeping and mopping the floor even though there might be customers present. It meant interrupting any cooking that was going on in the kitchen. It meant taking staff away from customer service and using them to clean up. The tension that employees felt was reflected in their dealings with customers. The workers weren't rude, but they were stone-faced and obviously unhappy. Customers soon learned not to bother coming by between about 4:00 and 5:30 as they couldn't get service then. Or if they did, they would have to smell the mop water, raise their feet for the sweeper, etc. So the atmosphere inside the restaurant was tense. That disruption in customer flow eventually carried into later hours, causing business to fall off badly. By the time the entrepreneur figured out that he was killing his own business, it was too late."

Use high pay to justify overworking trained professionals

"Working in a hospital may sound glamorous and exciting. And I suppose it is—for a while. But when you work 12-hour shifts day in and day out, it soon loses its glamor. At first you focus on helping doctors and patients—making a meaningful contribution to the health and well-being of people. But over time your focus changes to getting through your shift and collapsing from fatigue. If you work in ER as I did for a while, this happens sooner rather than later because the long hours are coupled with extraordinary stress. They pay well for ER work but it isn't worth it. I had no social life. I lived on fast food and sleeping through rented movies or bad television. My dog was so neglected that he tried to get my attention by leaving 'presents' for me and 'watering' my furniture.

"Even though I quit ER, I find the long shifts and being on call difficult. Not just difficult to do and perform well while you are doing your job, but also difficult for life. It is hard to have one. You make dinner plans and have to cancel at the last minute because you get a call. Eventually you just quit making plans. There must be something better for someone with my skills and training, but I keep reminding myself that the pay is really very good."

Fail to structure jobs

"I have worked for eight different companies. Three of those were small companies, two were medium-sized ones, and the other three (including my current employer) were very large companies. One of the things I have learned is that small companies are not good places to work. They tend to be run by people who are bad managers and who, as a result, create bad jobs. You rarely know what you will be asked to do from day to day. Your hours will be at the whim of the bosses although you will get no overtime pay. You may well be asked to do personal things for the bosses as well—pick up dry cleaning, drop off mail, or the like. Giant companies, on the other hand, tend to have things spelled out in writing and are far better places to work."

LOW REWARDS AND POOR JOB SECURITY

Low Pay and Fringe Benefits

You ought (not) to be in movies

"What a glamorous job—working on a movie set! I'd get to meet stars and see how a movie was actually made. It would open up all sorts of doors for me, and I'd have a great career making movies. Boy was I wrong!

"Not only did I agree to do this for a share of the future earnings in lieu of actual pay (there never were any), but also I quickly learned that I would rarely be actually 'on the set.' I was usually somewhere else running errands—buying diesel fuel for generators, picking up props at a warehouse, returning rented trucks or trailers, and the like. When I was at the location where the filming was being done, I emptied garbage cans, ran errands like buying cigarettes, helped the catering company set up the food service and then clean up after everyone ate (maybe even getting something myself to eat from the leftovers), and ran other errands for just about anyone around. If I saw one of the actors, it was just a glimpse.

"What really got me, though, was I did this the first day for 30 straight hours; the second, third, and fourth days for 18 hours each; then up to around 20 for several days, and finally down to about 14 hours for almost a week. And then as I wandered about in a daze, the whole project abruptly ended—this crew was finished with its work.

"Isn't it illegal to require employees to work that many hours? You bet! But if you ever want to work in this industry, you keep your mouth shut, do what you are told, and hope that someone, somewhere, or sometime will notice you and give you a better job."

Casino work—a poor gamble

"I figured that working at a casino would be great. I could gamble on my breaks. I could eat from the buffet table. I'd get nice clothes to wear. I'd meet rich people who I could strike up friendships with and then use those contacts to get a really good job some day. Boy was I wrong!

"I was an attendant, and what I learned is that any job that has the word 'attendant' in its title is a crap job. I was not allowed to use the facilities—no gambling, no buffet table. I had to put down a clothing allowance or have it deducted from my meager paycheck. And, to really ice the cake, I was not allowed to fraternize with customers—even being 'too friendly' could get me chewed out. Instead of a really cool job despite the low pay, I had a crappy job with low pay. I have heard that some other jobs, like blackjack dealer, are not as bad. I don't think I will gamble on that. I already rolled the dice, and the casino lost as far as I am concerned."

Cleaning houses—no way to clean up on money

"Growing up, I learned how to clean house. All of us kids had chores to do, and we rotated them so that no one felt that he or she was working harder than the others were. So I learned to wash—dishes, clothes, windows, floors, everything. I learned how to dust—catching the dust in clothes to be shaken outdoors. I learned to sweep—with both brooms and vacuum cleaners. I learned to wax—furniture and floors. There wasn't much around the house that I couldn't do.

"So after I got married and our children went to school, I thought I could get a job with a maid service and make some money during school hours, doing something I knew how to do and was good at. The first thing I learned was that I would make very little money. Maid service may cost customers a lot, but it doesn't pay the 'maids' a lot—the money seems to all go to the owners.

"The second thing I learned was that we had so many houses to do that we really didn't clean them very much. What we did was make them look like we had cleaned them. We actually cleaned only a few places where the customers were most likely to look (and this varied with customers). We almost never moved furniture to sweep under it. Likewise, we dusted around things without moving them or lifting them. We wiped things out rather than washing them. The only thing we did half way right was windows and that was because the customers paid extra for that service.

"No real money for doing honest work. Not for me. I quit as soon as I could get another job."

When 40 hours is not full time

"I was out of work and getting desperate for money for rent, food, and car payments. So I was applying for everything I could find—full time and part time. I managed to find a part-time job in an office doing routine work—answering the phone, making copies, filing, making coffee, cleaning the breakroom—the usual. I gladly took the job and made a real effort to do well so that I could get a good recommendation should a full-time job come along.

"The office manager was impressed with my hours, efficiency, and conscientiousness, and asked me if I could work more hours. Anxious to earn even more money, I readily agreed. A month or so later, I was eating my lunch with a couple of others from the office and one of them asked me how I liked being full time. I thought he was talking about my longer hours, so I replied that I was pretty happy about it since I could use the extra money. He then said, 'And the fringes aren't bad either.' I asked what he meant. He seemed surprised and said that he was referring to the medical insurance and 401k plan. When I then indicated that I didn't know what he was talking about, both of them gave me a lot of details and seemed stunned that I didn't know anything about those benefits. They said that, when they were hired (as full-time employees), everything was explained to them and they filled out a bunch of forms.

"Needless to say, I soon asked the office manager about it. She told me that I was not eligible for those benefits since I was not full time. I said, 'What do you mean? I was part time when I came here, but now I work 8 hours a day or a bit more and 5 days a week. If that's not full time, I don't know what is!' She then explained to me that while I was working 40–42 hours a week, that I was still technically part time, an hourly employee, and not entitled to benefits. She had never offered me a full-time position, just more hours.

"Suddenly the job was no longer as attractive. Why put in the hours if you don't get all the advantages?"

Impressive job titles don't buy groceries

"You probably think that working in a savings and loan would be a good job. True, the buildings are nicely furnished, the workers are smiling when assisting customers, and you usually get Saturdays, Sundays, and all holidays off. But good job? Not necessarily.

"First, the wages are very high for the top person, okay for the next couple of people, and little better than minimum wage for everyone else. Like a pyramid with huge gaps in it. Second, in order to cover up the low wages, titles don't tell you much. Everyone other than probationary employees is a vice president. We even had a Vice President and Custodial Engineer, a janitor with a fancy title, at our location. I was a Vice President and Teller, which means I was a teller who was paid low wages.

"Low pay and fancy titles, though, don't tell the whole discouraging story. At my location, no one ever advanced. If an opening occurred for a higher-level position, they always recruited and filled the position from the outside. No teller ever became an account manager. Tellers were dead-end jobs. Working around a lot of money and working for high-level managers who make a lot of money means nothing except that top management is giving itself a lot of the money that should be paid to others farther down the line."

Lack of Job Security or
Advancement Opportunities

Freelancing may mean free work to "friends"

"I spent many hours learning about desktop computers and software programming for them and the Internet. While I still didn't have my degree, I would occasionally help out friends by working on their computers. Sometimes they wanted a home network set up; sometimes they wanted to install new software; sometimes they complained that their machines were running slow (removing spyware and adware, cleaning the registry, and reformatting generally took care of that); and sometimes they were getting a new computer and wanted to move stuff from the old to the new. Everyone seemed impressed with my work and knowledge. Some of them encouraged me to hustle a few steady clients and go full time rather than freelancing.

"Then one day a friend told me that a client of his was starting a business and wanted to hire someone to design a website for him and then become the webmaster. That looked like just the perfect way for me to get more pay and more training and still be able to finish my college degree. My friend had recommended me and the client was interested. This would mean moving from full time to part time student in terms of pursuing my degree, but it seemed like it would be worthwhile in terms of money and experience. I interviewed for the job and was hired immediately.

"I spent several weeks working long hours to design the client's website and get it up and running. Everyone seemed impressed with the website, and I even had a few calls from other small companies to design or redesign their websites.

"And then the client informed me that my 'contract' was up. Confused, I asked what did he mean and was told that he only wanted me to work long enough to get the site going. No mention of becoming a webmaster. End of job. Back to school full time, but not until next semester (too late to add classes this semester). But I was more street smart now—I realized that freelancers are easier prey than individuals who have a company behind them.

"I hope the guy's site starts malfunctioning and he comes to me to fix it. Then we'll talk about real money!"

Making music doesn't mean security

"A group of us after studying music in school formed a band upon graduation. We honed our skills by playing by ourselves and for ourselves for months, but when a family member of the drummer suggested that we were 'really good,' we felt that it was time to go get it. If we were good, then why not make some money? So we began to look for people who might pay to have us play.

"The first thing we discovered is that everyone wanted to know where you had played before or to hear your record or tape. Since we had never played anywhere else and had no record, they all turned us down. So we took on some freebies—school dances, wedding receptions, backyard parties, anything to get some experience and exposure. And we rented a recording studio and made a tape. By then our bass guitar had quit and been replaced, as had our lead vocalist. We changed the name of the band (it had featured the name of the bass guitarist before) and continued to try to get hired.

"We finally got hired but there were some 'conditions.' First, we had to agree to play in four different cities each about four hours drive from the others and to do so on the same weekend. This meant City One on Friday at 6:00 P.M., then City Two on Saturday at 2:00 P.M., City Three Saturday at 7:00 P.M., and finally City Four on Sunday at 2:00 P.M. Second, we had to agree to do that for a month. Third, if we couldn't draw a large enough crowd, we wouldn't get paid. That was it. The guy doing the hiring said, 'We'll see how it goes after that.'

"Each weekend another member of the band quit. So by the end of the month when we were told that there would be no renewal of our contract, I was the only one of the original group left. The band dissolved."

Hard work no guarantee of upward mobility

"The worst job I ever had was at X mart (I'm not giving the real name of course). I worked in women's clothing and most of my day was spent picking up clothes from where customers had dropped or thrown them, folding them or putting them back on hangers, locating where they belonged (customers frequently carried them some distance before dumping them), and putting them back while rearranging the display. I was also supposed to keep the floor clean (sweep and mop), replace price tags removed by customers, sort incoming merchandise, print price tags for new merchandise, and reprice everything for sales periodically.

"Most of the time I barely kept up. This was physically far more grueling work than I ever imagined. My legs and back ached every day. My eyes sometimes burned from the dyes on the fabrics. The pay was low, but X mart employment ads and brochures stressed how you could move up in the organization, so I tried to stick with it. I even tried my best to be nice to my supervisor, who was a total brute and incompetent besides.

"Eventually the prospect of moving up grew dim and having to pay for my own health insurance began to get more and more costly. So I decided to move on. And the top of my list for a new job was fringe benefits—they are worth more than just higher wages any day."

Proven skills not enough to get ahead

"When I got my degree and was offered a government job, I was thrilled. I would be part of the state government, part of providing necessary services for citizens, part of a very meaningful activity. While the job proved to be pretty boring, it was not hard work, and while the pay wasn't great, the benefits were, so I was quite satisfied. My boss was nice and my coworkers pleasant if a bit lazy, and I met some really great people through interaction with other agencies and the public. So all in all, I was pleased with my job and my career path.

"Several years later after I had been promoted a few times and always gotten consistently high performance evaluations, a higher-level position came open. I had done that job once before for 2 weeks while the regular employee took a vacation, so I knew that I could handle it. Because I had done it so well, the person who had held the job encouraged me to apply.

"I noted that among the requirements was a line that said, 'some graduate work desired.' Since it was only 'desired' and since I had actually done the job, I thought nothing of that requirement. When I did not even get an interview, I asked about it and was told that I didn't have any graduate education and so was not considered. I pointed out that it was only a 'desired' requirement and that I had done the job and then learned something new. The next job above this one required a graduate degree. They used the 'some graduate work' for this job to assure that by the time the person was ready for the next promotion, he would have the necessary graduate degree.

"I tried getting into grad school but my grades were not very good, and I could never handle those national multiple-choice tests. So my wonderful government career has now come to an abrupt halt. I have topped out and I'm not even 40 years old. This is crap. Degrees aren't really necessary, as I've already proved by doing the job well when I filled in. This is making me look around for another position—not in government though!"

BAD SUPERVISORS, COWORKERS, OR CLIENTELE

Bad Supervisors

Overqualified worker, insecure boss

"When my boss at a supermarket where I was working while in graduate school found out that I had a bachelor's degree, he fired me because he said that, while I was an excellent worker, I was overqualified and would not make a long-term employee. I later found out that he had a habit of this so that his unit almost always had good performance but high turnover. Since workers got 'learner wages' for the first several months on the job, firing them before they started getting full wages kept his costs down. That compensated for the high turnover. This was a bad place to work if you had any brains at all, as this insecure boss was apparently afraid of anyone who might know something that he didn't know."

Abusive supervisor changes personality of workplace

"I had been on the job for nearly 2 years when a new supervisor was hired. She was loud, shrill, and talked to employees (more accurately she shouted at or chewed out employees) so that everyone could hear her. Almost immediately she began to make changes that none of us liked. First came the breakroom. No more playing games, reading books, or listening to the radio while on break—you could go outside and smoke or you could sit at a table and do nothing. The microwave oven was removed, and the refrigerator became essentially off limits as frozen food and soft drinks were banned (frozen food because it would have required the microwave; soft drinks because they are 'not good for you').

"Next came the way we were treated. While we were all college graduates with several years of experience at our jobs, she constantly went over every bit of our work, 'correcting' it (sometimes using improper spelling or grammar), and having us redo it until it met her satisfaction. She quickly started having us route everything (including our email) through her. Not only did this slow things down, but her 'touch' frequently made the work of poorer quality.

"Next came our workspace. All walls were removed and replaced with low partitions so that she could hear and see each of us anytime she wanted. Then came the order that we were not to have any personal items on our desks or on the cubicle walls as that detracted from the professionalism of the office and could serve to make some people feel inferior to others.

"Within a year, everyone who could leave did so. The ones remaining in this now unhappy workplace either were close to retirement and were simply 'waiting it out' or were not all that competent themselves so that they really couldn't leave."

Overly controlling supervisor creates underproducing employees

"I have a degree in marketing and so naturally I worked in sales for a while. One firm I was with was terrible. I spent about 10–12 hours each week doing reports instead of selling. I did a report on each customer I contacted even if I didn't make a sale. I had to do detailed expense reports. I had to summarize everything I did during each week and what I planned to do the next week. But the worst part was that I could not make any decisions, even little ones, on my own. I had to check with someone, not just my supervisor, if I wanted to extend credit or offer a quantity discount to a customer. I had to get expenses approved ahead of time or eat the costs. I could have been far more productive had I been granted more leeway in doing my job."

Bad Coworkers

Rude workers affect morale and offend morals

"I was hired to work backstage for a local theatre. Most of the time, I helped move scenery and lights and did other odd jobs as needed, and, while it was sometimes fairly hard work, it was also fun to be involved with the different productions. When off-Broadway productions came to town, as one of the few females in the stage crew, I was also asked to help out in the women's dressing room. I could not believe how rude and crude the dancers and support people in these groups were. They would throw their costumes everywhere and expect me to pick them up, clean them off, and hang them up in the proper order for use at the next performance. They also constantly bragged about their encounters with men. I had heard that men did this but was shocked to find out that these dancers seemed to think that 'bedding' a man was the way to get one to marry them. They seem obsessed with 'getting a man.' This was very embarrassing to me, and I tried to get assigned to something else when I could."

Lazy, manipulative coworkers don't carry their weight

"A really bad job I had was because of my coworkers. They worked together on the weekends on another job and so knew each other well long before I was hired. They also had worked for the same supervisor for years and so knew her and how to manipulate her. One of our tasks was cleaning up the cafeteria line after it shut down for the night. They would clean up by eating everything they could get their hands on, especially if it was something particularly good. I was never able to eat anything good as they got it all first, even packing some of it to take home. They would not do any of the real work unless the supervisor was around. They would be nice to her, do their work, and belittle my performance so that the supervisor always treated them nice but never did me. I tried to get friendly with them but they would have none of it."

Temp means low status

"One of the worst jobs I ever had was a temp job loading trucks at a warehouse. All night long I loaded boxes and crates into trucks from out of the warehouse. The heat (in summer) and the cold (in winter); the noise of forklifts and conveyor belts; and the dust and dirt made the place almost unbearable. I soon discovered that temp workers were not issued uniforms like the regular workers and so 'stood out.' By 'stood out,' I mean that we were clearly identifiable as second-class citizens with none of the few privileges afforded the regular workers.

"Not only were the regular workers 'better' than us, but they were our 'inspectors' who judged whether or not we were stacking the crates and boxes correctly—crates on the bottom, boxes on top. In addition to being checked by the regular workers, there were security cameras everywhere. No one could have walked off with a speck of dust without it being caught by one of the cameras. The cameras weren't just there to catch anyone trying to steal something either. We had strict rules about breaks, rests, and 'visiting' with other workers; the cameras monitored those as well. As soon as I could, I found another job."

Nursing not given healthy status in healthcare hierarchy

"When I got my associate degree in nursing from a local community college, I thought that my career was set. I kept hearing about the shortage of nurses and assumed that meant there would be plenty of jobs and high-paying ones at that. Well, what I found out was that lots of hospitals and private clinics apparently would get by without nurses rather than use ones without 4-year college degrees (or more). Jobs for me were in public health clinics and doctors' offices (doing office work rather than nursing in most cases).

"People with my level of training might be entitled to be called nurses, but that didn't make us nurses in the eyes of doctors or RNs (registered nurses). They looked down on us, treated us poorly, relegated us to the dirtiest and smelliest jobs (you probably can guess what they involved!), and generally treated us like we were at best nurses' helpers and at worst janitors.

"I'm now planning to try to go back to school to get a 4-year degree, but I plan to major in something other than nursing."

Mean-spirited coworkers on the line

"Our city has lots of telemarketing firms, and so it is easy to get a job with one of them whenever you need some extra cash. I picked one that specializes in securing contributions for charitable organizations because I wouldn't feel bad asking for money for charity. It paid well and since it was for good causes, I thought it would be fun and relatively easy since it was all done by phone.

"I was prepared (I thought) for people yelling and insulting me for interrupting their lives, but I wasn't prepared for my coworkers. My coworkers stole my call sheets (they are used to determine who you will call and to document that you have done so for merit pay). They would sometimes switch earpieces or screw up your computer password. They just seemed to be immature, mean-spirited, and nasty. I soon quit that job as no amount of money is worth putting up with jerks if you don't have to. And I don't think I will feel bad in the future if I insult a telemarketer who rings my phone to ask for a charitable donation."

Bad Customers/Clientele

If Only They Had to Walk in Our Shoes

"Being a cashier is a pretty cushy job, yes? Actually, no! I worked as a cashier for several months while I was an undergraduate at a large university in the Southeast, and there I found out that this job is no picnic. First of all, there are 'rush hours'—times when numerous customers are wanting to check out at the same time so you are under a lot of pressure to work fast. That pressure can lead to mistakes, which can slow things down (exactly what you don't want) or be costly and come out of your pay (exactly what you cannot afford on a cashier's salary). Second, there are the customers. Some customers are fine; they are polite and patient. Others are anything but; they are rude, critical, angry, bossy, and sometimes even cuss you out. It is stressful and I would not want to ever do it again. I think everybody should have to work at least one day (preferably more) as a cashier so they could see what it's like. I think it would change their attitude if they had to walk in our shoes."

So, so (un)satisfied

"One of the hardest things to learn in sales is that there are a lot of bad customers out there who will make your job miserable. They will eat up your time and energy. They will have you emailing, phoning, and faxing them constantly. They are never satisfied, haggle over everything, rarely pay their bills on time, and are frequently rude. I got stuck with a bunch of them and the only way I could make my quota was to try to keep them happy. Since you can't please all of the people all the time, I gave up and got out of sales. I would love to see some of those customers have to do my job for even a few days, working with complainers like themselves."

One bad apple

"My job is made miserable by this one big customer. She blames me or the product or the company for everything that goes wrong in her organization. I try to please her because she is a big customer and because she is so well connected in the industry that if she badmouths us, it could cost us plenty. So I take careful notes of all of her complaints and try to deal with them, but I also make sure that my supervisor is aware of everything 'just in case.'

"I think there comes a time when it's just not worth the effort it takes to keep a customer. For this customer, that time has come, as far as I'm concerned. I hope management will soon agree with my assessment."

Thieves on the loose

"If it weren't for customers, this wouldn't be a bad job. Actually, not all customers, just the bad ones. I work for _____, which is a major electronics retailer. We have customers who look for items that are heavily discounted to lure customers into the store. They will buy them and then offer them for sale on eBay or Amazon.com to try to make a profit on them. That doesn't bother me personally, as they could argue that that's just good, old-fashioned American entrepreneurship in action.

"Still other customers—the really bad ones—buy items that have a rebate, apply for the rebates, return the items, and then buy them back for a lower price as 'open box' items. That is dishonest, and I have a hard time holding back my instinct to tell them that they are cheaters. We have had a couple of cases even worse than that, though, where the customer purchased a computer, took out the hard drive, then returned the computer the following day. We put it back on the shelf at an opened-box price, and a few days later another customer wanted us to start it up before he bought it. That's when we found something wrong, opened up the computer, and discovered the missing drive. Sure, it's not my money that's being lost, but it's so dishonest that it makes you not trust anyone. I would bet that that person would yell loudest of all if a thief came into his house and took something."

Tanning salon patrons not always pretty

"I recently took a second-shift job for a tanning salon that requires me to work until closing time at 9:00. For just above minimum wage, I answer the phone, schedule appointments, handle walk-ins, and keep the place clean. Keeping the place clean means sweeping once a night, making sure the restroom is in order (it is seldom used except by me), and cleaning the tanning booths. After a booth is used, I wipe the sweat and lotion off the mats and the floor.

"These duties don't make for a really bad job, but for a young woman in here at night, in particular, it can be 'uncomfortable.' Male (and some female) customers look me over in very suggestive ways, ask me to help them apply lotion, and try out lame pick-up lines on me. I also wish that there was someone else around when I close at 10 so that I wouldn't worry about going alone to my car in the parking lot. Most of our customers are just younger women like me, who want to look good, and they are pleasant to have around. But there are a few guys in particular that I would never think from looking at them, that they cared about their personal appearance. That's why I say that some of my customers make this an unattractive job."

SECTION IV

NOW WHAT?

CHAPTER 11

WHAT DO WE KNOW?

The main goal of the future is to stop violence.
The world is addicted to it.

—Bill Cosby

Now that you've been through 10 chapters, some points of convergence regarding workplace violence should be apparent. Whether you are a manager or a nonmanager, your ability to reduce the propensity for workplace violence in your organization will be greater if you always strive to be a successful, effective, efficient member of your organization, with high performance standards. At the same time you should always strive to be observant, honest, ethical, fair, respectful, and trusting of people. Be open in your communications and to ideas and suggestions and understanding of others and their situations. That will assure that you, at least, are not contributing to workplace violence.

Always continue learning and keeping yourself mentally active. Read—read current works in your field and read for relaxation. It's not so much what you read as the fact that you are reading. Take classes offered by your organization, professional associations, local organizations, church groups. Again, it's not so much what you are studying as the fact that you are stretching your mind and making yourself more interesting and more interested. But while you are exercising your mind, don't neglect your body; it needs exercise, too.

Violence at Work: What Everyone Should Know, pp. 269–275
Copyright © 2014 by Information Age Publishing
All rights of reproduction in any form reserved.

For all of you who have read this book, we wish you the best and hope that your experiences don't mirror those in the anecdotes presented as section appendages throughout the book. As a further step in reducing the likelihood of violence in your organization, we offer the following concluding comments and recommend that you take a few minutes to work through the numbered Exercises following this chapter.

IMPLICATIONS FOR MANAGERS

In addition to the points made earlier, if you are a member of management—a manager—try your best not to be a "backwards boss": a double SOB. Just as the physical and fiscal resources of an organization are precious and need to be protected and developed, so, too, an organization's human resources are vital and need to be protected and developed. Try your best to hire the right people and then get to know them. Get to know those with whom you work—superiors, peers, and especially subordinates. Get out of your workspace and into theirs—but for the right reason. Talk to them, listen to them, understand them, and be sure to develop your own managerial skills.[1] A well-run organization is like an orchestra—it works best when everything is in harmony.

Matching Individuals and Jobs

An important factor to keep in mind is the match between individuals and jobs. Each job necessitates not only particular skills and abilities but also certain levels of effort for the jobholder to perform effectively. Whether those skills and abilities are acquired through education or experience—that is, formally or informally—is not as important as their presence. Also, matching individuals with jobs includes considering the individual's values, needs, and expectations. Only with a complete match will job holders have the "can do" necessary to perform successfully. Our philosophy is, "Give me the person with the right attitude and desire, and I can see that he gets the skills, whereas I cannot guarantee that I can develop the right attitude and desire in a skilled worker."

Obtaining Goal Acceptance and Compliance

Another important factor in determining performance involves what we might call "marching to the same drummer." Make sure that everyone understands and accepts the vision and mission of the organization. From there, work with your people to translate those into goals and objectives that are clear, understandable, achievable, and measurable. Move this line of thinking all the way down to specific tasks and job requirements. Clarify (make sure everyone knows what they are supposed to do) and get "buy in"—if not active commitment, at least get acceptance and compliance. As goals are established and agreed upon, ensure that the focus is on positive expectations for jobholders.

Even though people understand and accept the goals, and even if there is a good match, performance still depends upon other factors, one of which involves appraisal and feedback. How is performance on the job measured and evaluated, and how is that then communicated or fed back to the jobholder? If the jobholder sees the performance appraisal process as arbitrary or political, performance is likely to suffer. It is best if jobholders are involved in some way in establishing the objectives against which their performance will be measured and in the design of the measurement so that they accept the results as accurately reflecting their performance. Unless jobholders know how they are doing, they may have little incentive to try to do better. Self-control and feedback are vital components to achieving good performance.

One recommendation for assuring that people do understand and accept the goals is to establish S.M.A.R.T. goals. S.M.A.R.T. is an acronym that originally stood for specific, measurable, attainable, relevant and time-bound (or time-based or time-framed).[2] However, frequently other authors use the R for realistic and the T for timely. Fuzzy goals don't motivate as well as clear, specific ones. Having the ability to measure or verify the extent to which progress is made toward a goal provides a further incentive. But obviously if the goals are not really achievable or relevant to the task at hand, they don't serve to motivate people either. And finally, goals must have some sort of time limit—trying to achieve something in a month is clearly different than if you had 3 months or no specified time period at all.

Rewarding Performance

A third important factor in determining performance involves rewards. People do what is rewarding to them, so both the formal and informal reward structure must support good performance. You should recognize and reward good performance—even a simple thank you, atta boy, or some other form of recognition can go a long way. And always remember to praise in public but criticize in private. Rewards include more than praise, recognition, and compensation. Rewards include benefits, job assignments, titles, and access to resources as well. All of these should support good performance.

Of course the nature of the job itself can also impact performance. Highly monotonous jobs and jobs with little perceived significance don't have much appeal and are not likely to stimulate high levels of performance. Consider how you could modify jobs to allow a greater level of skill variety or so that the jobs are recognized as more important to the functioning of the organization. But most of all, permit job holders to exercise some control over their jobs. More control over the when, where, and how so long as quality, quantity, and timeliness goals are met has been shown to have strong links to effective performance.

If problems do develop, inform the individual(s) involved. This should be part of your normal feedback process but may on occasion need to be done sooner than normal processes permit. Prompt, informed action is needed for all of the situations described in this book. And, as noted earlier, when all else fails, termination carried out quietly and professionally may be the only solution.

Table 11.1 is designed to assist managers in recalling the information presented in Chapters 3, 6, and 9:

Table 11.1. Implications for Managers

Dealing With Managers	Dealing With Nonmanagers	Dealing With Jobs
Don't abuse power	Hire the right people	Improve undesirable workplaces
Control your anger	Be aware	Try to modify organizational culture/ climate
Learn new management skills	Understand reinforcement	Select better workers and outside contacts
Become competent and secure	Provide feedback	Increase pay, job security, and advancement opportunities
Hire and keep the right workers	Provide training	Redesign jobs
	Assist the exit	

IMPLICATIONS FOR NONMANAGERS

Beyond what has already been said, the most important issue for nonmanager employees and coworkers is communication. Whether the issue is a bad manager, one or more bad coworkers, or a bad job, you need to talk with someone about the situation. Keeping everything bottled up inside your will only lead to more problems over time. However, avoid being a whiner or complainer while doing so. Remember, you have only four options: (1) accept and adapt; (2) try to bring about a change in your situation by talking with those involved; (3) report/discuss the problem to a manager, the Human Resources department if one exists, or an ombudsperson if one exists; or (4) find another job.

Try to Cope

In trying to cope, you need to "get your house in order" by making sure that your own performance is good. Keep yourself healthy by eating and sleeping right, exercising, and trying to maintain some positive relationships at work. Start looking for another job but don't "jump ship," as a "panic move" may result in a situation that is no better and may even be worse. Make sure that you have things to do off the job that you enjoy—a hobby, recreation, family, church, or whatever. Your objective at the moment is to be sure that at least some part of your life is not miserable.

Try to Solve the Problem

If you choose the change route, make sure that you have good information before you start: good information about yourself, your manager, your coworkers, or the job, whichever is the target of desired change. Prepare an "action plan" that identifies the problems as you see them and what might be done to reduce or eliminate them. It's a good idea to have someone else, a confidant or mentor, help you with this plan to assure that your action plan is objective and attainable. Carefully consider who else is going to be involved and have the plan ready to share with them.

Unless the problem is simple and limited, we would caution you not to be too optimistic about effectively bringing about a change just by talking to the person you identify as the offender. If you are wanting to change your manager, for most problems you will need to communicate with him or her before you take your "case" to Human Resources or a superior manager in the organization. You are more likely to persuade a manager to change if others in the organization work with you. And you almost certainly will have to work with your manager if you are hoping to change the nature of your job and possibly the many issues that may surround your coworkers as well. Any meetings with others in the organization will need to be on "neutral ground," possibly even off the premises. Focus on what really matters to you—if you could make one and only one change, what would it be (and would it be enough or at least a good start)?

Table 11.2 is designed to assist employees or coworkers in recalling the information presented in Chapters 4, 7, and 10.

Table 11.2.   Implications for Nonmanagers

Dealing With Managers	Dealing With Nonmanagers	Dealing With Jobs
Analyze yourself	Be polite and professional	Change or adapt to workplace
Analyze your problem	Don't ignore the problem	Try to deal with organizational culture
Be polite, professional, and not disparaging	Identify your values	Change or adapt to bad managers, coworkers, and outside contacts
Exercise your options	Practice avoidance	Reevaluate career
	Focus on life off the job	
	Try to change the person	

But in the final analysis, be prepared to change jobs. Hopefully you will find help in that endeavor by concentrating on the following advice.

Find a New Job

If you become a job seeker, your goal is to try to avoid ending up employed by an organization that has a high potential for workplace violence. Your ability to research people and jobs is limited, of course, when you are not already employed by an organization and hence have access to inside information and people. An interview can help you learn a great deal more. You should try to find out as much as you can, though, about the organization and the job before the interview, and definitely before you accept or turn down a job. Our next chapter (Chapter 12, "Moving On") includes ideas for researching the organization and interviewing, including questions to ask interviewers, managers, and nonmanagers. Chapter 12 also offers ideas on evaluating the job and the workplace after the interview.[3]

Accepting a new job is always risky. What you want to do is to minimize the risk and be as prepared as you can for what lies ahead.

WHAT NEXT?

This chapter summarizes many of the suggestions about actions you may take to reduce the propensity for violence in your organization.[4] For those readers who may give up on the task and place themselves in the job market, just reading about the bad behaviors should be helpful in keeping their eyes and ears open for undesirable characteristics of a job, its workers, and its managers. This applies especially to those characteristics and behaviors that make the workplace vulnerable to violence.

NOTES

1. Griffin, R. W., & Van Fleet, D. D. (2013). *Management skills: Assessment and development*. Mason, OH: SouthWestern/Cengage Learning.
2. Doran, G. T. (1981). There's a S.M.A.R.T. way to write management's goals and objectives. *Management Review, 70*(11), 35–36.
3. Griffin & Van Fleet, *op. cit.*, Appendix B.
4. Van Fleet, D. D., & Van Fleet, E. W. (2010). *The violence volcano: Reducing the threat of workplace violence*. Charlotte, NC: Information Age Publishing.

CHAPTER 12

OPTION 4

Moving On

---

*It is the great sadness of our species that we have not found a way to
eliminate the conflict and to eliminate violence as a device to resolve our
conflicts throughout the entire history of the human race.*

—Neale Donald Walsch

Throughout this book we have noted that you have only four options. Earlier chapters focused on the first three of those options: cope, try to change the behavior of others, and seek help at higher levels of the organization. Now it is time to think about the fourth option: finding another job and moving on.

A rather obvious way in which to avoid bad jobs is to have sufficient training, education, and experience to qualify for jobs that are more likely to be good jobs. With higher levels of qualifications, you should be able at least to avoid the lower paying jobs that also offer little security. Thus, one piece of advice from us is to keep learning. Stay in school; go back to school; take advantage of training programs from local organizations or your current organization; keep developing your skills and broadening your qualifications. But given "where and who you are," what can you do to avoid getting into a bad job?

Ideally, the time to start thinking about avoiding organizations that may have a higher potential for workplace violence is when you are searching for a job, but identifying those organizations ahead of time can be quite difficult. Think about each of the groups of "bad" (managers, nonmanagers, workplaces/jobs) described earlier. How would you determine, before you join the organization, whether such "bads" exist? Individuals tend to be on their best behavior during job search processes, so "what you see" in an interview may well not be "what you get" after you're hired. On the other hand, if you don't like what you see during that time of best behavior, think seriously about pursuing the job further unless you absolutely have no other alternatives available to you. In some instances and for some individuals, any job may be better than no job, so an applicant may not wish to be too fussy in the first place. The best you can do is try to find out all you can about the organization, its reputation, and those who currently work there. Research the organization, visit the job site if you can, interview and follow up, and then evaluate the job and the organization.

Some of the items that job seekers are normally told to consider include job duties, the level of accountability, supervisory duties, education and experience required, human relations skills required, and the budget involved. Our anecdotes seem to suggest that job seekers should look for and ask for very specific information about the jobs they are interested in. That information should consist of the physical environment including location, noise, temperature and the like; the social environment including relations with coworkers; the managerial environment, particularly immediate supervision; the economic environment, including compensation, benefits, opportunities for advancement, and possibilities of reassignment if the organization has more than one location for the type of position that you are seeking. Accepting a new job is always risky. What you want to do is to minimize the risk and be as prepared as you can for what lies ahead.

DO YOUR HOMEWORK

First, do your homework—research the organization. That means trying to find out all you can about the organization, the job, and of course its people before you apply and interview for a job. If possible, browse the organization's Employee Handbook or talk with union representatives for clues as to how autocratic or progressive the organization is in its approach to human relations. Some companies share this information readily. Others keep strict control of their Handbook, so plan to get your information some other way.

Print and Web-Based Media

Both print and web-based media can provide general job/career information and somewhat more specific information about safety and health issues, competitive salaries, and financial security. Your local library may have access to sources that could be quite useful to you as well.

As a starter, check the Internet, especially the organization's website. Dig deeply, and try to read between the lines of press releases, annual reports, and newsletters. Use your browser to see what positive and negative things you can find about the organization, but be aware that (a) what you see may be distorted and (b) finding nothing is not a guarantee that there is nothing negative about the organization; it just means that nothing has been posted online yet. Much information can be gleaned by checking online sources such as *Dun & Bradstreet*, *Moody's*, and *The Wall Street Journal*. Even Wikipedia can supply interesting facts, such as the company's history, which may help you show your interest and thoroughness when you interview with the organization later. Look for endorsements and outside ratings such as *Fortune*'s "Best Companies to Work For" and *Newsweek*'s rankings of "Best Places to Work."

Internet blogs are a modern-day way of getting some inside information. See if the organization you are considering shows up on any of them and what is said. On the other hand, there are many sites in which people can air their grievances—legitimate or not—against individuals and organizations. Be careful, as many of these sites do not screen the individuals who are posting comments. As you are well aware, we cannot trust everything we read on the Internet or in print. Frequently, only the negative gets publicized. On the other hand, the company can post exaggerated positive comments.

Having said this, we should warn you that you are not likely to find very useful specific information on the Internet or in print about the work atmosphere or the bosses' behaviors. What you will find is more general information about the organization rather than the particular job and its supervisors.

The Community

While all information can be useful, your best bets may be the employees and the people with whom they talk outside of work. If possible, talk to the people who live and shop in the area—the people with whom the workers in the organization come into contact on a day-to-day basis. This may include people whom you know or meet through church connections, clubs, or professional organizations. They hear the good and the bad from their neighbors and clients who work with the coworkers that you will meet. Casually ask a waitress, barber, grocery checkout clerk, or church member in the area what they know or have heard about the organization as a place to work. Ask indirect questions like, "What's the organization's reputation for hiring, firing, and promoting?" or "What are the people who work for the organization really like?" Don't expect to get straightforward answers most of the time. Instead, listen for clues like, "They have a hard time keeping employees, so anybody can get a job there if you can read and write" or "Everybody wants to work there, so they're very selective, and that means there's a lot of cat fighting and dog fighting to move up."

The Job Site

If possible, visit the organization itself or meet with an acquaintance who works there before the interview and ask specific questions. How clean or dirty is the area? What is the temperature? Are there any unpleasant odors or loud noises? Is the equipment up-to-date and in good working condition? Observe how people dress and act. Are they busy but pleasant, or busy and looking stressed? Do they appear to be organized so that they can perform their jobs without sitting idle to wait for direction? This sort of information will greatly assist you in understanding the job before you accept it.

Sometimes you can get a feel for the atmosphere of the organization by visiting the employee breakroom to observe its condition and to read any signs or notices posted there. Watch how people act, and listen to what break or lunch conversations are about. Notice whether some individuals are left out of conversations and informal groups. Who are the leaders? The followers? The isolates? The employees who are left out? Also, you may be able to engage in conversations in this more informal setting and may want to ask other questions that have emerged based on what you see or hear in such a visit.

See if you can informally ask what people think of their bosses, the organization in general, and its culture (the Interview section below suggests questions to gain a perspective about an organization's culture). Maybe you can learn whether any coworker has experienced any kind of personal emergency and how the boss and the organization responded to that emergency. Maybe it wasn't an emergency but childbirth, bereavement, domestic problems, or a prolonged illness. How bosses and organizations respond to unusual events can also suggest a great deal about what your life would be like should you accept a job at the organization. Again, the important thing is to find out as much as you can before you accept a job at the organization. Information is the key to a successful job search.

PREPARE FOR THE INTERVIEW

Once you get to an interview, the information available to you changes. A good interview is a two-way process—the organization learns about you and you learn about the organization. Treat it as a way to see as well as to be seen. Generally, much of this learning takes the form of questions and answers, so you should have a list of written questions with you. Those questions should deal with details not covered in the job advertisement or prior contacts with the organization (many of these were suggested earlier in this book). In particular, you should try to find out as much as you can about the job details, the manager, and the coworkers. Ask the person setting up the interview to schedule you for a visit to the actual job site or office so you can get a firsthand feel for what it is like. You may be able to chat briefly with those who work there, which could be helpful.

Be prepared to talk to several people during the interview process. Obtaining input from different individuals will give you a more complete understanding of the job before you accept it or reject it. See also the questions that appear below. You will probably be able to ask only 4–5 questions of any individual, so the following are guides from which you can select your questions.

Immediately after the interview, write down specifics about the job, the organization, the interviewer, and anything else you think is pertinent. This will come in handy when preparing to follow up the interview.

Answering Questions

As stated earlier, the interview should be a two-way street—the organization is evaluating you, and you are evaluating the organization. So you should be prepared to answer questions about your qualification, expectations, and such. Questions that interviewers ask vary immensely by field of work, company, job, job applicant, and interviewer. Some of them are intended to get helpful information about your job qualifications; others are designed to find out more about you as a person or coworker. You may wish to answer some of them without hesitation but provide indirect answers to other questions (e.g., salary). Here are a few questions (used mostly for nonmanagers) to think about before a personal or telephone interview:

- Why do you think you want to work for this company?
- What can you do for this company?
- Why should we hire you instead of someone else with the same qualifications?

- Why are you leaving (Why did you leave) your job?
- What was your biggest accomplishment/failure in that position?
- What major challenges and problems did you face? How did you handle them?
- What were your responsibilities at your current (or last) position?
- What is the most difficult situation you have faced?
- What are some of the things you and your supervisor have disagreed on?
- Tell me about a time when you had to deal with a coworker who wasn't doing his/her fair share of the work. What did you do and what was the outcome?
- Tell me about yourself.
- Tell me about your skills.
- Tell me about your greatest assets or strengths.
- Tell me about your greatest shortcomings or weaknesses.
- How do you measure success?
- What motivates you?
- What do you enjoy doing during your "spare time"?
- What would you do differently if you could start your working life over?
- What does your budget say that you need to earn, or what were your starting and final levels of compensation?

Sometimes a company representative will ask questions that are inappropriate or even illegal; for example, marital status, religion, sexual preference, children (present or planned), spouse's employer, and the like. If so, you will want to think twice before accepting a position there; but at the time of the interview, you may nevertheless struggle to know what you should say. What is legal versus illegal varies with location as various federal, state, and local jurisdictions have different regulations regarding what a prospective employer can ask. In any case, legal questions must be related to the particular job in question. If you are asked a question that you suspect may be illegal, basically you have three choices open to you—each of which has some degree of risk involved.

One alternative is to refuse to answer the question. For example, if the interviewer asks where you were born, you have a legitimate right to indicate that you don't see how this is pertinent to the job. However, if you refuse to answer a question, no matter how graciously you handle the situation, you run the risk of appearing uncooperative or, even worse, confrontational. In most cases, this will reduce your chances of getting the job, so you should carefully consider the consequences before exercising that choice.

Another choice is to answer the question as asked. You incur some risk as well when you exercise this option, as your response may provide the interviewer with material that could limit your probability of getting the job. For example, if you answer the question about how many children you have or plan to have, the interviewer may decide that childcare will be a problem that affects your attendance or even your commitment to the job. If you answer that you have no children and no plans for children, the interviewer may conclude that you are self-centered or do not appreciate family values. If you divulge your birthplace, you may also create a bias in the mind of the interviewer.

Still another choice is to answer the question as you think it should have been asked. If you exercise the third choice, be careful that you don't appear negative or sound like a wisecracker or "smart aleck," as such perceptions would reduce your chances of getting the job. For example, if the boss asks "Who's going to take care of your children while you're at work?" you could respond by saying that you have that detail taken care of or "under control." If asked your age, you could respond that you are of legal adult age and qualified to handle the job.

ASKING QUESTIONS ABOUT THE JOB

So you need to have questions that you want to ask them as well—not just about the job duties, pay, and benefits, but also about the supervision and its impact. These sorts of questions will help you understand the organization, its managers, its employees, and the job you are considering. If any of the responses seem vague or unclear, don't hesitate to ask for clarification. Make sure that you allow enough time for the interviewer to respond to your questions—waiting silently can sometimes elicit information that otherwise might not have been forthcoming. Ideally, talk with others who already work for the prospective boss and even the former jobholder if at all possible. Don't be embarrassed or apologetic about having your questions in writing to aid your memory.

Now it's time to focus your questions on the job itself. Many of your questions will be covered by the interviewer or other managers, and much of the information you can get by keeping your eyes and ears focused. Seek as much detail as you can, as this is the most important aspect of your search. So from this set of questions, look for several that are pertinent to your particular job search.

- With whom will I work and what are their backgrounds?
- What skills, experience, and traits are needed for this job?
- What is the worst thing about this job?
- What significant changes do you foresee in the future?
- Describe a typical day for someone on this job.
- What are you looking for in the successful candidate?
- What do you see as my strengths and shortcomings in this position?
- How does my background fit with your requirements for this position?
- When was the last time someone left this job, and why did that person leave? And the person before that?
- How often has this position been filled in the past 5–10 years, and where have those people gone
- What are some of the long-term objectives you would like completed?
- What is most pressing? What would you like to have done within the next two or three months?
- What are the key milestones you expect me to reach and within what period of time?
- In what ways were you most pleased with the performance of the last person who held this position?
- Where is the greatest room for improvement?
- What would you like done differently by the next person who fills the job?
- What are some of the more difficult problems one would face in this position? How do you think these could be handled best?
- What freedom would I have in determining my work objectives, deadlines, and methods of measurement?
- How is performance on the job evaluated?
- A year from now, if I do an excellent job for you, what type of increase can I expect? How does this compare to the average increase?

Asking Questions About Employees

Ask about the individuals who will be your coworkers and try to determine if any of them might fall into the groups previously identified as bad nonmanagers/coworkers. These and questions like the following will help you understand the organization, its managers, and its employees as much as possible before accepting a job. Note that you will probably be able to ask only 3–5 questions, so these are guides from which you should select a few to ask. In any event, consider questions like the following. Prioritize them, as you may be given time to ask only 2–3 questions.

- What can you tell me about the employees with whom I would be working?
- What are some of the common characteristics of employees in this work group?
- Describe an employee who is thought to be a poor worker. What does that person do or not do to earn that label?
- Describe an employee who is thought to be an excellent worker. What makes that person special?
- What causes the most stress in the work group?
- Why is this job available? What happened to the person who previously held this job? If he or she was terminated, why and how long did the person stay in the position?
- How is performance evaluated? By whom? How often?
- What freedom would I have in determining my own work objectives, deadlines, and methods of measurement?
- What are some of the more difficult problems I would face on this job? What is the worst thing about this job?
- How are situations handled when there's too much work for employees?
- What were the main reasons for the turnover?

Asking Questions About the Organization

You may now ask one or two questions about the general nature of the organization to get an "overall" feel for it:

- Describe the organization's culture and values.
- Are there organizational training programs for employees?
- Is there tuition reimbursement or other support for training and education?
- What is your perception of the job and department?
- When did you start here and why do you stay?

- Are there opportunities for upward evaluations and feedback? Does the organization use 360-degree feedback for its supervisors and managers?
- What rotational policies and work arrangements are available (e.g., flexible schedules, compensatory time, or telecommuting)?

Avoid too many questions regarding pay, time off, bonuses, retirement benefits, rules, grievance procedures, and similar topics that may suggest that you are not as interested in the job as you are in those things (one CEO that we know refuses to hire a person who asks about retirement during the interview). You want to show an interest in growing with the job, of course, but too many questions about advancement opportunities, salary increases, and bonuses may suggest that you are not really committed to this particular job and could be a "short-timer." Also, questions regarding pay and benefits can be answered by the Human Resources department after the interview if there is mutual interest in the job. The best way to determine company rules and grievance procedures is to read the company's employee handbook.

Ask Your Closing Questions

Having said all of this about asking questions, we think it is also important to note that it is possible to ask too many questions. While it may be a good tactic to ask a couple of "impressive" questions to show that you have done your homework, your questions should be primarily about things that matter enough for you to take the interviewer's time. When you have many questions, consider asking different questions of different interviewers or departmental employees with whom you meet. You do not want to leave the impression that you are overly concerned, too uptight, or a person who worries too much.

Finally, ask some general questions to wrap things up. These may be questions that just naturally occur as the interview process comes to a conclusion and could even be asked as you are walking out.

- What are the questions that I did not ask you but should have?
- What is the next step in this process? When can I expect to hear from you?
- May I have your business card?
- When may I call you to follow up?

EVALUATE YOUR JOB SEARCH

Even if you have not yet been offered a job, take time to sit down and evaluate your experience. The general impression you get during your job-hunt process can be quite revealing about the nature of the organization and its willingness or unwillingness to tolerate bad employees. So you should be observant as to how you and the process are handled and who is involved. Are you treated respectfully or more like a part on an assembly line? Is the process open and interactive or rigid with only one-way communication? Do you meet several people with whom you would be working or only one or two HR people or supervisors? Did the workers seem relaxed or stressed? Consider the interview process in general; your interaction with the interviewer, managers, and nonmanagers; and your initial analysis of what you know at this point about the job, its rewards, and its advancement opportunities.

Your Interaction With Interviewer and Managers

First, think back to the way in which the organization and the individuals handled the interview process. Were they willing to accommodate your schedule and needs, or did they assign you a "take it or leave it" time? Did you get the impression that you are just a number or "one of the pack," or did they treat you as an individual and show genuine interest? Did they ask you questions that you felt were inappropriate or perhaps illegal? One possible tip-off to future problems may be noted by illegal questions asked during an interview. Were any of the questions inappropriate—marital status, present or planned children, where spouse is employed, and the like?

These impressions can be revealing about the nature of the organization and its willingness to tolerate bad managers and nonmanagers. If the human touch is not there in the interview process, it likely won't be there once you're hired either. Be alert to how you and the process are handled. On the other hand, recognize that the Human Relations people who are your primary contacts at this stage are not necessarily representative of the department in which you will be working.

Much of what you learn in the interview process is subjective and perceptual, but here are a few suggestions of things you should probably notice:

- How accommodating was the organization to your schedule?
- What information did they provide ahead of time to help you prepare? Whom did you meet and what were they like?
- Were you given clear and accurate instructions for getting to the interview location?

- Were you kept waiting?
- Was the interview threatening or pleasant?
- Were you voluntarily provided helpful details about the job and the company?
- Did you leave the company with a clear idea of what the job would be like on a day-by-day basis?
- Did you learn why the previous person had left the job?
- What were your impressions of the workers and managers that you saw? Did they seem busy and content? Friendly with one another? Loud or much too restrained? Groomed and attired as you would have expected?
- What were your impressions of the surroundings—Pleasant? Noisy? Busy? Clean and well-kept? Overcrowded? Sophisticated?
- Were you given skills tests? Personality tests?
- Think back to the questions that you were asked—what seemed most important to the interviewers? Were there any clues as to their likes and dislikes?
- All in all, does this seem to be the kind of place where you would like to work?

These questions or evaluations will help you form a general impression that becomes the background for your decision to accept or reject an offer if one is forthcoming.

Your Interaction With the Workers

Also evaluate the people you met and the process itself. What was the mix of people you met? Are the people you met homogeneous (same race, same age bracket, same sex, same organization level, same department, same everything)? That may suggest aspects of the organization that you may or may not like. Did everyone ask you the same questions? If so, they may be reluctant to deviate from a predetermined set of questions—which may or may not suggest the kind of organization that you want to work for.

Take note of the people you met during the interview process, but remember that they were probably on their best behavior. What were they like? How personable or friendly did they seem? Did they talk openly and freely about the job, the boss, and the organization; or did they talk in vague, general terms sharing little specific information? Were they almost too friendly? Did the place seem too dirty, too disorganized, too quiet, or too noisy for the work being performed?

Also note what questions you were asked. Were they inappropriate—marital status, religion, sexual preference, children (present or planned), spouse's work, and the like? Were they focused on your "tolerance," asking questions such as "Can you work with others who do so-and-so?" or "We do so-and-so around here. Would you have any problems with that?" Think twice before accepting a position in an organization that asks these kinds of questions, particularly if dangerous risks might be involved.

Did you detect any hints that any of the employees with whom you would be working might lack interpersonal skills or have attitude problems? Did their personal appearance seem appropriate to your concept, or are they over- or underdressed? Were there any hints that the employees are experiencing too much pressure or some type of problems with others in the organization or from clients/customers? Did you detect any subtle indicators of potential bad coworkers?

FOLLOW UP

Following up after an interview is one more way in which you can get a sense of what the organization's culture or climate is like. Is your follow-up ignored, responded to in a very mechanistic way, or warmly dealt with? Don't assume that a failure to respond promptly is tantamount to "no thanks." Some companies prefer not to be bothered with additional contacts (often because they receive so many applications), so they respond only when they invite the applicant to interview and when they issue a job offer. On the other hand, to some companies, following up is important and can actually influence whether you get the job. Following up suggests to them that you are interested in the job. It also suggests certain personal charactcristics such as resolve, attention to detail, and the ability to follow through. If you don't know the expectations of the persons with whom you interviewed, err on the safe side by following up.

There are several ways to follow up. Telephone calls are generally frowned upon as they disrupt the receiver and take too much of his time. Written approaches are generally more professional although that can vary by industry or organization. Using regular postal service or email, you can send a simple card, note, or letter indicating that you appreciated the opportunity of an interview and look forward to hearing the decision in the near future. You may wish to add a sentence about your continued interest and mention something specific about the interview to build some rapport with interviewee. Or you could develop a letter even further by reiterating your strengths and accomplishments that are relevant to the job and possibly bring in information that did not get conveyed during the interview. Usually, it is best to keep it brief.

The important thing about following up is that you do it. Following up not only can make a difference in whether you get an offer, but it may also furnish you with important perceptions about what working for the organization would be like. It may also help you in the future. Who knows, even if you don't get this job, maybe the organization will have another one in the future.

WHAT NEXT?

Hopefully, you will not need to be searching for a new job. But if that should be the case, this time you will use what you have learned to try to find a place that will at least be safe, and preferably more pleasant in other ways. Not all problems that you could encounter have been anticipated and covered in this book, but we hope that enough have been identified to arm you with useful information. The recommendations are not intended to be all-inclusive but rather to suggest the complexity of some things you can do to avoid "bad" situations. Also, keep engaging in self-evaluation so you can rest assured that you will not aggravate or become part of a problem.

We hope that you have found, or will find, this book useful. Put the suggestions into practice and pass the word—maybe then incidents of workplace violence will subside. Continue to learn about workplace violence—how to prevent it, how to deal with it, and most of all how not to become a part of it.

EXERCISES

As further assistance to you, we provide three assessment exercises and an appendix with checklists of psychopathy.

- The first assessment exercise is designed to help you focus on those specific aspects of your work situation that you feel might push you or others toward an increased propensity for workplace violence.
- The second exercise uses the same format but focuses on your organization to help you see how it could be improved so that it is not contributing to an increased propensity for workplace violence.
- The third exercise is an assessment instrument from an earlier publication and consists of a detailed list of items that can contribute to an increased propensity for workplace violence in an organization.

Violence at Work: What Everyone Should Know, pp. 291–304
Copyright © 2014 by Information Age Publishing
All rights of reproduction in any form reserved.

EXERCISE 1: SELF-ASSESSMENT EXERCISE

Step 1—List

On this page or on a sheet of your own paper, write down up to 15 items that you dislike about your current work situation. Don't worry about whether they deal with people, places, things, or whatever; don't worry about details either—just write them down. And don't try to put them into any particular order. *This list is very important, so take all the time you need to compile it.*

1. _____
2. _____
3. _____
4. _____
5. _____
6. _____
7. _____
8. _____
9. _____
10. _____
11. _____
12. _____
13. _____
14. _____
15. _____

Step 2—Categorize

Now put each of your 15 (or fewer) items into one of three categories. Reevaluate and rearrange them until you are satisfied that you have correctly categorized them.

1. = Things I Dislike: This makes the job unpleasant and harder to live with, but I can survive it.

2.   = Things I Hate: I probably can live with this, provided other changes are forthcoming.
3.   = Things I Cannot Tolerate: I will probably leave if this problem is not corrected.

NOTE: While we are providing only 5 "slots" for each category, you may put all your items in one category or have any other grouping that you feel is appropriate.

Things I Dislike:

1. _____
2. _____
3. _____
4. _____
5. _____

Things I Hate:

1. _____
2. _____
3. _____
4. _____
5. _____

Things I Cannot Tolerate:

1. _____
2. _____
3. _____
4. _____
5. _____

Step 3—Identify and Review

At this point, you need to identify your items in terms of what or to whom they pertain. Which are manager items? Which are nonmanager items? Which are workplace items? **Hint**: In the left margin, put an M (for manager) or N (for nonmanager) or W (for workplace).

Next, examine the third category, "Things I Cannot Tolerate." This is the most important category. Do all or most of the items in this category deal with the same group (either manager, nonmanager, or workplace)? Put them in priority order where the most bothersome item is ranked #1—the one thing that you would most want changed. Into which group does that one fall: Manager? Nonmanager? Workplace?

This then tells you which set of chapter suggestions to review. For instance, if you are a *manager* and you identify your main "I Cannot Tolerate" item as pertaining to the *workplace* rather than another manager or a nonmanager, you would now want to go back and review Chapter 9. On the other hand, if you are a *nonmanager* and you identify the main "I Cannot Tolerate" item as the *nonmanager group* (your coworkers), you would want to review Chapter 7.

Step 4—Develop an Action Plan

With your attention now focused on what you have identified as THE main item of your concern, it's time for action. Using the suggestions from the appropriate chapter, determine what steps need to be taken and the best sequence for them. Prepare a written plan of action based on those suggestions, and get a mentor or a very good friend to go over it with you to make sure that you have "covered all the bases."

Step 5—Put the Plan Into Action

Take a deep breath and go for it. Be sure to follow the exact steps that you outlined and their sequence. Meanwhile, resolve to close your eyes and ears temporarily to all your other complaints, which are important only if you solve the make-or-break problems.

Step 6—Monitor Progress

Pay careful attention to everyone and everything around you as you initiate your Action Plan. If things start to go wrong, be ready to stop or adjust your plan for these changing circumstances.

GOOD LUCK!

EXERCISE 2: ORGANIZATIONAL ASSESSMENT EXERCISE

Step 1—List

In Chapter 1, we noted that "Workplace Violence refers to willful or negligent acts, including either proscribed criminal acts or coercive behavior, that occur in the course of performing any work-related duty and that lead to significant negative results, such as physical or emotional injury, diminished productivity, and/or property damage."

With this in mind, on this page or on a sheet of your own paper, write down up to 15 items that you feel could potentially lead to some incident of violence in your organization. Don't worry about whether they deal with people, places, or things; don't worry about details either—just write them down. ***These are important, so don't feel rushed to complete your list.***

1. _____
2. _____
3. _____
4. _____
5. _____
6. _____
7. _____
8. _____
9. _____
10. _____
11. _____
12. _____
13. _____
14. _____
15. _____

Step 2—Categorize

Now put each of your 15 (or fewer) items into one of three categories:

1. Things That May Lead to Violence Eventually
2. Things That May Lead to Violence Soon
3. Things That May Lead to Violence Now

Then reevaluate and rearrange until you are satisfied that you have correctly categorized them.

NOTE: While we provide 5 "slots" for each category, you may put all your items in one category or have any other grouping that you feel is appropriate.

1. _____
2. _____
3. _____
4. _____
5. _____

Things That May Lead to Violence Eventually:

1. _____
2. _____
3. _____
4. _____
5. _____

Things That May Lead to Violence Soon:

1. _____
2. _____
3. _____

4. _____

5. _____

Things That May Lead to Violence Now:

1. _____

2. _____

3. _____

4. _____

5. _____

Step 3—Identify, Prioritize, and Review

Next, identify your items in terms of what or to whom they pertain. Which pertain to managers? Which refer to nonmanagers? Which are workplace items? Hint: In the left margin, put an M (for manager) or N (for nonmanager) or W (for workplace) alongside each item.

Next, examine the "Things That May Lead to Violence" Now category. This is the most important category. Put these items in priority order where the first or highest is the one item that you feel should be changed immediately. Into which group does that one fall: Manager? Nonmanager? Workplace?

Do all or most of these items deal with the same group—either manager, nonmanager, or workplace? This then tells you which set of suggestions from the text to review. For instance, if you are a manager and you identify the main "Things That May Lead to Violence Now" item as pertaining to the workplace rather than your managers or nonmanagers, you would now want to go back and review Chapter 9. If you are a nonmanager and you identify the main "Things That May Lead to Violence Now" item as the nonmanager group, you would want to review Chapter 7.

Step 4—Develop an Action Plan

Having now focused your attention on what you have identified as THE main item of your concern, it's time for action. Using the suggestions from the appropriate chapter, determine what steps need to be taken and the best sequence for them. Prepare a written plan of action based on these and get a mentor or a very good friend to go over it with you to make sure that you have "covered all the bases."

Step 5—Put the Plan Into Action

Take a deep breath and go for it. Be sure to follow the exact steps that you outlined and their sequence.

Step 6—Monitor Progress

Pay careful attention to everyone and everything around you as you initiate your Action Plan. Stay positive. If things start to go wrong, be ready to stop or adjust your plan for these changing circumstances.

GOOD LUCK!

EXERCISE 3: IDENTIFYING YOUR ORGANIZATION'S PROPENSITY FOR VIOLENCE

Which of the Following Are True For Your Organization?

This list of indicators is by no means inclusive but rather is suggestive of the kind of organizational environments that are conducive to workplace violence. The higher the number, the greater the propensity for violence.

Use This Scale—The Higher the Number, the Greater the Propensity for Violence

1. = not true at all
    2. = rarely or hardly ever true
        3. = sometimes true, sometimes not
            4. = mostly true
                5. = completely or always true.

☐ 1 ☐ 2 ☐ 3 ☐ 4 ☐ 5   Managers take undue or unfair advantage of their employees.

☐ 1 ☐ 2 ☐ 3 ☐ 4 ☐ 5   Managers yell at employees.

☐ 1 ☐ 2 ☐ 3 ☐ 4 ☐ 5   Managers use offensive language.

☐ 1 ☐ 2 ☐ 3 ☐ 4 ☐ 5   Managers belittle, demean, or degrade employees.

☐ 1 ☐ 2 ☐ 3 ☐ 4 ☐ 5   Managers display angry outbursts and tantrums.

☐ 1 ☐ 2 ☐ 3 ☐ 4 ☐ 5   Managers abuse their power.

☐ 1 ☐ 2 ☐ 3 ☐ 4 ☐ 5   Managers threaten employees.

☐ 1 ☐ 2 ☐ 3 ☐ 4 ☐ 5   Managers take undue or unfair advantage of their employees.

☐ 1 ☐ 2 ☐ 3 ☐ 4 ☐ 5   Managers are heavy-handed in the treatment of employees.

☐ 1 ☐ 2 ☐ 3 ☐ 4 ☐ 5   Violence/threats are accepted or overlooked as "part of the job" by managers and others in the organization.

☐ 1 ☐ 2 ☐ 3 ☐ 4 ☐ 5   Managers exhibit poor management skills.

☐ 1 ☐ 2 ☐ 3 ☐ 4 ☐ 5   Managers micromanage.

☐ 1 ☐ 2 ☐ 3 ☐ 4 ☐ 5   Managers perform performance appraisal poorly or not at all.

☐ 1 ☐ 2 ☐ 3 ☐ 4 ☐ 5   Managers show favoritism.

☐ 1 ☐ 2 ☐ 3 ☐ 4 ☐ 5   Managers do not do real "due diligence" in investigating complaints against other managers.

☐ 1 ☐ 2 ☐ 3 ☐ 4 ☐ 5   Managers use meetings inappropriately.

☐ 1 ☐ 2 ☐ 3 ☐ 4 ☐ 5 Managers are insecure and/or incompetent.

☐ 1 ☐ 2 ☐ 3 ☐ 4 ☐ 5 Managers try to cover up insecurity or incompetence.

☐ 1 ☐ 2 ☐ 3 ☐ 4 ☐ 5 Managers avoid making decisions.

☐ 1 ☐ 2 ☐ 3 ☐ 4 ☐ 5 Managers cannot accept criticism.

☐ 1 ☐ 2 ☐ 3 ☐ 4 ☐ 5 Many managers use authoritarian styles of management.

☐ 1 ☐ 2 ☐ 3 ☐ 4 ☐ 5 Coworkers lack interpersonal skills.

☐ 1 ☐ 2 ☐ 3 ☐ 4 ☐ 5 Coworkers are inconsiderate.

☐ 1 ☐ 2 ☐ 3 ☐ 4 ☐ 5 Coworkers have attitude problems.

☐ 1 ☐ 2 ☐ 3 ☐ 4 ☐ 5 Coworkers disregard appearance and/or hygiene.

☐ 1 ☐ 2 ☐ 3 ☐ 4 ☐ 5 Coworkers lie and manipulate.

☐ 1 ☐ 2 ☐ 3 ☐ 4 ☐ 5 Coworkers threaten.

☐ 1 ☐ 2 ☐ 3 ☐ 4 ☐ 5 Coworkers harass.

☐ 1 ☐ 2 ☐ 3 ☐ 4 ☐ 5 Coworkers bully.

☐ 1 ☐ 2 ☐ 3 ☐ 4 ☐ 5 Coworkers engage in theft or sabotage.

☐ 1 ☐ 2 ☐ 3 ☐ 4 ☐ 5 Coworkers take or subject others to unnecessary risks.

☐ 1 ☐ 2 ☐ 3 ☐ 4 ☐ 5 Coworkers engage in behavior that is potentially harmful to others or organizational assets.

☐ 1 ☐ 2 ☐ 3 ☐ 4 ☐ 5 Coworkers engage in behavior that is potentially harmful to themselves.

☐ 1 ☐ 2 ☐ 3 ☐ 4 ☐ 5 Coworkers don't carry their own weight.

☐ 1 ☐ 2 ☐ 3 ☐ 4 ☐ 5 Coworkers have poor or inefficient work habits.

☐ 1 ☐ 2 ☐ 3 ☐ 4 ☐ 5 Coworkers don't carry out instructions.

☐ 1 ☐ 2 ☐ 3 ☐ 4 ☐ 5 Coworkers are absent from work.

☐ 1 ☐ 2 ☐ 3 ☐ 4 ☐ 5 Coworkers are absent on the job.

☐ 1 ☐ 2 ☐ 3 ☐ 4 ☐ 5 Numerous workers have poor credit records.

☐ 1 ☐ 2 ☐ 3 ☐ 4 ☐ 5 Numerous workers have poor driving records.

☐ 1 ☐ 2 ☐ 3 ☐ 4 ☐ 5 Numerous members of the organization have extreme political views.

☐ 1 ☐ 2 ☐ 3 ☐ 4 ☐ 5 Numerous members of the organization have extreme religious views.

☐ 1 ☐ 2 ☐ 3 ☐ 4 ☐ 5 Reported incidents or violence are not carefully investigated.

☐ 1 ☐ 2 ☐ 3 ☐ 4 ☐ 5 Members of the organization file frequent complaints or grievances.

☐ 1 ☐ 2 ☐ 3 ☐ 4 ☐ 5 Members of the organization have experienced domestic violence issues.

☐ 1 ☐ 2 ☐ 3 ☐ 4 ☐ 5 Members of the organization are not required to report incidents or threats of violence.

☐ 1 ☐ 2 ☐ 3 ☐ 4 ☐ 5 Members of the organization do not feel that they are treated with dignity and respect by others in the organization.

☐ 1 ☐ 2 ☐ 3 ☐ 4 ☐ 5 Members of the organization generally do not feel "safe" when they are at work.

☐ 1 ☐ 2 ☐ 3 ☐ 4 ☐ 5 Members of the organization frequently feel unnecessarily stressed.

☐ 1 ☐ 2 ☐ 3 ☐ 4 ☐ 5 Members of the organization are not encouraged to communicate information about potentially threatening clients or visitors.

☐ 1 ☐ 2 ☐ 3 ☐ 4 ☐ 5 Managers do not inform members of the organization about violent incidents.

☐ 1 ☐ 2 ☐ 3 ☐ 4 ☐ 5 Members of the organization are not very satisfied with their jobs.

☐ 1 ☐ 2 ☐ 3 ☐ 4 ☐ 5 Members of the organization are not very satisfied with management.

☐ 1 ☐ 2 ☐ 3 ☐ 4 ☐ 5 Members of the organization don't understand or accept the organization's mission.

☐ 1 ☐ 2 ☐ 3 ☐ 4 ☐ 5 Members of the organization work in high-crime areas.

☐ 1 ☐ 2 ☐ 3 ☐ 4 ☐ 5 Members of the organization work with drugs.

☐ 1 ☐ 2 ☐ 3 ☐ 4 ☐ 5 Members of the organization work with cash.

☐ 1 ☐ 2 ☐ 3 ☐ 4 ☐ 5 Members of the organization work with patients or clients who have a history of violent behavior or behavior disorders.

☐ 1 ☐ 2 ☐ 3 ☐ 4 ☐ 5 Members of the organization work in isolated work areas.

☐ 1 ☐ 2 ☐ 3 ☐ 1 ☐ 5 There is no training about workplace violence prevention.

☐ 1 ☐ 2 ☐ 3 ☐ 4 ☐ 5 Members of the organization are not carefully screened prior to hiring/using them.

☐ 1 ☐ 2 ☐ 3 ☐ 4 ☐ 5 There are a lot of management/labor disputes.

☐ 1 ☐ 2 ☐ 3 ☐ 4 ☐ 5 There are a lot of injury claims.

☐ 1 ☐ 2 ☐ 3 ☐ 4 ☐ 5 There are a lot of occupational stress claims.

☐ 1 ☐ 2 ☐ 3 ☐ 4 ☐ 5 This organization or its members have experienced violent behavior, assaults, or threats from within the organization.

☐ 1 ☐ 2 ☐ 3 ☐ 4 ☐ 5 This organization or its members have experienced violent behavior, assaults, or threats from outside the organization.

☐ 1 ☐ 2 ☐ 3 ☐ 4 ☐ 5 There is a highly diverse workforce.

☐ 1 ☐ 2 ☐ 3 ☐ 4 ☐ 5 Higher level managers ignore bad lower level managers.

☐ 1 ☐ 2 ☐ 3 ☐ 4 ☐ 5 Higher level managers uphold bad or improper decisions of lower level managers.

☐ 1 ☐ 2 ☐ 3 ☐ 4 ☐ 5 Higher level managers set poor examples for lower level managers.

☐ 1 ☐ 2 ☐ 3 ☐ 4 ☐ 5 Jobs are unsafe or too physically demanding.

☐ 1 ☐ 2 ☐ 3 ☐ 4 ☐ 5 Jobs are in inconvenient locations.

☐ 1 ☐ 2 ☐ 3 ☐ 4 ☐ 5 There are many unpleasant or unsafe workplaces.

☐ 1 ☐ 2 ☐ 3 ☐ 4 ☐ 5 Many workplaces are uncomfortable.

☐ 1 ☐ 2 ☐ 3 ☐ 4 ☐ 5 There are numerous bad bosses.

□ 1 □ 2 □ 3 □ 4 □ 5 There are numerous bad coworkers.

□ 1 □ 2 □ 3 □ 4 □ 5 There are numerous bad customers or clients.

□ 1 □ 2 □ 3 □ 4 □ 5 Many jobs are low paying and/or have little by way of fringe benefits.

□ 1 □ 2 □ 3 □ 4 □ 5 There is little job security.

□ 1 □ 2 □ 3 □ 4 □ 5 There is little opportunity for advancement.

□ 1 □ 2 □ 3 □ 4 □ 5 There are many incompetent managers.

□ 1 □ 2 □ 3 □ 4 □ 5 Many managers are dishonest.

□ 1 □ 2 □ 3 □ 4 □ 5 Many managers are unethical.

□ 1 □ 2 □ 3 □ 4 □ 5 The organizational environment is generally threatening.

Source: Van Fleet, D. D., & Van Fleet, E. W. (2010). *The violence volcano: Reducing the threat of workplace violence* (pp. 205–209). Charlotte, NC: Information Age.

APPENDIX

PSYCHOPATHY INDICATORS

H. M. Cleckley's List

1. Considerable superficial charm and average or above average intelligence.
2. Absence of delusions and irrational thinking.
3. Absence of anxiety: considerable poise, calmness and verbal facility.
4. Unreliability, disregard for obligations, no sense of responsibility.
5. Untruthfulness and insincerity.
6. Antisocial behavior.
7. Inadequately motivated antisocial behavior.
8. Poor judgment and failure to learn from experience.
9. Pathological egocentricity: total self-centeredness; incapacity for love and attachment.
10. General poverty of deep and lasting emotions.
11. Lack of any true insight; inability to see oneself as others do.
12. Ingratitude for any special considerations, kindness, and trust.
13. Fantastic and objectionable behavior: vulgarity, rudeness, mood shifts, pranks, entertainment.
14. No history of genuine suicide attempts.
15. An impersonal, trivial, and poorly integrated sex life.
16. Failure to have a life plan and to live in any ordered way.

R. D. Hare's List

* Factor 1: Corporate psychopaths score *high* on this factor.
** Factor 2: Corporate psychopaths score *low to moderate* on this factor

1. * GLIB AND SUPERFICIAL CHARM: smooth, engaging, charming, slick, verbally facile.
2. * GRANDIOSE SELF-WORTH: grossly inflated view of one's abilities and self-worth, self-assured, opinionated, cocky, a braggart.
3. ** NEED FOR STIMULATION or PRONENESS TO BOREDOM: excessive need for novel, thrilling, and exciting stimulation; taking chances and doing things that are risky.
4. * PATHOLOGICAL LYING: in moderate form, shrewd, crafty, cunning, sly, and clever; in extreme form, deceptive, deceitful, underhanded, unscrupulous, manipulative, and dishonest.
5. * CONNING AND MANIPULATIVE: use of deceit and deception to cheat, con, or defraud others for personal gain.
6. * LACK OF REMORSE OR GUILT: lack of feelings or concern for the losses, pain, and suffering of victims; disdain for one's victims.
7. * SHALLOW AFFECT: emotional poverty or a limited range or depth of feelings; interpersonal coldness in spite of signs of open gregariousness and superficial warmth.
8. * CALLOUSNESS and LACK OF EMPATHY: a lack of feelings toward people in general; cold, contemptuous, inconsiderate, and tactless.
9. ** PARASITIC LIFESTYLE: intentional, manipulative, selfish, and exploitative financial dependence on others, low self-discipline and inability to meet one's responsibilities.
10. ** POOR BEHAVIORAL CONTROLS: irritability, annoyance, impatience, threats, aggression and verbal abuse; inadequate control of anger and temper; acting hastily.
11. PROMISCUOUS SEXUAL BEHAVIOR: brief, superficial relations, numerous affairs, and an indiscriminate selection of sexual partners.
12. ** EARLY BEHAVIOR PROBLEMS: prior to 13, lying, theft, cheating, vandalism, bullying, sexual activity, fire setting, glue sniffing, alcohol use, and running away from home.
13. ** LACK OF REALISTIC, LONG-TERM GOALS: inability or persistent failure to develop and execute long-term plans and goals; a nomadic existence, aimless, lacking direction.
14. ** IMPULSIVITY: unpremeditated behaviors that lack reflection or planning; inability to resist temptation; foolhardy, rash, unpredictable, erratic and reckless.

15. ** IRRESPONSIBILITY: failure to fulfill or honor obligations and commitments; not paying bills, defaulting on loans, performing sloppy work, being absent or late to work.
16. * FAILURE TO ACCEPT RESPONSIBILITY FOR OWN AC-TIONS: low conscientiousness or dutifulness, antagonistic manipulation, denial of responsibility, and manipulation.
17. MANY SHORT-TERM RELATIONSHIPS: inconsistent, undependable, and unreliable commitments in life, including in marital and familial bonds.
18. ** JUVENILE DELINQUENCY: ages of 13–18 crimes or antagonism, exploitation, aggression, manipulation, or callous, ruthless tough-mindedness.
19. ** REVOCATION OF CONDITION RELEASE: a revocation of probation or other conditional release due to technical violations.
20. CRIMINAL VERSATILITY: a diversity of criminal offenses; taking pride at getting away with crimes or wrongdoing.

Source: Adapted from Tillier, W. D. (2012). *Review of psychopathy.* Retrieved from www.positivedisintegration.com/psychopathy.htm#a4

ORIGINAL SOURCES

Babiak, P., & Hare, R. D. (2006). *Snakes in suits.* New York, NY: HarperCollins.
Hare, R. D. (1993). *Without conscience.* New York, NY: Guilford.
Hare, R. D. (1991). *The Hare psychopathy checklist-revised (PCL-R).* Toronto, Canada: Multi-Health Systems.
Cleckley, H. M. (1941). *The mask of sanity.* St. Louis, MO: C. V. Mosby.

BIBLIOGRAPHY

Aarons, G. A., & Sawitzky, A. C. (2006). Organizational culture and climate and mental health provider attitudes toward evidence-based practice. *Psychological Services, 3*(1), 61–72.

Adriansen, D. (2008). *Workplace violence prevention training*. Saarbrücken, Germany: VDM.

Aguirre, B. E. (2008). Sports fan violence in North America. *Contemporary Sociology: A Journal of Reviews, 37*(2), 157–158.

Albanese, A., & Van Fleet, D. D. (1985). Free-riding: Theory, research, and implications. *Academy of Management Review, 10*(2), 244–255.

Albanese, R., & Van Fleet, D. D. (1985). The free riding tendency in organizations. *Scandinavian Journal of Management Studies, 2*(2), 121–136.

American Psychiatric Association (APA). (1994). *Diagnostic and statistical manual of mental disorders* (4th ed.). Washington, DC: American Psychiatric Association.

ASIS International. (2011). *Workplace violence prevention and intervention* (ASSIS/SHRM WPVI.1-2011). Alexandria, VA: ASIS International, p. 3.

Babay, E. (2012). Local workplace violence cases. *The Examiner*. Retrieved from http://washingtonexaminer.com/local-workplace-violence-cases/article/112964

Baron, R. A., & Neumann, J. H. (1996). Workplace violence and workplace aggression: Evidence on their relative frequency and potential causes. *Aggressive Behavior, 22*, 161–173.

Bates, C. A., Bowes-Sperry, L., & O'Leary-Kelly, A. M. (2006). Sexual harassment in the workplace: A look back and a look ahead. In E. K. Kelloway, J. Barling, & J. Joseph Jr. (Eds.), *Handbook of workplace violence* (pp. 381–416). Thousand Oaks, CA: Sage.

Berdahl, J. L. (2007). Harassment based on sex: Protecting social status in the context of gender hierarchy. *Academy of Management Review, 32*, 641–658.

Bondi, M. A., & Violence Prevention Committee. (2013). *Domestic violence and the workplace.* Washington, DC: Partnership for Prevention. Retrieved from www.caepv.org/membercenter/files/Partnership%20For%20Prevention%20briefing%20%28confidential%20document%29.pdf

Booth, B, Vecchi, G. Finney, E., Van Hasselt, V. & Romano, S. (2009). Captive-taking incidents in the context of workplace violence: Descriptive analysis and case examples. *Victims and Offenders, 4,* 76–92.

Bowie, V., Fisher, B. S., & Cooper, C. L. (Eds.). (2005). *Workplace violence: Issues, trends, strategies.* Devon, UK: Willan.

Bramson, R. (1994). *Coping with difficult managers.* New York, NY: Fireside

Braverman, M. (1999). *Preventing workplace violence: A guide for employers and practitioners.* Thousand Oaks, CA: Sage.

Bryngelson, J. (2000). *CARE (Courtesy and respect empower).* Billings, MT. In J. Bryngelson & R. McMillan (Eds.), *The path of dialogue: Why smart people do dumb things and how they can stop.* A presentation at the Executive Forum's *Management Forum Series, March 24, 1999.* Lake Oswego, OR: Executive Forum.

Bureau of Justice Statistics. (2012). *Data collection: National crime victimization survey (NCVS).* Retrieved from http://www.bjs.gov/index.cfm?ty=dcdetail&iid=245

Cameron, K. (2008). A process for changing organizational culture. In T. G. Cummings (Ed.), *Handbook of organizational development* (pp. 429–445). Thousand Oaks, CA: Sage.

Cameron, K. S., & Quinn, R. E. (2011). *Diagnosing and changing organizational culture: Based on the competing values framework* (3rd ed.). San Francisco, CA: Jossey-Bass.

Carbo, J., & Hughes, A. (2010). Workplace bullying: Developing a human rights definition from the perspective and experiences of targets. *WorkingUSA, 13,* 387–403.

Catrantzos, N. (2012). *Managing the insider threat: No dark corners.* Boca Raton, FL: CRC/ Taylor & Francis.

Chambers, H. (2004). *My way or the highway: The micromanagement survival guide.* San Francisco, CA: Berrett-Koehler.

Christensen, L. W. (2005). *Surviving workplace violence: What to do before a violent incident, what to do when the violence explodes.* Boulder, CO: Paladin.

Coleman, L. (2004). The frequency and cost of corporate crises. *Journal of Contingencies and Crisis Management, 12*(1), 2–13.

Corporate Alliance to End Partner Violence. (2013). *Workplace statistics.* Retrieved from http://www.caepv.org/getinfo/facts_stats.php?factsec=3

Crothers, L. M., & Lipinski, J. (Eds.). (2014). *Bullying in the workplace: Causes, symptoms, and remedies.* New York, NY: Routledge/Taylor & Francis.

Deneberg, R., & Braverman, M. (2001). *The violence-prone workplace: A new approach to dealing with hostile, threatening, and uncivil behavior.* Ithaca, NY: Cornell University Press.

Deutschman, A. (2005). Is your boss a psychopath? *Fast Company, 96,* 44–51. Retrieved from www.fastcompany.com/53247/your-boss-psychopath

Doran, G. T. (1981). There's a S.M.A.R.T. way to write management's goals and objectives. *Management Review, 70*(11), 35–36.

Drake, H. A. (Ed.). (2006). *Violence in late antiquity: Perceptions and practices.* Burlington, VT: Ashgate.

Einarsen, S., & Mikkelsen, E. G. (2003). Individual effects of exposure to bullying at work. In S. Einarsen, H. Hoel, D. Zapf, and C. L. Cooper (Eds.), *Bullying and emotional abuse in the workplace: International perspectives in research and practice* (pp. 127–144). London, UK: Taylor & Francis.

Elias, S. M. (2013). *Deviant and criminal behavior in the workplace.* New York: New York University Press.

Employers Against Domestic Violence. (2013). *Effects on the workplace: How does domestic violence affect the workplace?* Retrieved from http://employersagainstdomesticviolence.org/effects-on-workplace/workplace-dv-stats/

Federal Bureau of Investigation. (2004, March). *Workplace violence—Issues in response*, p.13.

Geddes, D., & Stickney, L. T. (2011). The trouble with sanctions: Organizational responses to deviant anger displays at work. *Human Relations, 64*(2), 201–230.

Gill, M., Fisher, B., & Bowie, V. (Eds.). (2002). *Violence at work: Causes, patterns and prevention.* Cullompton, Devon UK: Willan.

Globe Risk International. (2013). *Kidnap & ransom.* Retrieved from www.globerisk.com/kidnap.php

Goulet, T. (2007). *Why bad employees don't get fired.* Retrieved from http://www.cnn.com/2007/Living/worklife/11/06/not.fired/

Greengard, S. (1997). 50% of your employees are lying, cheating & stealing. *Workforce Magazine, 76*(10), 44–53.

Griffin, R. W., & Lopez, Y. P. (2004). *Toward a model of the person-situation determinants of deviant behavior in organizations.* Paper presented at the 64th annual meeting of the Academy of Management.

Griffin, R. W., & Lopez, Y. P. (2005). Bad behavior. In Organizations: A review and typology for future research. *Journal of Management, 31*, 988–1005.

Griffin, R. W., & O'Leary-Kelly, A. M. (Eds.). (2004). *The dark side of organizational behavior.* San Francisco, CA: Jossey-Bass.

Griffin, R. W., O'Leary-Kelly, A., & Collins, J. M. (Eds.). (1998). *Dysfunctional behavior in organizations: Violent and deviant behavior.* Stamford, CT: JAI.

Griffin, R. W., & Van Fleet, D. D. 2013. *Management skills: Assessment and development.* Mason, OH: SouthWestern/Cengage Learning.

Gustin, J. F. (2013). *Workplace violence and the facility manager.* Lilburn, GA: Fairmont.

Hafner, J. C., & Gresham, G. (2012). Managers' and senior executives' perceptions of frequency and type of employee-perpetrated information sabotage and their attitudes toward it—The results of a pilot study. *Journal of Behavioral and Applied Management, 13*(3), 151–167.

Hankwitz, H. (2013). Domestic violence statistics and your workplace. *CPI.* Retrieved from www.crisisprevention.com/Resources/Article-Library/Prepare-Training-Articles/Domestic-Violence-Statistics-and-Your-Workplace

Harrell, E. (2011). *Workplace violence, 1993–2009.* Washington, DC: Bureau of Justice Statistics. Retrieved from http://www.bjs.gov/content/pub/pdf/wv09.pdf

Harrell, E. (2012). *Workplace violence against government employees, 1994–2011.* Washington, DC: U. S. Bureau of Justice Statistics. Retrieved from http://www.bjs.gov/index.cfm?ty=pbdetail&iid=4615

Haynes, M. (2013). Workplace violence: Why every state must adopt a comprehensive workplace violence prevention law. *Cornell HR Review.* Retrieved from www.cornellhrreview.org/workplace-violence-why-every-state-must-adopt-a-comprehensive-workplace-violence-prevention-law/

Hearn, J., & Parkin, P. W. (2002). *Gender, sexuality and violence in organizations.* Thousand Oaks, CA: Sage.

Hemp, P. (2004). Presenteeism: At work—But out of it. *Harvard Business Review, 82*(10), 49–57.

Heskett, S. L. (1996). *Workplace violence: Before, during and after.* Waltham, MA: Butterworth-Heinemann.

Inness, M., Barling, J., & Turner, N. (2005). Understanding supervisor-targeted aggression: A within-person, between-jobs design. *Journal of Applied Psychology, 90*(4), 731–739.

Jackson, D., Clare, J., & Mannix, J. (2002). Who would want to be a nurse? Violence in the workplace—A factor in recruitment and retention. *Journal of Nursing Management, 10*(1), 13–20.

Jackson, G. M. (2012). *Predicting malicious behavior: Tools and techniques for ensuring global security.* Indianapolis, IN: John Wiley & Sons.

Jacobs, J. L., & Scott, C. L. (2011). Hate crimes as one aspect of workplace violence: Recommendations for HRD. *Advances in Developing Human Resources, 13*(1), 85–98.

Janocha, J. A., & Smith, R. T. (2010, August 30). Workplace safety and health in the healthcare and social assistance industry, 2003–07. *Bureau of Labor Statistics.* Retrieved from www.bls.gov/opub/cwc/sh20100825ar01p1.htm

Johnson, P. R., & Gardner, S. (1999). Domestic violence and the workplace: Developing a company response. *Journal of Management Development, 18*(7), 590–597.

Kalleberg, A. L. (2011). *Good jobs, bad jobs.* New York, NY: Russell Sage.

Kalleberg, A. L., Reskin, B. F., & Hudson, K. (2000). Bad jobs in America: Standard and non-standard employment relations and job quality in the United States. *American Sociological Review, 65*(2), 256–278.

Keashly, L., & Neuman, J. H. (2004). Bullying in the workplace: Its impact and management. *Employee Rights and Employment Policy Journal, 8*(2), 335–373.

Kelloway, E. K., Barling, J., & Hurrell, J. J. (Eds.). (2006). *Handbook of workplace violence.* Thousand Oaks, CA: Sage.

Kerr, K. M. (2010). *Workplace violence: Planning for prevention and response.* Waltham, MA: Butterworth-Heinemann.

Kirschner, R., & Brinkman, R. (2012). *Dealing with people you can't stand* (Rev. & exp. 3rd ed.). New York, NY: McGraw-Hill.

Lanier, S. L. (2003). *Workplace violence: Before, during and after.* Alexandria VA: ASIS International.

LeBlanc, M. M., & Barling, J. (2004). Workplace aggression. *Current Directions in Psychological Science, 13*(1), 9–12.

Levs, J., & Plott, M. (2013). *Boy, 8, one of 3 killed in bombings at Boston Marathon; Scores wounded.* Retrieved from http://www.cnn.com/2013/04/15/us/boston-marathon-explosions

Litzky, B. E., Eddleston, K. A., & Kidder, D. L. (2006). The good, the bad, and the misguided: How managers inadvertently encourage deviant behaviors. *Academy of Management Perspectives, 20,* 91–103.

Liu, D., Liao, H., & Loi, R. (2012). The dark side of leadership: A three-level investigation of the cascading effect of abusive supervision on employee creativity. *Academy of Management Journal, 55,* 1187–1212.

Longo, J., & Sherman, R. O. (2007). Leveling horizontal violence. *Nursing Management, 38*(3), 34–37, 50–51.

Magan, C. (2012). *Minneapolis workplace shooting the deadliest of its kind in Minnesota.* Retrieved from www.twincities.com/localnews/ci_21655126/minneapolis-shooting-is-deadliest-incident-workplace-violence-minnesotas

Markoff, J. (2013, April 2). DDoS (Distributed Denial of Service). *The New York Times,* p. D7.

Martinko, M. J., & Zellars, K. L. (1998). Toward a theory of workplace violence: A cognitive appraisal perspective. In R. W. Griffin, A. O'Leary-Kelly, J. M. & Collins (Eds.), *Dysfunctional behavior in organizations: Violent and deviant behavior* (pp. 1–42). Stamford, CT: JAI.

McGoey, C. E. (2013). Robbery facts: Violent crime against persons. *Crime Doctor: Your Prescription for Security & Safety.* Retrieved from www.crimedoctor.com/robbery1.htm

Moore, M. H., Petrie, C. V., Braga, A. A., & McLaughlin, B. L. (Eds.). (2003). Deadly lessons: Understanding lethal school violence. Case studies of school violence committee. *National Research Council and Institute of Medicine.* Washington, DC: National Academies Press.

Morgan, L. A. (2013). Workplace violence statistics & information. *Chron.* Retrieved from http//:work.chron.com/workplace-violence-statistics-information-13144.html

Mr. X. (1995). *Fired? Fight back!* New York, NY: American Management Association.

Namie, G., & Namie, R. (2000). *The bully at work: What you can do to stop the hurt and reclaim your dignity on the job.* Naperville, IL: Sourcebooks.

National Safety Council. (n.d.), Information can be found at www.nsc.org/pages/home.aspx

Neider, L. L., & Schriesheim, C. A. (2010). *The "dark" side of management.* Charlotte, NC: Information Age.

Neuman, J., & Baron, R. (1998). Workplace violence and workplace aggression: Evidence concerning specific forms, potential causes, and preferred targets. *Journal of Management, 24*(3), 391–419.

Nixon, W. B. (2009). *Workplace violence prevention: Assessing the risk to your business.* Retrieved from http://www.collegerecruiter.com/blog/2011/01/27/assessing-the-risk-of-workplace-violence-to-your-business/

Nixon, W. B. (2013). *Prevention outweighs reaction. The workplace violence fact sheet.* Lake Forest, CA: National Institute for the Prevention of Workplace Violence.

O'Bryan, B. (2013, June 24). How "see something, say nothing" trumps policy and impacts workplace violence. *HR and Employment Law News.* Retrieved from hr.blr.com/HR-news/Health-Safety/Violence-in-Workplace/How-see-something-say-nothing-trumps-policy-and-im?goback=.gde_3876184_member_254572429

Occupational Safety & Health Administration (OSHA). (n.d.). Retrieved from www.osha.gov/

O'Leary-Kelly, A., Bowes-Sperry, L., Arens-Bates, C., & Lean, E. R. (2009, June). Sexual harassment at work: A decade (plus) of progress. *Journal of Management, 35*(3), 503–536.

O'Leary-Kelly, A., Griffin, R. W., & Glew, D. J. (1996). Organization-motivated aggression: A research framework. *Academy of Management Review, 21,* 225–253.

O'Leary-Kelly, A., & Reeves, C. (2007). The effects and costs of intimate partner violence for work organizations. *Journal of Interpersonal Violence, 22*(3), 327–344.

Ontario, Canada. (2011). *Ontario's Health & Safety Act.* Retrieved from http//:www.e-laws.gov.on.ca/html/statutes/english/elaws_statutes_90o01_e.htm

Paetzold, R. L., O'Leary-Kelly, A., & Griffin, R. W. (2007). Workplace violence, employer liability, and implications for organizational research. *Journal of Management Inquiry, 16,* 362–370.

Paludi, M. A., Nydegger, R. V., & Paludi, C. A. (2006). *Understanding workplace violence: A guide for managers and employees.* Santa Barbara, CA: Praeger.

Perrewé, P. I., Zellars, K. L., Rogers, L. M., Breaux, D. M., & Young, A. M. (2010). Mentors gone wild! When mentoring relationships become dysfunctional or abusive. In L. L. Neider & C. A. Schriesheim (Eds.), *The "dark" side of management.* Charlotte, NC: Information Age

Perryman, A. A., Sikora, D., & Ferris, G. R. (2010). One bad apple: The role of destructive executives in organizations. In L. L. Neider & C. A. Schriesheim (Eds.), *The "dark" side of management* (pp. 1–25). Charlotte, NC: Information Age.

Philpott, D., & Grimme, D. (2009). *The workplace violence prevention handbook.* Lanham, MD: Government Institutes/Scarecrow.

Pierce, J. L., & Newstrom, J. W. (2011). *The manager's bookshelf* (9th ed.). Upper Saddle River, NJ: Prentice Hall.

Porath, C. L., & Erez, A. (2007). Does rudeness matter? The effects of rude behavior on task performance and helpfulness. *Academy of Management Journal, 50,* 1181–1197.

Porath, C. L., & Erez, A. (2009). Overlooked but not untouched: How incivility reduces onlookers' performance on routine and creative tasks. *Organizational Behavior and Human Decision Processes, 109,* 29–44.

Reio, T. G., Jr. (2011). Supervisor and coworker incivility: Testing the work frustration-aggression model. *Advances in Developing Human Resources, 13*(1), 54–68.

Romano, S. J., & Rugala, E. A. (2008). Workplace violence: Mind-set of awareness. Spokane, WA: Center for Personal Protection and Safety.

Royle, T., & Towers, B. (2002). *Labour relations in the global fast-food industry.* New York, NY: Routledge.

Rugala, E. A., & Fitzgerald, J. R. (2003). Workplace violence: From threat to intervention. *Clinics in Occupational and Environmental Medicine, 3*, 775–789.

Schein, E. H. (1990). Organizational culture. *American Psychologist, 45*(2), 109–119.

Schein, E. H. (2004). *Organizational culture and leadership* (3rd ed.). Indianapolis, IN: John Wiley & Sons.

Segarra, M. (2012). *Stopping workplace violence. CFO*. Retrieved from www3.cfo.com/article/2012/12/workplace-issues_workplace-violence-workplace-fatalities-bureau-of-labor-statistics

SIW Editorial Staff. (2012). Feds: Workplace violence caused nearly 17 percent of all fatal U.S. work injuries in 2011. *Security Info Watch.com*. Retrieved from http://www.securityinfowatch.com/news/10834285/feds-workplace-violence-caused-nearly-17-percent-of-all-fatal-us-work-injuries-in-2011

Society for Human Resource Management (SHRM). (2012, February 29). *Workplace violence*. Retrieved from http://www.shrm.org/Research/SurveyFindings/Articles/Pages/WorkplaceViolence.aspx

Sommers, J. A., Schell, T. L., & Vodanovich, S. J. (2002). Developing a measure of individual differences in organizational revenge. *Journal of Business and Psychology, 17*(2), 207–222.

Smith, M. D. 1988. *Violence and sport*. Toronto: Canadian Scholars' Press.

Tepper, B. J., Moss, S. E., & Duffy, M. K. (2011). Predictors of abusive supervision: Supervisor perceptions of deep-level dissimilarity. Relationship conflict, and subordinate performance. *Academy of Management Journal, 54*, 279–294.

Tiesman, H., Gurka, K., Konda, S., Coben, J., & Amandus, H. E. (2012). Workplace homicides among U. S. women: The role of intimate partner violence. *Annals of Epidemiology, 22*, 277–284. Retrieved from http://www.annalsofepidemiology.org/article/S1047-2797(12)00024-5/abstract

Truman, J. L., & Rand, M. R. (2010). *Crime victimization, 2009*. Washington, DC: Bureau of Justice Statistics.

United Nations International Labour Organization (ILO). (2003, October 8–15). *Code of practice on workplace violence in services sectors and measures to combat this phenomenon*. Retrieved from www.ilo.org/wcmsp5/groups/public/@ed_protect/@protrav/@safework/documents/normativeinstrument/wcms_107705.pdf

U. S. Department of Labor, Bureau of Labor Statistics. (2006). *News: Survey of workplace violence prevention, 2005*. Washington, DC. Retrieved from http://www.bls.gov/iif/oshwc/osnr0026.pdf

U.S. Department of Labor, Bureau of Labor Statistics, (2012, October). *Statistics: Safety & health*. Retrieved from http://www.dol.gov/dol/topic/statistics/safety.htm

U.S. Department of Labor, Bureau of Labor Statistics. (2013). *Labor force statistics from the current population survey, household data annual averages: Table 39. Median weekly earnings of full-time wage and salary workers by detailed occupation and sex*. Retrieved from http://www.bls.gov/cps/cpsaat39.htm

U.S. Department of Labor, Occupational Safety and Health Administration. (2013). *OSHA fact sheet 2002*. Retrieved from www.osha.gov/OshDoc/data_General_Facts/factsheet-workplace-violence.pdf

Van Fleet, D. D., & Griffin, R. W. (2006). Dysfunctional organization culture: The role of leadership in motivating dysfunctional work behaviors. *Journal of Managerial Psychology, 21*(8), 698–708.

Van Fleet, D. D., Peterson, T. O., & Van Fleet, E. W. (2005). Closing the performance feedback gap with expert systems. *Academy of Management Executive, 19*(3), 38–53.

Van Fleet, D. D., & Van Fleet, E. W. (1996). *Workplace violence: Moving toward minimizing risks* [Curriculum module]. Minerva Education Institute.

Van Fleet, D. D., & Van Fleet, E. W. (2001). How terrorism affects companies. *Scottsdale Airpark News, 21*(11), 36–39.

Van Fleet, D. D., & Van Fleet, E. W. (2006). Internal terrorists: The terrorists inside organizations. *Journal of Managerial Psychology, 21*(8), 763–774.

Van Fleet, D. D., & Van Fleet, E. W. (2007). Preventing workplace violence: The violence volcano metaphor. *Journal of Applied Management and Entrepreneurship, 12*(2), 17–36.

Van Fleet, D. D., & Van Fleet, E. W. (2010). *The violence volcano: Reducing the threat of workplace violence*. Charlotte, NC: Information Age.

Van Fleet, D. D., & Van Fleet, E. W. (2012). Towards a behavioral description of managerial bullying. *Employee Responsibilities and Rights Journal, 24*(3), 197–215.

Van Fleet, D. D., & Van Fleet, E. W. (2013). Future challenges and issues of bullying in the workplace. In L. M. Crothers & J. Lipinski (Eds.), *Bullying in the workplace: Causes, symptoms, and remedies*. New York, NY: Routledge/Taylor & Francis.

Van Fleet, E. W., & Van Fleet, D. D. (1998). Terrorism and the workplace: Concepts and recommendations. In R. W. Griffin, A. O'Leary-Kelly, & J. Collins (Eds.), *Dysfunctional behavior in organizations: Violent and deviant behavior. Vol. 23, Part A.* (pp. 165–201) Greenwich, CT: JAI.

Van Fleet, E. W., & Van Fleet, D. D. (2007). *Workplace survival: Dealing with bad bosses, bad workers, bad jobs*. Frederick, MD: PublishAmerica.

Walter, L. (2011). Workplace violence claims the lives of two workers every day. *EHS Today*. Retrieved from http://ehstoday.com/safety/news/workplace-violence-two-death-daily-1007

Wann, D. L., Melnick, M. J., Russell, G. W., & Pease, D. G. (2001). *Sport fans: The psychology and social impact of spectators*. New York, NY: Routledge;

Whitmore, B. 2011. *Potential: Workplace violence prevention and your organizational success*. New York, NY: Highpoint Executive.

Working America. (2011, July 28). *"My Bad Boss contest" grand prize winners announced*. Retrieved from www.workingamerica.org/press/releases/My-Bad-Boss-Contest-Grand-Prize-Winners-Announced

ABOUT THE AUTHORS

Ella

Dr. Ella W. Van Fleet, Founder and President of Professional Business Associates, has an impressive background that includes more than 35 years of experience in teaching, training, managing, and consulting, plus three interdisciplinary degrees in Business and Higher Education. Her primary focus was on entrepreneurship and workplace violence and terrorism. She conducted a study of sexual harassment in the workplace before it became a household word. Ella moved to Arizona in 1989 after 16 successful years as a practicing and teaching entrepreneur in Texas, for which the Texas House of Representatives passed H.R. No. 746 honoring her for outstanding professional contributions to the State of Texas.

Early in her career, Ella gained a unique perspective on violent behavior while interviewing prison inmates for the U.S. Department of Justice. Under contract to the U.S. Department of Commerce, she gained experience interacting with a variety of business owners. Later, as Associate Director of the Texas Institute for Ventures in New Technology, she managed diverse teams of engineering and business consultants in projects involving a diverse clientele and subcontractors. Her consulting with new and expanding businesses has been in strategic planning, marketing, and developing human resources for the future.

Ella was also a founding member of the Board of Governors of the Houston Enterprise Alliance, a member of the International Council of Small Businesses, and a member of the SBA Advisory Council for Region

IV. In addition to her research and business experience, she has designed and taught courses and seminars for six different universities in five states. At Texas A&M University, her course in Entrepreneurship won regional and national recognition for creativity and innovation and was also named by the students as the "Best Class at Texas A&M." She currently is retired from teaching due to health problems but still focusing her attention on workplace violence and terrorism, with special emphasis on workers who differ in age or gender.

David

Dr. David D. Van Fleet is a Professor of Management in the Morrison School of Agribusiness, W. P. Carey School of Business, at Arizona State University. He also is an Associate with Professional Business Associates, has over 40 years of experience including full-time graduate and undergraduate teaching experience, extensive editing work, over 280 publications and presentations, numerous officer roles in professional associations, extensive executive education experience, and active consulting both in the United States and abroad. His work focuses on leadership, strategy, workplace violence and terrorism, and management history.

In addition to publications jointly with Ella, David has co-authored several books, including *Management Skills*, *Contemporary Management*, *Behavior in Organizations*, *Military Leadership*, and *Organizational Behavior*. He is a past Editor of both the *Journal of Management* and the *Journal of Behavioral and Applied Management*. He has been President of several professional organizations in management. He is or has been a member of the Board of Governors, Academy of Management, Southwest Federation of Academic Disciplines, and the Southern Management Association; and was national Chair of the Management History Division of the Academy of Management.

Because of the extensiveness of these endeavors, David was named a Fellow of the Academy of Management and a Fellow of the Southern Management Association, and is listed in *Who's Who in America* (5th ed.) and *Who's Who Among America's Teachers* (Vol. V).

Joint Publications

Among their many publications authored individually or with others, the Van Fleets have also authored the following publications together: *Workplace Violence: Moving Toward Minimizing Risks*, a Project Minerva publication funded by OSHA; *The Violence Volcano: Reducing the Threat of Workplace Violence; Workplace Survival: Dealing with Bad Bosses, Bad Workers, Bad Jobs; Agribusiness: Principles of Management;* "Preventing Workplace Violence: The Violence Volcano Metaphor," *Journal of Applied Management and Entrepreneurship;* "Towards a Behavioral Description of Managerial Bullying," in *Employee Responsibilities and Rights Journal;* "Future Challenges and Issues of Bullying in the Workplace," in *Bullying in the Workplace: Causes, Symptoms, and Remedies;* "Internal Terrorists: The Terrorists Inside Organizations," in the *Journal of Managerial Psychology;* "Closing the Performance Feedback Gap with Expert Systems," in *Academy of Management Executive;* "How Terrorism Affects Companies," in *Scottsdale Airpark News;* "Terrorism and the Workplace: Concepts and Recommendations," in *Dysfunctional Behavior in Organizations.*